WHISPERERS

WHISPERERS

THE SECRET HISTORY OF THE SPIRIT WORLD

J. H. BRENNAN

OVERLOOK DUCKWORTH
NEW YORK • LONDON

This edition first published in hardcover in the United States and the United Kingdom in 2013 by
Overlook Duckworth, Peter Mayer Publishers, Inc.

NEW YORK
141 Wooster Street
New York, NY 10012
www.overlookpress.com
For bulk and special sales, please contact sales@overlookny.com,
or write us at the above address

LONDON
30 Calvin Street
London E1 6NW
info@duckworth-publishers.co.uk
www.ducknet.co.uk

Cataloging-in-Publication Data is available from the Library of Congress

Book design and typeformatting by Bernard Schleifer

Manufactured in the United States of America
2 4 6 8 10 9 7 5 3 1
ISBN US: 978-1-59020-862-5
ISBN UK: 978-0-7156-4591-8

For a lost friend, Nick, and his dear wife, Clare,
with thanks for their hospitality, their help,
and, most of all, their inspiration.

Portions of this book originally formed part of my master's dissertation on *Spirit Communication: An Examination of a Key Phenomenon within Western Esotericism* at the University of Exeter, England. I would like to thank my professor, the late and much missed Nicholas Goodrick-Clarke, for the extraordinary range of reading he suggested, and my supervisor, Dr. Christopher McIntosh, for some interesting comments on the finished work.

CONTENTS

PREFACE

I S IT POSSIBLE THAT YOUR PRESENT SECURITY AND FUTURE WELL-BEING MAY be controlled by spirits . . . even though you don't believe in them? Is it possible that political decisions about peace and war, the food you eat, the welfare of your friends and family, your religious faith and moral foundations have sprung from discarnate voices whispering in the ears of popes and prophets, politicians and prime ministers, dictators and kings?

It seems incredible, yet there is overwhelming evidence not just that such whisperings are possible but that they have occurred, again and again, from prehistoric times to the present day, subtly directing the course of human history.

This is a phenomenon entirely ignored by historians and scientists, although they are fully aware that it exists. But with academic reputations (not to mention funding) at stake, few are in a hurry to investigate such a disreputable field as spirits. As a result, no one, to this day, can say with any certainty what "spirits" actually are or what they represent. They may be what they (variously) present themselves to be: the souls of the dead, ghosts, gods, discarnate entities, evolved minds, hidden masters, or aliens from outer space. But they may equally well be aspects of the unconscious mind. Or they may also be something else entirely.

Since the past generates the future, it is no exaggeration to say that the life you live today has come about, at least in part, through the hidden urgings of spirit voices. In such circumstances, it would surely make sense to undertake a full and open examination of the phenomenon . . . and try to discover who or what these shadowy advisers really are.

Fifty years ago, conventional scientific opinion held that "spirit communication" was essentially a question of the medium talking to himself. Unconscious contents erupted into consciousness to deliver messages, visions, and the occasional hallucination. The mechanism by which these gifts became personified as pseudospirits was not clearly understood, but psychologists, by and large, were convinced about the origins.

Today, some scientists are not so sure. Carl Jung, one of the founding fathers of modern psychology, observed that spirits sometimes knew more than the medium who channeled them. How, one might ask, could an unconscious projection contain more information than the mind that projected it? Clearly, if there is a purely psychological explanation of spirits, it must be a good deal more complex than the early idea that they simply represent fantasies of the subconscious mind. For many, of course, there is no mystery at all. To them, spirits are exactly what they claim to be: disembodied intelligences capable of communicating with humanity.

Throughout my research of the spirit world, I found myself increasingly dissatisfied with all of the current theories. It was a little like the wave-particle duality of quantum physics. Sometimes spirits behaved like bodiless intelligences communicating from the Beyond, sometimes like the contents of a medium's mind. To confuse matters still further, I discovered that it was possible to *create* a spirit, a purely artificial entity that would manifest in exactly the same way natural spirits have been reported to do throughout the centuries. Worse, artificial spirits proved capable of action and intent outside the control of their creators.

Discoveries like this, personal friendships with spirit mediums, and a lifelong interest in scientific psychical research eventually led to the writing of the present book. In it, I have aimed to present a history of spirit contacts throughout the ages in an attempt to show how prevalent the influence of spirits really was and is, and to investigate the nature of spirits without preconception or prejudice.

It proved to be a journey with an unexpected ending.

—J. H. (HERBIE) BRENNAN, Ireland, 2013

INTRODUCTION

O N JULY 2, 1936, A COTERIE OF HIGH-RANKING NAZIS, INCLUDING
the national Labor Front leader Robert Ley and Deputy Führer
Martin Bormann, descended on the central German city of Quedlinburg as guests of Reichsführer-SS Heinrich Himmler. They found the streets
newly swept and houses freshly painted. Nazi banners hung from the
rooftops, and walls along the major thoroughfares were decked with garlands.

The group was greeted by the local chapter of Hitler Youth ranked three
abreast with flags hanging from long poles. Accompanying them with lively
marching tunes was an SS band. Ranks of steel-helmeted, black-uniformed
SS troopers lined their route as Himmler himself led the party through wind-
ing cobbled streets to the city's Castle Hill.[1] The occasion was the one thou-
sandth anniversary of the death of Heinrich the Fowler (876–936 CE), the
medieval king who founded the Ottonian dynasty and pushed the Slavic tribes
across the River Elbe to establish new boundaries for his budding empire.
To the Nazis, he was the most Germanic of all the ancient German kings.
For Himmler, there was a more personal interest.

The Reichsführer and his party stopped briefly to admire the city's
magnificent castle, then moved on to their ultimate destination, the medieval
Quedlinburg Cathedral. There, in the colonnaded crypt beneath the nave,
Himmler laid a wreath on the empty tomb of King Heinrich, praised his
courage, and vowed to continue his mission in the east.

To historians, the ceremony at Quedlinburg reflected Himmler's passion for history and hopes to rebuild Germany in an heroic image,[2] but there
seems to have been more to it than that. A year after the wreath-laying, he
had the bones of King Heinrich carried into the cathedral in solemn procession to be reinterred in the original tomb. This was, he announced, a sacred
site to which Germans might now make pilgrimage. Another year later, he

ordered the cathedral shut to Christian worship and proceeded to turn it into a sort of SS shrine. Himmler was known for his desire to replace Christianity with a more thoroughbred Aryan religion, reviving old German gods like Wotan. Quedlinburg seems to have been the focus for this ambition. From 1938 to the arrival of American troops in 1945, the cathedral functioned as a mystical Teutonic sanctuary where Christian ritual was abandoned in favor of torch-lit SS ceremonials. In at least one of these, so author Lynn Nicholas assures us, spectators were treated to the apparently magical appearance of the Reichsführer-SS himself . . . through a secret compartment specially built in the church floor.[3]

From a twenty-first-century viewpoint, it all seems rather silly, but in 1972, while researching my own book on the esoteric beliefs and practices of Nazi Germany,[4] I stumbled on an arresting suggestion that changed the whole complexion of these curious antics. Himmler, it seemed, had not confined himself to conjuring tricks. There were intimations that he had held midnight séances in the cathedral crypt designed to put him in contact with the spirit of Heinrich the Fowler, from whom he sought political advice.

I found this revelation chilling. Himmler was not only Reichsführer of the SS but head of the Gestapo—Nazi Germany's infamous secret police—and the official ultimately responsible for the "Final Solution to the Jewish Problem," a program of industrialized murder that resulted in some six million deaths. Was it possible that such a man had based his decisions on the whisperings of a spirit? What struck me as the horror of the situation was its mind-numbing irrationality. This was not a question of whether spirits existed but of Himmler's perception of them. Had millions died because one silly little man believed he could talk to ghosts?

At first, I could find little reliable confirmation of the claims about midnight séances. All sorts of rumors were current—then and now—about Himmler's activities at Quedlinburg, but popular opinion does not constitute proof. Indeed, several reliable historians have mentioned Himmler's conviction that he was the reincarnation of Heinrich the Fowler, a belief that would surely rule out contacting the king as an independent spirit. But despite the problems, there eventually proved to be evidence.

Throughout much of his adult life, Himmler suffered grievously from stomach cramps, possibly nervous in origin. As Reichsführer, he found they often interfered with his work, but the efforts of Nazi doctors brought him little relief. Then, in 1942, a colleague recommended a Finnish masseur named Felix Kersten. Kersten held a degree in "scientific massage" awarded in Helsinki but had gone on to study a Tibetan system of bodywork under a Chinese practitioner named Dr. Ko. To Himmler's surprise, Kersten's ministrations dissolved his pain completely and while it returned when he was under pressure, Kersten's magic hands could be relied upon to give him relief. After a few treatment sessions, Himmler issued an invitation for Kersten to become his personal masseur. Kersten, fearful of his life if he refused, moved to Berlin and took up his new post.

At first, Himmler remained firmly in charge, but gradually the balance of their relationship changed. Kersten discovered he could manipulate Himmler, particularly when the Reichsführer was in pain, and eventually used this ability to save Jewish lives. At the same time, Himmler came to trust Kersten implicitly and, while on the massage couch, would share confidences he was unlikely to reveal to many other people. Among these was the claim that he could call up spirits.

The choice of words is important. A spiritualist séance is a passive affair. In essence a medium will sit quietly and wait for spirits to make contact. In more primitive cultures, a shaman communicates by means of trance journeys to the spirit worlds. But *calling up* spirits implies a conjuration, some form of magical rite that places the necromancer in a position of power. Did Himmler, who was master of so much in Nazi Germany, believe himself to be the master of spirits as well? According to Heinz Höhne, this is exactly what Himmler believed.

Höhne, who died in 2010, was a respected German historian specializing in the Nazi period. Among several other works, he produced a definitive history of the SS.[5] In it, he had this to say:

> Himmler was continually entering into contact with the great men of the past. He believed he had the power to call up spirits and hold regular meetings with them, though only . . . with the spirits of men who had been dead for hundreds of years. When he was half asleep, Himmler used to say, the spirit of King Heinrich would appear and give him valuable advice.[6]

Almost certainly, the term *half asleep* refers to the hypnogogic state between sleeping and waking, which is the closest most of us get to full-blown trance. If so, it marks Himmler as a medium as well as a necromancer, for psychical research has shown the hypnogogic state is a gateway to peculiar experiences, including visions of spirit entities. Furthermore, writing specifically about Quedlinburg and Heinrich the Fowler, Höhne states:

> On each anniversary of the King's death, at the stroke of midnight in the cold crypt of the cathedral, Himmler would commune silently with his namesake.[7]

Of course, even among the Nazi hierarchy, Himmler was an unusual, eccentric, sometimes diabolical figure. General Friedrich Hossbach, Hitler's onetime military assistant, called him "Hitler's evil spirit." General Heinz Guderian, who in 1944 became acting chief of staff, thought of him as "a man from another planet." Carl Burckhardt, high commissioner of the League of Nations, found him "sinister . . . inhuman" and with "a touch of the robot" about him. Armaments Minister Albert Speer thought he was "half schoolmaster, half crank."

Evidence of the crankish aspect is not difficult to find. In 1935, Himmler founded an elite research organization called the Ahnenerbe. Encouraged (and funded) by the Reichsführer, the Ahnenerbe's multiple institutes investigated such pressing matters as the magical properties of the bells in Oxford cathedrals (which had clearly protected the city from Luftwaffe attack), the strength of the Rosicrucian fraternity, the esoteric significance of the top hat at Eton and whether Hitler shared the same Aryan ancestry as Guatama Buddha.[8] Even his crowning achievement, the establishment of the sinister SS, involved an extreme irony—incredible though it sounds, the organization was structurally based on the Jesuit Order.[9]Against such a background, belief in spirits and claims to command them are not entirely surprising, and might easily be dismissed as the delusions of a lone fanatic. But when I investigated further, I discovered a whole historical mythology suggesting Himmler was not the only Nazi listening to spirit voices. I also discovered that spirit advice was not confined to Germany.

Many people use the term *spirit* to mean only a soul of the dead, but this is a limited definition. Every major world religion has its tradition of angels and demons. Folklore is crammed with tales of elves, fauns, fairies, sylphs, undines, and other elemental creatures. All are associated with spirit worlds of one sort or another. Even Almighty God is, for most believers, a spirit. Consequently, academics have now largely adopted the expression "intermediary beings" to describe the type of phenomena that arose in Nazi Germany. The use of the word *spirit* or *spirits* should be taken to mean one or other of the intermediary beings of contemporary academic study, with its precise interpretation drawn from the context.

Historical examination shows that this is a reasonable definition. Although a spirit may seem a long way from an angel or a demon, recorded belief in such intermediaries emerged mainly from a combination of Jewish and Greek ideas about noncorporeal entities (i.e., spirits) capable of influencing human life. A gradual metamorphosis is clear in the development of such beliefs. Interestingly, demons were not at first seen as evil. The Greek word *daimōn* was originally used to mean a god or divine power, and later extended to denote the sort of influence on human affairs that we would translate as "fate." In the sixth century BCE, the Greek poet Hesiod characterized the people of the Golden Age as "pure demons, dwelling on the earth . . . delivering from harm and guardians of mortal men"—that is to say, entirely benevolent creatures. Soon it seemed that mortal men themselves became demons after death, still without negative connotations. The Greek philosopher Socrates (c. 470–399 BCE) was famously advised by a daimon, whose inward voice spoke to him only when he was about to make a mistake. Nor was he unique. There was a widespread belief in personal daimons as tutelary spirits. In his *Meditations*, the Roman emperor Marcus Aurelius remarked that "Zeus has given a particle of himself as leader and guide to everybody."

But daimons did not remain benevolent, although the process of transformation was gradual. One of the earliest signs of things to come were the teachings of the third-century BCE philosopher Chrysippus, who claimed the gods punished the unrighteous through the use of evil demons. An ancient hermetic text, *Asclepius*, tentatively dated to the first century CE, contains the intriguing information that the statues of the gods seen in temples might prove harmful if certain demons were conjured into them. This was not to suggest that *all* demons were wicked, but it certainly pointed to the fact that *some* were now believed to be.

At much the same time, the idea arose that demons living in the air played an important role in the fate of human souls. It was believed that after death a chief demon would act as a judge to decide whether the individual merited punishment or reward. It is easy to see how this notion foreshadowed more developed religious ideas of God's postmortem judgment separating saints from sinners, with the latter condemned to eternal punishment at the hands of the chief demon himself, Satan. By the second century CE, the *Chaldean Oracles* show the modern distinction between good and bad daimons, with the former now usually called "angels" and the latter "demons."

A developing Judaism began by accepting that other peoples were entitled to their own gods but then insisted any other god (not to mention several classes of mythological beings) must be subservient to JHVH in his royal court. And even this grudging acceptance eventually collapsed when it was decided that foreign gods must actually be evil. "All the gods of the heathen are devils," sang the psalmist.[10] Christianity, and later Islam, adopted these ideas wholesale, populating their own anti-pantheons with hellish hosts. But however wicked they became, demons remained essentially spirits. They inhabited an otherworld and could be visited or summoned.

The development of angels followed a somewhat similar and equally convoluted path. At first, the distinction between good and evil seemed largely arbitrary, even where the entity was perceived to be on God's side. The Destroying Angel who slaughtered the firstborn of Egypt[11] was working under JHVH's orders, as was the case when he returned to murder selected Israelites following David's census.[12] Satan himself underwent a gradual metamorphosis from simple messenger of God[13] (the Greek *angelos* means "messenger") to the dislikable Accuser of Job at the heavenly court[14] to the archenemy not only of humanity as a whole but of God himself. The Fall of Satan seems to mark the clearest demarcation point between angels and demons, although his followers were still at times called "fallen angels." The situation was neatly rationalized in the Qumran community where it was believed that God created two important entities, the Spirit of Truth, aka the Prince of Light, and the Spirit of Lies, often called the Prince of Darkness. As a consequence, two classes of beings appeared—the Sons of Light and the Sons of Darkness. Inevitably, they went to war.

Early Christians were quick to adopt and combine the various forms of Greek and Jewish demonology/angelology that existed in their day. In the Gospels, Jesus frequently confronts demons of one sort or another, from his temptation by Satan in the wilderness[15] to his banishment of evil spirits into swine.[16] New Testament references to angels are equally frequent, and in the Annunciation we find an angel in its archetypal role of messenger. As mentioned above, the original Greek of "angel" translates as "messenger," but the entities were, of course, believed to be much more than that. The Christian theologian, Clement of Alexandria, quotes an Orphic hymn that refers to angels surrounding the throne of God and caring for humanity. In the Near East, the old pagan gods, including Zeus and Jupiter, sometimes attracted the term *angelos*, and in the dark, crypt-like adyton under the temple of Apollo at Clarus, the gods themselves delivered an oracle in which they claimed to be "only a small part of [the Supreme] God . . . his angels." Their statement is preserved to this day on a wall in the Lycian city of Oinoanda, now in southwestern Turkey.

Neoplatonism brought a further refinement to humanity's ideas about angels by expanding the term to mean the various levels of being between heaven and earth, thus allowing for paradoxical concepts like angelic demons. It had all become very convoluted, but the complications arose from human interpretations, not from the entities themselves. The same held true for less well-known intermediary beings. The inhabitants of folklore were reported in a multitude of differing forms, from elves to elementals, but could reasonably be classified as spirits in their essence. Thus, daimons remained daimons and, as we shall see, daimon spirits were everywhere. Nor is any of this an academic exercise. As spirits changed their form of manifestation down the centuries, one thing remained constant: the flow of reports that claimed humans could and did communicate with these Whisperers.

This is a hugely important and overlooked aspect in most histories. We talk about the influence of religion and various belief systems on politics and society, but the supernatural is still mostly taboo. Yet my studies—and, indeed, personal experience in the field—all indicate that the supernatural, real or not, has had a profound effect on certain individuals, and through them on society as a whole . . . often in astounding ways. Thus the same basic question returns to haunt us: to what extent has contact with a "spirit world"—whether one believes in such a thing or not—influenced the course of human history?

For conventional historians, the answer seems to be *not at all*. But this conclusion is reached by ignoring the evidence rather than examining it. Spirit contact lies at the heart of shamanism, the prehistoric belief system that guides, to this day, tribal communities throughout the world. It lies at the heart of almost every ancient religion, including those of the classical civilizations that laid down the intellectual and political foundations of our twenty-first-century world. It appears in the visions of prophets and psychics whose doctrines are accepted by men and women in positions of power. It arises, often heavily disguised, in systems of modern psychology and the experiences of individuals moved to experiment with mind-altering drugs or mystical techniques.

In examining these factors, and more, this book aims to correct the record by investigating a recurring theme that most historians elect to ignore. The results are just as chilling, but far more wide-ranging, than Himmler's antics in the crypt of Quedlinburg Cathedral, for it has become clear that, whether we realize it or not, your life and mine have been profoundly influenced by voices from the Beyond.

PART ONE

GODS AND MEN

T
HERE IS SOLID EVIDENCE THAT CONTACT WITH A SPIRIT
world has been an important—indeed even vital—part
of human experience long before the dawn of history.
But the contact was dynamic. With the advent of civilization, the
early spirit journeys of the tribal shaman evolved into a much
wider two-way interaction between humanity as a whole and
spirit entities considered to be gods. These entities were not the
cold, impersonal forces of later philosophies, nor the mystical
abstractions of some Oriental religions, but personalities taking
a direct and intimate interest in the individuals who worshipped
them.

But when these "gods" eventually withdrew, possibly under
the pressure of a population explosion, the evolutionary process
continued. In a desperate attempt to renew contact, humanity
developed new institutions, including oracular mediums and an
interpretive priesthood. These laid the foundations of the three
major monotheistic religions, Judaism, Christianity, and Islam,
and changed common perceptions of spirits from an accepted,
everyday aspect of human existence to denizens of a distant
domain, tightly controlled by a centralized Church.

1. FIRST CONTACT

DURING THE SUMMER OF 1877, EVERARD IM THURN (NOT YET SIR Everard, as he became later) arrived in British Guiana to take up his appointment as curator of the museum and begin his practice of a new branch of science, social anthropology. In pursuit of the latter, he began a series of trips to the interior of the colony and there managed to charm the indigenous Macusi people to such an extent that they permitted him to take up residence in one of their tribal villages. There he fell on an experience so bizarre that his account of it reads like the exotic adventure fiction of the Victorian author Rider Haggard.

The whole thing began when he developed a slight fever and headache. He had, at the time, been attempting to forge a relationship with the local *peaiman*, or witch doctor, apparently successfully since the man promptly offered to cure him of his illness.

An hour or two after dark, Thurn turned up at the *peaiman*'s home equipped, as previously instructed, with his hammock and a pocketful of tobacco leaves. He slung his hammock and handed the tobacco to the *peaiman*, who steeped it in a calabash of water and placed it on the ground, surrounded by several bunches of green boughs he had cut from bushes on the savannah. The *peaiman* was not alone. Some thirty Macusi had crowded into the house, attracted, as Thurn wrote later, "by such a novel performance as the peai-ing of a white man."[1] Someone closed the door and doused the fire, leaving the chamber in total darkness. (Macusi houses had neither windows nor chimney.) Thurn was instructed to climb into his hammock and was sternly warned not to set foot on the ground, otherwise the *kenaimas* (spirits), who would soon be on the floor, might catch him and do dreadful things to him.

It seemed the stage was set for the healing to begin, but the *peaiman* suddenly had second thoughts. He was, it appeared, wary of working in front of a white man. Thurn tried to reassure him by swearing he would not stir from his hammock, nor look at anything, nor attempt to lay hands on anything that might touch him. The *peaiman* reluctantly agreed to go on with the ceremony.

For a moment, there was utter silence, then the darkness exploded with "a burst of indescribably . . . terrible yells . . . roars and shouts which filled the house, shaking walls and roof."[2] The noise ebbed and flowed in a steady rhythm, sometimes rising to a roar, sometimes sinking to a distant growl, but continuing without pause for six full hours. Thurn knew very little Macusi, but it seemed to him that questions were being roared out and answers shouted back. A Macusi boy, whose hammock was close by, did his best to translate and confirmed that the *peaiman* was roaring out his commands and questions to the *kenaimas* and the spirits were yelling and growling back their answers.

At intervals through the cacophony, something even more weird occurred. There was a sound, indistinct at first, but growing louder, like that of some great winged creature approaching the house, then passing through the roof to settle with a thud on the floor. As it did so, distant yells came closer and reached their peak as it landed. Then, so it seemed, the thing lapped tobacco water from the calabash while the *peaiman* shouted questions. After a time, it seemed the creature took flight again and passed through the solid roof to return the way it came. Each time this happened, Thurn felt the air of its wings on his face. This was, he decided, the *kenaimas* coming and going. In the darkness, his imagination gave them forms—tigers, deer, monkeys, birds, turtles, snakes, and even Indians of the Ackawaoi and Arecuna tribes. Each shouted hoarsely in tones appropriate to their nature, each apparently promised the *peaiman* not to trouble Thurn anymore. As the last of them prepared to depart, a hand was laid briefly on Thurn's face.

The effect on the anthropologist was as strange as the performance itself. Before long he ceased to hear the whispered explanations of the boy and passed into something akin to a mesmeric trance where, incapable of moving, he seemed suspended somewhere in a ceaselessly surging din. Occasionally, when the noise died away and it appeared as if the *peaiman* had passed through the roof and was shouting from a distance, Thurn began to awaken. But when the *peaiman* returned and the noise increased, he would again sink into a stupor.

Toward morning, the ceremony ended and the noise stopped. When the door was opened, Thurn rushed out into the open savannah. It was still dark, a wild night with heavy rain and incessant thunder. As lightning flashed, he could catch glimpses of the far-off Pacaraima mountain range. Although without hat, shoes, or coat, Thurn stayed out in the storm until dawn. It felt strangely refreshing after the noise and the darkness of the stuffy house.

Spectacular though it was, the ceremony did not appear to be a therapeutic success. Thurn subsequently reported:

> It is perhaps needless to add that my head was anything but cured of its ache. But the *peaiman*, insisting that I must be cured, asked for payment. He even produced the *kenaima*, a caterpillar, which, he said, had caused the pain and which he had extracted from my body at the moment when his hand had touched my face. I gave him a looking-glass which had cost fourpence; and he was satisfied.

Despite falling into trance, Thurn was quick to rationalize the whole experience:

> It was a clever piece of ventriloquism and acting. The whole long terrific noise came from the throat of the *peaiman*; or perhaps a little of it from that of his wife. The only marvel was that the man could sustain so tremendous a strain upon his voice and throat for six long hours. The rustling of the wings of the *kenaima*s, and the thud which was heard as each alighted on the floor, were imitated, as I afterwards found, by skilfully shaking the leafy boughs and then dashing them suddenly against the ground. The boughs, swept through the air close to my face, also produced the breezes which I had felt. Once, probably by accident, the boughs touched my face; and it was then that I discovered what they were, by seizing and holding some of the leaves with my teeth.

Everard Thurn was not the only European to disapprove of *peaiman*s. Contact with them (under several different names) began in the sixteenth century with the early exploration of the Americas. It was a particularly difficult time for anyone claiming contact with spirits. Witches were being burned throughout Europe, a custom carried enthusiastically to the New World where, notably in Central and South America, colonial and church authorities joined forces to torture and kill literally thousands of indigenous people for the crime of following their tribal traditions. Attitude and mind-set were neatly summed up in the writings of a French Franciscan named André Thévet.

In 1557, Thévet found himself in Rio de Janeiro, then the first European colony in Brazil, and undertook to gather information about the area's native inhabitants, the Tupinamba. He quickly discovered that "these people—being thus removed from the truth, beyond the persecutions they receive from the evil spirit and the errors of their dreams—are so outside of reason that they adore the Devil by means of his ministers, called *pagé* . . . or *Caribo*."[3]

Thévet had little good to say about the *pagé*, whom he described as "people of evil custom" who had given themselves over to the Devil's service in order to deceive their neighbors. The *pagé* apparently had a nomadic streak, or perhaps simply favored the solitude of the forest in order to practice their profession, but Thévet saw this as a failing as well, claiming that they chose not to reside permanently anywhere, in order to disguise their nastiness. They did no honest work, but were supported in ones and twos by villages who inhabitants superstitiously believed them to carry messages from the spirit realm.

What a *pagé* actually did in order to receive such messages was described in some (not entirely unprejudiced) detail by Thévet. First the witch doctor constructed a brand-new hut, where no one had ever lived before, and furnished it with a white bed. He then moved in large quantities of supplies, notably a native drink made from a plant called *cahoiun* along with flour ground from its roots. For a total of nine days, the *pagé* abstained from sexual intercourse, then entered the hut where he was ceremonially washed by a young virgin girl of ten or twelve years. The girl withdrew, as did any villagers standing close to the hut, and the *pagé* stretched out on the bed to begin his "diabolical invocations."

Thévet was not privy to exactly what went on in the hut, but he noted that it lasted for more than an hour, at the end of which the spirit—the *evil* spirit in Thévet's account—would make itself heard by "whistling and piping." He was told by some of the Tupinamba that no one ever saw the supernatural creature but only heard the howling and other noises it made.

When the consultation was finished, the *pagé* emerged and was immediately surrounded by his people, who stood by while he described what he had heard. Few important tribal decisions were made without spirit advice, so the *pagé* was typically the recipient of many "caresses and presents."

Brother Thévet summed up his analysis of the experience with a brutal recommendation:

Of this magic we find two main kinds, one by which one communicates with evil spirits, the other which gives intelligence about the most secret things of nature. It is true that one is more vicious than the other, but both are full of curiosity . . . Such curiosities indicate an imperfect judgment, ignorance, and a lack of faith and good religion . . . I cannot cease to wonder how it is that in a land of law and police, one allows to proliferate like filth a bunch of old witches who put herbs on their arms, hang written words around their necks, and many mysteries, in ceremonies to cure fevers and other things, which are only true idolatry, and worthy of great punishment.[4]

Thévet's attitude was typical of his day, nor was it confined to church professionals. The Spanish navigator Gonzalo Fernández de Oviedo, a layman through and through, encountered old men who communicated with spirits on the island of Hispaniola and subsequently commented on their activities in terms that would do justice to the most rabid prelate:

They worship the Devil in diverse forms and images . . . they paint, engrave or carve a demon they call *cemí* in many objects and places . . . as ugly and frightful as the Catholics represent him at the feet of Saint Michael . . . not bound in chains, but revered . . . they prayed to him and had recourse to him in all their needs . . . And inside [the house] there was an old Indian . . . whose evil image was standing there; and it is to be thought that the Devil entered into him and spoke through him as through his minister; and . . . he told them the day on which it would rain and other messages from Nature . . . and they did not undertake or carry out anything that might be of importance without considering the Devil's opinion in this way.[5]

The old men, so anxious to carry out the Devil's work, did so by means of tobacco smoke that they inhaled through hollow canes until they fell down drunk or unconscious. They were then carried to their hammocks by their wives (noted by de Oviedo as "numerous") and subsequently awoke to prophecy future events and advise on proper courses of action, as dictated to them by the spirits.

A century later, as Russia began to colonize Siberia, explorers discovered similar individuals in its chill interior. Here too were men and women, claiming, like their American counterparts, to commune with spirits, heal or harm, influence the weather and game. In the east of the country, the Tungus peoples called them *saman* or *shaman*, the latter term destined to become a worldwide generic in describing the profession. Once again, there were priests impatient to condemn them. The conservative Russian cleric Avvakum Petrovich, in the first written account of shamanic practice, denounced the object of his study as "a villain of a magician who calls the demons" and, like others before him, suggested trickery might also be involved.

With the dawning of the Enlightenment at the beginning of the eighteenth century, the theory of fraud became more widespread and more all-encompassing. Shamans were no longer looked on as demonologists who sometimes used tricks but as tricksters through and through who only pretended to truck with spirits. It was not an entirely unwelcome development since it took away the excuse used by the religious to execute them. But even the rationalists could be harsh in their judgments. A German professor of chemistry and botany, Johann Georg Gmelin, spent ten years studying Siberian shamans. After watching one performance marked by much leaping, shouting, sweating, and "infernal racket," he dismissed the whole thing as humbug and remarked that "we wished in our hearts that we could take him and his companions to the Urgurian silver mine, so that there they might spend the rest of their days in perpetual labor."[6]

The French Jesuit missionary Joseph-François Lafitau, who spent five years among the Amerindian tribes near Montreal, also decided their shamans worked largely through "tricks of skill" but retained doubts that this was the whole story. He found them to have "some innate quality" that reminded him of the divine. He had witnessed them enter states of ecstasy in which a spirit appeared to take possession of them, throwing them into "frenzies of enthusiasm and all the convulsive movements of the Sibyl."[7] Interestingly, Lafitau remarked that the voice of the spirits, speaking from the depths of the shamans' chests, led to their being considered ventriloquists—an example, surely, of a genuine phenomenon masquerading as a fake, rather than vice versa. It is also difficult to reconcile trickery with his observation that the power of spirit sometimes raised shamans into the air or gave them greater stature than they normally possessed.

Lafitau, despite his religious convictions, stands out as one of the most open-minded of the early investigators of shamanism. It proved a rare enough quality. Even after the distinguished German-American anthropologist Franz Boas established the principle, in the late nineteenth century, that indigenous cultures should be appreciated on their own terms, there was a noteworthy

Humanity's first contact with the spirit world arose in prehistoric times from individuals like this Siberian shaman.

tendency toward lip service when it came to evaluating shamanism. Western observers might conscientiously report the claims of the shaman *as if* they were true, but the unspoken assumption was that no civilized person could possibly believe them. In 1904, Waldemar Bogoras was careful to place the word *spirits* in inverted commas when he published his study of shamanism among the Chukchee peoples of the North Pacific.

This situation endured throughout the first half of the twentieth century and only really began to break down when a handful of intrepid anthropologists took the unprecedented step of trying out some shamanic techniques for themselves. Few were intrepid enough to face the prolonged fasting and other, sometimes life-threatening, ordeals of traditional shamanic training but concentrated instead on the use of plant narcotics. Limited though it was, this approach produced striking insights.

The first recorded example of the approach dates back to 1957 and involved not a professional anthropologist, but an American banker named R. Gordon Wasson. With his friend Allan Richardson, Wasson approached a Mexican shaman named Maria Sabina and asked for her help in experiencing the secrets of a "divine mushroom" used in certain religious rites. The woman agreed and the two Americans found themselves drinking chocolate with some eighteen Mixtecos, all dressed in their best clothing. After the chocolate, they each ate their way through twelve acrid-tasting, evil-smelling mushrooms. The effect was, in Wasson's own word, staggering.

As the final candle was extinguished shortly after midnight, Wasson and Richardson were plunged into a visionary experience—or, if you prefer, began to hallucinate—and the visions continued at high intensity for fully four hours. They included art motifs in vivid colors, palaces set with semiprecious stones, and a chariot drawn by some great mythological beast. The walls of the house dissolved and Wasson left his body to float in midair viewing mountain landscapes with camel trains crawling across slopes which raised tier upon tier until they reached the very heavens. The figure of a beautiful, enigmatic woman appeared, leaving him with the impression that he was viewing a different world in which he played no part. He had become nothing more than a disembodied eye, poised in space.

From time to time, the shaman would make oracular utterances that, Wasson knew, were accepted by her native audience as the words of God. At one point something even stranger occurred. The shaman's daughter, herself a shaman, began a rhythmic dance during which she produced claps and slaps that came from unpredictable directions in complex rhythms, sometimes appearing close at hand, sometimes distant, sometimes above, sometimes below. Wasson described them as "ventriloquistic," although it is clear that if ventriloquism really was involved, it was nothing like ventriloquism as we know it in our present culture.

Wasson's published account, in *Life* magazine, aroused considerable interest but may have been somewhat devalued within the academic community since he was not an anthropologist. With the dawning of the 1960s, however, the American anthropologist Michael Harner underwent an experience of the plant psychedelic ayahuasca that led, nineteen years after his drug-induced visions, to his establishing the Foundation for Shamanic Studies, an organization dedicated to the investigation and preservation of shamanic techniques.[8] Harner lived for several years among the Jívaro and Conibo peoples of the Western Amazon and there drank more than a pint of the brew in order to understand the religious beliefs of the natives. On the instruction of his guide, a shaman named Tomás, he lay down on the bamboo platform of the tribe's communal house and waited.

At first his visions were unspectacular: faint lines of light and a sound like that of a distant waterfall. But then dim figures appeared and gradually resolved into a "supernatural carnival of demons" surrounding a gigantic crocodile head that gushed huge quantities of rushing water.[9] He became aware of other, even more disturbing spirit creatures—giant reptilian entities that resided at the base of his brain, where the skull met the spinal cord. They showed him planet Earth as it had existed in prehistoric times and he watched hundreds of black specks dropping from the sky to resolve themselves into huge whalelike dragons with stubby pterodactyl wings. They told him they were fleeing an enemy in outer space and had created the earth with its myriad life-forms as a place to hide. They were, they said, the true masters of humanity and, indeed, the entire planet. Harner went on to meet humanoid bird-headed spirits that reminded him of the traditional portrayals of Egyptian gods, but it was the dragons he found most disturbing and had eventually to ask his shamanic friends for medicine to bring the visions under control.

When his experience ended, Harner was left with a feeling of threat brought about by the thought that he now held a dangerous secret—humanity's unwitting slavery to the reptilians. His mood was not helped when two missionaries pointed out similarities between his vision and passages from the biblical book of Revelation, with the disturbing suggestion that the dragons he had seen might actually be aspects of Satan. Later, however, he was greatly reassured when he told a Conibo shaman of the dragons' claims that they were masters of humanity. The man grinned and said, "Oh, they're always saying that. But they are only the Masters of Outer Darkness."[10]

Another pioneer of direct shamanic experience was Barbara Myerhoff, who studied anthropology at the University of California–Los Angeles and, in 1974, decided to accompany the Huichol Indians of Mexico on a desert pilgrimage to search for supplies of their sacred peyote cactus. To prepare herself for the trip, she undertook to sample the cactus under the direction of a shaman named Ramón Medina Silva. After eating a dozen of the small, green peyote buttons, she lay down with closed eyes and eventually experienced a growing euphoria. Time and space evaporated and images arose into her consciousness. She began to experience her life as a series of discrete events, like booths at a carnival, thus allowing her to move backward in time to revisit earlier incidents. She found herself impaled on the Tree of Life, forming an image identical, it transpired, to a Mayan glyph she did not see until several years later. A vivid red speck flitting through the forest transformed itself into a spectacular bird that landed on a nearby rock. Myerhoff questioned the creature about myths and it responded by saying that myths could only be approached on their own terms, as themselves, and not interpreted according to preconceived ideas of what might be real and what not. But she missed a more important message—a message she believed to be the essential purpose of her experience—when her Western rationality prevented her from fully encountering another spirit being.

Since that time, various other anthropologists and academics have followed the trail blazed by these early pioneers. Harner's work in particular, with its emphasis on shamanic drumming techniques, has led to the phenomenon of the "urban shaman," men and women from First World countries who embark on their own shamanic adventures as a lifestyle choice. One result has been a deeper understanding of shamanism itself and a growing respect for practices that were once dismissed as fakery or Devil's work. The University of Chicago professor Mircea Eliade, who died in 1986 but whose books arguably remain the most authoritative academic sources on the subject, described the shaman as "medicine-man, priest and psychopomp."

> He cures sicknesses, he directs the communal sacrifices and he escorts the souls of the dead to the other world. He is able to do all this by virtue of his techniques of ecstasy, that is, by his power to leave his body at will.[11]

Contrary to the New Age idea that anyone can become a shaman by banging a drum in their living room, Eliade insists there are only three roads into the profession: spontaneous vocation (seen as a "calling" from the spirits), hereditary transmission from parent to child, or personal quest by means of which the candidate attempts to seek out his spirit allies. But whatever the route, a shaman is only a shaman after he or she has received the proper initiation, which involves a twofold transmission of knowledge. Part of this knowledge, passed on by an older, master shaman, is purely technical—details of the techniques for achieving trance, the names of the spirits, the secret shamanic language used by the given culture, tribal myths, traditions, and genealogy. The remainder, arguably more important, is imparted directly by the spirits during ecstatic visions, dreams, and trances. Thus prepared, the candidate faces the initiation itself, which may be an elaborate tribal ceremony but may equally be a wholly inward, visionary experience. Either way, an ordeal is often involved. Siberian shamans maintain that they die as part of the process and lie inanimate for up to a week. During this time, they are cut up by spirits, the flesh scraped from their bones and their body fluids drained. The spirits then carry what remains of them down to hell, where they are locked in a house for three years.

It is at this stage that the actual initiation takes place. The candidate's head is cut off and set carefully to one side so he can watch the remainder of the process. The spirits then hack his body to pieces, which are distributed among the spirits of various illnesses. (This gives him the power to heal when he becomes a full-fledged shaman.) His bones are then covered with new flesh.

This fearsome initiation can be, and often is, itself the result of illness. Says Eliade:

> It becomes clear that initiatory sicknesses closely follow the fundamental pattern of all initiations: first, torture at the hands of demons or spirits, who play the role of masters of initiation; second, ritual death, experienced by the patient as a descent to hell or an ascent to heaven; third, resurrection to a new mode of being—the mode of "consecrated man," that is, a man who can communicate with gods, demons and spirits.[12]

This then is the crux of the matter. For all his dreams, visions, and (perhaps) fakery, the shaman remains at his deepest essence, an individual with one all-encompassing power: the ability to communicate with spirits. It is the spirits who help him heal, who find the game, forecast the weather, predict the future, and generate the tribal customs. Spirit influence on primitive communities is both enormous and widespread—Michael Harner claims it is virtually universal: "the practice of shamanism existed on all inhabited continents."[13] A less sympathetic Sir James Frazer described primitive man as "a slave . . . to the spirits of his dead forefathers, who haunt his steps from birth to death, and rule him with a rod of iron."[14] Animism, the belief that spirits inhabit every hill, tree, stone, stream, pool, cloud, or breeze in Nature, proved so widespread among primitive cultures that an Oxford anthropology professor once proposed it as the origin of all religion.[15]

And the influence goes back a very long time. According to anthropologist Forest E. Clements,[16] there was a belief in spirits in western Asia more than ten thousand years ago and the "witch doctor" who dealt with them was

Were cave paintings, like this one at Lascaux, France,
an attempt to depict spirits?

a member of a profession that seems to have originated even earlier. A painting, apparently depicting a shaman, in the cave of Les Trois Frères at Lascaux in the French Pyrenees dates to ca. 14,000 BCE,[17] while Dr. Jean Clottes of the French Ministry of Culture argues that the function of *all* Paleolithic rock art was shamanic.[18] Since the primary work of the shaman is spirit contact, this suggests an interaction between humanity and spirits dating back as far as thirty thousand years.

2. COMMUNION WITH THE GODS

THE EARLIEST CIVILIZATION TO HAVE LEFT WRITTEN RECORDS IS THE Sumerian culture that arose in the fertile crescent of ancient Mesopotamia between the Tigris and Euphrates Rivers. Although populated from early times, the area was first settled between 4500 and 4000 BCE by a people referred to as Ubaidian,[1] who knew nothing of the local language but arrived from outside as a markedly civilizing influence. They drained the marshes, established agriculture, then created industries that included metalwork, leatherwork, masonry, pottery, and weaving. From this base, they developed a flourishing trade with neighboring regions.

But the people we now call Sumerian, whose tribal tongue became the prevailing language of the territory, did not arrive on the scene until 3300 BCE, probably from Anatolia. Within a few hundred years, the country had developed twelve separate city-states: Kish, Erech, Ur, Sippar, Akshak, Larak, Nippur, Adab, Umma, Lagash, Bad-tibira, and Larsa. Each comprised a walled city with its surrounding villages and land. Their earliest political system was a democracy of sorts, with power vested in the people. This gave way to a theocracy controlled by various independent groups of high priests, but growing rivalry between the states seems to have called for a more centralized form of authority so that one by one they each adopted the institution of kingship.[2]

There was, according to their written records, a universal belief in spirit beings. Each city had its patron god. In the early days of the civilization these numbered only ten—Anu, Enlil, Enki, Inanna, Ki, Nanna, Ningal, Ninlil, Ninurta, and Utu—but by 2000 BCE, the Sumerian pantheon had grown to some thirty-six hundred deities. However, we must not assume such belief was only a matter of religious faith. Julian Jaynes, a Princeton professor of psychology, has warned not to impose such a modern-day prejudice. Following a thorough study of the period, he was led to the astonishing conclusion that the ancient texts should be taken literally: not only did the spirits speak, but their voices were heard by entire urban populations.[3] In a carefully reasoned thesis, Jaynes presents a wealth of compelling evidence to suggest that whole civilizations were founded and functioned on the orders of these preternatural entities. They were, he claims, far more intrusive even than they are today, taking on visible form and directing the actions of a humanity that functioned at a level little better than an army of robots. We were, at that time, literal playthings of the gods, utterly unable to disobey their edicts or resist their plans.

Jaynes, who died in 1997, was the son of a Massachusetts minister. He studied at Harvard and McGill, received a doctorate (in psychology) from Yale, and lectured at some twelve other universities including Princeton and Cornell. In 1976, he dropped a bombshell on the academic world with his publication of a work later described by the prominent Darwinist Richard Dawkins as "one of those books that is either complete rubbish or a work of consummate genius, nothing in between."[4] The book in question groaned under the unwieldy title of *The Origin of Consciousness in the Breakdown of the Bicameral Mind*, but read, in many respects, like an intellectual thriller. In it, Professor Jaynes argued that prior to about 1250 BCE—a date that permits the establishment of several ancient civilizations—the whole of humanity was guided by spirit voices. No medium was involved. These voices manifested to everyone with apparent objectivity, sometimes accompanied by materializations—or at least visionary experiences—and were accepted as instructions from the gods.

Jaynes's starting point was the *Iliad*, Homer's epic poem chronicling the events of the Trojan War and itself one of the oldest extant works of Western literature. His initial analysis of the document revealed something strange. The heroes of the *Iliad* all seemed, without exception, to be in constant communication with their gods—and almost incapable of taking any action that did not spring from divine instructions.

> The characters of the Iliad do not sit down and think out what to do . . .
> When Agamemnon . . . robs Achilles of his mistress, it is a god that grasps
> Achilles by his yellow hair and warns him not to strike Agamemnon. It is a
> god who then rises out of the gray sea and consoles him in his tears of wrath

on the beach by his black ships, a god who whispers low to Helen to sweep her heart with homesick longing, a god who hides Paris in a mist in front of the attacking Menelaus, a god who tells Glaucus to take bronze for gold, a god who leads the armies into battle, who speaks to each soldier at the turning points, who debates and teaches Hector what he must do, who urges the soldiers on or defeats them . . . It is the gods who start quarrels among men that really cause the war, and then plan its strategy. It is one god who makes Achilles promise not to go into battle, another who urges him to go and another who then clothes him in a golden fire reaching up to heaven and screams through his throat across the bloodied trench of the Trojans, rousing in them ungovernable panic . . . The beginnings of action . . . are in the actions and speeches of gods . . . When . . . Achilles reminds Agamemnon of how he robbed him of his mistress, the king of men declares, "Not I was the cause of this act, but Zeus."[5]

To most modern readers, of course, the gods are no more than a poetic invention, a device intended to render the narrative more vivid and interesting. But the events of the *Iliad* are *already* both vivid and interesting. The poem is about action and the action is constant. There is no need to "cut to the chase"; in the *Iliad* the "chase" is all there is. Any further poetic device, any invocation of fictional gods, is patently unnecessary. Yet there it is, in line after line of the epic. More to the point, it is integral to the work itself. Both the *Iliad*'s author and the Iliadic characters are agreed in their acceptance of a divinely managed world. Faced with these puzzles, Jaynes took the courageous step of considering the possibility that the gods of the *Iliad* were not poetic inventions at all, but a wholly accurate account of the world as it was at the time of the Trojan War. What if, he speculated, both Greeks and Trojans really were listening to mysterious voices and sometimes looking on the very faces of their gods? What if it was all true, exactly as the *Iliad* described it? In such circumstances, "to say the gods are an artistic apparatus is the same kind of thing as to say that Joan of Arc told the Inquisition about her voices merely to make it all vivid to those who were about to condemn her."[6]

From this starting point, Jaynes went in search of further evidence that the world of our early ancestors may have been quite different from the world we experience today. He speculated that the earliest form of universal spirit contact occurred simultaneously with the development of urban living around 9000 BCE. A study of the Natufian settlement of Eynan, some twelve miles north of the Sea of Galilee, showed a town of more than two hundred people supported partly by hunting and partly by a primitive form of agriculture, with a social structure based on the rule of a king. The king's tomb at this site was a circular edifice some sixteen feet in diameter housing two complete skeletons. One wore a shell headdress and was presumed to be the king's wife. The other, the king himself, was partly covered in stones and partly propped upright, with his cradled head facing the distant Mount Hermon. The entire grave was surrounded by a wall, painted in red ocher, supporting a roof of large flat stones. On this roof, the Natufians had built a hearth, surrounded by a second wall, again roofed with stone slabs. Topping the entire structure were three large stones set central and surrounded by a ring of smaller ones.

Primitive though it was, this curious edifice has a religious feel about it, like the stupas found beside Himalayan roadways. Jaynes speculates that this is precisely what it was—a device that allowed the dead king to issue commands in spirit form, as he had done during life. When a holy fire was lit in the ceremonial hearth, its smoke, "rising into visibility for furlongs around, was, like the gray mists of the Aegean for Achilles, a source of . . . the commands that controlled the Mesolithic world of Eynan." This, says Jaynes, was the paradigm of what was to happen over the next eight millennia. The spirit of the dead king was transformed, in the imagination of the Eynans, into a god. The king's tomb was the god's house, the precursor of far more elaborate god houses and temples to be erected in the years ahead. Even the two-tiered formation of its structure was prescient of the multitiered ziggurats of temples built on temples (as at the ancient Sumerian city of Eridu) and the gigantic pyramids at Giza in Egypt.

Given that the plain people of Eynan heard the spirit voice of their dead king, their living king, his successor—who was also privy to the words of the spirit—would naturally designate himself as the dead god-king's priest or servant, thus ensuring his own authority until death permitted him to join with his predecessor as a god in his own right. Once established, this pattern spread throughout Mesopotamia and was particularly evident in ancient Egypt. As it did so, the tomb was gradually replaced by the temple (which contained no burial remains) while a statue took the place of the corpse—metaphors that continued to function admirably as an aid to spirit communication.

Jaynes spread his archaeological net and discovered that the basic plan for human group habitation from the end of the Mesolithic to relatively recent times was a god-house (temple or church) surrounded by man-houses. As cities expanded to embrace thousands of souls, so the god-houses became monumental, culminating in structures so large that they became the focus of spirit communication for miles around. He came across actual depictions of such communication. Two stone reliefs from an ancient site in Guatemala, for example, depicted a man prostrate on the grass as he was lectured by two divine figures. One clearly represents Death, the other is half human, half deer. Jaynes notes[7] that to this day the local *chilans* (prophetic shamans) adopt an identical posture for their peyote-enhanced conversations with spirits.

He discovered too that, as the centuries progressed, the tombs of kings, priests, politicians—indeed all who could afford it—were gradually filled up with grave goods . . . and even servants. The kings of Ur, for example, ruling during the first half of the third millennium BCE, were entombed with their entire retinues, often buried alive in a crouched position as if ready to spring up to offer service. The tombs also contained copious supplies of food, drink, clothing, weapons, jewelry, musical instruments, and even draft animals yoked to ornate chariots. Clearly these goods were assumed to be of use to the deceased. Jaynes further discovered that the burial of important personages as if they were still alive was common to almost all of the ancient cultures he surveyed. Nor was this bewildering custom confined to the rich and powerful. In Sumerian Lagash (now modern Tell al-Hiba) in about 2500 BCE, a commoner was buried with seven jars of beer, 420 loaves, two measures of grain, one garment, a head support, and a bed. The excavation of graves from the Indus civilizations of India revealed fifteen to twenty food pots per person. Similar finds were discovered in the Neolithic Yang-Shao cultures of China, not to mention the Olmec and Mayan kingdoms of South America.

> This practice has no clear explanation except that their voices were still being heard by the living and were perhaps demanding such accommodation.[8]

The lengths to which the living would go in order to placate the voices they heard is illustrated by the fact that some early Greek graves had feeding tubes that allowed broth to be poured down into the rotting mouths of the corpses below. Even more macabre is the painting on a mixing bowl dated to 850 BCE and now in the Metropolitan Museum in New York. This vessel depicts a boy tearing his hair with one hand while he stuffs food into the mouth of his mother's corpse with the other. To Jaynes, this was yet another indication that spirit voices had convinced the populace that the dead, despite appearances, lived on.

The advent of writing provided further support for Jaynes's contention that spirits of the dead were thought of as gods. An Assyrian incantation text makes the connection overtly. In it, the dead are referred to directly as *ilani* or gods. Records of the Aztec civilization quote the ancients as believing that when a man died he became a god—so much so that the expression "he has become a god" was used as a euphemism for death.

Alongside the grave goods and written traditions, Jaynes noted a veritable explosion in the use of figurines and life-size images during the millennia following the Eynan burial. The function of such figurines has been something of an archaeological mystery, with the most popular theory suggesting that they were fertility charms. Jaynes dismissed this idea as failing under logical analysis. Fertility charms would be of little use in areas where fertility was never a problem. Yet they were found in great numbers in such areas. Since many of these were stood upright in tombs, he took them to be more permanent substitutes for the propped corpse. Their function, he suggested, was to trigger the phenomenon of the spirit voices.

Jaynes found support for this conclusion in the figures themselves. Those of the Olmec civilization, to give only a single example, were created with open mouths and exaggerated ears, suggesting they had something to do with verbal communication. There was also the curious, and almost worldwide, convention of figures with exaggerated, staring eyes. Sometimes this was achieved by enlarging the eyes, sometimes by the use of rock crystal or gemstone inserts. Thousands of figures dating to about 3000 BCE, found in the upper branches of the Euphrates, had heads that consisted almost entirely of eyes enhanced with malachite paint. Analysis shows the diameter of the human eye is approximately one tenth the height of the human head, a measurement Jaynes elected to refer to as an eye index of one. His investigations showed that ancient statuary of gods had eye indexes as high as 18 and 20: "huge globular eyes hypnotically staring out of the unrecorded past of 5,000 years ago with defiant authority." The choice of the word *hypnotically* is deliberate. Jaynes became convinced that for our faithful ancestors, staring into the hypnotic eyes of their carved gods facilitated the state of mind in which they could more easily hear the sound of spirit voices. How can we know that such idols "spoke"? Jaynes asks rhetorically, then answers:

A Harvard professor has argued that statues like this Olmec figurine once 'spoke' directly to worshippers.

I have tried to suggest that the very existence of statuary and figurines requires an explanation in a way that has not previously been perceived . . . The setting up of such idols in religious places, the exaggerated eyes in the early stages of every civilization, the practice of inserting gems of brilliant sorts into the eye sockets of several civilizations, an elaborate ritual for the opening of the mouth for new statues in the two most important early civilizations . . . all these present a pattern of evidence at least.[9]

It is a pattern of evidence supported by the fact that cuneiform texts often refer to statues speaking while, closer to hand for most readers, the Old Testament tells how the king of Babylon "consulted with images" (Ezekiel 21:21). In South America, Aztecs told their Spanish conquerors that their history began when a statue from an ancient ruined temple spoke to their leaders, while nearby Peru was considered by the Spanish to be a kingdom commanded by the Devil, because Satan himself spoke to the Incas out of the mouths of their statues:

> It was commonly in the night they entered backward to their idoll and so went bending their bodies and head, after an uglie manner, and so they consulted with him. The answer he made was commonly like unto a fearefull hissing, or to a gnashing which did terrifie them; and all that he did advertise or command them was but the way to their perdition and ruine.[10]

It was evidence of this type that led Julian Jaynes to conclude these and similar statues were not *of* a god but were *themselves* the god.

> He had his own house . . . [which] formed the center of a complex of temple buildings, varying in size with the importance of the god and the wealth of the city. The god was probably made of wood to be light enough to be carried about on the shoulders of priests. His face was inlaid with precious metals and jewels. He was clothed in dazzling raiment and usually resided on a pedestal in a niche in the central chamber of his house . . . Since the divine statue was the owner of the land and the people were his tenants, the first duty of the steward-king was to serve the god not only in the administration of the god's estates, but also in more personal ways. The gods, according to cuneiform texts, liked eating and drinking, music and dancing; they required beds to sleep in and for enjoying sex with other god-statues on connubial visits from time to time; they had to be washed and dressed and appeased with pleasant odors; they had to be taken out for drives on state occasions; and all these things were done with increasing ceremony and ritual as time went on . . . The divine statues also had to be kept in good temper. This was called "appeasing the liver" of the gods and consisted in offerings of butter, fat, honey, sweetmeats placed on the table as with regular food . . . How is all this possible, continuing as it did in some form for *thousands* of years as the central focus of life unless we posit that the human beings heard the statues speak to them, even as the heroes of the *Iliad* heard their gods or Joan of Arc heard hers? And indeed *had* to hear them speak to know what to do?[11]

The social structure, as Jaynes conceived it, was complex. The common people were not privy to the words of the great gods who ruled from their ziggurats and temples. But even the lowliest commoner had his or her own gods embodied in idols or figurines living in household shrines. They too demanded their daily rituals and offerings, usually modest versions of the temple ceremonial. They too spoke to the citizens who served them and issued orders about what should be done and by whom. If, faced by some particularly fearful crisis or hugely important decision, a commoner wished to speak with one of the great civic gods, he could not do so directly but had to consult his personal house deity to act as an intermediary. Cuneiform tablets depict the practice, showing a great god seated while a lesser deity conducts the petitioner into the divine presence. The whole thing is somewhat reminiscent of later ideas about "guardian angels"—which might themselves be distorted memories of the earlier experience. In one sense, all spirit/god contact was personal. Every man and woman was capable of hearing the voice of her own deity. But the deities themselves formed a strict hierarchy, each answering to another, so that an important question or message could filter upward until it reached the city's great protector, who would then advise his personal servant—the king—on what should be done about it.

It was a structure that survived for millennia, but, manifestly, not indefinitely. Clearly, not everyone today is capable of hearing spirit voices—indeed, a sizeable proportion of the general population does not even believe in them. Jaynes realized that if his conclusions were correct, there was an age during which spirit intercourse with humanity increased to such a degree that it was all but universal, but that age eventually ended. He reasoned that for his theory to stand up, he had to find the point in history where things changed, the point when the gods withdrew and spirits ceased to speak directly to anyone who cared to listen. Consequently, he began to search for the turning point.

Jaynes was aware of the problems that could—indeed must—arise in any society whose members were constantly directed by spirit voices. As populations increased, so did the complexities of life . . . and the odds in favor of the spirits issuing contradictory orders. Once such contradictions reached critical mass, the basic structure of the society would collapse. Evidence of this was, he believed, writ large in the pre-Columbian civilizations of America where, time and again, whole populations suddenly deserted their cities to adopt a tribal lifestyle in the surrounding jungle. Such mass desertions, with no apparent cause, have remained a mystery to orthodox archaeology but were seen by Jaynes as a necessary flight from spirit instructions that no longer made any sense or had ceased to produce satisfactory results. This explanation also fitted an even more mysterious observation—the fact that given time, usually a century or more, there was often a drift back to the deserted cities, sustainable until the population once more increased to unmanageable proportions.

The linkage between population density and cultural collapse seemed to be confirmed by texts like the Sumerian epic *Atrahasis*, which opens with the words:

> The people became numerous
> The god was depressed by their uproar
> Enlil heard their noise
> He exclaimed to the great gods
> The noise of mankind has become burdensome.[12]

Interestingly, this text approaches the problem not from the viewpoint of a burgeoning population, but from that of the spirits themselves. And the spirits, it appeared, were not best pleased by the tendency of their worshippers to "be fruitful and multiply." The epic goes on to describe how they visited plagues, famines, and, eventually, a great flood on their followers in a brutal attempt to reduce population numbers. Clearly, whatever else may have been happening, the structure of the spirit-driven society was breaking down. By the end of the third millennium BCE, the problem was becoming increasingly evident. In Egypt, for example, the final century of this millennium saw the sudden, total breakdown of all authority. People fled the towns in an exodus reminiscent of the South American cities, brother fought brother, nobles scratched for food in the fields, children slaughtered their parents, tombs and pyramids were ransacked.

Orthodox historians postulate that the cause must have been some great natural disaster, without, however, being able to support their theory with hard evidence. Nor was there evidence of natural disasters in similar periodic breakdowns of the Mayan civilization mentioned earlier, or the collapse of Assur around 1700 BCE. But as we shall see shortly, natural disasters did hasten (but not cause) the population-generated breakdown in other areas. So did a wholly unexpected element, the invention of writing.

One of the founding fathers of modern psychology, Carl Gustav Jung, somewhere mentions the numinous quality of archetypes, a natural tendency

The deserted city of Palenque, in South America, was just one of those abandoned, for no apparent reason, at the height of their power.

to generate feelings of awe in those who encounter them. The same numinosity clings to spirits, as I witnessed some years ago when a medium agreed for the first time to publicly channel a spirit she introduced as an ancient Egyptian god. Her forty-strong audience consisted largely of professional people and included a judge, a medical doctor, a physicist, several academics, and an engineer. The medium fell into trance and the spirit entity spoke through her to deliver a brief address followed by a request for questions. None were forthcoming, but several members of the audience stood up to pledge themselves to the service of the god, despite the fact that, in our rational age, no one had asked for proofs or bona fides. Most people have a tendency to make unquestioned assumptions about the powers and authority of spirits, even when the communicating entities made no such claims for themselves. When a spirit requires something to be done, one feels an urge to carry out its wishes; and while it is perfectly possible to disobey, it feels uncomfortable to do so. If these observations represent the atrophied remnants of ancestral responses, it is easy to imagine the impact of a spirit command in the cultural context of a listener in, say, 4000 BCE, but only if the command was delivered directly.

Writing seems to have been developed in early societies as a means of keeping track of trade negotiations and possessions, but its scope was quickly extended to record city ordinances and countrywide legislation, both of which had, of course, come from the mouths of the gods. But if a law laid down face-to-face by a deity was virtually impossible to disobey, the same numinousness did not attach to the same law in written form. Writing was a convenience and, like most conveniences, spread very quickly through any culture that developed it. Soon it became the prime carrier of the wishes of the gods and, in so doing, weakened them.

The historical context of the final breakdown, which Jaynes eventually pinpointed to the second millennium BCE, was spectacular:

> [The era] was heavy laden with profound and irreversible changes. Vast geological catastrophes occurred. Civilizations perished. Half the world's population became refugees. And wars, previously sporadic, came with hastening and ferocious frequency as this important millennium hunched itself sickly into its dark and bloody close.[13]

The volcanic eruption at Thera, now firmly placed midway through this millennium, is one of the more striking examples of what Jaynes is talking about here. The Aegean island, some sixty-eight miles north of Crete, exploded with such violence that an estimated twenty-four cubic miles of material was thrown up into the atmosphere, darkening the sky for days and influencing the climate of the whole Northern Hemisphere for years. Nor were the consequences purely local. Climatic effects included crop failures in China. The immediate shock waves were equivalent to the simultaneous detonation of more than thirty H-bombs.[14] After the explosion, the population of Thera itself was obliterated and only a fraction of the island remained above water. A 490-foot-high tsunami devastated the northern coast of Crete, smashing two miles inland at 350 miles an hour to destroy the infrastructure of kingdom after kingdom.[14]

The disaster triggered a series of mass migrations and invasions that brought down both Hittite and Mycenaean empires. As the remnants of the old societies, with their different languages and customs, were forced to intermingle, what guidance could the spirits offer in the face of such overwhelming chaos? Their voices failed and, without divine guidance, humanity promptly made matters worse by embarking on wars of previously unimaginable brutality. The Assyrian king Tiglath-Pileser I staked whole populations alive from groin to shoulder and established a rule of law that amounted to what scholars of a later age would refer to as a "policy of frightfulness."[15] The chaos spread throughout the Mediterranean and the known world. Conflict and brutality took hold on a scale unknown throughout the preceding eight millennia. But these miserable developments were not the only change afoot.

Sometime around 1230 BCE, the Assyrian king Tukulti-Ninurta I commissioned a stone altar that bore his own likeness . . . twice. The first image is of a standing figure. In the second, the tyrant is on his knees before the throne of his god. This is an extraordinary representation, quite unlike earlier versions of the same scene. In these, invariably, the king would stand tall, locked eye to eye with the deity as he listened to its words. At no time, in the millennia-long history of spirit communication, did he kneel. More astonishing still, the throne before which Tukulti-Ninurta prostrates himself is empty. The god has gone.

In modern times we have become so accustomed to the idea of an invisible god that it is difficult to comprehend how shocking this representation really was. In tablet after tablet, altar stone after altar stone, cylinder after cylinder, the god was *always* depicted as an heroic humanoid figure, standing or sitting. Why then in Tukulti's reign is the god missing from this and other altars? Why, suddenly, was he represented by an abstract symbol on the cylinder seals? For Julian Jaynes there was no mystery at all. These scenes depicted reality as our Assyrian ancestors of the time experienced it. And the reality was that their god no longer appeared to them; their god no longer spoke.

Here at last was the turning point Jaynes had been looking for. In ancient Mesopotamia the spirits became silent at some point between the time of Hammurabi (died 1750 BCE), who was frequently depicted communing with his god, and that of Tukulti (1243–1207 BCE), whose deity seemed to have deserted him. Jaynes cast about for confirmation and discovered there were three clay tablets from the time of Tukulti that completely endorsed his conclusions. They were inscribed by a feudal lord named Shubshi-Meshre-Shakkan who began a sorry tale of woe with the words:

> My god has forsaken me and disappeared
> My goddess has failed me and keeps at a distance
> The good angel who walked beside me has departed.[16]

The disappearance of this lord's guardian spirits was only the beginning of his misfortunes. Without their guidance, he quarreled with Tukulti and consequently lost his position as ruler of a city. He fell prey to sickness and other misfortunes. He tried prayer, prostrations, and sacrifices, he consulted priests, but nothing brought the spirits back. (Interestingly, however, they did appear eventually in his dreams to assure him he had been forgiven his offenses and would henceforth prosper—the significance of which will become apparent later in this book.)

The change that was taking place was gradual, extending over some hundreds of years and moving at its own pace in different locations. Jaynes charts its progress as he analyzed it out from scores of ancient texts, scrolls, carvings, and tablets. The ancient hierarchical structure that flourished throughout the third millennium BCE permitted your personal god (with whom you communicated daily) to intercede with your city's god and even, in times of great emergency or need, with the kingdom's chief god, who generally communicated only with the king. Such intercessions were depicted in carving after carving showing the humble petitioner being presented to the great god by a lesser (personal) deity. But by the middle of the second millennium BCE the scenes change. As typified on Tukulti's altar stone, the major gods begin to disappear. Personal gods are seen presenting supplicants not to the ruling deity but only to his symbol. Then, by about the end of the second millennium BCE, there are changes in the representation of the personal god. He, or she, was no longer the purely humanoid deity he used to be but had in many cases metamorphosed into a bizarre half-human, half-avian creature.

Sometimes this new entity appeared as a winged man, reminiscent, in all but artistic style, of later depictions of angels. Sometimes it might appear as a bird-headed human, like the ibis-headed figure of Thoth in the ancient Egyptian pantheon. Sometimes it was a winged bull or lion. In the early stages of the change, such entities appear in presentation scenes, introducing the individual to the symbol of a major god. Later, however, such scenes disappear from the record altogether and the hybrid entities usually appear only as guardians, sometimes of places, sometimes of people, sometimes of kings. Each representation appears to have one thing in common: in no case do the entities speak. The spirits may still appear, but they remain strictly silent. Texts from the period show the reaction of whole populations to the change. There is general consternation and bewilderment. Why have our gods abandoned us? What have we done wrong?

Jaynes is quick to note that in these two archetypal questions lie the roots of the great themes found in every major religion of our modern world. Christ's last cry on the cross—*My God, my God, why hast thou forsaken me?*[17]—is answered not by God but by the great accusation of the Christian church, *Because humanity has sinned!* Nor, it transpired, could any penance or sacrifice atone for the mysterious transgression. When the father of history, the Greek author Herodotus, climbed the steps of the Etemenanki ziggurat in Babylon almost a thousand pleading, prayerful years after the time of Tukulti, he hoped to find a statue at the top, but there was only an empty throne.

As a psychologist, Professor Jaynes had his own theories about spirit contact that shall be examined in a later section of this book. But for the moment, his work is important in that it permits us to build up an intriguing, if somewhat puzzling, historical picture. If Jaynes's deductions are correct, that picture, in summary, is this:

At some point in deep prehistory, more (and possibly much more) than thirty thousand years ago, while humanity led a primitive, difficult, hunter-gather existence, certain individuals of the tribes became aware of spirit contacts and eventually developed techniques, some involving plant narcotics, that allowed them access to the spirit worlds. These individuals, whom we now refer to as shamans, believed they could rely on spirit advice in matters of healing and the location of game, both life-and-death essentials in the rigors of an Ice Age. Their consequent practice as doctors and prophets brought them prestige and a position within their tribe rivaling that of the chief himself. They formed primitive "guilds" to protect the secrets of their craft and adopted initiatory tests and rituals in their selection of candidates who wished to become shamans in their turn. Their work was of such importance to the tribe that (so many modern anthropologists believe) it was commemorated in cave art.

Throughout this whole period, the relationship between shaman and spirit might be characterized as one of cautious respect. Shamans found spirits often helpful, often reliable, but sometimes dangerous and occasionally untruthful. Although spirits could and would sometimes compel action, particularly in the matter of a tribesperson becoming a shaman in the first place, they were never, in any real sense, the masters. But nor were the shamans, whose title "master of the spirits" denoted no more than a skill at making contact and extracting direct assistance or useful information. Nobody actually commanded anybody. Instead, there was, generally speaking, a partnership based on mutual respect.

This situation remained essentially unchanged for tens of thousands of years and appears to have been beneficial to hunter-gatherer communities. But, if Julian Jaynes's patient detective work is correct, something happened approximately ten thousand years ago that marked a transformation—the gradual shift from hunter-gathering to farming, the move away from nomadic to urban lifestyle and larger communities. Whether this shift was prompted by spirit advice or simply a natural, evolutionary development, we have no means of knowing. But the shift itself certainly coincided—if we accept a literal interpretation of the archaeological evidence—with a new form of spirit communication. No longer was the shaman required. No longer were individuals forced to face life-threatening trials to contact spirit worlds. For reasons not yet clearly understood, the spirits stepped forward from their ancient domains and became accessible to entire human populations.

With this change came another: the traditional relationship between human and spirit quickly broke down. No longer was there an equality based on mutual respect. The spirits became masters and something in the new relationship persuaded us to accept the change with the submissiveness of sheep. When a spirit issued orders, some deep-seated instinct compelled people to obey like automata. But the dictatorship proved benevolent. Spirit decrees enabled happy, fulfilled lives, free from any serious degree of conflict. Under spirit leadership, towns became cities, trade developed with other spirit-guided cultures, bellies and purses were full. In gratitude, humans transformed the spirit contacts into gods and offered them worship as well as obedience. It was, in many respects, a golden age and is recalled as such in world mythologies.

The situation remained essentially static for millennia before a further change occurred. A gradual population increase reached critical mass and the hierarchical structure established by the gods could no longer support it. Spirit communications became confused, then counterproductive. Spirit advice could no longer be counted on to produce benevolent results. Society gradually descended into chaos and the day eventually arrived when the spirits themselves began to withdraw. This process too was gradual. Like the shamans of old, there were still some people who could see and hear the spirits, but for the majority, the gods first fell silent, then changed into lesser creatures, and eventually disappeared altogether.

For thousands of years every god had a specific terrestrial location as a statue in a temple or an idol in the home. Now the statues were silent and the idols lifeless lumps of wood or stone. Where had the spirits gone? Humanity supplied its own answer by deciding their deities had retreated into the sky, an identification with heaven (the ultimate home of the gods) that holds good to the present day. A new relationship began, based on unanswered prayers, individual isolation, and distant memories of a time when the gods had real immediacy and power.

But inevitably, there was a gradual adjustment to the new status quo. The priesthood became guardian of social custom, cultural tradition, and religious ritual. Each priest was looked on as a medium channeling cosmic forces, another way of saying that the powers of the gods flowed through him, but the majority asked for their powers to be accepted on faith. Their congregations believed them because belief was more comfortable than complete abandonment.

On a different level, the massive body of Mesopotamian magical texts, much of it concerned with divining the will of the gods or directly seeking their advice, suggests a widespread wish to communicate in the old style that was certainly not confined to the priesthood. Superstition and theological theory rushed in to fill the emotional vacuum. Sumerians came to believe in a gloomy afterlife inhabited by the souls of the dead and were not averse to attempting postmortem contact with their ancestors if they thought it might be beneficial. Enlil, one of whose titles was "Lord of the Land of Ghosts," was said to have gifted humanity with spells and incantations to compel the obedience of spirits, good and evil; and there were those who sought to use the gift to practical effect. Even more common were texts devoted to celestial observation and astrological lore, which attempted to discern the influences emanating from the highest spirit realms on human affairs.[18] But much of this is speculation. For more detailed information on how early civilization adjusted to the change—and established a new and different form of contact with its gods—we need to move away from Mesopotamia to examine another ancient culture whose copious, well-examined records will give us a clearer picture.

The jackal-headed god Anubis (left) was believed to communicate with the citizens of ancient Egypt.

3. THE EGYPTIAN EXPERIENCE

CONVENTIONAL WISDOM CURRENTLY DATES THE FOUNDATION OF EGYPT to the emergence of the first pharaonic dynasty ca. 2925 BCE,[1] a time when, according to Jaynes, widespread spirit communication was still commonplace. The broad sweep of Egyptology readily recognizes the astonishing engineering feats, cosmological preoccupations, and ubiquitous artworks that characterized it. Oxford philosopher Jeremy Naydler adds another dimension:

> The religious life of the ancient Egyptians was never really separate from the rest of their lives. The whole culture was infused with religious awareness, with an awareness that the spirit world interpenetrated all spheres of existence. Ancient Egypt was a sacred culture . . . When we "go back" . . . we are also "going down" to a deeper, more archaic level of human experience that is closer to the gods, closer to a half-forgotten awareness of transpersonal beings and primal encounters with archetypal realities.[2]

By "transpersonal beings," "primal encounters," and "archetypal realities," Naydler means spirits; and there can be little doubt that the ancient Egyptians, obsessed as they were with magic, carried that obsession into the realms of spirit contact long after their personal gods withdrew. The Leiden Papyrus, a New Kingdom copy of a manuscript tentatively dated 1850–1600 BCE, contains a spell to establish communication with the god Anubis. The spell, coming after the time the gods had begun to withdraw, may have been an act of desperation, but may possibly have been effective in that it created an experience of spirit communication. Certainly the structure of the rite set a pattern for similar "magical" spirit evocations in the centuries to come. According to the detailed instructions, one first engraves a bronze bowl with the figure of Anubis, then fills it with water and floats oil on the surface. The bowl is then placed on three new bricks, with four other bricks spread out beside it. Before beginning the rite, a child lies on his stomach on the surrounding bricks, with his chin on the brick on which the bowl is resting. His head is then covered with a cloth and a lighted lamp set on his right and a censer with fire on his left. Incense made up of frankincense, wax, styrax, turpentine, datestone, and wine is in the censer and a leaf of the Anubis plant[3] is placed on the lamp. One would then repeat the words "open my eyes" four times, "open my eyes, open thy eyes" three times, "open Tat, open Nap" three times, and "open unto me" also three times.

There follows a long, complex conjuration, repeated seven times, after which the child is required to open his eyes and look into the bowl. If the boy confirms that the god is beginning to appear to him, there follows a briefer finishing incantation, after which the god might be questioned. But not directly. Any communication, questions or answers, is passed on by the child.

To most modern ears, this sounds like superstitious hocus-pocus, but experience shows that scrying techniques of this sort, which include the use of black mirrors and (usually blue) water bowls with or without the oil, produce results. Staring fixedly into the bowl can engender a trancelike state, possibly due to self-hypnosis, during which visions will typically occur. Even the placing of lamp and flaming censer is significant. A variation of the technique, which requires a candle and mirror, is used to this day by occultists attempting to investigate past lives.[4] The use of a young child as a medium is confirmed time and again in later magical texts, based on the presumption that an immature mind is more open to this type of experience. The discovery of the technique, wrapped up though it might be in Egyptian religious and magical beliefs, confirms that when their gods withdrew, the culture of ancient Egypt was familiar with at least one workable method of continuing communication with spirits. There were others.

According to Sir Wallis Budge, onetime Keeper of Egyptian Antiquities at the British Museum and still considered an important authority on the culture, Egyptians believed that divine powers often made their will known through dreams.

> They attached considerable importance to them; the figures of the gods and the scenes which they saw when dreaming seemed to them to prove the existence of another world which was not greatly unlike that already known

to them. The knowledge of the art of procuring dreams and the skill to interpret them were greatly prized in Egypt as elsewhere in the East, and the priest or official who possessed such gifts sometimes rose to places of high honor in the state . . . for it was universally believed that glimpses of the future were revealed to man in dreams . . . [among those] recorded in the Egyptian texts may be quoted [that] of Thothmes IV, king of Egypt about B.C. 1450 . . .

A prince, according to the stele which he set up before the breast of the Sphinx at Gizeh, was one day hunting near this emblem of Râ-Harmachis, and he sat down to rest under its shadow and fell asleep and dreamed a dream. In it the god appeared to him, and, having declared that he was the god Harmachis-Khepera-Râ-Temu, promised him that if he would clear away from the Sphinx, his own image, the drift sand in which it was becoming buried, he would give to him the sovereignty of the lands of the South and of the North, *i.e.*, of all Egypt. In due course the prince became king of Egypt under the title of Thothmes IV, and the stele which is dated on the 19th day of the month Hathor of the first year of Thothmes IV proves that the royal dreamer carried out the wishes of the god.[5]

The perceived relationship between gods, spirits, and dreams is underlined by an account of demonic possession inscribed on a stele discovered in the temple of the god Khonsu at Thebes. During the fifteenth year of the reign of Rameses II, the Princess of Bekhten, who was the younger sister of the king's favorite wife, became ill and was diagnosed as having fallen victim of demonic possession. Her father consequently dispatched word to the king, begging him to send a god to help.[6]

Rameses was in Thebes when the messenger arrived and went directly to the temple of Khonsu Nefer-hetep where he asked the god to send his high priest, also named Khonsu, to Bekhten to exorcise the demon. The account on the stele gives no details of how the king communicated with Khonsu Nefer-hetep, but does record that the god agreed to the request and imbued a statue of himself with a "fourfold measure of magical power" to help with the cure.[7] (Since Rameses reigned from about 1303 to 1213 BCE, there may have been records or folk memories of the era during which statues spoke with spirit voices.) A procession of six boats then set off down the Nile, accompanied by a retinue of chariots and horses on each bank, the lead vessel carrying the magical statue, with images of different gods occupying the others.

Several months later, the party arrived in Bekhten and performed a magical ceremony over the ailing princess.[8] The demon immediately left her and struck up a remarkably friendly conversation with the god, during which they agreed to hold a great festival in the demon's honor. This was duly done and the demon then happily left the country.

The ruler of Bekhten, a remote African principality some distance from Egypt, was so impressed by the god's performance that he determined to keep him from returning to Egypt. The stele records that Khonsu Nefer-hetep did indeed remain in Bekhten for three years, four months, and five days. But one night the Prince of Bekhten dreamed the god had turned into a golden hawk and flown back to Egypt. When he awoke, the priest Khonsu confirmed the god had departed and advised that his chariot should be sent after him. The Prince of Bekhten agreed and sent the vehicle back loaded with gifts that were later housed in the temple at Thebes.

This story was not the only oddity to surface when archaeologists began to investigate ancient Egypt. Among the strangest was the practice of writing letters to the dead. Egyptian religion focused largely on survival of physical death. Tombs were known as Palaces of Eternity and those who could afford it ensured they were spacious and well enough equipped to provide a comfortable environment in which to spend the afterlife. "Thou shall exist for millions of millions of years," promised the Egyptian *Book of the Dead.* And the dead continued to exert an influence on the living—or so the living believed. Any misfortune visited on widows, widowers, or other survivors was attributed to neglect, even malevolence, on the part of the recently departed, who were failing to defend their loved ones as they should. It made sense to send them written reminders of their duty and practical results were confidently expected.

The letters themselves were usually inscribed on ceramic vessels, but papyrus or linen could also be used. They were then "posted" in a tomb, although not necessarily the tomb of the recipient. The afterlife, with its Palaces of Eternity, was seen as a continuum. The letter writers had absolute faith that their missives would find their way to their proper destination. What was written obviously varied from person to person, but enough of the letters have been discovered to show some typical patterns. One was the complaint that relatives were trying to defraud the rightful heir of the deceased's estate. Legal action might be threatened, but not necessarily against the relatives. One of the letters indicates that the writer was a widower convinced his current misfortunes were due to his late wife's ill will. In it, he takes pains to remind her what a model husband he had been, staying faithful to her, employing the best possible physician when she fell ill, then providing a first-class funeral and formally mourning her for a full eight months when death finally claimed her. Three years had passed since then, during which time he had not remarried, nor so much as touched any female member of his household, yet she had seen fit to behave like someone who could not tell right from wrong. In the circumstances, he found himself with no alternative but to mount a suit against her in the Divine Court of the West . . . a legal institution that formed part of the realm of the dead.[9] The obvious question, of course, is whether this could be seen as a practical approach. If so, the aggrieved husband must have been convinced that some method existed by which he could visit the afterlife and return to tell the tale.

For conventional Egyptologists this idea is absurd, as is the tale of the possessed princess. But perhaps we should not be too hasty in endorsing these conclusions. First it is beneficial to take a closer look at the individual central to the Bekhten story, although mentioned only once in Budge's account —the priest Khonsu.

Priesthood, in ancient Egypt, meant something very different from what it does today. We are accustomed to thinking of the clergy in terms of religious vocation, belief in God, pastoral duties, and so forth. In ancient Egypt, however, God was incarnate in the person of the pharaoh, whose duty it was to carry out the multiplicity of religious practices that ensured the country would continue to function in an effective manner. He was, in theory, obliged to perform every ritual in every temple throughout Egypt, but since, god or no god, he could not be everywhere at once, his priesthood stood in for him. No vocation, particular spirituality, or special relationship with the Almighty was involved. Nor was there anything remotely resembling pastoral work—the common people never entered the temples, let alone worshipped there. The priests were simply civil servants who carried out the duties Pharaoh could not manage for himself. Many of those duties were magical in nature.

But Egyptian magic, as Budge is quick to remind us, dated "from a time when the predynastic and prehistoric dwellers in Egypt believed that the earth, and the underworld, and the air, and the sky were peopled with countless beings, visible and invisible."[10] There are distinct echoes of the shaman in Budge's description of the typical priest-magician:

The temple at Philae

From the religious books of ancient Egypt we learn that the power possessed by a priest or man who was skilled in the knowledge and working of magic was believed to be almost boundless. By pronouncing certain words or names of power in the proper manner and in the proper tone of voice he could heal the sick, and cast out the evil spirits which caused pain and suffering in those who were diseased, and restore the dead to life, and bestow upon the dead man the power to transform the corruptible into an incorruptible body, wherein the soul might live to all eternity. His words enabled human beings to assume divers forms at will, and to project their souls into animals and other creatures; and in obedience to his commands, inanimate figures and pictures became living beings and things which hastened to perform his behests. The powers of nature acknowledged his might.[11]

The Egyptian priest was required to abstain from sex before embarking on a magical operation, the same prohibition observed by the *pagé* in Thévet's vivid account of shamanic practice quoted earlier. While the wearing of animal fibers such as wool was strictly forbidden, the *sem*-priest (high priest) was required to wear a leopard skin as a mark of his office[12]—reminiscent of shamanic practice in tribal Africa. Is it possible that the religion of ancient Egypt was, in its later manifestations, a return to shamanic practice, albeit modified by the specific needs of the times? For mainstream Egyptologists, the answer is a resounding no. Egyptian religion is well known and well studied. The consensus sees it as an exotic, faith-based creed, partly focused on funerary customs and preparations for the afterlife, partly on the ritual activities of the pharaoh, which guaranteed the well-being and prosperity of the state. Nonetheless, there are pointers in a different direction.

What are now known as the Pyramid Texts were a series of writings carved into the walls and sarcophagi of the Saqqara pyramids during the fifth and sixth dynasties of the Old Kingdom, between 2465 and 2181 BCE. The oldest of them have been dated, with reasonable certainty, to the period between 2400 and 2300 BCE but may reflect an even earlier oral tradition. Since they were discovered in 1881 by the French Egyptologist Gaston Maspero, the texts have generally been interpreted as a series of spells or "utterances" used to guide a dead pharaoh through the afterlife in his journey toward the heavens.

There are two problems with this interpretation. The first is that the texts were discovered randomly, with no way to tell for certain in what order they should be read: thus any picture of the pharaoh's journey can be no more

Texts discovered at Saqqara point to shamanic practice by the Egyptian pharaohs.

than guesswork. The second is that the texts themselves insist the pharaoh is not dead. Utterance 219, on the south wall of the sarcophagus chamber, begins with the words:

> Atum, this your son is here . . . whom you have preserved alive. He lives! He lives! This Unas lives! He is not dead, this Unas is not dead! He is not gone down, this Unas is not gone down! He has not been judged, this Unas has not been judged![13]

This jubilant passage, varied to address different gods, is repeated no less than twenty-two times, emphasizing again and again that the king is not dead. In Utterance 223, he is told to stand up, stir himself, and have some beer and bread. For conventional Egyptologists, these passages represent little more than a state of denial, a refusal to accept the reality of death, expressed in the pious hope that the king somehow survived in an afterlife. But the final sentence of the text as quoted above seems conclusively to give the lie to this interpretation. In Egyptian religion the dead were escorted by the god Anubis to the Halls of Judgment where their souls were weighed against a feather. This had to happen before they could proceed to their reward or punishment. There was no other way for a dead person to continue his journey. Yet the text clearly states that Unas has not been judged. If he was dead, for him to proceed without the final judgment would deny everything the Egyptians believed about the afterlife. The logical deduction, as the text itself insists, is that what is being described here are not the experiences of a dead king but of a living one.

Naydler reminds us that "death was, for the Egyptians . . . a realm of invisible forces, powers and beings. It was a spirit realm that existed in a more interior way than the outwardly manifest world that we perceive with our senses, but is nevertheless regarded as completely real" and "[this] spiritual universe of the ancient Egyptians . . . [has] a great deal in common with that revealed in the literature of shamanism."[14] Rather than describing the postmortem fate of a deceased pharaoh, is it possible that the Pyramid Texts actually refer to a shamanic journey carried out while he was very much alive?

According to Harner and Eliade, the shamanic universe consists of three "worlds," the Upper, Middle, and Lower. The Middle World is the familiar physical plane in which we live. The Lower is the home of animal spirits. The Upper is the realm of the gods. A shamanic journey to the Upper World would typically begin with an entranced shaman allowing himself to be carried upward by the smoke of a campfire or, in more recent times, a censer or incense stick.[15] There was also the possibility of entering nonordinary reality to discover a ladder or a flight of steps linking earth and heaven. Utterance 365 of the Unas texts reads, "The earth is beaten into steps for him towards heaven, that he may mount on it towards heaven, and he rises on the smoke of the great fumigation."[16] Had he previously visited the Lower World and made contact with his power animal,[17] he might learn from it, among many other things, the ability to shape-shift, which he could then use to take himself anywhere he wished to go. The coronation text of Thutmosis III describes him as rising to heaven in the form of a falcon.[18] When he reaches the Otherworld, he might find himself undergoing a complete dismemberment by demons or gods followed by a mystical reassembly that again conferred powers. Utterance 117 of the Unas Texts begins with its own description of this experience: "Osiris Unas, receive your head . . ." And Utterance 213 emphasizes above all that the pharaoh was not making this journey as the soul of a dead man: "O Unas, you have not gone dead, you have gone alive, to sit on the throne of Osiris, your scepter in your hand that you may give orders to the living, the handle of your lotus-shaped scepter in your hand."[19]

What is emerging here is a very curious picture indeed. It is a picture of ancient Egypt as a shamanic culture writ large. Where, in more primitive communities, the shaman transported himself to the spirit worlds for the benefit of his tribe, in ancient Egypt, the king transported himself to the spirit worlds for the benefit of the entire country. His ability to do so, like the shaman before him, was the ultimate source of his authority and power. That he could walk among the withdrawn gods, and return to earth unscathed, was the root of his divinity, which means a civilization that endured for some three thousand years did so under constant spirit guidance. But lest we are tempted to conclude that the structure of ancient Egypt is too remote to have any relevance to the present day, it may be useful here to introduce the earliest known foundation of a religion that remains to this day a major driving force in twenty-first-century culture.

The Hebrew prophet Moses was a teacher and leader who, in the thirteenth century BCE, delivered his people from Egyptian slavery and in so doing founded the religious community of Israel. As such, "his influence continues to be felt in the religious life, moral concerns, and social ethics of

Western civilization."[20] Although seldom mentioned or examined from any-thing but a purely faith-based standpoint, that influence was ultimately based on communications from a spirit voice.

The origins of Moses's story are lost in the depths of history. Even the term *Hebrew*, in its original form of *Habiru*, had nothing to do with ethnicity or race but referred instead to a class of people who lived by providing var-ious services for hire. As such they were a familiar sight in Egypt for many generations, apparently well assimilated culturally. But it would be wrong to view even the earliest of Hebrews as a scattering of freelance tradesmen. They clearly comprised a unified class within the overall society, living mainly in their own district, Goshen, and as years went by their numbers grew[21] to such an extent that they came to be perceived as a threat to the ruling authority. Who that authority was remains a matter for conjecture, but the best guess of modern scholarship points to Seti I, a pharaoh who reigned from 1318 to 1304 BCE. Whether or not this is correct, there is much more certainty that one or another Egyptian pharaoh moved to enslave the Hebrews and attempted to control their numbers by means of a brutal cull of newborn males. When the plan was first put into practice, the main instruments of the cull were to be Hebrew midwives—among them Jochebed, Moses's mother, and Miriam, his sister, herself still a child—but when the women refused to cooperate, the Egyptians sent bailiffs to seek out the babes and drown them.[22]

Jochebed herself became pregnant, but the child was born prematurely, thus allowing her to conceal the birth from the Egyptian bailiffs who, while they watched pregnant Hebrews carefully, were not expecting so early a delivery. She successfully concealed the baby for three months despite the fact that her home was guarded, but the father of the child, Amram, became increas-ingly concerned that it would be discovered, an eventuality that carried the certainty of death for them all. Consequently, he decided to leave his son's fate to God and ordered his wife to abandon the baby. Sources vary as to where the child was left—some claim it was on the shores of the Red Sea, others that he was floated away in an ark on a river, usually specified as the Nile. There is closer agreement on what happened next.

It appears to have been particularly hot in Egypt at the time and much of the population suffered from boils. Among them was Thermutis, a daugh-ter of the pharaoh, who went to bathe in the Nile to seek relief from her pains. There she saw a small ark floating in the water and suspected it might contain one of the infants exposed for drowning on her father's order. When her ser-

Angelic spirits watch over the infant Moses in this artistic depiction of his early legend.

vants refused to fetch it, afraid as they were of contravening the pharaoh's edict, Thermutis retrieved it herself. The little vessel did indeed contain a baby boy[23] whom she decided to name *Mose* (or possibly *Tutmose*) and bring up as her own.[24] Consequently, Moses was reared as a prince of Egypt, with the inference that he was educated in religious, political, civil, and military matters. For all this, he somehow discovered his Hebrew origins and went as a young man to visit Goshen. Tradition has it that he was so appalled by the treatment meted out to his people that he abandoned life at court to come and work among them. One day he witnessed an Egyptian taskmaster beating a Hebrew, probably to the point of death. Jewish legend has it that the Egyptian had previously slept with the man's wife and was anxious to get him out of the way. Moses was appalled by both the dishonoring of the woman (who became pregnant) and the beating. When no one else would intervene, he stepped in himself and killed the taskmaster.

It proved an act impossible to keep secret. Within days, two Hebrew brothers, Dathan and Abiram, betrayed him to the pharaoh who, according to some sources,[25] ordered his execution. Moses fled to northwestern Arabia, to what was then the country of Midian. There he married Zipporah, a daughter of the Midianite priest Jethro, and for some years he attended to her father's flocks. One day, while roaming the wilderness in search of pasture, he saw in the foothills of Mount Horeb a miraculously burning thornbush that somehow survived destruction by the flames. As Moses approached, a voice issued from the fire, introducing itself as the god of his forefathers and ordering him to deliver his people out of their slavery in Egypt.

The best-known version of this story, a precis in the scriptural book of Exodus, gives the impression that this was Moses's first brush with paranormal phenomena, a unique experience of divinity that shortly led to the establishment of the Jewish religion. In fact, if rabbinical tradition is to be believed, spirit voices and visions played an important part in the Mosaic dialogue right from the point of Moses's birth.

Moses's father, Amram, belonged to the priestly tribe of Levi and attracted a reputation for extreme piety even among that august company. When Jochebed became pregnant—apparently much to the surprise of all concerned—Amram found himself in a state of confusion: the pharaoh Seti had not only decreed a general separation of Hebrew couples in order to lower the rate of pregnancy, but he had issued his notorious order for the slaughter of any male children whom the couples nonetheless managed to conceive. In his perplexity, Amram turned to God for guidance and was rewarded by a spirit visitation in a dream: God "stood beside him in his sleep" and prophesied that:

> the child out of dread of whose nativity the Egyptians have doomed the Israelite children to destruction, shall be this child of thine and shall remain concealed from those who watch to destroy him and when he has been bred up, in a miraculous way, he shall deliver the Hebrew nation from the distress they are under by reason of the Egyptians. His memory shall be celebrated while the world lasts, and not only among the Hebrews, but among strangers also.[26]

Moses's sister, Miriam, seems also to have been prone to visions: she experienced a white light in the house at the moment of her brother's birth and prophesied he would grow up to redeem Israel. Later, when the babe was abandoned in the ark, Pharaoh's daughter is believed to have experienced a revelation of the archangel Gabriel and an appearance of the Shekinah (the feminine aspect of God) in the vessel with the child. When the boy was two years old, she had another spirit visitation, this time from an entity claiming divinity who endowed her with the name Bithiah, the "daughter of God." In a fascinating aside, the tradition mentions that in face of her pious deeds, she was permitted to enter Paradise alive—an echo of the pharaoh's own shamanic journeys into the spirit worlds.

Tradition records a further example of spirit intervention when Moses was two years old. During a banquet, the infant, who was seated on his mother's lap beside the pharaoh, took the crown from the king's head and placed it on his own. The act was interpreted as a significant omen and there was immediate discussion as to whether the child should be put to death. Pharaoh, however, decided the matter needed more deliberate consideration and called together a council of "all the wise men of Egypt." These worthies appeared with the disguised archangel Gabriel in their midst, who suggested testing the child with a choice between an onyx stone and a burning coal. Moses convinced everyone of his stupidity when he picked up the coal and tried to eat it, burning his lips and tongue. The act left him slow of speech for the rest of his life—something mentioned at a later point in the biblical version of his story—but saved him from execution.

Jewish folklore also suggests the burning bush was not the first instance of a spirit voice communicating with Moses himself. When he visited Goshen as a young man, witnessed Hebrew suffering for the first time, and made his decision to leave court and work among his own people, he heard a disembodied voice proclaim: "Thou didst relinquish all thy other occupations and didst join thyself unto the children of Israel, whom thou dost treat as brethren; therefore will I too put aside now all heavenly and earthly affairs and hold converse with thee."[27] There is also a tradition that when Moses eventually fled from Egypt after killing the overseer, he was led to safety by a vision of the archangel Gabriel.

There are substantially more mythic accretions to the Moses story, many of which are doubtless the miraculous fictions that attach themselves to every powerful religious figure. However, the examples already mentioned have a ring of veracity about them in that they follow a well-established pattern of voices and visions, culminating in a major revelation. Analysis of this revelation produces some interesting insights.

In the version given in Exodus, Moses had a vision of an angel who appeared in the midst of a flaming bush. Tradition identifies the angel as the archangel Michael, associated with the element of fire, and suggests he had appeared as a forerunner of the Shekinah who was shortly to descend from heaven. A voice within the flames then called out Moses's name, but when he went to investigate he was told to halt and remove his shoes for he was approaching holy ground. At this point in the biblical account, the voice introduces itself as "the God of thy father, the God of Abraham, the God of Isaac and the God of Jacob."[28] The expanded version of Hebrew tradition introduces an additional element of considerable interest to the present thesis: the voice that called to Moses was, recognizably, the voice of his father, Amram.[29] It was a long time since Moses had seen either of his parents and he had no way of knowing whether they were alive or dead.

The legendary interpretation of Moses's burning bush contact contains an apologia for this curious development. God realized that Moses was a novice in the art of prophecy and reasoned that if he spoke in a loud, godlike voice, the man would be alarmed. But conversely, if he spoke softly, Moses might not take his words seriously. Consequently he elected to mimic the voice of Amram, as a reassurance. After explaining the ruse to Moses, God then set about confirming his own bona fides by having the angel Metatron arrange a trip to the seven heavens accompanied by a thirty-thousand-spirit bodyguard. The descriptions of the seven heavens are fanciful in the extreme but carry hallmarks of genuine shamanic experiences, including the visions of Merkava mystics.[30]

Following this experience and a spectacular trip to hell, the voice then charged Moses with the task of freeing his people from their bondage in Egypt, which by now was under the rule of Rameses II, one of the most powerful pharaohs in Egyptian history. Not unreasonably, Moses demurred. The voice in the bush instructed him to explain to Pharaoh that he had been sent by YHVH (Yahweh), a name translated in the King James Bible as "I am that I am" but held in Jewish mystical tradition to be an acronym for the ultimate Name of God that must never be pronounced aloud. When Moses complained that he was unlikely to be believed, the entity taught him what amounted to three conjuring tricks—changing a rod to a serpent and back again, creating a temporary illusion of leprosy in one hand, and changing water into the appearance of blood—designed to impress Pharaoh. During Moses's subsequent meeting with the pharaoh, however, they did nothing of the sort and it was only after a series of plagues that the Egyptian king finally released the Hebrews from servitude.

Throughout his verbal battles with Pharaoh and during the long nomadic period that followed the Hebrew release, Moses was in almost constant communication with his spirit voice. Eventually it led him and his followers back to the familiar location of Mount Horeb (Sinai) where he had seen the burning bush and there delivered a major communication that was to change the social history of the entire Western world: the dictation to Moses of the Decalogue or Ten Commandments. The act took place in a dramatic thunderstorm, witnessed from a distance by Moses's followers. It created a social structure unlike any that preceded it, backed as it was by claims of divine authority. Scriptural sources give the uninterpreted rendering as follows:

> And God spake all these words, saying,
>
> "I am the LORD thy God, which have brought thee out of the land of Egypt, out of the house of bondage.
>
> "Thou shalt have no other gods before me.
>
> "Thou shalt not make unto thee any graven image, or any likeness of any thing that is in heaven above, or that is in the earth beneath, or that is in the water under the earth.
>
> "Thou shalt not bow down thyself to them, nor serve them: for I the LORD thy God am a jealous God, visiting the iniquity of the fathers upon the children unto the third and fourth generation of them that hate me;
>
> "And shewing mercy unto thousands of them that love me, and keep my commandments.
>
> "Thou shalt not take the name of the LORD thy God in vain; for the LORD will not hold him guiltless that taketh his name in vain.
>
> "Remember the sabbath day, to keep it holy.
>
> "Six days shalt thou labor, and do all thy work:
>
> "But the seventh day is the sabbath of the LORD thy God: in it thou shalt not do any work, thou, nor thy son, nor thy daughter, nor thy manservant, nor thy maidservant, nor thy cattle, nor thy stranger that is within thy gates:
>
> "For in six days the LORD made heaven and earth, the sea, and all that in them is, and rested the seventh day: wherefore the LORD blessed the sabbath day, and hallowed it.
>
> "Honor thy father and thy mother: that thy days may be long upon the land which the LORD thy God giveth thee.
>
> "Thou shalt not kill.
>
> "Thou shalt not commit adultery.
>
> "Thou shalt not steal.

"Thou shalt not bear false witness against thy neighbor.

"Thou shalt not covet thy neighbor's house, thou shalt not covet thy neighbor's wife, nor his manservant, nor his maidservant, nor his ox, nor his ass, nor any thing that is thy neighbor's."[31]

Interestingly, the spirit voice also gave Moses detailed instructions on how to construct a device that would aid communication from then on, the Ark of the Covenant, which, like the god-statues of old, was to provide a dwelling place for divinity. (Later scriptural reading shows, however, that it was more often used as a weapon of war.)

Although exhibiting an apparent simplicity, the commandments have been the subject of considerable scholarly debate. While the first is often claimed to be a statement of monotheism, this is clearly not the philosophical monotheism of modern Judaism, Christianity, or Islam. The spirit tacitly acknowledges the existence of other gods and insists only that they should be seen as subservient to Yahweh. There is controversy too about the ban on "graven images" used as objects of worship. On the face of it, this applies to the statues of other gods worshipped as divinities in their own right throughout the ancient world. As we have seen in an earlier chapter, the statue *was* the god, so that their prohibition would seem to represent little more than a step beyond the first commandment, which insisted other gods must accept the ultimate authority of Yahweh: now they must be banished altogether. But scholarly investigation suggests the prohibition originally applied only to images of Yahweh himself,[32] thus emphasizing the importance of direct communication with deity of the type Moses himself seems to have enjoyed throughout much of his adult life. At the same time, the ban on "taking the name of the Lord in vain"—now generally seen as a prohibition against swearing—has been interpreted by some scholars as attacking the use of the divine name for magical purposes, notably the evocation and control of other spirits.

There is, however, no controversy at all about the far-reaching influence of Moses's mediumistic activities on the history of Western humanity. Nor, as we shall see in later chapters, was he the only man to make contact with a spirit and in so doing change the world. But before continuing an examination of such individuals, the chronology of our narrative returns us to the more broadly based spirit contacts of other early civilizations.

4. MYSTERIES OF ANCIENT GREECE AND ROME

Accoding to Pliny the Younger, Rome's famous lawyer, author, and magistrate:

There was at Athens a mansion . . . of evil repute and dangerous to health. In the dead of night . . . a specter used to appear, an ancient man sinking with emaciation and squalor, with a long beard and bristly hair, wearing shackles on his legs and fetters on his hands . . . Hence the inmates, by reason of their fears, passed miserable and horrible nights in sleeplessness . . . The mansion was accordingly . . . abandoned to the dreadful ghost.

However, it was advertised . . . [and] . . . Athenodorus the philosopher . . . read the advertisement. When he had been informed of the terms, which were so low as to appear suspicious, he made inquiries, and learned the whole of the particulars. Yet . . . did he rent the house.

As evening began to draw on . . . the shaking of irons and the clanking of chains was heard, yet he never raised his eyes . . . The noise . . . approached: now it seemed to be heard at the door, and next inside the door. He looked round, beheld and recognized the figure he had been told of . . . and followed it. It moved with a slow step . . . and after turning into the courtyard of the house vanished suddenly and left his company.

On being thus left to himself, he marked the spot with some grass and leaves which he plucked.

Next day he applied to the magistrates, and urged them to have the spot in question dug up. There were found there some bones attached to and intermingled with fetters; the body to which they had belonged, rotted away by time and the soil, had abandoned them thus naked and corroded to the chains. They were collected and interred at the public expense, and the house was ever afterward free from the spirit, which had obtained due sepulture.

The above story I believe on the strength of those who affirm it.[1]

In this account, Athenodorus's practical, down-to-earth approach to the ghost reflects his culture. Ancient Greece was populated by an expansive pantheon of divinities who, while theoretically resident on the distant peaks of Mount Olympus, were intimately involved in every aspect of human life. The supreme deity, Zeus, guarded the home, ensured the sanctity of oaths, protected storehouses and supplicants, insisted on the gift of hospitality to strangers, and brought justice and safeguarded the city, among a host of other duties. His lesser companions took over where he left off: Eros was in charge of love, Selene governed the moon, Demeter protected agriculture, and so on, almost endlessly, so that spirit intervention was accepted as a rule of nature and a fact of life.

Scholarly analysis suggests classical Greek religion emerged from a blending of Cretan goddess worship and, later, more masculine elements personified in the mighty Zeus himself. But the roots run both deeper and wider than that. Any study of the subject will reveal an uneven, but clearly recognizable, development from primitive magical practice to official state religion. The progression extends from a type of nature worship where spirits were thought to animate the wind and the waters, to a more sophisticated religious expression in which the gods appeared in human form. Yet even at its most developed, the magical element remained, most noticeably visible in popular cults that simply associated natural forces, flora, and fauna with specific gods and goddesses. Overall, religious expression in classical Greece was an amalgamation of early Aegean and later Indo-European elements, with the former including Minoan and Mycenean survivals dating back to the Bronze Age. Against such a background, it comes as little surprise to discover evidence of widespread spirit contact. Among the most intriguing sources were the Greek Mysteries.

Although often referred to as a religion, the Mysteries were actually an induced religious experience. Tradition has it they were founded by Orpheus, the legendary singer who charmed beasts, birds, rocks, rivers, and trees with voice and lyre. Ancient genealogies date him to a time prior to the thirteenth century BCE, but scholarly investigation is content to fix a later date, somewhere in the fifth or sixth century BCE, which saw the emergence of Orphic groups dedicated to a life of purity, with dietary restrictions and sexual abstinence. The similarity to shamanism has been noted and shamanism is accepted as one of the roots of Orphism. Its main expression, in those early days, was its staunch support of the individual, leaving one free to choose

The ruins of Eleusis, which was once the heart of a religion that held out the promise of direct spirit contact.

whatever form of worship he or she wished—a novel idea at the time. There is some suggestion of spirit contact, notably in the activities of the priest-prophet Pythagoras, who around 500 BCE, seems to have channeled Orpheus in some of his writings. He certainly attributed portions of his own work to Orpheus without, however, establishing any satisfactory historical provenance. The emphasis within Orphism on "Orphic" poetry, with its traditional evocation of the Muse—herself a spirit creature—is another small pointer in the same direction. But the prime manifestation was in the Mysteries themselves.

Historically, the first location of the ritual Mysteries was the small Greek town of Eleusis, a coastal city on the Isthmus of Corinth, between Athens and Megara. Ceremonies were held there in honor of the goddess Demeter. Among them were local initiations of town burgesses, in rites that were more political than religious and strictly confined to Eleusinian townspeople. But the practice underwent a profound change when Eleusis was annexed by Athens around 600 BCE. This meant Athenians were now entitled to initiation and many of them claimed the right. Greeks from other areas soon began to follow suit.

At about this time, there was a change in the nature of the rite as well, which moved in emphasis from political to mystical. Participation was no longer a matter of becoming a town burgess but of undergoing a literally life-changing experience. When the Ptolemaic (Greek) pharaohs became established in Egypt, their Alexandrian capital expanded to include a new suburb named for Eleusis, with its own cult of Demeter offering initiations patterned on the Greek originals. The influence of Eleusis spread to another popular cult, the ecstatic rites of Dionysus. As god of wine, Dionysus had long encouraged his followers to seek the transpersonal in group dancing, drinking, and sexual release. Now the emphasis slowly shifted toward individual salvation.

The Mysteries, from whatever source offered, were open to everyone able to speak Greek, whether they be male or female, freeman or slave, but the initiate was bound by oath to hold the rites absolutely secret. While tens of thousands learned it, that secret was kept, a telling tribute to the power of the central experience. To this day, our knowledge of what really happened in the Mysteries is extremely fragmentary, but there are hints, clues, and small revelations from both archaeology and ancient documents that permit us to patch together a broad picture.

Focus of the rites was the great telesterion (initiation hall) at Eleusis, on the site of which, archaeological digs have confirmed, were a series of buildings from prehistoric times onward. But before the rites could begin, the initiate had to be carefully prepared. A Homeric Hymn, one of thirty-three anonymous Greek texts celebrating individual gods, throws some light on the preliminary rituals. Initiation, it seems, began with a purification. This was carried out by a priest or priestess of the Mysteries while the candidate was seated on a stool, with his head veiled and one foot resting on a ram's fleece. No record exists to describe the nature of the purification, but there are hints that it may have involved fire. Exactly how is open to speculation: simple censing seems the most likely approach, although more rigorous tests of faith like fire-walking cannot be completely ruled out.

Purification was followed by a nine-day fast, during which the candidate was allowed neither food nor wine, although it is unclear whether other liquids were permitted. Given a maximum daily temperature of 26.7°C (80.06°F),[2] it is possible to survive for nine days without water, but only at the risk of near-terminal dehydration. Nonetheless, if the aim of a Mysteries initiation was to induce an altered state of consciousness, a risky ordeal of this sort may have been considered acceptable. During or immediately after the fast period, the initiate was obliged to take part in a vigorous all-night festival (*pannychis*), which involved torchlit dances around the well Callichoron, still visible at the entrance to the Eleusinian sanctuary to this day.[3] Here too one can see the possibility of an altered state.

The fast was broken with a special drink combining barley, water, and pennyroyal. Although pennyroyal oil is highly toxic, indeed lethal, in quite small doses the herb itself was used in a culinary capacity in ancient Greece and to flavor wine. Taken as an infusion, one of its medicinal properties is to promote sweating. Some authorities have speculated that the barley used in the preparation might have been (purposely) contaminated by ergot, a fungus known to induce hallucinations. Thus, if we take the preliminaries as a whole, their similarity to shamanic preparations involving exhausting ordeals and psychotropic plants becomes evident. What evidence we have clearly points to initiation as the induction of a mind-altering experience.

When Athens took over the Eleusinian Mysteries, the preliminaries became more complex and a new structure was introduced formalizing what was known as initiation into the Lesser Mysteries. These rites took place in Athens, while the ultimate initiation of the Greater Mysteries remained centered on Eleusis. Purification was still an important preliminary and now included a sort of baptism in the River Ilissus. Here too there is a possibility that the aim was an altered consciousness. In a later era, the famous Qabalistic rabbi Isaac Luria developed a system of total immersion designed to trigger higher visionary states. Adepts in this system first entered a river, lake, or special ritual bath called a *mikvah*. Before immersing themselves completely, they were required to engage in a complex meditation on the term *mikvah*, then on the word *nachal*, a stream. When this was completed, they were instructed to immerse themselves fully in the water, then emerge with the words *Im tashiv miShabbat raglecha*, a quotation from the book of Isaiah that translates, "If you rest your foot for the Sabbath." Although the meditative sequence, which involved the divine names of God, was an intellectual powerhouse, it seems from texts left by Luria's pupils that the act of immersion was the main thing. Breath retention, which forms such an important part of Oriental yoga systems, combined with visualization and other forms of meditation is another tested route to mystical experience. One school of thought even holds that early Christian baptism was not the symbolic sprinkling used in churches today, nor even the (brief) total immersion of some fundamentalist denominations. Instead it is argued that the earliest Christians were held under water at the literal risk of their lives until oxygen starvation forced a change of consciousness with visionary experiences analogous to the life of a drowning man flashing before his eyes. But whatever might have been experienced, initiation into the Lesser Mysteries at Athens was seen as no more than a preparation for entering the Greater Mysteries later in the year. Consequently, the ceremonies had an instructive content, although scholars have yet to discover exactly what knowledge was imparted.

The Greater Mysteries were held in the month of Boedromion (September –October) from the fifteenth to the twenty-third day. Two grades of admission were on offer, with a full year between them and admission to the second grade dependent on initiation into the first. This final grade was known as the *epopteia*, perhaps tellingly, since the word translates as "vision." The opening day of the ceremony began with a solemn gathering in Athens and the arrival of certain sacred objects, carried in special boxes, from Eleusis. A priest commenced proceedings with a proclamation naming the classes of people who were forbidden participation in the Mysteries—basically those who could not speak Greek and criminals. The following day there was a grand procession to the coast, with the candidate for initiation accompanied by a live pig, an animal sacred to Demeter.[4] Both pig and candidate were required to take a ritual bath in the sea.

Another procession took place on the nineteenth or twentieth of the month, this time a fourteen-mile journey to Eleusis itself. We know it was called the Iacchus Procession after Demeter's son who personified the ritual cry of joy uttered during the march. On the way there was dancing, various ceremonies, the singing of hymns, and sacrifices. Curiously, it was also traditional for participants to lighten the more sober aspects of the celebration by telling obscene jokes about prominent citizens. The arrival at Eleusis was marked by further dancing before the candidate retired to rest in anticipation of his initiation the following day.

What happened during an initiation is less certain than the foregoing descriptions of the preliminaries. Archaeological investigation shows that the ceremony took place in a huge square hall of fifty-one-meter sides with wide, stepped tiers of seats capable of accommodating an astonishing four thousand spectators. There is speculation that a small room once stood in the center of this vast space, functioning as a sanctuary for the hierophant who conducted the ceremony.[5] Evidence of the ceremony itself is largely drawn from a Latin work of fiction, the *Metamorphoses* of Apuleius, and the suspect writings of disapproving Christians. Nevertheless, there are just enough correspondences between the various accounts to allow us a reasonable degree of certainty about the broad outlines of what went on.

The ritual was divided into three parts—*legomena*, or "things spoken," *dromena* or "things performed," and *deiknymena* or "things revealed." The first of these was almost certainly brief. We have it on the authority of Aristotle that candidates for initiation did not go to learn but to be put in a particular frame of mind. The emphasis was always on emotion and experience, points reiterated by other writers in the ancient world.

"Things performed" may have included the enactment of a sacred marriage between Hades and Persephone, or possibly Zeus and Demeter. Bishop Asterius of Amasea (ca. 350–410 CE) suggests this involved a sex act between the hierophant and a priestess, a possibility that may have been more spiritual than it must have appeared to the bishop. There is a technique of Oriental tantra in which a couple identify with a specific god and goddess during the sex act in order to communicate with the divinities and/or channel their energies. The tantric "magic" works by changing the consciousness of the participants in such a way that permits an experience of direct spirit communication. It is possible that some similar technique could have been developed within the Greek Mysteries.

Another known aspect of "things performed" was a light show that accompanied the revelation of certain sacred objects to the candidate. An inscription at Eleusis tells of the hierophant "coming from the shrine and appearing in the luminous nights." Another describes the scene as "clearer than the light of the sun."[6] The light show seems to have immediately preceded the final act of the Mystery—the revelation. Hippolytus of Rome, a third-century CE theologian, claimed this was nothing more than a single ear of corn, dramatically produced by the hierophant amid many fires. Although widely quoted and supported by academics to the present day, this seems unlikely. Initiates of the Greater Mysteries were described as joyous, having been granted a far more positive view of both life and death than was offered by orthodox Greek religion. In short, they underwent a profound and lasting change. This seems a tall order for a single ear of corn, even if the plant was closely associated with the goddess Demeter. If we consider the various elements that made up the Greek Mysteries—the fasting, the ordeals, the breath control, and the possibility of a mind-altering drink—the parallels with shamanic practice become obvious. In view of this, the likelihood is that the final initiatory experience, guided and to some extent controlled by the ceremonial, was a visionary meeting with the goddess herself—in other words, a spirit contact. If so, it would not be the only spirit contact to influence the culture of ancient Greece.

Today, Epidaurus in southern Greece is a vast, multilevel archaeological site surrounded by rocky heights thinly covered in Mediterranean shrub. In classical times, it was a small but thriving city and contained arguably the most popular tourist attraction of the known world. The great Doric temple of Asclepios measured eighty meters in length and, according to an inscription discovered at the site, took almost five years to complete. But it was not its architectural splendor that attracted visitors, nor even the exquisite gold and ivory statue of the god. The thousands who flocked there, not merely from Greece but from surrounding countries and beyond, came mainly in the hope of a cure for their ills. For the Asclepion was a place of healing, with a reputation for producing miracles.

But while there was a hall where patients might sleep—the Abaton—any further resemblance to a modern hospital was almost entirely coincidental. The shrines of Asclepios—at Epidaurus, Cos, Pergamum, and many other sites throughout Greece—were impressive examples of architecture and landscaping. Cypress groves enclosed springs, baths, long colonnades, and peristyles, as well as huge open-air altars and soaring temples to a variety of gods. Epidaurus had its own tiered ampitheater, Pergamum a library. A visitor to the shrine typically passed through an imposing entrance along a well-trodden path past a small temple of Artemis to the altar of Asclepios himself. There he might make sacrifice—an ox if he was rich, a cockrel sacred to the god, or a body part in precious metal signifying the area of illness. From there he might proceed to the Tholos, or purifying bath of waters drawn from a sacred spring. Depending on his condition, medical priests could insist on several days of a cleansing diet before the real healing began.

Once cleansed, he was permitted to enter the Abaton. This was essentially a dormitory administered by white-robed priests. It was also the home of a great many nonvenomous snakes, creatures sacred to Asclepios. Within this extraordinary environment, the patient was put to bed and encouraged to sleep. In his dreams, the god would come and either effect a cure directly so that he awoke restored, or prescribe a course of treatment for him to follow. When morning came, the priests of the temple would help him remember his dream and interpret its meaning in those cases where it was not already clear.

Sometimes the god might not enter the dream in person but send one of his totem animals—a dog, rooster or snake—in his place.

Although dream incubation of this type is today open to a purely psychological explanation—the patient's expectations are aroused by the temple visit so that his unconscious ensures he dreams of the god—to the ancients themselves it was, without question, an example of spirit communication. Whether psychological or paranormal, it worked. Six marble tablets, all that remained of a great many more, were discovered along the inner wall of the northern colonnade that bordered the sacred enclosure. They contained a remarkable record of *iamata* or cures, some bordering on the miraculous, carried out in the sanctuary.

Although Strabo records that the earliest temple of Asclepios was at Trikka, the birthplace of the god, the healing temple at Epidaurus claimed primacy and its methods proved so effective that similar Asclepions were established at Cos, Pergamum, and eventually throughout the whole of the country, usually in settings of awe-inspiring natural grandeur. Soon they too were recording their own *iamata*. In the Lebena Asclepion on Crete, archives describe how the god performed a surgical operation on Demandros of Gortyn while he was asleep. Even more oddly, a sleeping woman was cured of her infertility through the use of a cupping instrument known as a *sikya*.[7] She became pregnant soon after leaving the sanctuary. The exact nature of these two Cretan cures is not entirely clear from surviving descriptions. It is possible that the surgical operation literally took place and involved some form of anesthesia, which may have involved the administration of an herbal drug or the use of hypnosis—priests at the temple were known to be able to induce "sleep" in certain patients, an indication that an early form of hypnotism formed part of the treatment regime. The fact that the surgery was attributed to the god could easily be a religious convention, with the actual operation carried out on his behalf by a priest. The case of the infertile woman is also suggestive of actual physical treatment. Cupping, now mainly used by acupuncturists, involves placing a small quantity of flammable material on a (protected) area of the body, setting it alight, then immediately covering it with a cup or similar vessel. As the fire consumes the oxygen inside the cup, a partial vacuum is created that sucks on the area underneath the cup to therapeutic effect. A *sikya*, in Ancient Greece, was a vessel used for this type of treatment.

But despite these indications of physical intervention, the *iamata* leave no doubt at all that the main healing technique in the various Asclepions was the incubation of dreams for spirit contact. Some of these produced bizarre results if the records are to be believed. Pandarus of Thessaly, for example, suffered from an embarrassing mark on his forehead. After he entered the Abaton at Epidaurus, Asclepios appeared to him in a dream and placed a bandage around his head, warning him not to remove it until the god had gone. Pandarus did as instructed and later took off the bandage, to find the mark had been transferred from his forehead to the cloth. When he awoke, the physical mark had disappeared as well.[8] As an act of gratitude, Pandarus sent his friend Echedorus—who had a similar mark on his forehead—to Epidaurus with a gift of money to pay for the erection of a statue of Athene in the shrine. But Echedorus was untrustworthy and kept the cash for himself. When he went to sleep, however, Asclepios appeared to him in a dream and asked about the money. Echedorus flatly denied having received it but promised to paint a picture and dedicate it in place of the proposed statue. The god was not satisfied with the offer and wrapped the bandage used by Pandarus around the head of Echedorus. When Echedorus awoke, the forehead marks of Pandarus had been added to his own.

Other recorded dream cures included that of Euhippus who suffered from a broken spear point embedded in his jaw. During an induced dream in the Abaton, the god drew out the point and carried it away, leaving the patient free from pain (and presumably from the spear point) when he awoke. Clinatas of Thebes was rid of a lice infestation when Asclepios appeared in his dream to brush him down with a stiff broom.

The *iamata* can be unclear at times about what happened in a dream and what in the waking state. To the Greek mind, the two were almost interchangeable: actions carried out on the dream body were automatically transferred to the physical. Sometimes there was an observable crossover. One patient who presented himself at the Asclepion had an ulcerated toe. He dreamed that a handsome youth treated his affliction with a special remedy and woke cured. But priests on duty at the temple claimed the cure had actually taken place when one of the sacred snakes licked the toe.

Dreams were not thought to be subjective experiences, as they are today. The Greeks appear to have believed the dream state was something akin to another world that people could visit in sleep. Consequently, it was perfectly possible to dream on behalf of someone else. When Arata of Laconia fell foul of dropsy and was too ill to travel, her mother journeyed to Epidaurus to incubate a dream for her. In the Abaton the mother dreamed that the god removed her daughter's head and drained it of liquid before restoring it to her shoulders. Curiously, Arata had the same dream and was free of her affliction by the time her mother returned home.

Sometimes a worthy patient did not find his way to an Asclepion of his own accord—he might be summoned by the god in a dream or, more rarely, a waking vision. The second-century CE writer Aelius Aristides recorded a personal experience of this phenomenon is his diary, which he later published as *Hieroi Logoi* or "Sacred Tales." Aristides lived in Smyrna, an ancient Greek city located on the Aegean coast of Anatolia and ruined his health on a rigorous midwinter journey across the Balkans to the Adriatic and Rome. By the time he came home again, he was suffering from convulsions, breathing difficulties, and periodic paralysis. In this sorry state, he had a dream during which he was summoned to become a devotee of Asclepios at his Pergamum shrine. For seventeen years, Aristides placed himself entirely in the hands of the god—and cold hands they turned out to be. Asclepios prescribed exhausting fasts, emetics, purges, bloodletting, naked winter runs around the temple, plunges into frozen rivers and lakes, special foods, and long periods when he was forbidden to wash. Not altogether surprisingly, Aristides eventually tired of this treatment and turned to human physicians for help, but Asclepios promptly punished him for his faithlessness by inflicting him with chills, digestive ailments, and catarrh. On the positive side, however, Aristides believed the god protected him in times of plague, brought him favor with the authorities, and arranged for the defeat of his literary rivals.

Although by far the most popular, Asclepios was not the only god of healing in Greece—Apollo was probably second favorite, but there were many others. As their following increased, the technique of dream incubation for spirit contact spread beyond the boundaries of the country. In the third century BCE, Ptolemy I established Greek rule in Egypt and shortly thereafter was visited in a dream by a god who introduced himself as Serapis and demanded that his statue be brought from the Black Sea coast and established in Alexandria, the new Egyptian capital. Although Serapis promised benefits to the kingdom, Ptolemy procrastinated so that the god had to come again, with threats this time, in a second dream. This time Ptolemy caved in at once and not only fetched the statue but had a new Serapeum built in Alexandria to house it. True to his word, Serapis thereafter began to appear in the dreams of the sick, with therapeutic effect. But he was a more demanding deity than Asclepios and induced in his devotees at Memphis and elsewhere a state

Serapis, the healing god established in Alexandria following spirit instructions given in a pharaoh's dream

An artist's impression of a Delphic priestess, whose trance communications with spirits guided the ancient world

called *katoche* during which they were compelled to obey his commands until released into normal consciousness.

Serapis shared his Memphis shrine with a native Egyptian deity named Imhotep—a real person who was deified after his death as Imouthes. Imouthes was as demanding in his own way as Serapis and just as unpredictable. When a scribe failed to publish a book on Imouthes's healing miracles, this god struck him down with a fever as punishment, then appeared in a dream to cure him with a single look.

That dream incubation spread to Egypt was predictable enough, since Egypt was now ruled by a Greek pharaoh, but the reason for its spread to Rome was bizarre in the extreme, if contemporary accounts are to be believed. According to these sources, Rome was suffering the ravages of plague in 292 BCE and sent a deputation to the Greek oracle at Delphi in the hope of advice. The oracle told them to visit Epidaurus. When the mission arrived, its members were greeted by a huge serpent that appeared from under a statue of Asclepios and then boarded the Roman ship and went to sleep beneath a tent. Firm believers in omens, the Romans left it where it was and sailed for home. The snake swam ashore at Antium, where it remained for three days coiled around a tree before boarding the ship again. When the ship entered the Tiber, it went ashore on Tiber Island and disappeared . . . as, almost at once, did the raging plague. The grateful Romans built their first Asclepion on the island and established worship of the healing god under his Latin name, Aesculapius.

The Delphic Oracle that advised this deputation was another, considerably more famous, example of spirit communication in the world of ancient Greece. According to the Greek historian Diodorus, the Delphic Oracle came into being because of the activities of a goat. A goatherd watched the animal peer into a crack in the ground known as the "Delphic chasm," then begin to leap about in an extraordinary manner. Other goats approaching the chasm exhibited the same peculiar behavior. So did the goatherd when he went to investigate, but with one important difference: he immediately began to utter prophecies. Word of the phenomenon quickly spread and vast numbers of people made pilgrimage to see for themselves. Unfortunately many were overcome by the fumes and sent tumbling into the chasm so that the authorities proclaimed it a health hazard and decreed that henceforth only a single, specially appointed woman would be permitted to prophecy. She was supplied with a tripod to sit on so she would not fall in.

Although a great many authors, ancient and modern, have passed on the theory that Delphic *pythia* (oracular priestesses) were intoxicated by volcanic fumes,[9] there is no archaeological evidence of any fissure under the Delphic temple. Proponents of the Diodorus theory suggest it may well have closed over during an earthquake, but the Roman author Lucan proposed a different explanation altogether. He held that the priestess was able to prophesy because she was temporarily possessed by the god Apollo.

Lucan never visited Delphi in person, so his description of a *pythia* rushing around in the grip of divine madness is suspect, but other accounts do little to dispel the idea that some form of mediumship was involved. Certainly Delphi was presented to a believing public as the voice of Apollo, who selected the spot by killing the "blood-reeking bane"[10] of a female dragon that had been terrorizing the countryside. The idea that gods or other spirits spoke through oracles had wide popular currency. In his play *Elektra*, Euripides writes how Orestes attributes the words of an oracle to an *alastor* or mischievous spirit when it advises him to kill his mother. No member of his audiences would have found the suggestion unlikely.

It is worth remembering that the ancient Greeks had no holy scriptures they could turn to for guidance, nor did their priesthood offer living advice in anything analogous to the modern Sunday sermon. But people then and now had the same deep-rooted human need for direction so that Delphi, despite its fame, was far from the only oracular temple in the Greek world. There were others spread across the entire country with Dodona, Claros, and Didyma among the more popular sites. Most of these subsidiary oracles, like Delphi itself, were dedicated to Apollo and virtually all made their pronouncements through an entranced medium, male or female, speaking with changed voice and personality as the temporary incarnation of the god. Often their answers were garbled, leading to the widespread belief that the gods had little time for rash inquiries (which seemed to be most inquiries pertaining to mundane human affairs) and were not above confusing or even misleading their authors. As a consequence, a structure of questioning developed within which the querient was not permitted to hear the medium's actual reply but only its interpretation, delivered in verse by a priest. There was also expense involved. At Delphi, a single question could cost the equivalent of two days' wages, plus additional "freewill" offerings. But this was the minimum cost only for private inquiries. Governments and individuals in positions of power could expect to pay ten times as much. Many were happy to do so and their questions, related to potential wars and similar matters of life and death, ensured that the political fate of whole provinces and even countries rested on spirit utterances.

But it would be quite wrong to assume the spirits of Greece influenced only her contemporary cultures. Greece is widely acknowledged as the cradle of Western civilization, which allows us to deduce that many of the philosophies we embrace so instinctively today were bequeathed to us by ancient spirit voices. Moreover, even the most superficial study of history shows a similar bequest was made to us by that other great classical civilization, the military culture of ancient Rome.

According to Livy, the very foundation of Rome was marked—and marred—by spirit contact. Having decided to found a new settlement, the twins Romulus and Remus began to quarrel about which of them the town should be named for and who should govern it. Since they could reach no agreement, they decided to ask the tutelary gods of the countryside to make the decision for them by augury. The brothers then retired to separate hills—Palatine and Aventine—to await their respective signs. Remus was the first to hear from the spirits when six vultures appeared, but shortly afterward twelve of the same birds appeared to Romulus. Livy writes, "The followers of each promptly saluted their master as king, one side basing its claim on priority, the other upon number. Angry words ensued, followed all too soon by blows, and in the course of the affray, Remus was killed . . . This, then, was how Romulus obtained the sole power. The newly built city was called by its founder's name."[11]

It is difficult to know how much truth lies in this intriguing tale. There is no archaeological evidence of the original settlement and historian Robert Hughes describes Rome's accepted foundation date, 753 BCE, as "wholly mythical."[12] What is certain is that augury of the type Livy described did not end with Romulus and Remus but came to dominate the thinking of patricians, politicians, and plebeians alike across the centuries as the settlement became a city and the city became an empire. Tradition has it that King Romulus established a College of Augurs sometime between 735 and 716 BCE. At this period it had no more than three members, but by 81 BCE the number had increased to fifteen. For several centuries, serving augurs elected new members to the college, but this right disappeared in 103 BCE and the appointment of augurs was politicized.

Augury itself was not, as many assume, a procedure designed to foretell the future, nor even to determine a correct course of action. Rather it sought to discover whether a particular decision, *already made*, found favor with the gods and thus should be acted upon or abandoned. In other words, it was a system of communication with spirit beings created to ensure their approval of human actions. As such, it is worth noting, a favorable augury could only really be judged in retrospect. If the signs appeared favorable, but the outcome proved catastrophic, then the augur must have misread them in the first place.

College augurs handed down the techniques of their craft to new members of the profession—a profession that carried with it enormous prestige and power. Augurs were consulted prior to every major undertaking in Roman society, both public and private. Their findings determined matters of trade, diplomacy, war, and even religion. To make those findings, an augur would first don the *trabea*, a state robe edged with purple, reserved for members of his profession, kings, and certain priests and knights. He would then retire to high ground, or sometimes a tower, cover his head with a special cowl, and place his left foot on a boulder.[13] From this elevated position, he turned his face eastward and used a short, straight rod with a right-angled bend at one end to mark out the heavens into four quarters. Then he waited for a sign from the gods, related to the undertaking in question. When such a sign appeared, it was not considered a valid augury until confirmed by a second sign of the same type. There were several groups of omens to which particular attention had to be paid. The first, and arguably most important, were signs in the heavens themselves—a flash of lightning, a roll of thunder, the appearance of a meteorite or comet, or the behavior of birds, notably vultures, eagles, owls, and crows. The augur might take note of whether thunder came from his right or left, whether lightning produced an odd or even number of strokes, the appearance and direction of a flight of birds, or possibly even the sounds they made. When the augur dropped his eyes from the heavens, he might typically watch out for the appearance of a wild animal like a fox or a wolf, interpreting the direction from which it came and whether it crossed the horizon or ran parallel to it.

A more artificial, but extremely popular, method of divining the will of the gods involved the use of sacred chickens.[14] Birds reserved for this purpose were kept in a coop and generally consulted by the augur early in the morning. In a short but solemn ceremony, he would order a moment of silence, then throw down a handful of corn and open the coop. If the chickens swooped directly on the food and ate heartily, it indicated that the gods were pleased about the undertaking in question. But if the chickens refused to eat, flew away, or scattered the food with their wings, the augur would pronounce the omen unfortunate and predict trouble ahead if the proposed course of action was carried through. There was, apparently, no way of avoiding the will of the gods. Prior to the naval Battle of Drepana in 249 BCE, the consul Pulcher ordered a chicken-based augury for his planned attack on the harbor. When released, the chickens refused to eat, but instead of abandoning his plans, Pulcher snapped, *"Bibant, quoniam esse nolunt"* ("Let them drink if they won't eat") and threw the birds overboard. The move reassured his crew sufficiently to follow him into battle, but the attack failed miserably, the battle was lost, and almost all of Pulcher's ships were sunk.

Running parallel to the work of the augurs were the activities of the haruspices, with whom augars are sometimes confused in popular modern accounts. A haruspex was a priest trained in the art of divining the will of the gods by examining the behavior and entrails of sacrificed animals. Typically, the animals offered in sacrifice would be sheep or poultry. The haruspex would carefully observe the animals' behavior and condition before they were killed, and the condition of their entrails—notably the liver—after death. If the *caput iecoris* (head of the liver) was missing, this was seen as a particularly bad omen. In Euripides's play *Elektra*, an incomplete liver signaled the impending death of one of the characters.

To the modern mind, there seems little to choose between the oracular practices of augury and haruspicy. Both seem superstitious, even silly, and curiously lacking in any real spirit contact. But one ancient tale may provide a hint as to why we should not rush to judgment—at least on the question of augury. Livy's *History of Rome*, written in the first century BCE, describes how the third king of Rome, Tullus Hostilius, received word of a shower of stones that had fallen on the Alban Mount, the second-highest peak of the Alban Hills near Rome. The mount was a long-extinct volcano and this indication of renewed activity quickly persuaded Hostilius to send an investigatory expedition.

When the men arrived at the mount, they discovered it was indeed mildly active—they were greeted by their very own hailstorm of pebbles—but not so much that it prevented a climb. When they did so, they received a great augury at the *lucus cacumen*, the hill's topmost grove. A spirit voice emerged from the trees to dictate instructions concerning religious observances. Hostilius was sufficiently impressed to order a nine-day festival to mark the event, a celebration repeated when there were subsequent reports of stony rains.

The incident on the Alban Mount was not the only example of verbal augury. The accepted list of omens to be considered by every member of the College of Augurs included "unusual incidents," such as the hearing of strange voices and the appearance of apparitions. In the *De Divinatione* ("Concerning Divination"), our best source of information on the divinatory practices of Roman times, Cicero is careful to distinguish between the sort of "cookbook" augury that could be learned by rote and the divinely inspired communication with the gods that took place in an ecstatic trance. A similar distinction was made by Plato,[15] suggesting that at least some examples of augury, and possibly even haruspicy, involved neo-shamanic techniques of spirit communication.

The same suspicion hangs over another popular Roman institution, the Mithraic Mysteries, which flourished from about the first to the fourth centuries CE and were strongly supported by the Roman military. Like their Elusion counterparts in Greece, little is definitively known about the Mysteries of Mithras. The Roman Mysteries were bound by oaths of absolute secrecy and no text recounting their innermost activities has survived. But a multitude of subterranean temples have, and archaeological investigation has enabled us to piece together a "best-guess" scenario of what went on.

The Romans themselves believed these Mysteries originated in Persia—*Mithra* is a Persian god and *Mithras* the Greek adaptation of his name—but modern scholarship fashionably claims that the cult was indigenous to Roman imperialism and may even have arisen as a counterbalance to early Christianity. There is less controversy about its symbolism. Reliefs of the young Mithras slaying a bull have led scholars to believe the worship likely involved bull sacrifice, while a multitude of eating vessels and implements found at Mithraic sites strongly suggests feasting as part of the ritual. We can also be certain that the Mithraic Mysteries were initiatory—and with that certainty come important pointers toward the sort of spirit contact embodied in the Greek Mysteries. There were seven grades in all, ranging from *corvex* (crow or raven) through *nymphus* (male bride), *miles* (soldier), *leo* (lion) *Peres* (Persian), *heliodromus* (sun-runner), to the supreme grade of *pater* (father). Entry into each grade was conditional on the candidate having survived a particular ordeal, often in a pit dug into the floor of the Mithraeum. The emperor Commodus (r. 180–192 CE) is alleged to have introduced

Mithraic trials specifically designed to kill the candidate as a sop to his own sadism, but even the more routine tests, involving exposure to heat, cold, and other perils, were dangerous. If the candidate survived, he immediately came under the protection of the god associated with his new grade—Mercury for corvex, Venus for nymphus, Mars for miles, Jupiter for leo, Luna for Perses, Sol for heliodromus, and Saturn for pater. On achieving the grade of leo, the candidate's ethical emphasis became that of purity. The resemblance to shamanic rites in which purifications and life-threatening ordeals led to the knowledge and protection of certain spirit entities is too obvious to require further comment.

Another, more subtle link with the institutionalized spirit contacts of ancient Greece—and indeed ancient Egypt—may lie in the curious figure so often discovered in Mithraic temples that today attracts the scholarly designation of *leontocephaline*. The figure, as the name suggests, depicts a (naked) man with the head of a lion, often openmouthed and threatening. An enormous serpent coils around his body. In the version found in the Mithraeum at Ostia Antica there is an engraved tablet behind the figure, a caduceus and chicken at his feet. Other representations elsewhere include the figure of a god. Serpent, rooster, and dog are all symbolic companions of Asclepios, while the caduceus is associated with Mercury, messenger of the gods and guide of the dead. The Egyptian association with this near-ubiquitous figure lies in the lion head. The Egyptians typically experienced their gods as animal- or bird-headed humans, itself a curious link with ancient shamanism. There is even a lion-headed deity—Sekhmet—in the Egyptian pantheon, although unlike the Mithraic figure, she was conceived of as female.

Although the signs of spirit communication are less obvious in ancient Rome than they are in ancient Greece or Egypt, there are pointers to the possibility that such communication existed. Beyond this, there is absolute certainty that the Roman people firmly believed that spirit beings played a part in their everyday lives and went to considerable lengths to ensure their benevolence. Thus, here again, we have clear evidence of spirit influence on an ancient culture and one, in this instance, that bequeathed us the entire foundation of our Western legal system. Furthermore, if we consider the Roman empire as a whole, we find within its far-flung confines the early indications of a spirit contact that was to influence profoundly the whole of Western esoteric thought.

In 598 BCE, the Babylonian emperor Nebuchadnezzar launched a massive attack on the little kingdom of Judah. It was a grossly uneven conflict and within a year the remnant Israelite community had all but collapsed. By 597 BCE, the capital Jerusalem surrendered. But despite appearances, the war was far from over. A resistance movement sprang up and hostilities renewed. In an attempt to break the spirit of the Israelites, Nebuchadrezzar instituted a policy of mass deportation, concentrating on the brightest and best of the conquered people. Among those who joined the earliest forced marches to Babylonia was a temple priest named Ezekiel.

Ezekiel was well thought of by his fellow exiles and quickly became spiritual adviser to their leaders. He seems to have been a flamboyant character, given to grand gestures. On one occasion he ate a scroll in order to make a point. On another, he lay on the ground pretending to fight with unseen opponents. He was likely to fall on his face or be struck dumb for long periods of time. But despite these peculiarities, people took him very seriously—and with good reason. While Jerusalem was under siege, his wife became terminally ill and the force of his grief convinced him to make a grim prophecy: the city would be destroyed "and your sons and daughters whom you left behind shall fall by the sword." All too soon his prediction came true.

The Babylonian exile left Ezekiel at Tel-abib by the river Chebar, a canal that formed part of the Euphrates irrigation system in what is now southern Iraq. On July 31, 592 BCE, he was walking on the banks of the Chebar when something quite bizarre occurred. Ezekiel later described it in his own words:

> And I looked, and, behold, a whirlwind came out of the north, a great cloud, and a fire infolding itself, and a brightness was about it, and out of the midst thereof as the color of amber, out of the midst of the fire. Also out of the midst thereof came the likeness of four living creatures. And this was their appearance they had the likeness of a man. And every one had four faces, and every one had four wings. And their feet were straight feet and the sole of their feet was like the sole of a calf's foot: and they sparkled like the color of burnished brass. And they had the hands of a man under their wings on their four sides and they four had their faces and their wings. Their wings were joined one to another they turned not when they went they went every one straight forward.

As for the likeness of their faces, they four had the face of a man, and the face of a lion, on the right side: and they four had the face of an ox on the left side they four also had the face of an eagle. Thus were their faces: and their wings were stretched upward two wings of every one were joined one to another, and two covered their bodies. And they went every one straight forward: whither the spirit was to go, they went and they turned not when they went.

As for the likeness of the living creatures their appearance was like burning coals of fire, and like the appearance of lamps: it went up and down among the living creatures and the fire was bright, and out of the fire went forth lightning. And the living creatures ran and returned as the appearance of a flash of lightning.

Now as I beheld the living creatures, behold one wheel upon the earth by the living creatures, with his four faces. The appearance of the wheels and their work was like unto the color of a beryl: and they four had one likeness: and their appearance and their work was as it were a wheel in the middle of a wheel. When they went, they went upon their four sides: and they turned not when they went. As for their rings, they were so high that they were dreadful and their rings were full of eyes round about them four.

And when the living creatures went, the wheels went by them: and when the living creatures were lifted up from the earth, the wheels were lifted up. Whithersoever the spirit was to go, they went, thither was their spirit to go and the wheels were lifted up over against them: for the spirit of the living creature was in the wheels. When those went, these went and when those stood, these stood and when those were lifted up from the earth, the wheels were lifted up over against them: for the spirit of the living creature was in the wheels.

And the likeness of the firmament upon the heads of the living creature was as the color of the terrible crystal, stretched forth over their heads above. And under the firmament were their wings straight, the one toward the other: every one had two, which covered on this side, and every one had two, which covered on that side, their bodies. And when they went, I heard the noise of their wings, like the noise of great waters, as the voice of the Almighty, the voice of speech, as the noise of an host: when they stood, they let down their wings. And there was a voice from the firmament that was over their heads, when they stood, and had let down their wings.

And above the firmament that was over their heads was the likeness of a throne, as the appearance of a sapphire stone: and upon the likeness of the throne was the likeness as the appearance of a man above upon it. And I saw as the color of amber, as the appearance of fire round about within it, from the appearance of his loins even upward, and from the appearance of his loins even downward, I saw as it were the appearance of fire, and it had brightness round about. As the appearance of the bow that is in the cloud in the day of rain, so was the appearance of the brightness round about. This was the appearance of the likeness of the glory of the Lord.[16]

This "vision of Ezekiel," as it came to be called, was so peculiar that several twentieth-century authors—including a former NASA engineer—decided the priest must have witnessed a spaceship landing. Generations of rabbis have disagreed. To them, Ezekiel was granted a vision of God.

The term merkava, sometimes spelled merkabah, is Hebrew for "chariot" or "throne" and has the latter translation in the passage above.[17] The throne described by Ezekiel came increasingly to function as the focus of contemplation for early Jewish mystics. By 40 BCE, the year Judea became a Roman province, Jewish holy men had begun to experiment with a visionary system that would allow them to share the experience of Ezekiel. By the first century CE, Merkava mysticism was flourishing in Palestine. Six centuries later, it had not only spread to Babylonia, but centered itself there, in the home of Ezekiel's original vision.

The mystical experience is common to all the world's religions and is characterized by a realization of ultimate unity. But the interpretation of the experience tends to be colored by the cultural background and belief system of the individual. Thus, while a Buddhist or Hindu might speak of transcendent unity with the cosmos, a Jewish—and, indeed, Christian—mystic will often describe what has occurred as union with God. The experience itself will sometimes arise quite spontaneously, but more often it results from the application of certain techniques. While the most important of these—prayer and fasting—have religious connotations, others are more occult, with a distinct crossover between mysticism and magic.

The tzenu'im, Merkava initiates, were drawn from a select few judged to be of the highest moral caliber. They had to prepare themselves for their experience by fasting, then embarked on what was believed to be an extraordinarily dangerous visionary journey through seven "heavenly dwellings," each one guarded by a hostile angel. It was in these heavenly dwellings that the magical element of Merkava training came into play. The initiate used specific magical formulas—referred to in Merkava literature as "seals"—in order to control, or at least placate, the guardians. It was believed that use of the wrong seal could prove fatal, or at best result in serious injury.

Once the journey through the celestial spheres was completed, these explorers of the supernatural world (*Yorde Merkava*) were convinced they would be granted sight of the divine throne—the same vision encountered by Ezekiel on the banks of the Chebar.

Although initially viewed with distrust by mainstream Judaism—the Talmud suggests that half of those who take the celestial journey will die or go mad—Merkava doctrines evolved over centuries to become the mystical heart of the Jewish religion. In developed form, they constitute that body of teaching now known as the Holy Qabalah. It is a body of teaching that has profoundly influenced the practice of magic and the techniques of spirit contact in the Western world right down to the present day. But it is important to note that the influence of spirit contact has not been confined to the Western world.

5. SPIRITS OF
THE ORIENT

THE HINDU TERM *JATI*, WHICH TRANSLATES LITERALLY AS "BIRTH," refers to a set of social groupings that have existed in India for millennia—the tenacious caste system. Although some *jati*s are named for specific occupations, the linkage is limited. Whatever their actual career, members of a particular caste are expected to marry within their own *jati*, follow its dietary restrictions, and interact with other *jati*s in accordance with their position in the social hierarchy. Although there are actually more than two thousand *jati*s, virtually all of them are assigned to one of four *varna*s, social groupings with specific traditional functions. These groupings are the Brahmins, the priestly caste who head the social hierarchy, followed in descending order of prestige by the Kshatriyas, or warriors, the merchant Vaishyas, and the Sudras, artisans or laborers. A fifth group, known variously as the Untouchables, Harijan ("Children of God"), or Dalit (the oppressed), exists outside the social groupings altogether. The origins of caste are lost in the depths of Indian prehistory, but some clue to its beginnings may be gleaned from the little-known claim that there was a secret system of initiation within the Brahmin *varna* designed to train candidates in the techniques necessary to contact spirits.

The claim was made by Louis Jacolliot, a French barrister, colonial judge, and author, who spent several years in India investigating what he believed to be the roots of Western occultism. When he published his findings in 1875, he quoted his major source of information as a Sanskrit text entitled the *Agrouchada-Parikchai*. At the time, the Western world was only just beginning to learn about the practice of Hinduism and the source was initially accepted without question. Later, however, scholars failed to find copies of the *Agrouchada-Parikchai*, decided the book was Jacolliot's personal invention and branded him unreliable, a label that has stuck to the present day. But if the book was fictional, Jacolliot's real sources were not. Most recent scholarship has traced the roots of his material to the *Upanishads*, a collection of some two hundred philosophical texts considered to be the foundation of the Hindu religion, and the massive corpus of the Brahmanical *Dharmasastra*, dealing with natural law and religious and legal duty. From these, and from personal experience—some of which has since been confirmed by later writers —he constructed the following picture:

According to the *Manava Dharma Shastra* (Laws of Manu), the ancient Vedic text that laid the foundations of domestic, social, and religious life in India:

> The life of mortals, mentioned in the Veda, the desired results of sacrificial rites and the supernatural power of embodied spirits are fruits proportioned among men according to the character of the age . . . To Brahmanas (Brahmins) he assigned teaching and studying the Veda, sacrificing for their own benefits and for others, giving and accepting of alms.[1]

The text, and others similar, underpin the faith of the general populace in the Brahmin priesthood, as references to the Last Supper might underpin claims of transubstantiation by the Roman Catholic Church. That faith included a near-universal belief in spirits[2] and a similar conviction that Brahmins had the power to summon, dismiss, and otherwise control them. But it would be a mistake to assume that either the spirits themselves or Brahminic powers concerning them were entirely faith based.

According to Jacolliot, there were three levels of initiation into the practice of the Brahmin priesthood. The first of these, conferred at an early age, appears to have been little more than instruction on how to conduct various religious ceremonies and sacrifices, how to comment on the Vedas, and how to engage in pastoral work among the people. But the second degree of initiation, offered only to suitable candidates who had functioned effectively in the first degree for at least twenty years, was considerably more esoteric. It included training in the evocation of spirits, exorcism, soothsaying, and prophecy, based on a study of the *Atharvaveda*, a Vedic text that incorporates much of India's earliest traditions of healing and magic. Public demonstrations of the powers conferred by this initiation were commonplace.

The powers of a third-degree initiate were less often on display and were reserved for the most special of occasions. Initiates, who had to complete many years in the second degree and were thus by definition elderly, were obligated to undertake an exclusive study of all physical and supernatural forces of the universe. Their reputation in this area could scarcely have stood higher. Jacolliot quotes a popular Sanskrit saying, *Dêvadinam djagat sarvam, Mandradinam ta devata, Tan mantram brahamanadinam, Brahmana mama devata*, which translates as "Everything that exists is in the power of the gods, The gods are in the power of magical conjurations, Magical conjurations are in the power of the Brahmins, Therefore the gods are in the power of the Brahmins."

Jacolliot gives a vivid description of the manifestation of these powers as part of a festival known as the *Oupanayana*. On the second day of celebrations, all married women among the guests were asked to go together into the forest looking for a nest of white ants. When they found one, they were required to fill ten earthen pots with earth disturbed by the insects and, on their return to their fellow guests, plant a different kind of seed in each pot and water them all from a sacred vessel. The Brahmin then covered the pots with a fine cloth and recited an invocation to the spirits requesting their manifestation through an auspicious omen. To achieve this, he held his hands above the covered pots and chanted the words *Agnim Pa Patra Paryaya Paroxa* eighty-one times. The words themselves seem to have little significance beyond their inherent meaning—*agnim* translates as "sacred fire," *pa* as "holy water," while *patra* means a "purified vessel," *paryaya* means "magical vegetation," and *paroxa* means "invisible." Nonetheless, eyewitnesses report that the cloth began slowly to rise during the Brahmin's chant, a visible indication that the spirits were present. The Brahmin then removed the cloth to reveal that the seeds had not only germinated but had grown into flower and fruit-bearing shrubs standing as tall as his forehead.

It has always been widely accepted in India that Brahminic abilities included authority over spirits, notably ancestral spirits. No marriage or funeral ceremony could be carried out without the evocation of these *pitris*. It is probably safe to suggest that many such evocations were formalities, but it is clear from Jacolliot's investigation that some could go far beyond empty ceremonial. His description of an evocation in the first degree shows this clearly. The rite begins in a darkened portion of the room and calls for a vase of water, a lamp, some powdered sandalwood, boiled rice, and incense. The practitioner traces magic circles before the doorway to prevent entrance by evil spirits. He then uses a series of breathing exercises to induce an ecso-matic state in which his consciousness vacates his body, allowing it to be temporarily animated by the spirits he wishes to evoke. This is, of course, a classic description of the mechanics of deep-trance mediumship during which a communicating entity may take over the body of the medium and speak using the physical larynx and vocal chords. Only the breathing exercises are missing from common Western practice. It appears, however, that Brahmin evocation techniques are more sophisticated than their Western counterparts. Having permitted a spirit to share his physical vehicle, the practitioner uses his own essence to create what Jacolliot calls an "aerial body," which the spirit then enters in order to manifest visibly within the incense smoke. Once again, Jacolliot's description, based on the ancient texts, leaves little doubt about what is happening:

Pronouncing the sacred word *aum* three times and the magic syllable *djom* nine times, he should impose his hands above the lamp and throw a pinch of incense upon the flame saying: "Oh sublime Pitri! O illustrious penitent narada whom I have evoked and for whom I have formed a subtle body from the constituent particles of my own, are you present? Appear in the smoke of incense and take part in the sacrifice that I offer to the shades of my ances-tors. When he has received a suitable answer and the aerial body of the spirit evoked has appeared in the smoke of the incense, he should then proceed to perform the oblations and sacrifices as prescribed. The sacrifices having been offered, he should hold converse with the souls of his ancestors . . . Having extinguished his lamp, in darkness and in silence he should then lis-ten to the conversation of the spirits with each other and should be present at the manifestations by which they reveal their presence.[3]

The description of a prayer to the goddess Nari also underlines the mediumistic nature of Brahmin practice—and all the more convincingly since the prayer is in no way part of a public performance. After paying hom-age to the goddess and asking that after death the practitioner might be admitted to the higher spheres, the Brahmin is instructed to place both hands above a copper vessel filled with water and evoke a sage from times past. This is a popular evocation technique common to many countries and cultures. The water in the darkened bowl acts to fixate the gaze and induce an autohyp-notic trance that facilitates a vision of spirits. In this particular instance, any manifesting spirit is requested to join in the Brahmin's praises to his goddess.

There are practices that may suggest shamanic roots to the spirit manipulations of Brahminic Hinduism. At the highest level of initiation, for example, the practitioner retires to his pagoda equipped with a wand, calabash, and gazelle skin. There he meditates in total darkness for several hours, all the while attempting to persuade his consciousness to leave his body in order to converse with the *pitris* "in infinite space."[4]

For several thousand years, up to and including the present day, Indian society has been ruled by the Brahmin caste, not necessarily directly, for the country assuredly had its rajas and maharajas and now has its democratically elected politicians, but covertly in terms of social, political, and religious influence. Since it is now clear that the Brahmins themselves were guided—and, according to Jacolliot, at the very highest level *exclusively* guided—by their spirit contacts, then we must conclude that all social, domestic, and political aspects of Indian life have been shaped by the intervention and guidance of spirit voices.

Nor was India the only major Asian country to be so guided. There is a silk painting of Fu Xi on display at the National Palace Museum in Taipei, China. It shows a strong-featured, mildly threatening man dressed in an elaborate robe of furs and leopard skin. He is staring pensively to his left while being watched from close proximity by a tortoise. Above him is a range of Chinese characters.

The artwork, created by court painter Ma Lin during the Song dynasty (960–1279 CE), is a commemoration of the first Chinese king, a distinguished ruler who introduced the domestication of animals, the art of cooking, fishing with nets, the creation of a calendar, the breeding of silkworms, the invention of several musical instruments, and the use of iron weapons.[5] Yet for all his accomplishments, Fu Xi does not appear on the conventional list of rulers as compiled by Western academics. For them, Chinese history begins with the Shang dynasty, probably established in 1600 BCE. Since Fu Xi is reputed to have lived around 2900 BCE, this places him firmly in the realm of myth.

But while the Shang dynasty was the first to leave written records, there are now indications that this earliest of emperors may not have been so mythic after all. Although there are traces of anatomically modern humans in China as long ago as forty thousand years BPE (Before Present Era),[6] archaeologists were once united in their belief that the first villages of the Yang Shao culture (indicative of the shift from hunter-gathering to a developed urban civilization) only appeared in the Yellow River valley about 4500 BCE. Subsequent excavations shifted the dating progressively back, until now it is accepted that by the sixth millennium BCE there were cultures in China using most of the inventions credited to Fu Xi, including that most typical of Chinese activities, the production of silk.

But if Fu Xi really existed, neither silk, nor calendars, nor iron weapons were seen as his crowning achievement. According to Ban Gu, the first-century CE Chinese historian:

> In the beginning there was as yet no moral or social order. Men knew their mothers only, not their fathers. When hungry, they searched for food; when satisfied, they threw away the remnants. They devoured their food hide and hair, drank the blood, and clad themselves in skins and rushes. Then came Fu Xi and looked upward and contemplated the images in the heavens, and looked downward and contemplated the occurrences on earth. He united man and wife, regulated the five stages of change, and laid down the laws of humanity. He devised the eight trigrams, in order to gain mastery over the world.[7]

The first three sentences of this quotation might be interpreted as referring to a primitive Paleolithic existence before the discovery of cooking. The remainder requires some elaboration.

According to legend, Fu Xi was born in Chengji (now tentatively identified with Lantian County in China's northwestern Shaanxi Province) on the middle reaches of the Yellow River. While he was still a young man, a great flood swept across the land, killing everyone except his sister Nüwa and himself. With a special dispensation from the emperor of heaven, Fu Xi married his sister and set about procreating the human race. Prior to the flood, Chinese society was a primitive matriarchy in which birth was considered a miraculous process involving only the mother. After the deluge, the role of the father came to be recognized and society moved toward a more patriarchal culture. Nonetheless, Nüwa's contribution to a newly restored humanity was much more than that of a brood mare. She was said to have repaired the pillars of heaven and the broken corners of the earth, both of which had been damaged in a fit of anger by a monster named Kung Kung.

All this is fairly standard mythological fare, but, surprisingly, geological investigation suggests there might be some (distorted) truth behind it. Toward the end of the Pleistocene era, about 9500 BCE, vast tracts of China underwent violent tectonic convulsions, resulting in massive changes to the natural environment. Among them was the elevation of the Great Han Hai, an inland sea that occupied what is now the Gobi basin and stretched westward from the volcanic peaks of the Khingan Shan some two thousand miles to meet the Pamirs. With a north-south reach of seven hundred miles, a stretch of water covering 1.4 million square miles drained into the surrounding countryside in a flood of biblical proportions.

To the people who lived through these convulsions—and there is no doubt at all that China had a human population at the time—they must have seemed like the work of some supernatural monster and certainly left the "corners of the earth" in need of repair. At the same time, the Han Hai flooding was so devastating and so extensive as to take on the appearance of a truly universal inundation that threatened the very existence of the human race. Thus environmental conditions did at one time mirror the surviving myth, albeit at an earlier period than the myth suggests.

The myth also depicts Fu Xi and his sister as civilizing influences. She repaired damage left by the flood, he was credited with the list of cultural achievements mentioned earlier. Was it possible the myth may have mirrored an additional reality? Could China have developed civilization at a much earlier period than is now generally supposed? The proposal addresses several difficulties arising from the orthodox picture. For example, China's first supposed civilization, the Shang, has always seemed far too advanced for a culture gradually emerging from the Stone Age. A sophisticated philosophy of life was already in place. Not alone did it have a fully developed form of writing, but early texts are just as subtle and poetic as later works. There were imposing buildings, impressive tombs, horse-drawn chariots, wheel-thrown pottery, exquisite metalwork. And all this apparently emerged fully formed. The myth presents a different, some would say more logical, picture. It depicts Fu Xi and Nüwa as representatives of an earlier civilization, all trace of which disappeared beneath the waters of a devastating flood. It depicts them, like survivors everywhere, as determined to rebuild what had been lost.[8]

If, however, we accept the legend of Fu Xi as a picturesque representation of something that actually happened, we are still left with a mystery. The myth lists several aspects of the earlier culture that we would certainly expect survivors to restore as a matter of urgency—efficient ways of hunting and fishing, the institution of marriage to safeguard the family unit, the working of metal, and the techniques of building. But above them all is set the carefully preserved mention of "five stages of change" and "eight trigrams" that enabled Fu Xi to gain mastery over his world. What do these terms mean and what was he doing when he "looked upward and contemplated the images in the heavens, and looked downward and contemplated the occurrences on earth"?

The answers to these questions are embodied in the oldest known examples of China's most profound speculative philosophy. First came the question of what existed before the universe came into being. Chinese sages managed to imagine the almost unimaginable: a field phenomenon of pure potential that they labeled *Wu Chi*. This state of nothingness, beyond description or even speculation, is nonetheless the state out of which everything we experience arises. It precedes and, so to speak, "stands behind" matter, energy, space, and time. It is the ancient background to what physicists today refer to as the Quantum Foam, the ultimate substratum of reality created by the appearance, from nowhere, of fundamental subatomic particles that exist momentarily, then disappear again.

The genius of the ancient Chinese lay not in their recognition of this state but in their realization that its sole knowable characteristic had to be that of change. Without change, nothing could have emerged from the *Wu Chi*. Without change, it would have remained pure potential forever. But change it did, as we deduce in retrospect: the *Wu Chi* became the *Tai Chi* or Grand Terminus, the totality of our manifest universe, known and unknown, including our planetary world and the humanity that inhabits it.

Against this background, the Chinese made one further, vital deduction. If change was inherent in the great *Wu Chi–Tai Chi* transformation, then change was likely to remain inherent in the *Tai Chi* itself; indeed, likely to be its most fundamental aspect. Contemplation of these ideas led to further conclusions. In its original, pristine form, *Wu Chi* was a single unity. Once *Tai Chi* manifested, duality came into being; and this too must be an aspect of our universe. In fact, the manifest universe continued to mirror the processes that brought it into being. Inherent in its very structure was perpetual change, leading to the potential becoming actual, then transforming in its turn.

These are not particularly easy concepts for the Western mind to grasp (and worse is to come), but a modern exponent of the ancient philosophy,

Jou Tsung Hwa, puts forward a helpful analogy in the formation of tornadoes. He begins with the calm before the storm. The air is still and there is no tornado. This is the state of *Wu Chi*. Then the first hint of a breeze springs up, begins a circular motion, and eventually turns into a tornado. This is the state of *Tai Chi*. The state of calm, which once was all there was, has now become a duality: the original state of calm and the current tornado. But the tornado cannot last forever. The winds die down, a state of calm returns: *Tai Chi* has once again become *Wu Chi*.[9]

Observation of natural phenomena persuaded the Chinese that *everything* involved duality. Anything there was at any given time, any object, any event, had a part that changed and a part that stayed the same. Even when the hurricane was raging, there were parts of China that enjoyed calm weather; and in the heart of the hurricane there was also an area of flat calm, the eye of the storm.

All this is symbolized in the myth of Fu Xi looking upward to contemplate the heavens, and downward to discover what was happening on earth. He decided to call the unchanging part of phenomena yin and the part that changes yang. For convenience and practical application, he symbolized yin and yang as broken and unbroken lines. In doing so, he laid the foundations of the most influential oracle in the history of China—the *I Ching* or Book of Changes. Historically, that influence was most obvious in the Imperial Court. Courtiers, whose lives literally hung on the whim of their emperor, used the book constantly to divine their fate and seek advice on safe conduct. Sages used it as a basis for their advice to the emperor himself. Philosophers took up the work, allowing its insights to shape their own thoughts, which in turn shaped the society they lived in. How profoundly the *I Ching* influenced Chinese society as a whole is underlined by the fact that Confucius, who wrote his own commentaries on the oracle, claimed that were he to live his life again, he would devote it entirely to a study of the *I Ching*. Confucian thought continues to shape Chinese society to the present day, as, directly and indirectly, does the oracle Confucius so much admired.

In its developed form, the *I Ching* is a lengthy and complex work, daunting to the Western mind. It incorporates a binary system similar to that which drives modern computers and interprets a total of sixty-four figures known as hexagrams, each comprising a different pattern of interacting yin/yang lines. Since the meaning of every line varies with its position in the hexagram and any line is capable of modifying the meaning of the whole, the oracle offers a multitude of possible answers. In the earliest times, the lines were generated by heating a tortoiseshell until it cracked—hence the appearance of the little tortoise in Ma Lin's picture. If the crack was a single unbroken line, it was seen as yang; if broken, as yin. Later, bunches of dried yarrow stalks were used, as were coins. The exact method was unimportant, so long as it enabled the questioner to "tune in" to the currents of change pertinent to his query.

We have it on the authority of Carl Jung that the *I Ching* is capable of producing meaningful answers. When he tried it for himself, he concluded that "had a human being made such replies, I should, as a psychiatrist, have had to pronounce him of sound mind."[10] The question, however, is how. There have been many convoluted answers—Jung's theory of synchronicity is often evoked, for example—but the Chinese themselves were in no doubt. They attributed the *I Ching*'s accuracy to the intervention of spirits.

There are indications that this belief may be based on something more than simple superstition. One of them is the *I Ching*'s long association with yarrow stalks. Any good horticultural reference will list yarrow as a temperate-zone plant that grows across the British Isles, Europe, and much of the United States. In China, there is a tradition that it may be found growing wild in areas devoted to sacred ceremonies. What few sources mention is that the herb, when correctly prepared, has psychotropic properties.

The *I Ching* itself can also be used shamanically, as the American travel writer William Seabrook confirmed firsthand while visiting an apartment above New York's Times Square. Some friends were experimenting with the oracle, and one of them, a Russian émigré named Magda, decided to try an unusual technique that promised direct access to the oracle's wisdom. She generated a hexagram in the usual way using fifty yarrow stalks, but instead of finding its interpretation in the text, she entered a meditative state in which she visualized the figure painted on a wooden doorway. When the door opened of its own accord, she expected entry into a visionary experience that would clarify the meaning of the hexagram.

When nearly half an hour passed without anything happening, Magda's companions became bored and began to talk among themselves. But they were soon interrupted by a loud groan from Magda and the announcement that she was running in the snow, naked except for a fur coat. As they crowded around her she became agitated and began to growl like an animal. Her companions realized she was in some sort of trance, but when they attempted to waken her, she attacked them fiercely. They managed to subdue her eventually and when she woke she reported that entering the hexagram doorway had taken her into an environment not unlike the wilder parts of her native Russia, but in the process she had become possessed by the spirit of a wolf. Interestingly, the hexagram Magda generated was named *Ko*, which translates as "revolution." The original Chinese text equates it with molting, the means by which an animal changes its coat.[11]

Magda was not the only one to suspect the intervention of a spirit in the workings of the *I Ching*. By the time he came to admit it publicly in 1949, when his introduction to the classic Wilhelm/Baynes edition was first published, Carl Jung had been using the oracle for personal guidance and as part of his analytical practice for close to thirty years. He too liked to evoke synchronicity as an explanation of the oracle's effectiveness but privately admitted that the answers were prompted by "spiritual agencies" that formed the "living soul of the book."[12] Nor should the remarks be taken figuratively. Although in his earlier years Jung insisted apparitions and even physical manifestations must be "projections" of the unconscious, from personal experience he was convinced that a purely psychological explanation would not do. In a footnote to a lecture he gave to the Society for Psychical Research in London, reprinted in the 1947 edition of his *Collected Works*, he admitted that he now doubted whether an exclusively psychological approach could do justice to the phenomena. A year earlier, in a private letter to the psychotherapist Fritz Kunkel, he stated bluntly that "metaphysic phenomena could be explained better by the hypothesis of spirits than by the qualities and peculiarities of the unconscious."[13]

Underlying these insights is the little-known but time-honored Chinese Yarrow Stalk Ritual, which in its original form went well beyond the simple counting of stalks as practiced in the West—and indeed much of China—today. Portions of the ritual, pieced together from various sources, suggest it involved an altar spread with a cloth of the elemental color associated with the question asked.[14] A copy of the *I Ching* was placed in the southern quadrant of the altar, its cover facing south. A second, smaller and lower, altar was placed to the south of the main altar. On this was set an incense burner and a pouch containing the yarrow stalks. The questioner would move to the southern quarter of the room, then kneel to perform three kowtows northward toward the altars. The incense was then lit and the first yarrow stalk selected.[15]

Analysis of this ritual produces an important insight. The book is placed on the southern quarter of the altar because individuals of authority in ancient China traditionally faced south when granting an audience. The book itself, placed in this quarter, is seen as no more than the physical embodiment of a spiritual presence. When the questioner kowtows, facing north, it is the most profound indication of respect he could bestow on such a presence. And for the questioner, the presence is undoubtedly there, visible or invisible, ready and willing to answer the queries presented. The manipulation of the yarrow stalks represents no more than the establishment of a line of communication, as one might manipulate the buttons on a mobile phone in order to dial the number of a friend. In other words, the Yarrow Stalk Ritual is an act of spirit evocation.

The influence of a spirit oracle on ancient Chinese thought comes as little surprise in face of the fact that shamanism was Asia's oldest religion. Its reach extended beyond China itself to encompass Mongolia, Siberia, Russia, India, Tibet, Nepal, and even Persia. Japan's aboriginal practice of Shinto, now largely a faith-based religion focused on spirit and ancestor worship, betrays its own shamanic origins. Folk Shinto, one of Shinto's five modern manifestations, includes divinatory practice, spirit healing, and spirit possession.

Across this broad cultural spread, the influence of spirits on human beliefs and behavior has been pervasive, but nowhere so direct as in the institution of the Tibetan State Oracle. The term *oracle*, in Tibetan Buddhist tradition, has a much more specific meaning than its Western usage. It refers to a spirit capable of entering into and communicating with our mundane world through the medium of *kuten*, men or women capable of becoming— at least temporarily—the spirit's physical basis.

According to local legend, Buddhism arrived in Tibet from heaven in a miraculous casket sometime prior to 650 CE. It was established—without mythic overtones—as the country's official religion more than a hundred years later during the rule of King Trisong Detsen (755–797 CE). Prior to then, Tibet's principal spiritual practice had been the shamanic techniques of Bön. Animistic Bön, the earliest and most basic expression of this ancient religion, was deeply concerned with spirit contact. The techniques in use were very similar to those found in Siberia. Bonpo shamans banded together in a clan-guild that passed on and protected their sacred knowledge, which was largely centered on possession by gods, elementals, demons, and the spirits of shamanic ancestors. Initiatory practices for shamans-in-training were closely similar to those in Siberia. Initial attention from—and often possession by—the spirits would typically result in a sort of divine madness, which could only be cured by the candidate's retreat into a wilderness where, alone with his visions, he would bear witness to his own death and dismemberment by the spirits. If he survived the ordeal with his sanity intact, he would return to his clan-guild where senior practitioners would teach him how to control his spirit visitations. One way of doing so was to become an oracular *kuten* and act as a physical vehicle for intelligences from the Beyond.

Academic consensus accepts that in these early days there were hundreds of such mediums throughout Tibet, offering spirit advice to those who sought it and, collectively, exerting a profound influence on the entire culture. The arrival of Buddhism from India made little difference to this practice, and indeed led quickly to its becoming institutionalized. This arose from the newly imported belief in five emanations of the Wisdom Buddha, related to corresponding principles of Body, Mind, Speech, Qualities, and Activities. Each emanation was personified and chief among them was Pehar, king of the principal of Activity. Guru Padmasambhava, the Indian Master who helped establish Buddhism in Tibet, appointed Pehar as protector both of the new religion and Tibet itself. At once the Tibetans cast about for a *kuten* who could contact Pehar and his fellow kings. They eventually established communication with an emissary, Dorje Drak-den, and established a succession of monks to act as mediums for the entity. By the sixteenth century, the lineage, based in Nechung Monastery, was officially sanctioned and the current medium, a monk named Drag Trang-Go-Wa Lobsang Palden, appointed the country's first State Oracle.

The lineage endures to the present day, with ritual consultations virtually unchanged from those of centuries past. Prior to the Chinese invasion of 1950, the oracle was formally consulted each New Year and at other times depending on political circumstances. Access to the oracle was exclusive to the ruling Dalai Lama, high lamas of the major monasteries, and ministers of state. What happened during a consultation has been vividly described by the Fourteenth Dalai Lama,[16] who continues to seek the oracle's advice in exile:

Having prepared himself for the work through a lifetime of meditation and special rituals, the *kuten* dons an elaborate costume of several layers culminating in an ornate robe of golden silk brocade, embroidered in traditional designs in bright reds, blues, greens and yellows. A scrying mirror of polished steel surrounded by turquoise and amethyst clusters hangs on his chest and over it all he wears a heavy harness supporting four flags and three victory banners. The combined weight of the garments and accoutrements is more than seventy pounds, to which is added during the ceremony an enormous ornamental helmet weighing a further thirty. As a result, the oracle is scarcely able to walk unaided and is often helped to his place by fellow monks.

But the difficulty in movement is mysteriously overcome during the ritual itself. The ceremony begins with a generalized chanting of invocations and prayers, accompanied by cymbals, horns, and drums. In a short time, the oracle begins to show signs of trance and his assistants help him onto a small stool set before his questioner—generally the Dalai Lama himself. The first prayer cycle ends and a new one begins. The trance state deepens. It is at this point that the decorative helmet is placed on the *kuten*'s head. A wildness enters his expression and his face begins to swell, his eyes to bulge. Steady breathing changes to short, sharp pants and he begins to hiss violently. Abruptly his breathing stops altogether. His assistants take this as a sign and tie the helmet in place with a tight knot. Moments later, his entire body begins to expand visibly.

Although the *kuten* is wearing a costume weighing in excess of one hundred pounds and could previously only move with the help of his assistants, he now leaps to his feet unaided, grabs a sword from an assistant, and begins to dance. The scene is distinctly threatening, but the oracle merely approaches his questioner and bows from the waist so that his helmet actually touches the ground. It seems as if his spine must snap, but instead he leaps up with "volcanic energy" and moves about the room "as if his body were made of rubber and driven by a coiled spring of enormous power."[17]

Dorje Drak-den is now in full possession of the medium who manifests a persona that combines the dignity of a wise elder with the wrathful appearance of an ancient lord. He makes ritual offerings to the Dalai Lama, then awaits his questions and those of the ministers of state. Before replying, he throws himself into another violent dance, waving his sword above his head like some fierce warrior chieftain, then frames his answers in poetic verse and symbolic gestures. Once Dorje Drak-den has finished speaking, his physical vehicle makes one final offering, then collapses inert as the entity withdraws. The *kuten*'s assistants rush to remove the ornamental helmet, which might result in strangulation if left in place, then carry him off to recover—a process that may take a week or more.

The present Dalai Lama has maintained[18] that while he consulted—and at time of writing still consults—the oracle regularly, he does not always take the spirit's advice. Rather, he gives weight to its opinions in the same way he might give weight to the opinions of his ministers or his own judgment. Nonetheless, there is no doubt that important political decisions—including the Dalai Lama's own flight from Tibet a decade after the Chinese invasion—have been based directly on oracular predictions, just as they were in the West during the period of the classical civilizations. And just as we have seen how spirit influence in the Orient has permeated through to the present day, so it is possible to trace the pathways of spirit influence in the Western world following the fall of the classical civilizations.

6. DARK AGE CONJURATIONS

OR ANCIENT ROME, THE LAST OF THE GREAT EARLY WESTERN CIVILIZA-
tions, the problem had always been Germany. The barbarian hordes
beyond the Rhine had sometimes been subdued, sometimes temporarily pacified, but never fully conquered. In the later years of the empire, the
Romans began to realize they had disturbed a hornet's nest. The Germanic
tribes were no longer content to defend their own territory but set their sights
increasingly on lands ruled by Rome. For years, the seasoned Roman army
held them off. Then in the third century CE Roman soldiers pulled back from
the Rhine-Danube frontier to fight a civil war in Italy, leaving the borderlands
largely undefended. Gradually the northern tribes began to overrun the former
Roman territories in Greece and Gaul. Eventually the invaders penetrated
Italy and a ragtag army was soon camped outside the gates of Rome itself.
In 476 CE that army moved and the German general Odovacar overthrew the
last of the Roman emperors, Augustulus Romulus.

Germanic rule proved less than effective. The great engineering works
of ancient Rome were left to fall into disrepair. Without the disciplined legions
for protection, travel became unsafe. A cultural malaise set in so that farmers
no longer tilled their fields. Without goods from the farms, trade and business
began to disappear. The once mighty Roman Empire was visibly crumbling.
In an almost unimaginably brief period of time, it disappeared altogether.
The Dark Ages had begun.

But while hardly evident in conventional histories, widespread spirit
influence survived the fall of classical civilization. The prologue to a first-
century CE treatise on astrological botany, attributed to the Greek physician
Thessalos of Tralles, gives an account of evocation indicating that the use of
professional intermediaries was still the norm.

In the final years of his medical studies in Alexandria, Thessalos stumbled on a treatise attributed to an obscure Egyptian pharaoh, Nechepso, that detailed twenty-four cures for various diseases based on the signs of the zodiac. Impressed by the antiquity of the work, Thessalos boasted about his amazing discovery to friends, family, and colleagues in Alexandria, only to discover that the cures did not actually work. The discovery almost drove him to suicide. In desperation, he decided to look for divine revelation.[1] To this end, he traveled to Thebes where he found a priest willing to summon up Asclepios, the god of medicine.

The priest led him into a darkened room and chanted an incantation that caused the god to appear as a vision in a bowl of water. Thessalos was able to converse with the apparition, which explained in detail why King Nechepso's approach had failed, then dictated the genuine secret to Thessalos on the condition that he would never reveal it to the profane.[2] Ian Moyer comments that the description penned by Thessalos "reveals an awareness of similar narratives current in literature of the period."[3] Most of these typically involved the input of a professional who stood between the spirit and his client, acting to pass on messages and interpret their content. The intermediary was a priest in the case of Thessalos, among the last few of his profession to act openly as an intercessor with the spirit world. But by the time Thessalos discovered his mysterious book, Saint Paul was busily preaching to the Athenians and sending open letters to the Corinthians and Ephesians in an ultimately successful attempt to convert the pagan Greeks. Only a century or so later, Coptic Christianity had become the majority religion in Egypt. Soon the creed of the crucified god spread out of the Mediterranean and North Africa to conquer Europe. The Church of Rome was swiftly established as a major player—then *the* major player—in the politics and cultural life of the Continent. And the Church of Rome did not approve of spirit communications.

There were several biblical authorities for this stance, beginning with Saint John's comparatively mild admonition, "Beloved, believe not every spirit, but try the spirits whether they are of God: because many false prophets are gone out into the world."[4] John suggested a simple test. If the spirit professed belief in Jesus it was good; if not, it was a minion of the Antichrist. The Church paid scant attention to such a gentle approach, but concentrated instead on harsher passages:

> Regard not them that have familiar spirits, neither seek after wizards, to be defiled by them: I am the LORD your God.[5]

And the soul that turneth after such as have familiar spirits, and after wizards, to go a whoring after them, I will even set my face against that soul, and will cut him off from among his people.[6]

And he made his son pass through the fire, and observed times, and used enchantments, and dealt with familiar spirits and wizards: he wrought much wickedness in the sight of the LORD, to provoke him to anger.[7]

Moreover the workers with familiar spirits, and the wizards, and the images, and the idols, and all the abominations that were spied in the land of Judah and in Jerusalem, did Josiah put away, that he might perform the words of the law.[8]

And pounding like a leaden drumbeat across the Middle Ages:

Thou shalt not suffer a witch to live.[9]

A witch, as was made clear in the Old Testament story of the Witch of Endor,[10] was someone with the ability to contact spirits.

Christianity was never very happy about spirits, despite the Annunciation, the voice at Jesus's baptism, and Paul's experience on the road to Damascus. Christ, his immediate disciples, and many early saints encountered them, but the entities are almost invariably described as "unclean" or "evil." When the Lord granted his disciples the power to command spirits, the gift came with a warning: "Notwithstanding in this rejoice not, that the spirits are subject unto you; but rather rejoice, because your names are written in heaven."[11] As it grew in strength, the Church moved away from its initial position of caution to a decision that anyone who dealt with spirits was guilty of heresy. Since there was no apparent distinction between good and evil spirits, cynical historians might be tempted to see the move as an attempt to defend ecclesiastical power from possible competition. Certainly the heresy was vigorously pursued. In 1231, Pope Gregory IX set up the Papal Inquisition. His initial targets were the Waldensians and Cathars, two sects that shamed the Church by leading lives of Christlike simplicity, but eventually the Inquisition's remit was extended to take in a long list of heresies, including sodomy, polygamy, blasphemy, and usury.

While later institutionalized, the Inquisition was at first little more than a legal method. The old ecclesiastical court system was replaced by single officials (Inquisitors) with the authority to demand information from anyone they believed to possess it and, if necessary, take action on any heresy revealed. The Inquisitor's work was governed by strict, complex guidelines that limited the maximum punishment he could impose; in these early years, a simple penance was often the most that was imposed. But Gregory IX died in 1241 and just twenty-one years after the establishment of the Inquisition, a new pope, Innocent IV, authorized the use of torture.

Within 150 years, there were Inquisitors assigned throughout Europe, with brutally extended powers. Now they could impose prison sentences, up to and including life. Some enthusiastic Canon lawyer had even discovered a loophole to get around the ban on the Church taking life. Those condemned to death by an Inquisitor—the apostate who retracted his confession, the stubborn heretic who refused to confess at all—were simply handed over to the civil authorities who happily carried out the sentence. A favorite form of execution was burning alive. It reminded heretics of their fate in the afterlife and encouraged last-minute repentance. It was, in short, an act of mercy.

On August 22, 1320, a papal bull was issued specifically authorizing a French Inquisitor to investigate all those who used images or sacred objects to make magic and those who worshipped or made pacts with demons. Since by this time the Church tended to define all spirit communications as demonic, every mediumistic intermediary with the spirit realms was immediately at risk. Nor was the risk merely hypothetical. The first sorcery trial was held in Carcassonne just a decade after the bull. Five years later, Inquisitor Bernardus Guidonis condemned eight defendants to the stake, one on the basis of her confession that she had learned the secrets of evil from a goat. By 1350, the Inquisition had tried over one thousand French citizens for sorcery and burned more than half of them. For some, this hideous form of death may have been a blessed relief.

Typical of Inquisitorial justice was the case of Pierre Vallin. By the time the Inquisition caught up with him, Vallin was an old man and understandably frightened. He confessed at once to having sold his soul to the Devil some sixty-three years earlier, then gave the court an imaginative account of everything he thought the Inquisitor might want to hear, detailing a life of evil that included raising tempests, flying on a broomstick, and having sex with a succubus. When asked about his accomplices in this nefarious existence, he gave the names of four "witches" whose death had placed them beyond the reach of the Inquisition forever. Unfortunately, his Inquisitor suspected he was holding something back and ordered that Vallin be "put to the Question," a euphemism for interrogation under torture.

In the Dark Ages, those suspected of spirit contact frequently found themselves in the torture chambers of the Inquisition.

By the time of Vallin's trial, the Inquisition had refined its approach to torture. There were now several stages to the process. For the first, often recorded as "without torture," he was stripped, bound, flogged, stretched on the rack until his bones cracked, then crushed with thumbscrews until his fingers burst. This treatment persuaded Vallin to give five more names—not, unfortunately, enough to satisfy his Inquisitor, who ordered him taken to the kitchens of the Castle of Quinezonasium where he underwent three sessions of *strappado*, a procedure during which his hands were tied behind his back, then fastened to a rope fed through a pulley high above in the roof. He was then slowly hoisted upward some fifteen or twenty feet and left dangling in agony for several hours. Five further names were extracted. Vallin was lucky his Inquisitor left it at that. The *strappado* sessions were recorded as "ordinary torture." A further level of persuasion by pain, "extraordinary torture" typically left victims permanently crippled or dead. One favored practice was to burn off a victim's foot, then present him with the charred bones in a bag as a souvenir.

Against this background, it is easy to appreciate why the professional intermediary—priest, medium, oracle, shaman—disappeared so quickly from the public eye in medieval Europe. But this is not to say that spirit contact ceased. Advice from the Beyond was so useful, or perhaps just so alluring, that there remained those prepared to risk torture and death in order to receive it. Such individuals were wizards and witches, magical practitioners who sometimes used herbal drugs like thorn apple[12] to stimulate visionary experiences, and participated in rituals designed to conjure spirits. From the eighth to the eleventh centuries CE, Qabalistic texts like the *Sepher Yetzirah* made their way into European Jewish circles and, based as they were on the experiences of the Merkava mystics, promised spirit contact at the highest level. Even though Talmudic doctrine warned about the dangers of esoteric practice, several mystical fraternities were established in France, Spain, and Germany. But medieval forms of contact generally differed from those of the classical world in one important respect. Throughout the Dark Ages, belief in the Devil and his minions as living, breathing, and, above all, intervening, entities was strongly fostered by the Church and all but universal. But while the doctrine inspired fear in the many, for a certain minority mind-set, it was a short step from trying to avoid Satan to attempting to enslave his minions. Church disapproval ensured that the day of the openly practicing intermediary was gone, so the onus of spirit contact was thrown, for the first time in centuries, on the individual who sought their aid. The question was how to do it. The answer was provided by an increasing proliferation of grimoires, the notorious "black books" of magic. Specialist authority, Sir Keith Thomas writes:

> Since classical times, it had been believed that, by following the appropriate ritual, it was possible to get in touch with supernatural beings . . . Many such rituals were extant during the Middle Ages . . . Usually they circulated in manuscript and were guarded with the utmost secrecy by their owners: which was hardly surprising, since for much of the period, the conjuration of spirits was a capital offence . . . These works opened up to the reader the possibility of invoking the whole hierarchy of angels and demons, each with their own names and attributes. The rituals for such spirit-raising varied, but usually involved such procedures as drawing chalk circles on the ground, pronouncing incantations, observing ritual conditions of fasting and prayer, and employing such apparatus as holy water, candles, sceptres, swords, wands and metal lamina. There is no doubt whatsoever that these rituals were extensively practiced, both by contemporary intellectuals and by less educated would-be

magicians. The so-called "Books of Magic" . . . contain quite explicit formulae for invoking spirits and there is no shortage of evidence for such *séances* in the manuscript "Books of Experiments" which have survived.[13]

A study of the grimoires indicates a distinct change in attitude toward spirit entities during this period, possibly occasioned by an unconscious acceptance of Church doctrines. Where the spirits of ancient shamanism were treated with respect and the speaking statuary of Jaynes's investigations approached with awe, medieval conjurers viewed communicating entities as servants or slaves to be commanded, cajoled, threatened, or bullied into submission. The following extract from one of the most popular grimoires, *Clavicula Salomonis* or "Key of Solomon," gives a flavor of the new approach. In it, the wizard is instructed on what to do if the spirits prove recalcitrant in the face of milder conjurations:

> If they then immediately appear, it is well; if not, let the master uncover the consecrated pentacles which he should have made to constrain and command the spirits, and which he should wear fastened round his neck, holding the medals (or pentacles) in his left hand, and the consecrated knife in his right; and encouraging his companions, he shall say with a loud voice:—
>
> Here be the symbols of secret things, the standards, the ensigns, and the banners, of God the conqueror; and the arms of the almighty One, to compel the aerial potencies. I command ye absolutely by their power and virtue that ye come near unto us, into our presence, from whatsoever part of the world ye may be in, and that ye delay not to obey us in all things wherein we shall command ye by the virtue of God the mighty One. Come ye promptly, and delay not to appear, and answer us with humility.
>
> If they appear at this time, show them the pentacles, and receive them with kindness, gentleness, and courtesy; reason and speak with them, question them, and ask from them all things which thou hast proposed to demand.
>
> But if, on the contrary, they do not yet make their appearance, holding the consecrated knife in the right hand, and the pentacles being uncovered by the removal of their consecrated covering, strike and beat the air with the knife as if wishing to commence a combat, comfort and exhort thy companions, and then in a loud and stern voice repeat the following conjuration:—
>
> Here again I conjure ye and most urgently command ye; I force, constrain, and exhort ye to the utmost, by the most mighty and powerful name

of God EL, strong and wonderful, and by God the just and upright, I exorcise ye and command ye that ye in no way delay, but that ye come immediately and upon the instant hither before us, without noise, deformity, or hideousness, but with all manner of gentleness and mildness.

I exorcise ye anew, and powerfully conjure ye, commanding ye with strength and violence by him who spake and it was done; and by all these names: EL SHADDAI, ELOHIM, ELOHI, TZABAOTH, ELIM, ASHER EHEIEH, YAH, TETRAGRAMMATON, SHADDAI, which signify God the high and almighty, the God of Israel, through whom undertaking all our operations we shall prosper in all the works of our hands, seeing that the Lord is now, always, and for ever with us, in our heart and in our lips; and by his holy names, and by the virtue of the sovereign God, we shall accomplish all our work . . .

But if ye be still contumacious, we, by the authority of a sovereign and potent God, deprive ye of all quality, condition, degree, and place which ye now enjoy, and precipitate ye into and relegate ye unto the Kingdom of Fire and of sulphur, to be there eternally tormented. Come ye then from all parts of the earth, wheresoever ye may be, and behold the symbols and names of that triumphant sovereign whom all creatures obey, otherwise we shall bind ye and conduct ye in spite of yourselves, into our presence bound with chains of fire, because those effects which proceed and issue from our science and operation, are ardent with a fire which shall consume and burn ye eternally, for by these the whole Universe trembleth, the earth is moved, the stones thereof rush together, all creatures obey, and the rebellious spirits are tormented by the power of the sovereign creator.[14]

It is worth noting the second major change in spirit communication during this period—the overwhelming reliance on Judeo-Christian imagery in the evocation rituals. Claims to speak with the authority of God and Jesus Christ seem to be a universal feature of the grimoires, despite the Church's stance on the practice of evocation. Reading the "black books," one is left with the distinct impression that their authors were highly religious men, or at least absolute believers in the sovereignty of Jehovah and/or his Christian Son. Hand in hand with this conviction was the assumption that enslaving demons was a legitimate activity, since it gave them an opportunity to do some honest work for a change. Calling on the angels, for which instructions are given in some of the grimoires, usually produced a change of tone. The heavenly messengers were begged rather than commanded to appear, although even in supplication the arrogance of the conjurer was never far from the surface. But the practice of evocation was not confined to infernal and celestial spirits. The medieval scholar Michael Scot (c. 1175–c. 1234) wrote that contemporary occult practice included necromancy, the conjuration of the spirits of the dead.[15]

With few exceptions, conventional historians see spirit communications as a hidden (and unimportant) influence on society throughout the Middle Ages, largely ignoring the fact that the Church's vigorous attempts to stamp it out suggest a serious problem. But even the most conventional cannot entirely ignore two striking examples of spirit contact of glaringly obvious historical import—and twenty-first-century implications.

7. ROOTS OF ISLAM

THE DARKNESS THAT ENVELOPED EUROPE DURING THE EARLY MIDDLE Ages was not a worldwide phenomenon. The lights of learning that went out across Europe, as the Romans retreated, remained lit throughout the Middle East where Arab respect for and development of the sciences was a beacon to the world. Yet, as in every earlier civilization, contact with the spirit world remained. Prior to the advent of Islam, Arabs "lived and died with magic—they spoke to the good genii, the Djinns."[1] Against this cultural background, in 570 CE, there occurred the birth of a child who was destined literally to change the world. His name was Abū al-Qāsim Muḥammad ibn ʿAbd Allāh ibn ʿAbd al-Muṭṭalib ibn Hāshim. Today he is known more simply as Muhammad.

The boy's parents, ʿAbd Allāh and Āminah, belonged to the ruling tribe of Mecca responsible for guarding the city's most sacred shrine, the Kaʿbah, while his grandfather, ʿAbd al-Muṭṭalib, was a community leader. Nonetheless, his earliest years proved hard. His father died before the boy's birth. In accordance with the custom held by all the great Arab families at the time, his mother, Āminah, sent him as a baby to live among the Bedouin tribesmen of the deep desert. The belief held was that life in the desert taught a boy nobility and self-discipline, while giving him a taste for freedom. It took him away from the potential corruption of the city and offered escape from the cruel dominance of time. In some ways most important of all, it exposed him to the eloquent Arabic spoken by the Bedouin and instilled in him special skills as a speaker. The desert was seen as a place of sobriety and purity. To send a child there was to renew a bond that had existed for generations.

During his sojourn in this empty wilderness, Muhammad had his first spiritual experience:

A desert encampment similar to that in which the Prophet Muhammad had his first spiritual experience during his sojourn with the Bedouin as a child

There came onto me two men, clothed in white, with a gold basin full of snow. Then they laid upon me and, splitting open my breast, they brought forth my heart. This likewise they split open and took from it a black clot which they cast away. Then they washed my heart and my breast with the snow.[2]

When Muhammad was six years old, his mother died, and he was placed in the care of his grandfather. But the old man himself died just two years later and the boy's upbringing was entrusted to an uncle, Abū Ṭālib. Apparently he did a good job, for Muhammad grew into a young man whose character eventually earned him the nickname al-Amīn, or "Trusted One." Citizens of Mecca took to seeking him out as an arbiter in their disputes. Muhammad's appearance was, according to early sources, quite striking:

[He] was neither tall nor lanky nor short and stocky, but of medium height. His hair was neither crispy curled nor straight but moderately wavy. He was not overweight and his face was not plump. He had a round face. His complexion was white tinged with redness. He had big black eyes with long lashes. His brows were heavy and his shoulders broad. He had soft skin, with fine hair covering the line from mid chest to navel. The palms of his hands and the soles of his feet were firmly padded. He walked with a firm gait, as if striding downhill. On his back between his shoulders lay . . . a mole.[3]

The mole, first noticed by his guardian Ḥalīmah immediately after the vision of the two men in white, was important. Its placement identified it as the Seal of Prophethood, a visible sign of the young man's destiny.

Muhammad was first married at the age of twenty-five. He accepted the proposal of his employer at the time, a wealthy Meccan woman named bint al-Khuwaylid, who bore him two sons and four daughters. Both boys died young. Ten years later, Muhammad was one of the most respected figures in his native city. He was still being asked to arbitrate on disputes, but by now these were as often civil as personal and sometimes extremely important. On one occasion, for example, the main tribes of the region were at odds over the question of which of them should place the holy black stone in position in the newly restored Ka'bah. Muhammad was called in to resolve the situation, which he did by placing the stone on his cloak, which was spread on the ground, then having representatives of each tribe lift a corner of the cloak until the stone reached a height where it could be set into the wall.

By now, Muhammad was spending much of his time in prayer and meditation, often in the solitude of the desert. The practice brought him religious visions, some of which he described as like "the breaking of the light of dawn."[4] In the year 610 CE, when Muhammad was forty years old, one of his desert trips brought an experience that was to change his life. Meditating in the cave of al-Ḥirā' in the Mountain of Light (Jabal al-Nūr) near Mecca, a spirit with the appearance of a man embraced him and demanded that he "recite." When Muhammad demurred, the entity embraced him again three times and began to dictate a lengthy message. Muhammad panicked—he thought he might be at risk of possession by *djinn* or demons—and fled from the cave. The voice pursued. Arab tradition holds that at this point it told Muhammad he was the messenger of God, while the voice itself belonged to the archangel Gabriel. Muhammad believed none of it and ran down the mountain. But then he looked back and discovered that the sky had turned green and was filled in whatever direction he looked by the immense form of an angel.

When Muhammad reached home, he told his wife of the experience. She accepted his story without hesitation and sent for her cousin Waraqah, a particularly devout Christian who nonetheless confirmed that Muhammad had indeed been chosen as God's prophet. Muhammad himself had a second revelation shortly thereafter. It was the beginning of a process that was to last twenty-three years and resulted in the *Qur'ān* (Koran), the sacred scrip-

*The Mountain of Light, near Mecca, where Muhammad
first encountered the Archangel Gabriel*

ture of Islam that contains, in Muslim belief, the word of God revealed through Gabriel to the Prophet Muhammad. According to early traditions, Gabriel brought the Qur'ān directly to the Prophet's heart, suggesting an emotional rather than intellectual transference. Gabriel is represented on the Qur'ān as a spirit whom the Prophet could sometimes see and hear. Apparently, the revelations occurred in a state of trance, accompanied by heavy sweating. They carried their own conviction, strong enough to split a mountain from fear of God, according to the scriptures themselves. The Qur'ān describes itself as the transcript of a heavenly book written on a preserved tablet with no earthly source.

It took Muhammad three years before he gained the confidence to preach his revelation to the public at large, although he did explain the message to his family, and even a few close friends, in the interim. A tiny group formed around him, but small though it was, this group proved to be the seed from which the whole of Islam eventually grew. It was not an easy growth. Most influential figures in Mecca rejected the new doctrine, which preached a strict monotheism, opposed idolatry, and consequently threatened trade. At the time, the Ka'bah was the focus of almost all Arab religious cults and a magnet for lucrative pilgrimages. If the new religion took hold, who could tell what would happen to the Ka'bah's favored status? Who could tell what would happen to commerce?

Despite everything, Islam did manage to grow, although opposition increased as its influence spread. Early converts found themselves persecuted and even tortured. But in 619 CE, Muhammad himself underwent his supreme religious experience while spending the night in an open sanctuary attached to the north wall of the Ka'bah. While traditions vary slightly, there is general agreement that he was transported by Gabriel on a winged horse to the city of Jerusalem. There they went to the rock on which Abraham was prepared to sacrifice his son[5] and hence to heaven itself, ascending through higher states of being toward God. At one point, Gabriel told Muhammad he could go no farther because to do so would risk burning his wings in the glory of the Almighty. Muhammad, however, was permitted to continue until, prostrate before the divine throne, he received the ultimate storehouse of Islamic knowledge, including the final form and number of the daily prayers.

The idea of spreading the message of Islam beyond the city of Mecca, something that had been preying on Muhammad's mind, received an unexpected boost in 621 CE when a delegation arrived from Yathrib, a city to the north, inviting him to take up residence there as civic leader. The following year, the Prophet reached an agreement with the people of Yathrib (now modern Medina), promising leadership in return for protection. He then ordered his followers to travel to Yathrib in small groups to avoid undue attention and await him there. Muhammad himself escaped from Mecca only just in time. His enemies attacked his home, with murderous intent, shortly after he had fled. His arrival in Yathrib on September 25, 622, CE marked the establishment of Islam as a religion and the introduction of the Islamic calendar.

Today, Islam is the world's second-largest religion after Christianity. According to a study released by the Pew Research Center in 2011, it has 1.62 billion adherents, only a little short of one person in four throughout the world. All follow a lifestyle and belief system arising from the revelations of a spirit voice in an Arabian cave more than thirteen centuries ago.

Islam was not, of course, the first religion to have stemmed from spirit revelations, nor was it the last. But spirits have also had effects that were almost entirely political—and far-reaching. As such it ably illustrates both the direct contemporary influence of a spirit contact and its implications for the course of history, even when those who believe in it are limited in numbers.

PART TWO

WORLD CHANGERS

WHILE THE WORLDWIDE GROWTH OF INSTITUTIONAL-
ized religion changed public perceptions of the
spirit world, there remained individuals who were
unwilling to accept the need of priestly intermediaries to bring
them otherworldly aid and doctrines. For some, their convictions
came in the form of spontaneous spirit voices and visions. Others
were driven to seek contact by eccentric beliefs, a will to power,
desire for knowledge, or just simple curiosity. Some were larger-
than-life personalities, destined by fate to play a major role in the
political decisions of their day. All were guided by the Whisperers, those muted voices that had forged the course of human history since time immemorial.

This section presents portraits in context of a representative
example of such individuals, including a pious zealot, a courageous clairvoyant, a royal adviser . . . even the founder of a dynamic new religion. They are as diverse a collection as it is
possible to imagine, but the lives of all of them were changed by
spirits, allowing them to become world changers in their turn.

8. THE VOICES AND
THE MAID

THE HUNDRED YEARS WAR WAS AN INTERMITTENT STRUGGLE BETWEEN England and France in the fourteenth and fifteenth centuries, over who was the proper successor to the French crown and several other less pressing disputes. Despite the name, it actually lasted more than one hundred years, starting in 1337 and ending in 1453. Toward the end of the period, spirits intervened in the conflict so dramatically that they have earned a prominent place in every history of the late Middle Ages. Their channel was a rustic French girl named Jehanne. Today, she is best known in the English-speaking world as Joan of Arc.

Joan was born on the Feast of the Epiphany, 1412, in the village of Domrémy, in northeastern France. Her parents were peasant farmers, Jacques and Isabelle d'Arc, who worked fifty acres of land along the upper Meuse valley. Her birth date has a certain significance, for the baby grew into a likeable and pious child who worked diligently and went to church often. She developed a special devotion to the Virgin Mary and took to bringing candles in her honor to the Notre Dame de Bermont chapel. A fellow villager recalled her as "greatly committed to the service of God and the Blessed Mary." Another added that she helped the sick and gave alms to the poor.[1] In the summer of 1424, while in her father's garden, she heard "a voice from God" and was very much afraid.[2]

The voice, which she believed was sent by the Almighty to help guide her behavior, came at a complex and turbulent time in French history. The crown of France was in dispute between the Dauphin Charles (later Charles VII), son and heir of the Valois king Charles VI, and the Lancastrian English king Henry VI. Henry's armies were in alliance with those of Philip the Good, Duke of Burgundy, and were occupying much of the northern part of the kingdom. Joan's village lay on the turbulent frontier between lands controlled by the Dauphin and those occupied by Henry and Philip. Her father had already pooled resources with another farming family in order to rent the Château de l'Ile, an island fortress on the Meuse that he hoped would provide a sanctuary for the villagers and their livestock.

Joan's voice in the garden came from the direction of the Church of St. Rémy close to her home. It was accompanied by a light and she quickly decided it was the voice of an angel. The exact sequence of events, as given in Joan's own account,[3] is a little confused at this point, but it appears that the initial communication turned into a full-blown vision of the archangel Michael, who was, among other things, a patron saint of the Royal French Army. With him came "many angels from heaven" seen by Joan as if physically present. The archangel told her Saint Catherine and Saint Margaret would soon come to her and that she was to obey them in what they told her to do, since they were acting on God's order. After he delivered the message and left, she broke down in tears: she wanted to go with the angels back to their celestial abode.

The experience proved to be the first of many. Voices, which she understood to be those of the promised saints, came to her two or three times a week. Initially, they simply told her to be good and attend church regularly but then, to Joan's dismay, the messages became political. She was instructed to travel into the territories loyal to the Dauphin and raise the siege laid on the city of Orléans. To this end, she was first to visit the town of Vaucouleurs where the garrison commander Robert de Baudricourt would provide her with troops. Joan protested that she did not know how to lead men into war, nor even how to ride a horse; besides, at age twelve, she was far too young for such an undertaking. She ignored the insistent voices and continued to do so for four years, but the spirits persevered.

Joan's visions did not exactly change her—she had always been a conservative, well-behaved, churchgoing girl—but they intensified her piety to an extraordinary degree. While her friends were singing and dancing, Joan would take herself off to church, where she spent hours in prayer. She went frequently to confession and worked hard in her home and in her father's fields. She ignored the other girls when they told her she had become "too pious." Meanwhile, all around her, the political situation continued to deteriorate. By the spring of 1428, it seemed as if the English would soon overrun the southern half of France. Joan decided she could no longer procrastinate.

The time had come to obey the spirit voices. She was just sixteen years of age.

On May 13, Joan traveled to the village of Burley-le-Petit to visit her uncle, Durand Lassois.[4] After she settled in for an eight-day stay, the real purpose of her visit became evident. She told him she needed to visit Vaucouleurs and he agreed to take her. Once in Vaucouleurs, she went searching for the garrison commander, Robert de Baudricourt. Although she had never seen him before, one of her voices pointed him out. Joan bravely marched up to him and told him she needed to go to the Dauphin to ensure he would be crowned as the rightful king of France. De Baudricourt was not impressed. He told Lassois to take her home and "give her a good slapping." Joan withdrew and returned reluctantly to Domrémy.

By the following October, the predicted siege of Orléans had begun. The city was surrounded by some four thousand English troops and was in imminent danger of falling by the winter months. In January 1429, with her spirit voices becoming more and more insistent, Joan again made plans to visit Vaucouleurs. She told her parents she was going to help Durand Lassois's wife, arranged for him to collect her, and, while en route to his home, persuaded him to take her to Vaucouleurs instead. There she stayed with family friends, Henri and Catherine le Royer. Once safely installed, she began to pester Robert de Baudricourt again, but he continued to ignore her. Nonetheless, Joan's reputation had begun to spread. She had taken to calling herself the Maid, frequently quoted an old prophecy that a virgin would be the salvation of France, and spoke freely of her voices and her mission. As a result, she was summoned to the sickbed of the Duke of Lorraine, who thought the devout young visionary might be able to cure him. Instead, Joan gave him a brisk lecture about his sins and offered to pray for his health if he would have his son and some men escort her to the Dauphin. The pro-English Duke declined but may have been taken by her boldness, as he gave her four francs. Joan returned to Vaucouleurs where her voices encouraged her to persevere with Robert de Baudricourt. She approached him twice and was twice turned down. Her voices predicted he would accede to her requests if she tried a third time. The prediction proved accurate. De Baudricourt authorized that she be escorted to the Dauphin's court at Chinon and even gave her a letter of recommendation.

By now Joan had developed friendships in Vaucouleurs. An escort was quickly put together and Joan was supplied with some made-to-measure male clothing, spurs, greaves, sword, and a horse.[5] The party then took to the road. Joan predicted that if they met soldiers on the way, God would clear a route for them, for this was what she had been born to do.

After a long, arduous journey, Joan was eventually escorted into a packed audience hall at Chinon. Her reputation had preceded her. There were more than three hundred men-at-arms milling around and the Dauphin had withdrawn to the end of the chamber to test her powers. But her voices proved up to the occasion and guided her directly to him. She introduced herself as Jehanne la Pucelle (Joan the Maiden), assured him that he was the rightful heir to the throne of France, and predicted that he would eventually be anointed and crowned in the town of Rheims. Eyewitness accounts of the meeting suggest Charles was pleased enough with what he heard, but he was also a cautious man. Although she frequently evoked the name of God, he badly needed to know whether she was in genuine contact with the Almighty. Consequently he ordered that she be thoroughly examined by a committee of high-ranking clerics, prelates, and theologians to determine whether or not he should believe her. The examination took a little over three weeks, part of them spent in Poitiers. At one point, when asked to provide a (supernatural) sign of her bona fides, she told her questioner bluntly, "I did not come to Poitiers to produce signs; but send me to Orléans; I will show you the signs for which I was sent!"[6] The type of signs she meant might be inferred from the contents of a letter she sent subsequently to the English commanders besieging Orléans. In it she told them she had been appointed by Christ to push them out of France.

In March 1429, the theologians at Poitiers handed down their verdict:

> The King . . . must not prevent her [Joan] from going to Orléans with his soldiers, but must have her conducted honourably, trusting in God. For to regard her with suspicion or abandon her, when there is no appearance of evil, would be to repel the Holy Spirit and render himself unworthy of the aid of God.[7]

To celebrate the verdict, Joan's voices found her a sword: the weapon, they said, would be discovered behind the altar of the church at St. Catherine-de-Fierbois; as indeed it was, rusting and buried in the ground. Clergy of the church cleaned it up and sent it to her. Although delighted by the gift, Joan never carried it into battle. Her only "weapon" was her personal banner depicting Christ holding the world, flanked by two angels and the names

"Jesus" and "Mary." That way, she claimed, she would not have to hurt anyone. To prevent hurt to her, the king ordered a full suit of burnished steel-plate armor, specially made to measure, at a cost of 100 *livres-tournois*. Two months later, Joan traveled to the town of Blois to collect provisions and meet up with her promised army, whom she doubtless disconcerted by issuing an immediate set of orders banning swearing and looting, while the regular attendance at Mass and confession became compulsory. Camp followers were sent packing and any soldier with a mistress was told to marry her or leave the camp. Once the provisions arrived, Joan and her men marched for Orléans.

At this point the city was cut off on three sides by a chain of fortresses, some built from the ground up by the English, some the result of fortifying and occupying existing buildings. To reach the city itself, the Dauphin's army was obliged to cross the Loire, but this proved problematic since the transport barges were hindered by a high wind. Joan reassured her fellow commanders and a city representative sent to meet her that God himself had taken pity on Orléans, at which point the wind changed and the barges became operational. Joan was ferried across past the English positions and entered the city after nightfall, but there were not enough boats to transport the whole of her army, so less than half of her men accompanied her.

Now safely ensconced in Orléans, Joan sent a second letter to the English telling them to leave. Against the rules of war, the English imprisoned one of the two heralds who delivered her message and sent the other back with a response that berated Joan as a herder of cows and a bawd. Joan decided to try again in person and went to a spot within shouting distance of the English positions. There she called on the commander to surrender, in the name of God. The commander responded by threatening to burn her.

The following day (May 1) was a Sunday—the "truce of God" during which all fighting was temporarily suspended. Two of Joan's commanders took the opportunity to try to retrieve the remainder of her army, only to discover that without the inspiration of her presence, significant numbers had deserted. Joan herself used the truce to make another shouted appeal for an enemy surrender but was once again met with abuse. Three days later, the remainder of her army arrived, bringing supplies and reinforcements into Orléans with no opposition from the English. But this proved little more than the lull before the storm. A fresh English army was spotted marching to reinforce the besiegers and, while Joan was asleep, one of the Orléans commanders launched a fifteen-hundred-strong attack against an enemy position, the fortress of St. Loup. It proved impossible to hide anything from Joan's voices, however, since they woke her with instructions to attack the English. Her only problem was whether to attack the approaching army or one of the English fortresses. In the end, the decision was made for her when she learned of the fighting at St. Loup. The French attack on the fortress was not going well, but Joan's appearance made all the difference. The troops of Orléans rallied strongly at the sight of her standard, English morale collapsed, and within three hours the fort had fallen. By then, 114 of the English were dead and 40 taken captive. Joan instructed her men to attend confession and thank God for their victory. She then prophesied that the siege of Orléans would be lifted within five days. It proved a wholly accurate prediction.

The day following the fall of St. Loup, May 5, was another "truce of God" (the Feast of the Ascension) and Joan seized the opportunity to write a further letter to the English demanding their retreat. This time, rather than risk losing another herald, she had it shot into the English positions tied to an arrow. Despite their defeat at St. Loup, the English remained defiant. On May 6, hostilities began again, with a French attack on two of the remaining English fortresses. The English abandoned the first of them without a fight, quickly withdrawing to the second, a fortified monastery known as Le Bastille des Augustins. French commanders hesitated, then called off the attack. Joan appeared on horseback and insisted on leading the troops forward again. Her assault succeeded, the Bastille fell, and the few English survivors retreated hastily to their main fortification, les Tourelles.

With the French army now camped outside les Tourelles, Joan had another disagreement with her military commanders. They wanted to withdraw to Orléans and await reinforcements. She told them that having taken council from the Lord, she wanted them to attack at dawn. Once again she had her way. Morning found her at the head of her army, despite the fact that she had prophesied she would be wounded in the battle. The prediction came true after breakfast, as she was helping the men raise a scaling ladder. An English archer shot her between shoulder and neck, so that she was flung off her feet with the arrow protruding from her back. Her soldiers carried her to safety and suggested she use magic to heal the wound, but Joan refused, claiming that to do so would be a sin and against God's will. Military surgeons then stanched the bleeding by packing the wound with cotton soaked in a mixture of olive oil and bacon fat. According to Joan's later testimony, Saint Catherine appeared then to comfort her.

Demoralized by the wounding of their leader, the French commanders decided to call off the attack. Joan was dismayed when she learned of the decision and asked them to wait a little before retreating. She then rode off into a nearby vineyard where she remained for fifteen minutes deep in prayer. When she returned, she predicted that when the wind blew her banner against the wall of the fortress, it would fall at once to the French assault. She then rode out in sight of the English, who were completely demoralized by her unexpected reappearance. Her own troops attacked again with renewed ferocity, a soldier called out that Joan's banner had touched the wall, and the fortress fell to a pincer movement that met with little real resistance. French troops returned to Orléans to the sound of church bells and citizenry singing "*Te Deum Laudamus*" ("We Praise Thee, O God"). The following day, the English abandoned their siege.

By this point, there was no longer any lingering doubt that Joan was inspired by God, nor that she was almost single-handedly responsible for the breaking of the Orléans siege. Buoyed up by their success, the French quickly embarked on a series of campaigns aimed at rolling back the remaining English positions along the Loire. More clashes followed in other locations, with more successes for the French until, in June 1429, the decisive battle was fought at Patay and the entire English army put to rout, breaking its long stranglehold on the country. After a period of hesitation, the Dauphin finally marched on Reims and was there crowned King Charles VII later in the month, finally fulfilling Joan's initial prediction. He declined, however, to march on Paris—the one move that, if successful, would have established him securely on the throne. Instead, he pulled back to the Loire and disbanded his armies on September 22. But the wars were far from over and Joan, now a national heroine, took part in several more actions, all of them successful until, on May 23, 1430, her luck finally ran out. Leading a sortie against Burgundian troops laying siege to Compiègne, she was eventually outflanked by English reinforcements and compelled to retreat. In typical fashion, she held back to protect the rear guard as they crossed the River Oise. Minutes later she was unhorsed and, unable to remount, gave herself up. She was taken first to Margny, where she met with the Duke of Burgundy, then was sent by his ally John of Luxembourg to a castle in Vermandois. She tried to escape, so he sent her to an even more remote castle where she jumped from the top of a tower into the moat. Although knocked unconscious, she was not seriously injured, and when she recovered she was taken to Arras, the center of the Artois region in northern France and a town loyal to Burgundy. From there, John of Luxembourg sold her for 10,000 francs to Pierre Cauchon, the bishop of Beauvais, a supporter of the English who put her on trial in Rouen. The charge was heresy, the judges were Cauchon himself and Jean Lemaître, the Vice-Inquisitor of France.[8]

On February 21, 1431, Joan of Arc was taken before her judges and promptly proved as defiant as she had ever been with her military commanders. She demanded to attend Mass,[9] insisted she was morally free to attempt an escape, and refused to divulge any details of her conversations with the Dauphins.[10] One consequence of her stubbornness was that she was chained to a wooden block and watched day and night by guards assigned to her cell. She faced a total of seventy charges, including those of prophecy, disobeying commands of the church, endorsing her letters with divine names, and wearing male clothing. After a staunch defense, the original seventy charges were reduced to twelve, which were then forwarded for consideration to various eminent theologians in Rouen and Paris.

While the deliberations were in progress, Joan fell ill and clearly thought she was dying. (She asked to confess, to receive Holy Communion, and to be buried in consecrated ground.) Her captors reacted by threatening her with torture if she continued to evade the question of obedience to the Church, but she remained so stubborn that they eventually voted 10 to 3 that torture would be useless. On May 23, she was finally informed that if she persisted in her heresies, she would be turned over to the secular authorities—the ecclesiastical equivalent of a death sentence. The following day, she was taken to the graveyard at the church of Saint-Ouen for the sentence to be formalized. She asked leave to appeal to the pope, but her request was ignored. As her judges began to read the document that would transfer her to secular power, she recanted and declared she would do everything the Church required of her. She then signed an official form of abjuration and was formally condemned to life imprisonment. A few days later, Joan again put on men's clothes, then told her captors that the voices of Saints Catherine and Margaret had censured her for the treason of her abjuration. On May 29, her judges agreed unanimously to hand her over to civil authority. The following morning, she was taken to the Place du Vieux-Marché and burned at the stake. Her last request was for a crucifix to be held high so she could see it as she burned.

Her beliefs were eventually vindicated. On his entry into Rouen in

*Guided by her spirit voices, Joan of Arc chose to be burned alive
rather than recant their teaching.*

1450, Charles VII belatedly ordered an inquiry into the trial. Two years later
the cardinal legate Guillaume d'Estouteville made a second, more thorough,
investigation. In 1455, Pope Calixtus III instituted proceedings that revoked
her sentence. Joan was canonized by Pope Benedict XV on May 16, 1920.
Spirit guidance had made her a saint, and its influence reverberated down
the corridors of time.

9. THE EVOCATIONS OF NOSTRADAMUS

WITH THE ADVENT OF THE RENAISSANCE, SPIRIT INFLUENCE BECAME increasingly overt—although the Inquisition remained brutally active—and the numbers of grimoires in circulation actually increased under the stimulus of Renaissance Neoplatonism. Scholarly investigation of the occult arts and spirit evocation became widespread. This spirit renaissance is felt to the present day, due to the activities of a man who arguably became the world's second most famous prophet.

Michel de Nostradame was born at St. Remy in France on December 14, 1503, at the stroke of midnight. He was the elder of two brothers and studied mathematics, Greek, Latin, Hebrew, and the humanities at the feet of his maternal grandfather, Jean de St. Remy. He was also taught how to use an astrolabe, an instrument used by astronomers and astrologers for predicting planetary positions, and may have picked up some herbal lore through watching his grandfather—a physician—compounding potions and ointments. When Jean de St. Remy died, the boy moved back to live with his parents at St. Remy-en-Crau and was subsequently sent to the university at Avignon. To gain entrance, he had to pass examinations in grammar, rhetoric, and philosophy. He did so well that his examiners made him a teacher. His father later arranged his transfer to Montpelier Medical School where he remained for three years.

At the time, medical school examinations were conducted by dispute. For his finals, Michel sat from 8:00 a.m. to noon, arguing points of physics and logic with his professors so successfully that he was awarded the scarlet robe of a scholar. But to achieve the status of physician, he had to teach under supervision for three months and then survive a further, more rigorous, examination by dispute. For the ordeal, he presented himself in turn to four different professors, each of whom questioned him about the treatment and cure of a specific illness. This was followed, just over a week later, by a visit to the chancellor, who stuck a pin at random into a huge medical text in order to select the next disease for which the student was to prescribe. When he survived these tests, an aphorism of Hippocrates was selected—again at random—and he was required to prepare a thesis on it for delivery within twenty-four hours. His professors formally disputed his thesis for four hours in the Chapel of St. Michel. A week later, Nostradamus received his license to practice as a physician. Shortly afterward, bubonic plague swept through his native France.

Michel, now known by the Latin version of his name, Nostradamus, began to establish a medical reputation in his twenties when he devised treatments for plague that proved remarkably effective. By the time he was fifty, his name was known throughout Europe. In 1554, there was an outbreak of plague in Marseilles and Nostradamus was called in. Within days he was feted throughout the city as successful cure followed successful cure. The plague, known as the Blue Sickness or Black Death, hit Aix-en-Provence. Months into the outbreak, its parliament had closed down and courts and churches ceased to function. More than half its citizens fled and weeds began to grow in the streets. The city gates were shut and remained closed for a year in an attempt to isolate the disease. After a deputation begged Nostradamus for his help, he took up residence in the stricken city and soon the outbreak began to abate. Grateful authorities loaded him with gifts and voted him a permanent pension. The plague struck at Salon and again Nostradamus was called in. A rival doctor accused him of magical practice. The authorities ignored him and when the outbreak died down, Nostradamus was given more gifts.

By now in middle age, he had become a wealthy man. His first wife was dead for more than ten years and he had fallen in love with another woman, the widow Anne Ponsart Beaulme (née Gemelle). With a strong desire to marry again and settle down to a less hectic lifestyle, he proposed to Madame Beaulme and she accepted. But the less hectic lifestyle proved elusive. He continued his practice of medicine but soon added on a new and very different career, as a publisher. What he published (and wrote) was an almanac.

The first known almanac appeared in Europe in 1457 and set the style for those that followed. They were typically based around an annual calendar

The Black Plague, depicted here as a rampaging demon, first ushered the prophet Nostradamus into public prominence when his remedies proved effective against the disease.

of events and usually contained seasonal tips for farmers. But much of their content was devoted to weather forecasting and other astrological predictions. Nostradamus embarked on his own venture cautiously, publishing a trial edition designed to gauge public reaction. He found himself with an immediate success on his hands, largely due to the predictive four-line poems he had assigned to each month of the year.

Emboldened by his success, Nostradamus turned the almanac into an annual. His work on the publication seems to have given him a taste for prophecy, for he began to write a book called *Les Propheties* containing *Centuries and Presages* devoted to his predictions for a more distant future. Like the poems in his almanac, each presage was written as a quatrain.

The term *Centuries* refers not to a time period, but rather to a grouping of one hundred prophecies. By his death in 1566, he had written ten Centuries, or just short of a thousand prophecies (since one of the Centuries fell short of the requisite one hundred). His secretary at the time, Jean-Aymes de Chavigny, claims he was afraid of public reaction and kept his prophecies to himself for a long time before publishing them. However, the Lyons printer Macé Bonhomme eventually brought out a first edition in 1555. It contained three Centuries and fifty-three quatrains of a fourth.

The book was an instant success, despite its many obscurities. It was written in a mixture of French, Greek, Latin, and Italian, crammed with anagrams, initials, cryptic terms, and mysterious abbreviations. With few exceptions, the predictions were undated. Nonetheless, the work quickly found its way into influential circles. The French queen, Catherine de Medici, certainly had a copy. The book was issued toward the end of 1555. In the early months of 1556, Catherine wrote to the governor of Provence demanding that Nostradamus be sent to the Royal Court. By the time he received the summons, it was summer. He set out on July 14, 1556, for the court's summer seat at St. Germain-en-Laye. There Nostradamus had a brief meeting with the king (Henri II) before being closeted for a longer period with Queen Catherine. What happened at these meetings is not known, but Nostradamus obviously impressed the royal couple since he was given a gift of 130 écus.

Nostradamus's warm reception may have had something to do with an earlier prediction made by the Italian astrologer Luc Gauric. Gauric had forecast Henri's accession to the throne, a sensational duel in the early part of his reign, and the probability that Henri would lose his life in a similar event. By the time Nostradamus was summoned to court, the first two parts of this prediction had already come true. Henri was now king, and a sensational duel had indeed marked the early part of his reign. It took place between two nobles, Guy Chabot Jarnac and François Vivonne la Châtaigneraie, at St. Germain-en-Laye on June 16, 1547. King Henri attended and watched Châtaigneraie die. A phlegmatic Henri recalled the remainder of the prediction and remarked, "I care not if my death be in that manner more than any other. I would even prefer it, to die by the hand of whomsoever he might be, so long as he be brave and valiant and that I keep my honor." Catherine took the whole thing a lot more seriously. She called on Gauric to provide more details, and Gauric cast a horoscope that advised the king to avoid all single combat, particularly during his forty-first year, since he would be particularly susceptible to a head wound that would certainly blind him and might even cost him his life.

With this ominous prediction hanging over her husband, Catherine discovered that Nostradamus had, in his very first Century, written the quatrain:

> Le lion jeune le vieux surmontera
> En champ bellique par singulier duelle
> Dans cage d'or les yeux lui drevera
> Deux classes une, puis mouris, mort cruelle.
> (The young lion will overcome the old one,
> On the field of battle, by means of single combat
> In a cage of gold his eyes will be pierced.
> A double wound, a cruel death.)[1]

King Henri's emblem was the lion, and it occurred to the queen that Nostradamus was also predicting the king's death in a duel. Others came to a similar conclusion. At one point, the quatrain was so widely discussed at the French Court that the English ambassador alerted Queen Elizabeth I. When, three years later, Henri was indeed killed in single combat during a jousting accident that cost him the sight of one eye before he finally succumbed, Nostradamus's reputation as a prophet was firmly established. No one had the slightest doubt that this was the event he had foretold. As news spread, an angry crowd stormed through the Paris streets to burn him in effigy and demand he be turned over to the Inquisition on charges of sorcery. Only Queen Catherine's intervention saved him.

Despite the immediate reaction, Nostradamus's influence spread. All sorts of stories began to circulate about his prowess as a seer. One recounted how a servant of the wealthy Beauveau family lost a valuable hound that had been left in his care and called on Nostradamus to help him find it. Nostradamus was in his study, determined not to be disturbed, but after a time the noise of the man's knocking got too much for him. He opened an upstairs window and, without waiting to find out what the problem was, shouted down, "You're making a lot of noise over a lost dog—look on the Orleans Road: you'll find it there on a leash." According to the story, the servant subsequently found the dog where Nostradamus had predicted he would.

Nostradamus's reputation provoked challenges. On one occasion he was a guest at Fains Castle in Lorraine when his host, the Seigneur de Florinville, defied him to predict the fate of two pigs in the farmyard. Nostradamus told him the black pig would be eaten by the seigneur, while the white one would be eaten by a wolf. According to the story that circulated afterward, the seigneur issued secret instructions to his cook that the white pig should be slaughtered and served to his guests that night at dinner. When the pork was carried in, de Florinville remarked that no wolf was likely to get the white pig now since they were about to eat it, but Nostradamus insisted they were actually about to eat the black pig. His host then summoned the cook and invited him to prove Nostradamus wrong. But the embarrassed cook explained that while he had started to roast the white pig as instructed, a pet wolf cub belonging to one of the castle guards had stolen the meat off the spit. Not wanting to disappoint his lordship's guests, the cook then killed the black pig, which the guests were now about to eat.

Another story about Nostradamus came closer to genuine prophecy. While in Italy, he was on the road near Ancona when he met a group of Franciscans. To the astonishment of the monks he threw himself at the feet of one of them—a young friar named Felice Peretti—and addressed him as "Your Holiness," a term reserved for the pope. In 1585, less than twenty years after Nostradamus's death, Peretti became Pope Sextus V.

While it is possible, perhaps even likely, that these stories are apocryphal, there is no doubt at all about his influence. Both his book and the ongoing prognostications in his almanac—a total of more than six thousand predictions—spread his fame throughout France and led to requests for horoscopes and psychic consultations from members of the nobility and various influential people inside the country and beyond. After his death in 1566, his fame and influence actually increased. His prophecies remain in print to this day and have been translated into every major language of the world. During

World War II, Nostradamus's prophecies (some faked, all skewed in their interpretation) became part of the Allied propaganda effort to diminish Nazi morale. Following the 9/11 attack on New York's Twin Towers, Nostradamus predictions of the event—many highly suspect—flooded the Internet.

Despite an interest that has endured for centuries, very few people are aware of the source of Nostradamus's prophecies. When the question arises at all, most will readily accept the prophet's own claim that he had used only "judicial astrology"—a perfectly respectable art in his day—to produce them. But there is clear evidence that Nostradamus was lying when he made this claim. He was not even a particularly good astrologer: the surviving charts he drew up contain numerous errors.[2] The reason for his deception seems to have been fear of the Inquisition. Scholarly detective work has shown that the predictions were dictated to him by a spirit—and one that he evoked by means of magical ritual.

The first clue emerges in a document known as the Epistle to César, a public letter to his son, no more than a few weeks old at the time, which appeared as the preface to the first edition of his Centuries. Here Nostradamus wrote:

> And further, my son, I implore you not to attempt to employ your understanding in such reveries and vanities which wither the body and bring the soul to perdition, troubling the feeble sense: even the vanity of that most execrable magic, denounced already by the Sacred Scriptures and by the Divine Canons of the church—from which judgment is excepted judicial astrology, by means of which, and the divine inspiration and revelation, by continual calculations we have reduced our prophecies to writing. And, not withstanding that this occult philosophy was not reproved by the church I have not wished to divulge their wild persuasions, although many volumes which have been hidden for centuries have come before my eyes. But dreading what might happen in the future, having read them, I presented them to Vulcan, and as the fire began to devour them the flame, licking the air, shot forth an unaccustomed brightness, clearer than natural flame, like a flash from an explosive powder, casting a strange illumination over the house, as if it had been in sudden conflagration so that none might come to be abused by searching for the perfect transmutation, lunar our solar, or for incorruptible metals hidden under earth or sea, I reduced them to ashes.[3]

Although Nostradamus begins the epistle with the familiar claim that his prophecies were astrologically generated, in the second half of the quoted passage he admits to having owned "many volumes" of occult lore. The nature of these books is clear from his references to transmutation and incorruptible metals. They were works on alchemy and magic. He burned them, of course, but not before he read them. Even their destruction underlines their magical nature—they produced an unnatural flame. What were these books? Part of the answer may lie in the very first quatrain Nostradamus ever published outside of his almanac—Quatrain 1, Century 1—which reads:

> *Étant assis de nuit secret étude,*
> *Seul, reposé sur la selle d'airain,*
> *Flamme exigue sortant de solitude*
> *Fait prospérer qui n'est pas croire vain.*
> (Being sat secretly at night in his study,
> Alone, on the saddle of brass,
> A small flame emerges out of the void
> Causing a vain believe)[4]

This was followed by:

> *La verge en main mise au milieu de Branches*
> *De l'onde il mouille & le limbe & le pied:*
> *Un peur & voix frémissent par les manches:*
> *Splendeur divine. Le Divin pres s'assied.*
> (Grip the Branchus wand in the middle
> Wave it to wet the hem and the foot:
> A voice quivering with fear:
> Divine splendor. The Divine sits near.)[5]

It is worth noting that these verses echo, almost word for word, a passage in *De Mysteriis Egyptiorum* ("Concerning the Egyptian Mysteries"), which reads:

> *Foemina in Branchis fatidica, vel sedet in axe, vel manu tenet virgam, vel pedes aut limbum tingit in aquam et ex his modis impletur splendore divino, deumque nacta vaticinatur.*
> (The prophetess of Branchus sits wand in hand, places her foot and the hem of her robe in the water and in this way creates the divine splendor and calls the god by whom she prophecies.)[6]

De Mysteriis Egyptiorum was written by the Neoplatonic philosopher Iamblichus (or possibly a member of his school) somewhere around the third century CE. It deals with a type of "higher magic" operating through divine agencies. Much of the text is concerned with the ritual evocation of gods, demons, and other spirits.[7]

The similarity between the text and Nostradamus's opening quatrain is no coincidence. Further investigation of the prophecies shows that the conjuration of spirits was definitely one of his interests. The forty-second Quatrain of the first Century, for example, points to this as well as to familiarity with another magical tome:

> The ten Calends of April, according to Gothic measure,
> Are revived again by wicked people
> The fire goes out and the devilish assembly
> Looks for the bones of the Psellus demon.

The "Psellus" mentioned in the final line is Michael Psellus, the Byzantine philosopher, theologian, statesman, and Neoplatonist. His "demon" was a work he wrote in the eleventh century called *De Demonibus* ("About Demons"), which contained the following instructions for spirit conjurations:

The diviners take a basin full of water appropriate to the use of the demons. This basin full of water seems first to vibrate as if it would emit sounds nevertheless the water in the basin does not differ in appearance from natural water, but it has the property, by the virtue which is infused into it, of being able to compose verses which renders it eminently apt to receive the prophetic spirit. For this sort of demon is capricious, earthbound and subject to enchantments and so soon as the water begins to give out sounds, manifests its satisfaction to those who are present by some words still indistinct and meaningless, but, later, when the water seems to boil and spill over, a faint voice murmurs words which contained the revelation of future events.[8]

Here again, it is no coincidence that the final five words of the instructions link the conjuration to prophecy, as does Psellus's earlier reference to "prophetic spirit."

The two quatrains quoted earlier that begin the Nostradamus Centuries are not themselves prophecies. Instead, consensus scholarship has now concluded that they are descriptions of how his prophecies came about. The translation of Quatrain 1 is as follows:

> Seated by night in secret study
> Alone resting on the brazen tripod
> As slender flame licks out of the solitude
> Making possible what would have been in vain.

This was followed by Quatrain 2 :

> The rod in his hand is placed in the center of Branchus
> He moistens the hem of his robe, his limb and his foot
> A voice causes his arms to tremble with fear
> Divine splendor. The God sits close beside him.

What is being described here is a rite—and not any of the familiar Church rites to which Nostradamus so ostentatiously subscribed. Taken together, the verses summarize an extraordinary ceremony that involved a magical rod or wand, a brass tripod, a naked flame, and the appearance of a god in the midst of divine light: in other words, a ritual of evocation.

On the evidence of the quatrains alone, it would seem that the works of Psellus and Iamblichus were among the tomes "hidden from ancient time" that Nostradamus felt constrained to destroy. The "Branchus" referred to here—and in the Egyptian Mysteries of Iamblichus—is Branchus of Miletus (in what is now Turkey), a figure in Greek mythology who was fathered on a human woman by the sun god Apollo during a miraculous act of fellatio. The boy was walking in the woods one day when he met with his heavenly father and, struck by the god's beauty, kissed him. The result of this impulse was that Branchus was instantly endowed with the gift of prophecy.

Based on this myth, the Greeks established an oracular temple jointly dedicated to Branchus and Apollo at Didyma, south of Miletus. The sanctuary was in charge of the Branchids, a group of priests named after Branchus himself, and the prophecies generated there were reputed to have been a heady mix of inspiration and madness.

The Branchids seem to have betrayed their trust, for they were reputed to have collaborated with the Persian king Xerxes when he plundered and burned the temple in 494 BCE. Persians and priests both fled to Sogdiana, an ancient Asian country centered in the Zeravshan River valley, in what is now Uzbekistan. But the sacrilege caught up with their descendants when Alexander the Great conquered the country with considerable slaughter in 328 BCE. Another of Alexander's conquests, that of Miletus itself in 334 BCE, resulted in the oracle being resanctified. Due to the memory of their betrayal, no new Branchid priests were ordained. Instead, the oracle was administered by the municipal authorities who elected a prophet on an annual basis. Around 300 BCE, the Milesians began work on a new temple of Branchus planned to be the largest building in the Greek world but archaeological excavations in the early twentieth century showed it was never finished.

Iamblichus described the temple ceremony in these words:

> The prophetess of Branchus either sits upon a pillar or holds in her hand a rod bestowed by some deity, or moistens her feet or the hem of her garment with water, or inhales the vapor of water and by these means is filled with divine illumination and, having obtained the deity, she prophesies. By these practices, she adapts herself to the god, whom she receives from without.

Elsewhere in his works, he mentions that the priestess at Delphi sat upon a tripod in order to receive a "ray of divine illumination." Nostradamus mentions a tripod in his quatrains. He also wrote in his Epistle to César that the intellect could perceive nothing of the occult "without the aid of the mysterious voice of a spirit appearing in the vapor floating above the vessel of water and without the illumination of the magic flame in which future events are partly revealed as in a mirror."

It is clear from this textural evidence that Nostradamus was indeed interested in magic, an interest prudently well-hidden in the era of the Inquisition. By his own admission, he studied magical books, and while he suggested they were works on alchemy, the content of his own quatrains indicates that some were rituals of evocation linked to the art of prophecy. All of the evidence points to the Nostradamus prophecies being spirit driven.

This conclusion is reinforced by another of the stories attached to his legend. According to Hollywood-born author John Hogue,[9] the widowed Catherine de Medici summoned Nostradamus to the Château Chaumont in 1560 and demanded further insights into the future. On this particular visit, the prophet elected not to carry on his pretense about judicial astrology and instead requested the use of a large room in which he would not be disturbed.

There he traced a magic circle on the floor, fortifying it with holy names of power and angelic sigils. Before it he set up a magic mirror, a black concave surface of polished steel, the corners of which were traced in pigeon's blood with the names YHVH, Elohim, Mitratron, and Adonai. At the stroke of midnight the queen entered the dimly lit chamber, filled by this time with clouds of incense smoke. Nostradamus led her into the magic circle, then began an invocation to the angel Anael, a spirit believed to grant prophetic visions.

The vision granted on this occasion was of a room that somehow abutted the chamber in which they stood. Standing in it was Francis II, the queen's son. He walked once around it, then abruptly vanished. Nostradamus interpreted this as the boy's impending death. Another of the queen's children appeared, the boy who would become Charles IX. He circled the room fourteen times; Nostradamus predicted that he would rule for fourteen years. Then came the future Henri III, who walked around the room fifteen times, then François, Duke of Alençon, whose image was quickly transformed into that of Henry of Navarre, the man to whom Catherine was destined to marry her daughter Margot.

The interest of this story is not in the predictive accuracy of the vision— which may be the result of later embellishments—but in the fact that Nostradamus was thought to be so intimately involved with the highest in the land that he could safely conduct this necromantic experiment. The perception is largely correct. Nostradamus clearly did have friends in high places, friends who came to him for advice and were thus exposed to spirit influence one step removed. A similar situation existed in England, where an influential courtier also had the ear of his queen . . . and also communicated with spirits.

10. THE QUEEN'S CONJURER

My feet are swifter than the winds and my hands are sweeter than the morning dew . . . I am deflowered and yet a virgin: I sanctify and am not sanctified. Happy is he that embraceth me: for in the night season I am sweet, and
in the day full of pleasure. I am a harlot for such as ravish me, and a virgin
with such as know me not. Purge your streets, O ye sons of men, and wash
your houses clean: make your selves holy, and put on righteousness. Cast
out your old strumpets and burn their clothes and then I will come and dwell
amongst you: and behold, I will bring forth children unto you.[1]

THE WORDS ARE THOSE OF A SPIRIT, REVEALING ITS ESSENCE TO THE
Elizabethan magician, Dr. John Dee.
Dee was the son of a minor official at the court of Henry VIII.
He was born in Mortlake—now part of London, then a small village on the
Thames—in the summer of 1527, a time when the Renaissance had spread out
of Italy and opened up some of the best minds throughout Europe. He went to
school at Chelmsford, then on to Cambridge at the age of fifteen. Like Nostradamus, he proved to be a natural scholar. His diary records that he would
regularly spend up to eighteen hours a day in study. At the age of nineteen, he
was made assistant professor of Greek and became a Fellow of the newly
formed Trinity College. He also had a charge of sorcery leveled against him.
The charge followed his creation of a mechanical flying beetle for use
in a play. He was fascinated by toys and did his work too well. Superstitious
spectators insisted the beetle must have been powered by magic. Dee survived the accusations without much difficulty, but soon he really did take an
interest in magic. He went to Belgium's University of Louvain in 1547 and
there came across Cornelius Agrippa's *Occult Philosophy*, which influenced
him profoundly. He developed an interest in the Qabalah, which had accrued

Christian elements throughout the Renaissance. He also became friendly with Gerardus Mercator, the famous cartographer, and eventually brought back two of Mercator's globes and several newly invented astronomical instruments to England. Before that, Dee visited Paris, where his lectures on Euclid proved so popular that he was offered a professorship. He decided to turn it down in favor of a return to England, then ruled by Henry VIII's successor, the ten-year-old Edward VI. His reputation stood so high that the king's advisers recommended a pension. Dee accepted, but promptly sold the right to the income in return for two rectorships.

Despite his fame and academic credentials, money was a problem for Dee. Influenced by the occult visionary Jerome Cardan, he began to study alchemy in the hope of changing base metals into gold. But alchemical apparatus was expensive, and his economic situation worsened after his patron, the Earl of Northumberland, was beheaded. Things brightened slightly when Queen Mary came to the throne. His talent for astrology attracted royal attention and he was required to cast horoscopes for the queen and her prospective husband, Philip of Spain. Perhaps his astrological calculations foretold the brevity of her reign for he made little attempt to curry the queen's favor. Instead he made contact with Mary's younger sister, Elizabeth, then a virtual prisoner at Woodstock. He cast her horoscope (which is preserved today in the British Museum) but slipped up badly when he showed her the queen's birth map as well. This indiscretion was taken as evidence of a plot. Dee was accused of attempting to poison the queen or to cause her death by black magic. A trial for treason followed. Although finally acquitted, the force of the accusations kept him in prison until the latter part of 1555.

Three years later, Mary was dead and Elizabeth had succeeded to the throne. Dee's original horoscope must have impressed her greatly, for she required him to calculate an auspicious date for her coronation. From that point on, he was firmly, if discreetly, established at court. He often traveled to Europe on mysterious missions for Sir Francis Walsingham, who headed Elizabeth's intelligence service, and was assigned the code name "007" several centuries before James Bond. For six years, Dee engaged in these Continental wanderings, perhaps spying, perhaps simply searching for esoteric knowledge. In 1564, however, he returned to England and seems to have settled down for a full decade, living in his mother's home at Mortlake and engaging in his occult pursuits. Among them was the use of a "magic mirror," an autohypnotic device designed to produce visions similar to those seen in

Dr. John Dee, conjurer, Court astrologer, and close advisor to Queen Elizabeth I, was himself guided by the spirits he evoked.

a crystal ball. In 1574, Dee married for the first time. His emotional involvement with the woman appears to have been slight, for he did not even bother to name her in his diaries. She died only a year later. On the day of her death, the queen visited Dee's Mortlake home and demanded to see his "magic glass." Dee complied, but the courtiers, lacking the clairvoyant faculties necessary to make the device work, found it more amusing than impressive.

Two years later, when Dee was forty-nine, he married for the second time. His choice fell on Jane Fromond, an attractive girl considerably younger than himself, who was lady-in-waiting to Lady Howard of Effingham. The marriage was both happy and fruitful—it resulted in eight children. Dee continued to study esoteric matters: his diaries are full of dream records, spirit rappings, and other mysterious phenomena. In May 1581, there came a turning point in his career. Dee stared into a crystal and saw a vision. It is important to realize that Dee was not a born clairvoyant. Indeed he frequently claimed he had no psychic abilities whatsoever. As such, he was much more impressed by an isolated visionary experience than any natural psychic would be. Dee plunged into crystal gazing with enormous enthusiasm but saw no further visions and was eventually forced to employ mediums to work the crystal for him.

But for all of his learning and experience, John Dee was a poor judge of character. His first choice of psychic was a man called Barnabas Saul, so notorious a rogue that some modern historians speculate he had been sent by Dee's enemies to discredit him. In any event, Saul did not last long. He got into trouble with the law, renounced occult experimentation, and vanished from the scene.

Dr. Dee learned very little from the experience. Two days after Saul disappeared, an Irishman walked into his life, introduced himself as Edward Talbot, and offered to extend Dee's magical knowledge with the aid of fairies. Dee was dismayed by the thought of communicating with such pagan entities. Fortunately Talbot proved versatile, and when Dee confessed that what he needed was "help in my philosophical studies through the company and information of the blessed angels of God,"[2] Talbot assured him he was just the man for the job. Dee led him to his study for a trial. Despite the odd nature of his researches, Dee was essentially a religious man. While Talbot had undoubted charm, part of his appeal may have been that he represented a soul to be saved. Dee lectured him on the evils of black magic and explained that he prayed for guidance before each of his experiments. Talbot agreed to do the same and, after a period of enthusiastic prayer, claimed he saw the face of a cherub in the crystal. Dee was suitably impressed and identified the entity as the Qabalistic angel Uriel.

It was the beginning of a lasting, intimate relationship that survived the revelation that Talbot was not Talbot at all, but one Edward Kelley, born in Worcester and a former student at Oxford before some undisclosed problem caused him to leave abruptly. When he met Dee, he was just twenty-seven years old.[3] The relationship also survived an accusation of deception made by Dee's wife, the discovery that Kelley was a fugitive from justice who had been pilloried in Lancaster for forgery,[4] and the noticeable fact that he had had his ears cropped—a punishment reserved for coining (the shaving of precious metal from the edges of gold or silver coins). There were also suspicious connections with Catholicism and the possibility he might even have been a recusant priest.[5]

A veritable orgy of spirit communication began, with Kelley as its medium. Following the initial success with the crystal, Dee and Kelley's first full-scale experiment took place on November 21, 1582. The result was an appearance of a spirit named King Camara who told Kelley they needed a particular type of "most excellent" sanctified stone to ensure their success. The

*A spirit evocation in process. The conjurers within the magic circle
are Dr. John Dee and (possibly) his medium Edward Kelley.*

spirit promised they would have it forthwith. Kelley looked toward the study
window and reported the presence of a smallish angel who was offering Dee a
bright, clear, glistening jewel about the size of an egg. Camara commanded Dee
to go and take it. Dee, who could see nothing of the stone, the angel, or Camara,
obediently walked toward the window. When he was about two feet from where
the stone was supposed to be, he noticed a shadow on the ground. He reached
down and found a crystal. "Keep it sincerely," the spirit Camara instructed. "Let
no mortal hand touch it but thine own. Praise God."[6]

This apport, as it would be called in Spiritualist circles, was the closest Dee ever came to the physical materialization of something from the spirit world, and it is all too easy to imagine that the rascally Kelley may have left it on the floor for him to find. Later séances concentrated largely on philosophical discussions with the spirits, and these would have been even easier for Kelley to fake. When we learn that the angels eventually instructed the pair that they should "hold their wives in common" it is difficult to repress the conclusion that Dee, for all his learning, lacked the common sense to protect himself against the machinations of an obvious scoundrel. However, there are problems with any suggestion that Kelley simply made up his conversations with the angels.

From notes in his spiritual diaries,[7] it is clear that Dee relied heavily on Agrippa's work in constructing the rituals he hoped would persuade the blessed angels of God to visit his study.[8] Dee also owned a manuscript copy of the thirteenth-century *Sworn Book of Honorius*,[9] which contains the *Sigillum Dei Aemeth*, a complex symbol used in evocation. But as his work with Kelley progressed, Kelley's visionary angels gave instructions for the creation of equipment and formulas that were even more complex. Nowhere is this more apparent than in the series of séances throughout June 1583 during which an angel called Ave dictated a collection of Calls or evocations to the "Watchtowers of the Universe."

On angelic instructions, the two magicians created more than a hundred large tablets, each measuring about forty-nine by forty-nine inches, filled with a grid pattern of letters. When contact was made, Kelley typically reported sight of the angel in a crystal, along with the angel's own copies of the tablets. Using a wand, the angel would then point to certain letters on the tablets. Kelley would call out their position. Dee would then locate the letter in the same position in his tablet and write it down, gradually building up a written evocation. As a further complication, the Calls had to be dictated backward so their power would not be accidentally unleashed.[10] The result of such a system should have been gibberish, but it was not. As the Victorian students of the Golden Dawn later discovered, the Calls represented "a true language . . . [with] . . . syntax and grammar of its own and the invocations . . . are not mere strings of words, but sentences which can be translated, not simply transliterated into English."[11] It is (just) possible Kelley invented it, for artificial languages have certainly been created: Esperanto is a modern example. But it would have required a massive investment of time and effort, and since he was by then Dee's constant companion, it is difficult to imagine how he could have managed the work without arousing Dee's suspicions. Furthermore, having invented an entire language, Kelley would then have had to memorize the Calls—there are forty-eight of them—so perfectly that he was able to dictate them backward, letter by letter. If nothing else, the Calls suggest there was something going on at Dee's séances other than tricks played on a gullible old man.

But if Kelley seems to have shown some genuine mediumship, relations between the two were far from placid. Despite his marriage to a local girl, Kelley found it difficult to settle down and was forever sneaking off to London taverns and brothels. The spirits frequently denounced him to his employer, but Dee put up with it—and with Kelley's bad temper—because he badly needed a psychic.

The year Kelley joined him, Dee had another of his own isolated visions. He saw an angel floating outside his window holding an egg-shaped crystal. The archangel Michael appeared and commanded the doctor to take this gift and use it. Although the crystal is today displayed in the British Museum, most historians dismiss the story of its origin. But whether or not we feel the communications were genuine, Dee certainly believed in them.

It was a time of miracles and much soul-searching. Historians who consider Kelley a charlatan ignore the many indications of his mediumistic makeup. As such, he was prey to doubts. In Kraków, he had already told Dee bluntly that their "teachers" were deluders who had wasted their time for years. Later, Dee was to record, "There happened a great storm or temptation of E.K. of doubting and misliking our Instructors and their doings and of contemning and condemning any thing that I knew or could do. I bare all things patiently for God his sake."

But Kelley's problem was whether the spirits were good or evil, not whether they actually existed. He had little enough doubt on this point at the best of times, and less still when one of the spirits revealed a map of the world that he later found to agree with the mystical geography outlined by Cornelius Agrippa. The event shook him so much, he decided to ask the evil spirits of his black magical days to help him escape but then had a change of heart and confessed the whole thing to Dee instead. Nevertheless, he continued to question the validity of the messages they were receiving. Dee had no such doubts, largely, it appears, because the language of the spirits was pious enough for a sermon. But the content often concerned temporal matters. The spirits wished the map of Europe altered. They required some states changed, others destroyed altogether. There can be little doubt that Dee used every ounce of his influence to have these requests made political reality.

While Dee was concerned with changing the world, Kelley had his own problems. The archangel Gabriel appeared in the crystal to order him to burn his magical books. Kelley grudgingly compromised by burying them a week later. The spirits seemed to take this as a moral victory, for they pressured Dee into burning *his* books on April 10, 1586 (or, rather, having Kelley burn them for him). While the pair were with Count Rosenberg on April 30, however, all the volumes were miraculously restored intact. Those of a suspicious disposition might see the hand of Kelley in this miracle.

Despite lip service to the spiritual principles of his employer and apparently genuine, if brief, periods of conversion, Kelley generally labored under the weight of an old obsession: how to persuade the spirits to bring him treasure, or at the very least show him how to manufacture gold. Occasionally, desperation would drive Dee in the same direction, but all that he got were promises. When he pressed the matter too far, presumably by pointing out that he could not wait forever, Gabriel snapped back: "To talke with God for money is a folly; to talke with God for mercy is great wisdom. Silver and gold I give not, but my blessing is above the substance of the earth." Kelley became so upset by this that he refused to scry and Dee's young son Arthur was pressed into service as a medium. He saw lions, men with crowns, and various other visions but heard no voices. There was nothing else for it. Kelley had to start again.

Kelley stared into the crystal, saw the spirit-child Madimi, and received the revelation that he and Dr. Dee should henceforth "share all things in common," including their wives. It took Kelley some time and many protestations before he could bring himself to pass the message on. When he did, Jane Dee, who had viewed him with loathing from the day they met, was understandably upset. For a quarter of an hour she lay on the floor, trembling and weeping, after which she "burst forth into a fury of anger." John Dee did not take much to the suggestion either and went so far as rebuking the spirit for delivering unfitting advice. But he seems to have gotten used to the idea, for on May 3, 1587, the four people concerned signed a document binding themselves to angelic commandments. Even so, the women were not entirely happy and demanded a further scrying session to clarify the question of who should sleep with whom. Kelley piously refused. The original communication had to stand.

Regrettably, there is no record of how the experiment in partner-swapping went, but the Kelleys parted from the Dees soon after. Whether this was due to the strain of the situation or simply to Kelley's refusal to scry, is a matter of conjecture. On parting with his learned employer, Kelley drifted back into alchemy, and even took up scrying again, apparently with some success, for his reputation grew. But he was unable to control his worst instincts, and he eventually fell foul of the law and died in prison.

Dee returned to England, where he was received by the queen. But despite this initial indication of royal favor, he was actually embarking on a downward slide toward the end of his career. Vandals had broken into his Mortlake home and ransacked it, destroying many of his books and astronomical instruments. He petitioned the queen for employment but received nothing until 1595, when he was granted the wardenship of Christ College, Manchester. Judging by his records, it was not a post he particularly enjoyed. The city must have lost whatever little appeal it had for him when his wife died there of the plague.

He remained true to his occult interests, however, writing voluminously and keeping a record of his dreams. He even employed another scryer, Bartholomew Hickman. But this individual seems only to have told him what he wanted to hear, passing on messages from the archangel Raphael that he was on the point of discovering great secrets. Despite the promise, he never did. He died quietly at Mortlake in the fifth year of the reign of James I, a sovereign who had little time for magicians or their spirits.

In his public persona, Dr. John Dee strove hard to appear as a mathematician, scholar, and astrologer. Rather more discreetly, he was, as one academic study concluded, "one of a line of philosopher-magicians that stemmed from Ficino and Pico della Mirandola."[12] But while the Renaissance magic of Dr. Dee was both sophisticated and erudite, there was never a complete break with medieval practice.[13] Thus another of his biographers named him simply as the "Queen's conjurer"[14] and with some justification: when an image of the queen was found impaled by a pin in Lincoln's Inn fields, the Privy Council called on Dee to use his magic to counteract the spell. Dee himself would not have taken kindly to the title. In 1577, he became so impatient with rumors about his activities that he published an advertisement roundly denying "divers untrue and infamous reports" that he was a "conjurer or caller of divels . . . yea, the *great conjurer*; and so (as some would say) the *arch conjurer* of this whole kingdom."[15] If a conjurer is solely defined as a "caller of divels," then Dee was justified in his denials, but by any broader definition the advertisement was disingenuous. There is no doubt that Dr. Dee was engaged in practical magic, nor is there any doubt that part of his practice was the evocation of spirits.

For Dee, "the existence of spirits was as clear as the existence of God."[16] And while it might be possible to imagine an Elizabethan atheist, the description could never fit Dee. He was an intensely religious man. When, for example, he learned he had made an enemy of the papal nuncio in Prague, his reaction was, "Almighty God, the Creator of heaven and earth, who is our Lord, our preceptor and guide, this God himself will be our protector and liberator."[17] He was closely associated with those members of the court who concerned themselves with the cause of religious reform and, in a Europe riven by the schism between Protestants and Catholics, he stood out as a beacon of ecumenism.[18] He considered that a divided Christianity was a disaster for the world and worked hard to heal the rift.

His religious concerns invaded his esoteric pursuits. (It was angelic comments on corruption in the Catholic Church that earned him the displeasure of the papal nuncio.) Indeed, it might be argued that his esoteric pursuits were largely driven by religious and political interests. Where the typical sorcerer of the Middle Ages sought spirit help in finding gold or sex, there is little indication of such mundane concerns in Dee's records. His early dialogue with the spirit child Madimi sounds in places like a discussion between two theology students. Beyond that, spirit contact was "a way of beholding the universe in all its glory and understanding its manifold and mysterious workings."[19]

The influence of his spirit contacts on his political interests was just as obvious. Messages from the Beyond may even have helped create a turning point in history. When the Spanish Armada sailed against England in 1588, it appeared utterly invincible. Spain claimed to be the strongest nation in Europe, with a considerable degree of justification. Her quarrel with England over English sea power had led to a showdown that might well have put paid to Elizabeth's pretensions of international power. But the English sea defenses proved impregnable. Drake's ships, aided by a little luck, smashed the Armada completely. And the man responsible for England's sea defenses at the time, by appointment of the queen, was Dr. Dee, who turned to spirits when he needed advice.

Dee's political influence was destined to spread beyond his native

England. In 1583, the king of Poland's representative, Count Laski, was impressed by stories of Dee's conjurations and suggested they should all visit Prague to meet the emperor Rudolf II, himself an enthusiastic occultist. Dee took up the suggestion and in 1885, he and Kelley, their respective wives, and Dee's three children embarked with Laski for the Continent. Their wanderings were to last four years.

The king of Poland, Stephen Bathory, received them well at Kraków, where he listened with interest to warnings passed on from the spirit world. The restless Kelley may have slipped back into some of his old habits at this time, for his talk of having found a magical gold-producing powder at Glastonbury sounds suspiciously like a con man preparing potential victims for a sting. The party moved on to Prague, where Laski introduced the occultists to Emperor Rudolf. Once again, warnings from the spirit world were passed on, and Rudolf may well have acted on them. But Dee was becoming altogether too well known for his own good. The pope decided he was engaged in necromancy (magical operations involving the use of corpses or communication with the dead), and his nuncio in Prague passed on the accusation to the emperor on May 6, 1586. A few days later, the magicians were ordered to leave. Luck remained with them. The tsar of Russia made Dee the offer of a house in Moscow, a salary of 12,600 rubles a year—a small fortune in those days—and assured him he would be "honorably accounted as one of the chief men in the land." Simultaneously, Count Wilhelm Rosenberg extended an invitation to his palace in Trebon. Surprisingly, and probably to Kelley's chagrin, Dee accepted the latter offer. The party spent a peaceful eighteen months as Rosenberg's guests in Bohemia.

From the foregoing, it becomes clear that, acting through Dee and Nostradamus, the spirits influenced both the crowned heads of Europe and the queen of England. They were not the only channel for such influence, for Keith Thomas assures us Dee's experiments were in no way unique. "There is enough objective evidence relating to the manufacture of conjuring apparatus and the holding of conjuring sessions to show that spirit-raising was a standard magical activity. Spiritual beings were thought to offer a short cut to riches, love, knowledge and power of all kinds; and the Faustian legend had a literal meaning for its Elizabethan and Jacobean audiences."[20]

11. ENLIGHTENMENT SPIRITS

ATTEMPTS TO EVOKE SPIRITS CONTINUED LONG AFTER THE ELIZABETHAN era. Manuscript copies of the *Lemegeton* ("The Lesser Key of Solomon") circulated throughout the seventeenth century,[1] while Dr. Thomas Rudd's *Goetia* is dated to the eighteenth.[2] Solomonic traditions not only survived into the nineteenth century, but actually gained currency with the formation of the Hermetic Students of the Golden Dawn, a magical organization that attracted some notable and influential members. Similar Solomonic evocations, usually with some modification of the original techniques, continue to the present day, particularly in America.[3] But while Elias Ashmole could still record a visit to a conjurer in his diary in 1652[4]—the man, Jo. Tompson, summoned spirits and had responses "in a soft voice"— there was already change afoot.

The great religious upheaval of the Reformation, which began a decade before John Dee was born, introduced a new perception of the spirit world. Until then, the doctrine of purgatory had provided the theological basis for the return to earth of spirits of the dead. But the reformers denied the existence of purgatory and since heaven and hell were both permanent states, there was nowhere from which a spirit might come back. The (Protestant) powers-that-be took care to warn that apparitions should not be taken at face value. Thus the phantom spotted by Sir Thomas Wise during the reign of James I caused controversy between the local archdeacon, who thought it might have been an angel, and the theologian Daniel Featley, who pronounced it an evil spirit.[5]

But ghostly sightings like this were, of course, the very essence of the problem. Whatever doctrines the theologians propounded about spirits, people still kept seeing them. And given the intellectual currents of the time, it comes as no surprise to discover that among those who made the most influential sightings was a member of a newfangled breed—a scientist.

Emanuel Swedenborg was born in Stockholm, Sweden, on January 29, 1688. His father was a Lutheran priest who later rose to the rank of bishop. His mother, the daughter of a wealthy mine owner, owned a part interest in several iron mines and in so doing almost certainly helped shape her son's early career. Emanuel, the third of nine children, proved a highly intelligent youngster. Following home schooling that included study of Latin and probably Hebrew, he entered the University of Uppsala at the early age of eleven and elected to study with the philosophy faculty, which was, at the time, an umbrella discipline for the natural sciences. A year after his graduation in 1710, he sailed for London, England, a city that was, at the time, the frontier of work on the natural sciences. There he studied mathematics, Newton's newly developed calculus, and applied mechanics while developing close relationships with some of the world's leading scholars, including the astronomers John Flamsteed and Edmund Halley.

Toward the end of 1712, Swedenborg left England for Europe in search of further scientific knowledge. In Leiden, he met with Anton van Leeuwenhoek, who had just begun his pioneering work with the microscope. In Paris he discussed technical matters with leading lights in mathematics and astronomy. Wending his way home in late 1714, he sent to his brother-in-law a list of inventions that had occurred to him during his travels. These included such prescient scientific developments as a "flying carriage," a submarine, a siphon, sluices, pumps, and, almost a century and a half before the birth of Freud, "a method of conjuring the wills and affections of men's minds by means of analysis."[6]

Swedenborg eventually returned to Sweden in 1715 with such a well-established reputation that the following year King Charles XII made him Extraordinary Assessor to the Royal College of Mines. It proved a less impressive appointment than it appeared. The king died in 1718 and, due to the political instability that followed, Swedenborg did not actually take up his office until 1724. He followed his own scientific endeavors, however, and busied himself with inventing a method of transporting ships safely overland.

In 1733, he took leave of absence from the board of the Royal College of Mines in order to publish his first scientific work, the three-volume *Opera Mineralia*. In the first book he developed a nebular hypothesis to account for the formation of planets (which anticipated the work of Kant and Laplace) and an atomic theory of matter. The second and third volumes were scientific studies of iron, steel, copper, and brass. At this stage of his career, a less likely candidate for spirit contact could scarcely be imagined. Yet it happened.

Swedenborg, the Swedish scientist turned mystic whose communications with spirits enabled him to 'see' events hundreds of miles distant

It began with his dreams. Swedenborg started a travel dairy in 1743. The first ten entries were devoted to his waking experiences, but thereafter he took to noting down the contents of his dreams. Almost from the beginning, he took to interpreting them as well. In one vivid example, he found himself lying beside a woman whom he took to be his guardian angel. She told him he smelled bad, which he later interpreted as a comment on the state of his spiritual health. The dream marked the beginning of a period of great transcendent temptations, alternating eventually with more positive, near-mystical experiences. On the day after Easter, for example, he was abruptly cast prostrate on the floor to the sound of a peal of thunder. He began to pray and quickly sensed the presence of Jesus Christ, who asked him if he had a clean bill of health. When Swedenborg responded that Jesus should know best about this, Jesus suggested he should get one.

Come October, Swedenborg was seized by a sense of deep peace. Christ came again to him in a dream with the admonition that he should undertake nothing without divine guidance. By late 1744, the dream journal came to a close, but not, it transpired, his contact with spirits. He began to publish a series of books on religious themes, notably the story of creation, in which he expounded what he believed to be the deeper meaning of the book of Genesis. (He even returned to his Hebrew studies so he could read his sources in the original.) He rejected the doctrine of the Trinity, holding with most mystics that God's prime characteristic was unity, and called for a new Christianity that would expand on the original rather than replace it. He introduced one seminal volume with the words:

> The arcana which are revealed in the following pages are those concerning heaven and hell, together with the life of man after death . . . it has been granted me to associate with angels and to converse with them as one man with another, and also to see the things which are in the heavens as well as those which are in the hells and this for the space of thirteen years, and so to describe these things from what I have myself seen and heard.[7]

The works, which collectively amounted to a new theology, were issued anonymously, but in 1759 something happened that was to bring the question of authorship into the open.

In July of that year, Swedenborg had returned from a trip to London and was staying in Göteborg on Sweden's west coast. On the evening of the nineteenth, he went to dine with friends at the home of William Castel, a wealthy local merchant. Early on in the evening, he became disturbed and eventually withdrew from the company to take some fresh air in the garden. He returned with the news that a great fire had broken out in Stockholm not far from his home. The announcement may have been met with some skepticism—Stockholm is approximately three hundred miles away from Göteborg—but Swedenborg continued to report the progress of the fire to his fellow guests until, around eight p.m., he exclaimed with relief that the fire had been extinguished just three doors from his house.

Several other guests had homes in Stockholm, so that news of Swedenborg's curious pronouncement quickly spread. When it reached the provincial governor, he summoned Swedenborg to his residence the following day for a detailed firsthand account of what had happened. It was not until July 21 that a messenger arrived from Stockholm with a letter reporting the disaster. The details coincided in every respect with the account Swedenborg had given two days earlier. The story circulated rapidly and Swedenborg gained a reputation for having extraordinary powers. Soon people began to suspect he must be the author of the equally extraordinary books that had been appearing over the past several years.

The critical factor, for our present thesis, was not the expanded biblical theology propounded by Swedenborg, but his open admission—in his very first theological volume—that his doctrines were not intellectual constructs but a direct spirit revelation emanating from the very highest sources. In his analysis of Swedenborg's career, John Selwyn Gummer stresses that Swedenborg was not prone to trances, nor did he conduct any form of séance, but rather he engaged in regular direct communication with beings from heaven, experiencing them as physically present. According to Gummer, his religious writings, which included a guided tour of both heaven and hell, were literal reports of his experiences. Swedenborg himself had this to say:

> I am well aware that many persons will insist that it is impossible for anyone to converse with spirits and with angels during his lifetime in the body; many will say that such intercourse must be mere fancy; some that I have invented such relations in order to gain credit; whilst others will make other objections. For all these, however, I care not, since I have heard, seen and felt.[8]

Although fiercely attacked in his own day, by the philosopher Kant among others, Swedenborg's literary legacy was enough to guarantee him a following in later years. The first sign of things to come appeared ten years after his death in 1772 when a Church of England cleric named John Clowes established, in Manchester, a Society for Printing, Publishing and Circulating the Writings of the Hon. Emanuel Swedenborg. Clowes translated many of Swedenborg's works into English and preached Swedenborgian doctrines from the pulpit. Swedenborg's own writings predicted the formation of a "New Church," Christian in essence, but expanding on the Gospel message to include the insights Swedenborg had gained through his heavenly visions. In May 1787 a New Church movement was founded in England. Two years later, there were several physical churches opened across the country while the first General Conference of the New Church was held in London. Before long, missionaries were carrying the Swedenborg revelation to an international audience. One who brought them to the shores of America was the famous "Johnny Appleseed" (John Chapman).

Although membership of the New Church remains comparatively small in the twenty-first century, the large corpus of Swedenborg's visionary work is still in print, with fresh translations issued every few years. Consequently, his ideas continue to shine as an unlikely beacon from Enlightenment times, attracting the attention of theologians and to some extent esotericists, once again engendered by spirit contact and revelation.

Not all spirits carried the same weight as those that appeared to Emanuel Swedenborg, but spirit activity nonetheless remained lively throughout the period. The Faustian legend, accepted as a statement of literal truth, survived more or less intact until the Enlightenment, after which it reemerged in a different form. Interest in the art of ceremonial conjuration gradually waned, but the desire to contact spirits did not. Despite the intellectual rationalism characteristic of the Enlightenment, it would be a mistake to assume the period had much in common with our own. New habits of scientific observation were subject to psychological factors, so that microscopic examination of donkey semen revealed tiny donkeys and mermaids could still be spotted sunbathing on their rocks.[9] The scientific method, as we know it today, was still in its infancy and the scientific mind remained open to all sorts of fantastic possibilities. A herald of one such possibility was a physician named Franz Anton Mesmer.

Mesmer was born in Iznang, near Lake Constance in Swabia, in 1734. He was educated in two Jesuit universities—Dillingen and Ingolstadt—before attending medical school at the University of Vienna. His medical dissertation in 1766 postulated that the gravitational pull of the planets influenced human health by way of an invisible fluid permeating nature and the human body, an idea he almost certainly picked up from a prominent English physician named Richard Mead. But nine years later, Mesmer modified this theory: now it was no longer gravitation that influenced the fluid, but magnetism. He experimented with this idea—one patient was required to swallow a preparation containing iron, then endure magnets attached to her body—but while it appeared to work, Mesmer again modified his basic theory. Now he replaced ferrous magnetism with a speculative "animal magnetism" in which direct manipulation of the fluid produced therapeutic results. This idea too seemed to be borne out in practice, and soon Mesmer abandoned the use of magnets altogether. Instead he manipulated the fluid in his patients' bodies by making "magnetic passes" over them with his empty hands. As a therapy, the approach was astonishingly successful. Mesmer's reputation grew and his fame spread. In 1775, he was approached by a representative of the Munich Academy of Sciences to give an opinion on the work of a self-effacing Austrian priest named Johann Joseph Gassner, who was one of the most successful healers of his day.

Fr. Gassner was ordained in 1750 and began his ministry in the tiny village of Klösterle (in eastern Switzerland) in 1758. A few years later he noticed he had become prey to headaches and dizziness while celebrating Mass and hearing confession. The specific timing of his symptoms led him to suspect a Satanic attack. Fortunately the Church had techniques to combat such an eventuality. Fr. Gassner performed a ritual of exorcism, said the relevant prayers, and his troubles disappeared. Impressed by the result, he took to exorcising the sick of his parish, again with dramatic success. Soon he found patients traveling to see him from neighboring districts. Among them was the Countess Maria Bernadine von Wolfegg. When he successfully exorcised her as well, his fame began to spread like wildfire.[10]

Gassner distinguished between two kinds of illness—natural and preternatural. Natural illnesses he referred to a physician. Preternatural he divided into three categories: *circumsessio*, the symptoms of which masqueraded as natural illness but were, in fact, caused by the Devil; *obsessio*, illness caused by sorcery; and *possessio*, which was the result of possession by evil spirits. In all cases, he first subjected willing patients to a trial exorcism during which he asked the demon to manifest the disease symptoms. If nothing happened, he concluded the disease was of natural origin and sent the patient to a doctor. If symptoms appeared, he continued with the exorcism and drove out the spirits that were causing the problem.[11]

Although his methods were hugely successful in effecting cures, Gassner's basic theories were at variance with the new rationalism of the Enlightenment. Even at the height of his fame he was the focus of fierce controversy, and in 1775 Prince-Elector Karl Theodor appointed a commission of inquiry to investigate his cures. Mesmer was one of its members.

It is difficult today to think of Mesmer as a champion of the Enlightenment, but the fact was that he represented new ideas and methods that, within the milieu of the time, seemed strictly scientific. They certainly made no appeal to Satan and his minions for their justification. Mesmer examined the Gassner approach, then demonstrated that everything Gassner could do he (Mesmer) could do better. He concluded that while Gassner was an honest man, he was nonetheless mistaken in his conclusions. His cures were actually effected by animal magnetism, unconsciously applied. Exorcism had nothing to do with them.[12] Thus, in the turning point of 1775, Mesmer banished spirits from medical theory. But the spirits refused to stay banished and it was only a few years before they began to haunt mesmerism itself.

Despite (or possibly because of) the fact that Mesmer achieved some spectacular cures, Viennese physicians accused him of fraud, leading him to move to Paris in 1778. Interest in his theory of animal magnetism spread rapidly. Within a few years a correspondent of the Royal Society of Medicine wrote that "even the coolest heads in town talked of nothing but mesmerism," while a survey by the Society concluded that few sizeable towns in France lacked mesmeric treatment centers.[13] As the practice of mesmerism, professional and amateur, continued to spread, so did its associated phenomena.[14] Spirit contact arose when two brothers discovered a new form of somnambulistic mesmerism (now generally believed to be hypnosis) and found that one of their subjects could communicate with the dead.[15]

This proved to be no isolated event. In a letter to the *Société Harmonique* in Strasbourg, the Swedenborgian Exegetical and Philanthropic Society of Stockholm explained that "angels" had possessed somnambulists in Sweden, thus providing "the first immediate correspondence with the invisible world."[16] In Lyons, mesmerism was absorbed into two essentially spiritist cults, *La Concorde* and the secret *Loge Elue et Chérie*. In both organizations, mesmerized subjects channeled messages from God.

Table turning, a technique later associated with Spiritualism, in which invisible forces cause a small table to move, was at first attributed to the influence of the magnetic fluid. But while some mesmerists saw this only as the mechanistic manipulation of animal magnetism, others assumed spirit intervention: "Ask the table, that is, the spirit that is inside it; it will tell you that I have above my head an enormous pipe of fluid which rises from my hair up to the stars . . . by which the voice of spirits on Saturn reaches my ear."[17]

Clearly, the mesmeric manifestation of spirits was not an isolated phenomenon. In his *History of Hypnotism*, Alan Gault puts it bluntly: "A major treatise would hardly suffice to exhaust somnambules' descriptions of their contacts with the spirits of diseased persons, or with angelic or spiritual beings, and of their visions of, or visits to, heaven or Hades or limbo . . . Not infrequently the two kinds of voyage—astronomical and eschatological— are combined and the moon and the planets are represented as being the probationary homes of departed spirits. Often the voyages are conducted under the guidance of the somnambule's own particular guardian spirit, who also fulfils the more mundane role of medical and moral adviser."[18]

As a professor of psychology, Dr. Gauld is naturally wary of the claims of mesmerism in this respect. The subhead of the section of his book that deals with paranormal phenomena is prefaced by the word *ostensibly*,[19] and he takes care to point out that where his "magnetic somnambules" reported voyages to the moon or planets, "the accounts are frequently picturesque [but] the amateur astronomer will search them in vain for anticipations of modern discoveries."[20] He is, however, kinder to one of the better known examples of spirit contact: Frau Friedericke Hauffe, the "Seeress of Prevorst."

As a child, Frau Hauffe was prey to visions and prophetic dreams. She became increasingly introverted following an arranged marriage and began to exhibit symptoms of various illnesses from about the age of twenty-one.[21] As her symptoms worsened, her physician prescribed "magnetic passes and medicines" and soon Frau Hauffe decided she was being magnetized by the spirit of her dead grandmother. Poltergeist phenomena broke out around her, untypical in that objects floated slowly through the air rather than being thrown.[22] Later "she began to see another person behind the one she was looking at. Thus behind her youngest sister she saw her deceased brother, Henry; and behind a female friend, she saw the ghostly form of an old woman, whom she had known in her childhood at Lowenstein."[23]

Since only magnetic passes could alleviate the symptoms of her various illnesses, the seeress spent more and more of her time in the magnetized condition. This produced in her four distinct states: (1) what appeared to be a normal waking consciousness, but with heightened psychic sensitivity; (2) a magnetic state that produced vivid and sometimes prophetic dreams; (3) a transitional state between sleep and waking (now usually termed "hypnogogic") during which she would write and speak a mysterious "inner language"; and (4) a similar state to number 3, but with added clairvoyance, which allowed her to diagnose and prescribe for herself and others. In all of these states, she was liable to see apparitions.[24] Gauld points out the similarities with other clairvoyant somnambules of the time and adds the telling detail that she had a guardian spirit in the person of her dead grandmother.[25] In this she greatly resembled a new breed of clairvoyant waiting in the wings of history: the Spiritualist medium.

The confusion of the old ("superstitious") and the new ("scientific") in the practice of mesmerism did little for its reputation. In 1784 Louis XVI appointed a commission to examine Mesmer's methods. Their report was damning. They found Mesmer unable to substantiate his scientific claims and concluded the phenomena of mesmerism had nothing to do with any invisible fluid but could be explained by the action of imagination alone.

Mesmerism subsequently declined in France, but the British, ever suspicious of Continental conclusions, remained happy to import the practice in the early nineteenth century. Here, too, mesmeric abilities included communication with spirits. The O'Key sisters, who exhibited precognitive talents while mesmerized, insisted they did not have direct knowledge of the future, but had it described to them by a spirit who had first appeared when one of them fell ill.[26] A mesmeric experiment in Trinity College, Dublin, produced an observation from one mesmerized subject to the effect that great changes were taking place in the spirit world, including in the relations between men and angels.[27] Five years after King Louis's commission dismissed mesmerism as effectively as Mesmer himself had once dismissed exorcism, the spirits were back on Europe's political scene, making mischief on a scale unheard of before.

12. REVOLUTIONARY SORCERER

HE FRENCH REVOLUTION OF 1789 HERALDED THE MOST RADICAL changes in the political history of Europe since the fall of the Roman Empire. It marked the beginning of the end for absolute monarchy, the feudal system, aristocratic privilege, and the unquestioning acceptance of religious authority. Under sustained assault from new-formed left-wing groups, backed by discontented mobs in both town and country, old certainties perished, to be replaced by new principles of equality, liberty, and citizenship rights. Few historians recognize the part played by spirit influence in these massive changes or pay much attention to its channel, the rascally count Alessandro di Cagliostro.

Cagliostro, a rascally channel for spirit influence
in the French Revolution

Cagliostro was born Guiseppe Balsamo in Sicily in 1743, a wild child with considerable artistic talents to complement his second sight. He ran away from school several times and, following a disgraceful Scripture reading,[1] was finally expelled. Deciding to visit Rome, he posed as an alchemist in order to separate a wealthy goldsmith from his gold, but he was himself robbed later and thus reached Rome penniless. He lived on his wits and his artistic talents and somehow managed to survive.

Even at this early age, Balsamo's interest in the occult was profound. He was attracted to a Greek alchemist named Altotas who, in his search for the Philosopher's Stone, had stumbled on a valuable process for making flax fiber feel like silk. Together they visited Malta where Balsamo so impressed the Grand Master of the Knights of Malta (himself an alchemist) that this worthy gave him letters of introduction to several influential men in Italy. It was the first gust of a wind that was to blow the young occultist into the halls of the mighty.

On his return to Rome, Balsamo met and married Lorenza Feliciani, the beautiful fourteen-year-old daughter of an impoverished copper smelter. They traveled throughout Italy, on to Spain, and into France, where they met a man fated to become Europe's most famous libertine—Giovanni Jacopo Casanova. Back in Spain, Balsamo worked for the Duke of Alva, but a year later he turned up with his wife in London and was swiftly jailed for debt. Lorenza used her good offices with Sir Edward Hales to have him released. The knight offered him employment painting the ceiling of his family seat near Canterbury. Balsamo accepted, made a ruinous job of the ceiling, then embarked with his wife for France. On the boat, they encountered the French advocate Duplessis, who fell in love with Lorenza. He brought the couple to Paris and permitted them to live in the residence of the Marquis de Prie, to whom he was steward. After two months, Duplessis finally succeeded in seducing Lorenza and she moved into apartments in the rue Saint- Honoré. Balsamo promptly petitioned the king, with the result that Lorenza was jailed in 1773. She remained there for a year.

Whatever the fate of his wife, Balsamo's own fortunes took a turn for the better. He invented a skin lotion that actually worked and consequently made him money. His reputation as an alchemist was growing, so that he was able to take on paying pupils. By the time Lorenza was released from jail (with, apparently, no ill feelings toward the man who put her there), he had enough money for a flamboyant return to Italy, posing as the Marchese Pellegrini. He was foolish enough to visit his home in Palermo, where he was recognized by the goldsmith he had swindled and jailed.

Balsamo subsequently returned to London in 1776 and changed his name to Cagliostro (which was, in fact, the name of his Sicilian uncle). During this visit, both he and his wife became Freemasons, entering as apprentices on April 12, 1777.

Today the Masonic Order presents itself largely as a charitable organization. Although founded on a system of ritual initiations that contains some profound and interesting symbolism, it cannot readily be called an occult order in the generally accepted sense of the term. Masonry makes no claims to contact spirits or channel esoteric powers, but minds drawn to Masonic ritual are often drawn to ritual magic as well; and it is a fact of history that many magicians have also been Masons. It is also true to say that in earlier centuries, the search for arcane secrets within Masonry was carried out with much greater diligence than it is today.

Cagliostro was, of course, an occultist before he was a Mason and approached Freemasonry with the mind of an occultist. He discovered—or claimed he discovered—an Egyptian Masonic rite, incomparably older than anything worked by the Masons of his own day. On the basis of this rite, he set out to found an Order of Egyptian Masonry, headed by himself as Grand Copt and open only to Freemasons in good standing. Perhaps to add a little harmless excitement to the whole affair, he began to stir up a rumor that he had been a pupil of the founding prophets of the order, Elijah and Enoch, and thus was many thousands of years old.

About this time, his own prophetic abilities began to flower, but he was first and foremost a magician. He followed the traditional magical approach of using very young children as mediums to contact spirit entities and view the future.

Cagliostro began a tour of Europe preaching Egyptian Masonry and attempting, often successfully, to persuade more orthodox Masons to adopt his rite. His psychic abilities, which may have involved what we would now call "cold reading,"[2] helped him enormously in the superstitious environment of his day. Furthermore, the Egyptian Rite ended in a demonstration of clairvoyance. This must have appeared enticing to Masons fed on no more satisfying fare than symbolic chatter about rough and smooth ashlars, but as there is little doubt Cagliostro presented well as a psychic, there is even less doubt that he was a charlatan. During a demonstration in St. Petersburg, the child medium abruptly announced the whole thing was a put-up job. Cagliostro fled to Strasbourg, in Germany, where his reputation remained unimpaired. Crowds lined the route to watch the Grand Copt in his black coach with its enticing magical symbols.

Confounding those critics who looked on him as nothing more than a swindler, Cagliostro set up headquarters in a simple room in one of the poorer quarters of the city and promptly began charitable work healing the sick and distributing alms. His reputation increased enormously, and not simply with the poor. His patients included nobles like the Marquis de Lasalle and the Prince de Soubise. The latter had been abandoned by his doctors as a hopeless case. Cagliostro cured him in three days. The Baroness d'Oberkirch also visited and, though she never really came to trust him, she was forced to admit to his clairvoyant abilities: he informed her the empress of Austria had died three days before the news reached Strasbourg by more orthodox channels. At this time too, Cagliostro met Cardinal de Rohan, who was duly impressed and eventually persuaded him to come to Paris.

It is a curious fact that the lives of many famous occultists follow a similar pattern. From obscure beginnings, they move into a period of mixed fortunes. Then comes a time during which they achieve great prominence, followed by an eventual fall from grace. Often those concerned are the authors of their own misfortune, but in Cagliostro's case, he appears to have been caught up in a sequence of events outside his own control.

Despite his calling, Cardinal de Rohan was something of a womanizer. In the days when he was bishop of Strasbourg, the future queen of France, Marie Antoinette, passed through the city en route to her wedding with Louis XVI. Even at fifteen she was a beauty and as de Rohan gave her Communion, he fell in love with her. The infatuation was a lasting one, probably heightened by the fact that Marie Antoinette's husband failed miserably to take her virginity for several years—a fact that inevitably leaked beyond the nuptial bed. But if de Rohan loved the queen, the queen had very little love for de Rohan. No sooner had her husband succeeded to the throne than she had de Rohan dismissed from his post as ambassador to Austria. She also attempted to block his elevation to cardinal, although this time she was unsuccessful. One suspects a touch of the masochist in de Rohan's character, for the more Marie Antoinette attempted to humiliate him, the fonder of her he became. It was not, however, an exclusive infatuation. When de Rohan was fifty, he fell in love with the twenty-five-year-old Countess de la Motte Valois (a title unlikely to have been genuine). It proved a more satisfying relationship; he managed to seduce her on their second meeting. She became his mistress and he introduced her into court, where she quickly became a favorite of the queen.

Unfortunately for all concerned, the countess had formulated an unsavory plan to make herself a fortune. Aware of de Rohan's feelings toward the queen, she set about convincing him that the queen's own attitude was changing and Marie Antoinette was slowly warming toward him. Eventually she undertook to deliver the cardinal's letters to the queen and brought back what she claimed to be the queen's replies. In fact, the queen knew nothing of the correspondence. The cardinal's letters were destroyed. The queen's "replies" were forgeries.

The reason for all this double-dealing was a 1.6-million-livre diamond necklace, which the queen wanted but could not afford. Countess de la Motte Valois persuaded de Rohan that he should obtain it for her (on credit), with the understanding that he would be suitably recompensed for his actions. In fact, the countess planned to abscond with the necklace herself as soon as she got her hands on it. At one point in the affair, the countess arranged a secret meeting between de Rohan and the queen in the Gardens of Versailles. The shortsighted cardinal kissed the royal slipper, without apparently noticing the foot inside belonged to a young prostitute hired by the countess.

Subsequent developments in the "Diamond Necklace Affair" are well known. The first payment fell due in the summer of 1785. Countess de la Motte Valois forged a letter from the queen telling the cardinal she could not meet the demand. At this point, the countess's plan began to fall apart. She had been under the impression that de Rohan was fabulously rich and relied on his infatuation with the queen to make him quietly pay for the necklace himself. She may well have been right about the extent of his infatuation, but in the event, de Rohan could not raise the money. The jewelers went directly to the queen, who did not, of course, know what they were talking about. The king became involved and de Rohan questioned. When the whole story came out, Marie Antoinette was furious and insisted on the arrest of all concerned. Among those drawn into the net was Cagliostro.

A cool reading of history suggests Cagliostro was innocent. The worst that could be said of him was that he had once conjured an image of the queen into a bowl of water for the benefit of de Rohan. But despite his protestations, he was incarcerated in the Bastille for the better part of a year. His wife was also arrested, but she was released after seven months. There is unconventional evidence to suggest Cagliostro knew he would get his revenge. During a

Masonic meeting at the home of the Count de Gebelin, he used his knowledge of Qabalistic numerology to make a prediction. King Louis, he said, was to die on the scaffold before his thirty-ninth year—"condemned to lose his head." His queen, Marie Antoinette, was destined for an equally unpleasant fate. She would become wrinkled through grief, imprisoned, starved, and beheaded.

When he emerged from prison, Cagliostro was banished from France by the king. He went to London and mounted a lawsuit against the governor of the Bastille for the return of money stolen at the time of his arrest. The move was unsuccessful and, in something suspiciously like a fit of pique, he composed a pamphlet dated June 1786 and entitled *Letter to the French People*, which claimed the king had been deceived by his ministers, while Cagliostro himself was entirely innocent. The letter attracted considerable attention in Paris, possibly because it contained two predictions. Cagliostro attested that he would not return to France until the Bastille was pulled down to become "a public promenade," and he finished his pamphlet with the words:

> Yes, I declare to you, there will reign over you a prince who will achieve glory in the abolition of *lettres de cachet*, and the convocation of your States-General. He will feel that the abuse of power is in the long run destructive of power itself. He will not be satisfied with being the first of his ministers; he will aim at being the first of Frenchmen.[3]

Even to the most skeptical, the "prince" mentioned in this paragraph must sound at least a little like Napoleon.

Things were not going well with the French nobility. Although an innocent victim in the Diamond Necklace Affair, Marie Antoinette's popularity plunged sharply because of it. Mobs booed her each time she appeared in public, and the feeling of the country grew steadily more threatening. Countess de la Motte Valois, who had been condemned to public flogging and branding, added to the pressure with the claim that the queen had been having an affair with Cardinal de Rohan. Cagliostro's own embittered *Letter* helped the process along. Revolution was stirring in France. The country was at a turbulent turning point and an occultist who practiced contact with spirits was at the center of the storm.

But while now banned from France, Cagliostro was not particularly welcome in England either. Following an exposé in the *Courier de L'Europe*, a biweekly Anglo-French newspaper published in London, he and his wife went to Basel, then Turin. The police moved them on. They traveled to Roveredo, in Austria, with a similar result. They were in Trent when the Austrian emperor himself intervened, ordering them to leave the country altogether.

Cagliostro decided to return to Rome and there make an all-out effort to establish his curious brand of Freemasonry. Predictably, the Vatican reacted violently. Cagliostro was arrested and jailed in 1789. After his trial he was transferred to the Castel San Leo, where he was incarcerated in almost total darkness. The France he had left was plunging into the chaos of its revolutionary period. In 1792, Cagliostro's Qabalistic prophecies came true with a vengeance and Louis was beheaded. By 1797, French troops had taken the Castel San Leo. They mounted a search for the magician, who was now considered a revolutionary hero. But the search came too late. Cagliostro had died two years earlier at the age of fifty-two. Or at least so orthodox history records. The more credulous within the ranks of occultism are not so sure. As Grand Copt of the Egyptian Rite, Cagliostro had taught a twofold system of moral and physical regeneration. According to the French magus Eliphas Levi, his precepts of moral regeneration were as follows:

You shall go up Mount Sinai with Moses; you shall ascend Calvary; with Phaleg you shall climb Thabor, and shall stand on Carmel with Elias. You shall build your tabernacle on the summit of the mountain; it shall consist of three wings or divisions, but these shall be joined together and that in the centre shall have three storeys. The refectory shall be on the ground floor. Above it there shall be a circular chamber with twelve beds round the walls and one bed in the centre: this shall be the place of sleep and dreams. The uppermost room shall be square, having four windows in each of the four quarters; and this shall be the room of light. There, and alone, you shall pray for forty days and sleep for forty nights in the dormitory of the Twelve Masters. Then shall you receive the signatures of the seven genii and the pentagram traced on a sheet of virgin parchment. It is the sign which no man knoweth, save he who receiveth it. It is the secret character inscribed on the white stone mentioned in the prophecy of the youngest of the Twelve Masters. Your spirit shall be illuminated by divine fire and your body shall become pure as that of a child. Your penetration shall be without limits and great shall be also your power: you shall enter into that perfect repose which is the beginning of immortality: it shall be possible for you to say truly and apart from all pride: I am he who is.[4]

Levi considers this passage an allegory. He believed the "three chambers" to be physical life, religious aspirations, and philosophical life. The signatures of the genii represented a knowledge of the Great Arcanum and so on. But despite one spectacular attempt at spirit-raising in London, Levi was not a practicing magician, merely a student of occult theory. As such, he missed the point completely. But before examining what Cagliostro might really have been talking about—for the passage quoted is far more interesting than the allegorical jumble Levi saw in it—it is important to study the Grand Copt's system for achieving physical regeneration.

Cagliostro advocated a forty-day retreat once every fifty years. The retreat was to begin during the full moon in May, with only one "faithful" person for company. During the forty-day term, a partial fast was to be observed, the menu consisting of a large glass of dew (collected from sprouting corn with a clean white linen cloth), followed by new, tender herbs, and ending with a biscuit or a crust of bread.

After seventeen days of this treatment, Cagliostro forecast the onset of slight bleeding, which was the sign to begin taking "Balm of Azoth." The fifteenth-century physician and alchemist, Paracelsus, equates Azoth with the Universal Medicine, reputed to cure all ills including old age, but Levi suggests Cagliostro meant "Philosophical Mercury," an alchemical substance that can be extracted from any metallic body. Hopefully, he referred to something different from ordinary mercury, for his dosage of six drops, taken morning and evening and increased by two drops daily until the end of the thirty-second day, would quickly prove fatal.

If bleeding did not arise spontaneously on the seventeenth day, Cagliostro taught that it should be induced, presumably by lancing or leeching. At dawn on the thirty-third day, bleeding had to be renewed. The individual following these strenuous instructions was then advised to take to his bed and remain there until the end of the fortieth day. On the morning of the thirty-third day, after bleeding had recommenced, a grain of Universal Medicine (compounded of "Astral Mercury" and "Sulfur of Gold") should be taken. The effects of this medicine seem to be rather extreme: a three-hour faint, followed by convulsions, sweating, and much purging. To help fight them, a broth of lean beef had to be taken, seasoned with rice. Highlight of day 36 was a glass of Egyptian wine, while on the thirty-seventh, the last grain of Universal Medicine was to be taken. A profound sleep would follow, Cagliostro claimed, during which hair, teeth, fingernails, and skin would be renewed. Day 38 saw another warm bath, this time infused with the aromatic herbs previously used in the broth. Next day ten drops of "Elixir of Acharat" should be taken in two spoonfuls of red wine. The retreat ended a day later with "the aged man renewed in youth."

Despite the obvious difficulties of these accounts, they may not be entirely nonsense. What Levi missed was that the moral and the physical regeneration processes were, almost certainly, two aspects of the same operation. Nor were the moral regeneration instructions an allegorical description of a certain lifestyle, as Levi believed. They were, rather, detailed instructions for scenes that were to be built up vividly in the imagination of the operator during his forty-day retreat. They are similar in approach (if not in content) to the famous Spiritual Exercises of Saint Ignatius Loyola practiced by the Jesuit Order, and also to various psychological exercises practiced by occult orders in the present day.

It may be that such an inner working, which has profound affects on the consciousness of anyone who cares to try it, was designed to clarify the many obscurities contained in the outer working (like the exact nature of Balm of Azoth, Astral Mercury, Sulfur of Gold, Elixir of Acharat, and so on). This it might well do, for such exercises tend to throw up the most unlikely snippets of information from the unconscious mind and have often contributed greatly to the psychical abilities of magicians. But the most interesting aspect of all is the reference to the "seven genii." A geni or djinn is an elemental spirit. The breed was much publicized in the *Arabian Nights* where we find them bottled by magicians and forced to grant wishes in return for their release. Whatever we feel about such romantic fictions, the reference to receiving the seals of the genii indicates that Cagliostro believed the rite would help him communicate with spirits.

The exercise has an historical importance in that Cagliostro persuaded Cardinal de Rohan to undergo it, apparently without much regenerative success. But Cagliostro insisted it worked for him—hence the rumors that he had lived for centuries. Against this background stands a persistent legend that the Grand Copt did not die in the San Leo dungeons. Instead, he asked to make Confession and designated a priest to hear it. Some hours after the Father Confessor departed, the jailer entered the cell to find the man who left had actually been Cagliostro in the priest's garments. The priest himself lay strangled.

The story adds that Cagliostro lived on for many years, presumably working to influence later political events as profoundly as he had influenced those of pre-Revolutionary France . . . under the continuing guidance of his seven spirits.

13. HISTORY REPEATS

THERE ARE CURIOUS PARALLELS BETWEEN PRE-REVOLUTIONARY FRANCE and pre-Revolutionary Russia. Like Louis XVI, Tsar Nicholas II was fundamentally weak, pleasant enough in his personal relationships, but lacking in political insight. Like Louis, Nicholas was the last in a centuries-long line of absolute monarchs, and both had an almost fatal instinct for meddling in political affairs they did not understand while remaining blind to the dynamic social changes that were about to topple their thrones. These two monarchs vacillated on the vital question of establishing a workable parliament, and married foreigners who, like themselves, lacked political sense yet insisted on interfering with the political life of their adopted countries. Both were imprisoned at the end, both executed by their former subjects. There were similar rumors that one member of the two royal families had managed to escape. Finally, both imperial courts had their resident magician. In France, it was the mysterious Cagliostro, in Russia the shamanistic Rasputin. These magicians had many similarities themselves; they were both born of peasant stock, they both lost a parent in childhood, and they both exhibited second sight. Most important, both were in contact with spirits.

The history of pre-Revolutionary Russia is inextricably linked with the Romanov dynasty, an aristocratic family of little grandeur until the day in 1613 when sixteen-year-old Michael came to the throne in his troubled homeland. Contemporary records show he accepted his election with enormous reluctance, yet he nevertheless established a ruling lineage that lasted nearly three centuries. Members of the family were highly religious. According to the Romanovs' biographer E. M. Almedingen:

> The early Tsars were almost continually in attendance on the heavenly hierarchy and the business of governing was interwoven with the business of

*Grigory Rasputin, whose spirit contacts and mystic abilities gave him
enormous power over the Tsar and Tsarina of prerevolutionary Russia*

the Church. They ordered their year in strict accordance with the memorials
left by the Lord, the Lord's Mother and the company of saints. The Tsars'
work and leisure, their clothes and food, even their gait and demeanour were
all patterned in conformity to what they believed to be God's will for them.
Their wives never shared their board, and could share their bed only on such
nights as were sanctioned by the church ordinance. The season of Lent and
all the lesser fasts enjoined continence. So did all the great feasts since their
honour would have been polluted by sexual intercourse.[1]

Tellingly, Ms. Almedingen adds that the rigor practiced in the seventeenth century "had not altogether vanished in the 20th." By the time the
twentieth rolled around, Tsar Nicholas II was occupying the Russian throne
during a period of internal turmoil almost unequaled in the history of his
country. But a new and strange factor had entered the picture. It was neatly

summed up in a caricature by the artist Ivanov that showed a tiny tsar and tsarina seated like children on the lap of a towering Russian peasant, with grim features, deep-set, hypnotic eyes, and a long, black beard. The cartoon was satirically captioned RUSSIA'S RULING HOUSE. The peasant was Rasputin.

Grigory Efimovitch Rasputin was born, probably in the late 1860s, in the small Siberian town of Pokrovskoe. His father was a horse owner who worked as a coachman and was relatively well-to-do. In many ways, the young Rasputin was a very ordinary child. He loved horses, adored the life of the sweeping steppe, and hated schooling, of which, as it happened, he received very little. But one strangeness manifested early—he had "second sight," a catchall term for a wide-ranging psychical ability that includes an awareness of spirits.

Perhaps the earliest manifestation of his talent came before the age of twelve while he was ill with fever. A horse had been stolen in the village and a number of men gathered at the home of Rasputin's father (who was then village headman) to discuss the matter. During the course of the meeting, the boy sat up and flung an accusation at one of the peasants. He was not immediately believed—his father took some pains to placate the accused man—but two of the gathering were intrigued enough to investigate. They subsequently discovered that the thief was the man Rasputin named. In another example of his odd abilities, his daughter Maria has described how, as an adult during his days in St. Petersburg, her father was instantly able to detect a revolver concealed in a woman's hand-warmer—and possibly saved himself from assassination by doing so.

There was epilepsy in the family, a disease associated in shamanic cultures with an ability to speak to spirits. Rasputin's sister had it, and later his son did too. The sister was likely killed by a seizure; she fell into a river while washing clothes and drowned. It was a bad period for Rasputin in an otherwise happy childhood, for his mother and brother also died around this time and the family home was razed to the ground by fire. Rasputin survived the multiple tragedies to build up, during his teens, a reputation as a libertine. His approach, to judge from his behavior in later life, was direct in the extreme. Urged on by a monstrous libido—a more commonplace characteristic in mystics than one might imagine—he would often attempt to undress a woman during the first few minutes of their meeting. It is a tribute to the dynamism of his personality that many women did not bother to resist.

But sexual hedonism was not the only aspect of a complex character to manifest in those early years. Colin Wilson, who has written one of the better biographies of Rasputin,[2] remarks that he was "driven by a will to power that was stifled in Pokrovskoe." Perhaps a more complete assessment might be that he was driven by a will to occult power, for the occult was to become a central pivot of his life.

At the age of sixteen, Rasputin had occasion to visit the monastery of Verkhoture and stayed for four months. During that time he came into contact with an heretical sect of flagellants, the Khlysty, who held the belief that the kingdom of God could be attained on earth, at least by an elite. It is not known whether Rasputin practiced Khlysty techniques, although he was certainly drawn to their doctrines. But if he did, there is a chance the techniques opened the doors of his mind to visionary experience. Aldous Huxley, in his twin essays, *The Doors of Perception and Heaven and Hell*,[3] had much to say with a bearing on this point. Although Huxley's literary springboard was an experiment with mescaline, he makes the point that drugs are not the only means of influencing body chemistry toward mystical or pseudo-mystical experience. Such practices as flagellation, especially when the wounds are left unwashed and untreated, lead to a buildup of decomposing protein in the bloodstream, along with bacterial infections. This can, in certain circumstances, produce biochemical changes that influence brain function. Visions may follow. Nor was Huxley entirely satisfied that such visions were subjective hallucinations. He felt they might actually represent deeper insights into the nature of reality.

At the monastery, Rasputin also met the holy hermit Makary, whose blessing was eagerly sought by pilgrims. Makary, it seems, sensed something extraordinary in this brawling youth and took the trouble to advise him about his future. Whether he accepted this advice is open to question, for on leaving the monastery, Rasputin promptly returned to his old ways, drinking, whoring, and keeping a shrewd eye out for ways to grab another ruble—not all of them honest, as his brief imprisonment in 1891 attests.

About a year earlier, Rasputin had married Praskovie Fedorovna Dubrovine, a slim, blond, docile girl from a neighboring village. She subsequently bore him a son. But the baby died within six months and Rasputin underwent a change of character. He revisited Makary to discuss the meaning of death and began to study holy books and pray. In the spring, while plowing his fields, the upsurge of piety was rewarded with a vision of the Virgin Mary, who, he claimed, communicated something of great importance to him. Rasputin planted a cross to mark the spot, told his family of the vision, then went quickly to Makary for an explanation. The hermit advised a pilgrimage to strengthen his spiritual power. Rasputin agreed and, with the sort of determination difficult for the irreligious to comprehend, set out to walk the two thousand miles to one of Europe's oldest monastic communities at Mount Athos in Greece. But he was not impressed by the character of the monks when he got there and declined to become a novice. Instead, he decided to press on with his pilgrimage and walked a further thousand miles across Turkey to the Holy Land.

On his way home, Rasputin visited Kazan and called at the cathedral. Here he had an experience that moved him profoundly. His vision of the Virgin had been unusual in that she was not dressed as the icons in the local churches represented her. Rasputin had filed this fact away in his mind without being able to explain it. Now, in Kazan Cathedral, he was suddenly faced with a representation of the Virgin exactly as he had seen her in the fields. If ever he needed a justification for his pilgrimage, this must surely have been it.

The round-trip took him more than two years, and he returned home so changed that his own wife did not recognize him. Like many another magi, his wanderings had brought him a strange personal power and it communicated to the villagers. When he built an oratory in his backyard and began to hold prayer meetings in his house, they came in droves. A jealous village priest, Father Peter, suspected heresy and reported him to the bishop of Tobolsk. Subsequent investigations unearthed nothing unusual, but if Rasputin's outward observance was orthodox, the man himself was not. He had an intense hypnotic ability and appears to have developed impressive powers of healing. He was reputed to be able to expand and contract the pupils of his eyes at will, a trick that must have contributed greatly to the dominance of his gaze.

Wanderlust remained strong in him and he seemed unable to settle down again to village life. For a decade he traveled throughout Russia, building up his reputation as a holy man and healer. He returned home infrequently, but even in Pokrovskoe the people learned he had become a prophet, with his second sight so highly developed that it was impossible to fool him.

There are times in the history of nations when it is dangerous to exhibit psychic powers, for one runs the risk of burning, but there are also times when psychic powers become chic and fashionable, and one is perhaps in even greater danger—of becoming a pet to the rich and powerful. At the turn of the century, this was the situation in Russia. High society in St. Petersburg exhibited a fascination for astrology, magic, fortune-telling, and Spiritualism.

Among the most enthusiastic adherents was the Grand Duchess Militsa, who at one time seems to have led the tsarina herself to engage in table-tapping. (The tsarina's spiritual directors disapproved and she abandoned the practice.) It was the Grand Duchess, always searching for a new purveyor of miracles, who discovered Rasputin and invited him to St. Petersburg. He accepted in 1903.

The visit brought him into contact with the tsarina's confessor, Father John Sergeieff. Despite the priest's unease about psychical phenomena, the two got along famously, probably because they shared the same ultraconservative political views. This fact may have contributed to Rasputin's ready acceptance at court, although that was still some time in the future. It is entirely possible that the real turning point came when, during the canonization ceremonies of a monk named Seraphim, he predicted (accurately) that an heir to the Russian throne would be born within a year. But it was a further two years before he met the imperial family and embarked on a period of his life that was to make him the most influential man in Russia.

Rasputin returned to St. Petersburg in 1905 and was warmly welcomed by Grand Duchess Militsa. In a curious atmosphere where almost anything could happen, Rasputin cured a dog belonging to Militsa's brother-in-law, and the Grand Duke responded by paying for Rasputin's wife to come to St. Petersburg for an operation. But the broad-shouldered Siberian peasant was not the type to become a pet to anyone. His success did not depend on patronage. Within a short time, his name had become known throughout the city and crowds were literally queuing up to see him. He caused the lame to walk, cured the sick, and, according to one report, magically transformed a handful of earth into a blooming rose. On November 1, he met the tsar, who described him in his diary as "a man of God."

There is considerable controversy about the circumstances of this first meeting. Several biographers suggest Rasputin was dancing drunkenly at a gypsy encampment when a messenger arrived with news that the tsar's son was ill. Rasputin then cured the boy, partly by distant prayer and partly by some on-the-spot faith healing. At least one source claims he was called out from church by his friend Father Sergeieff, who had by this time become convinced of his therapeutic skills. In fact, it seems unlikely that anything very spectacular happened on this occasion and it is just possible that his healing abilities were not even involved. But if this was the case at first, circumstances changed radically in the years ahead.

The pivot of Rasputin's influence over the Russian royal family was the condition of the tsarevitch, the little boy whose birth he had foretold. The tsarevitch suffered from hemophilia, a blood disease inherited from his maternal grandmother, Queen Victoria. The condition prevents normal clotting. As a result, the slightest injury—even bruising—can lead to internal bleeding that, unless halted artificially, results in death. In 1907, the boy fell seriously ill and Rasputin was called, since court physicians appeared helpless. Almost instantly, the tsarevitch began to recover. The whole incident had such inherent drama that Rasputin was promptly accepted as a miracle worker. He became a daily visitor to the palace, impressing the tsar with his powers and engendering in the tsarina an emotion falling little short of worship. Neither his tactless habit of calling on her four teenage daughters in their bedrooms, nor his seduction of the children's nurse, shook the tsarina's faith in Rasputin as a holy man. Nor can one entirely blame her, for Rasputin's abilities were impressive. In September 1912, for instance, while Rasputin was away from St. Petersburg and the royal family were holidaying at Belovetchkaya, the tsarevitch developed hemorrhage and blood poisoning following a boating accident. When fever set in, the tsar's doctors feared for the boy's life, but the tsarina telegrammed Rasputin at his native Pokrovskoe, almost two thousand miles away. Instead of hurrying to the child's side, Rasputin merely sent a telegram back, remarking that the illness was not so serious as the doctors imagined. When the message arrived, the boy began to recover. Nor were his powers confined to healing. Two years earlier, while visiting his friend (and later his enemy) the monk Illiodor, Rasputin successfully carried out two exorcisms on women apparently possessed by demons.

But from about 1912 onward, Rasputin's second sight—or possibly his common sense—seems to have made him increasingly aware of the grim fate in store for his royal patrons. He prophesied that the throne would be safe only so long as he himself lived. In December 1916, with the prevision of his own death hanging heavily over him, he wrote a remarkable document in which he said, among other things:

> I feel that I shall leave life before January 1 . . . If I am killed by common assassins, and especially by my brothers the Russian peasants, you, Tsar of Russia, have nothing to fear, remain on your throne and govern, and you, Russian Tsar, will have nothing to fear for your children, they will reign for hundreds of years in Russia. But if I am murdered by Boyars, nobles, and if

they shed my blood, their hands will remain soiled with my blood, for twenty-five years they will not wash their hands from my blood . . . Tsar of the land of Russia, if you hear the sound of a bell that will tell you that Grigory has been killed, you must know this: if it was your relations who have wrought my death, then no one in the family, that is to say, none of your children or relations, will remain alive for more than two years. They will be killed by the Russian people . . . I shall be killed. I am no longer among the living.[4]

This fateful prophecy came true among circumstances as bizarre as any in the life of the man who made it. Rasputin's assassin did, indeed, prove to be a member of the nobility, Prince Felix Yusupov, a handsome homosexual with, to judge from his photograph, a striking resemblance to the silent movie actor Rudolf Valentino. Yusupov issued an invitation for Rasputin to visit him in his palace on the night of December 29 and, despite warnings from friends and his own precognitive forebodings, Rasputin agreed to go.

Details of the midnight visit are reminiscent of a horror movie. Yusupov, according to his own testimony, prepared a basement room with bottles of wine and a chocolate cake liberally laced with cyanide, a poison so virulent that it paralyzes in less than a minute and kills in less than four. Some of the wineglasses also had a sprinkling of powdered cyanide. Rasputin arrived at midnight, to the strains of a gramophone playing "Yankee Doodle." He was brought to the basement room where, again, according to Yusupov, he drank the poisoned wine and ate some of the poisoned cake, ingesting perhaps an ounce of cyanide in the process. It should have killed him instantly—as little as an eighth of an ounce is normally fatal—but, instead, he grew convivial and requested Yusupov to sing. Yusupov, who had a healthy respect for the magician's "demonic powers," excused himself and went upstairs to his fellow conspirators with the news that the poison had not worked. They discussed the possibility of strangling their victim but abandoned the notion in favor of shooting him. One of the men gave Yusupov a revolver and he returned to the basement. Rasputin was seated with his head slumped, complaining of sickness and a burning sensation in his throat. Yusupov suggested he should pray before a crystal crucifix in the room, and when Rasputin turned to it, Yusupov shot him in the back. A doctor among the conspirators examined him and pronounced him dead. Two of the conspirators left the palace. The remaining two, which included Yusupov, went back upstairs, leaving the corpse in the cellar.

Yusupov was not happy. At the back of his mind may have been the suspicion that this miracle worker could be capable of the greatest miracle of all—rising from the dead. He went back to look at the body. It was still there. Unconvinced by the evidence of his own eyes, Yusupov leaned over to shake it. Rasputin arose and tore an epaulette from his shoulder. The terrified Yusupov fled upstairs, but Rasputin followed, crawling on all fours. Somehow the "revived corpse" exhibited almost superhuman strength, bursting through a locked door to reach the outside courtyard. Another of the conspirators, Purishkevich, raced after him and fired four times with his revolver. Two shots hit Rasputin and he collapsed again. Purishkevich promptly kicked him in the head and a little afterward, Yusupov battered the body with a heavy steel press.

Incredible though it may seem, later evidence shows Rasputin was still alive at this time, although certainly unconscious. Taking no chances, the conspirators tied his hands, then carried him to a nearby river, where they dumped him through a hole in the ice. The freezing water revived him, for he actually managed to get one hand free and make the sign of the cross. But he was unable to break through the ice on the river and drowned.

This, then, was the man who advised the Russian leadership through one of the most critical periods of Russian history—an occultist so powerful he proved almost impossible to kill, a member of the esoteric Khlysty, a mystic with proven abilities to stare across the vista of the future, a channel for mysterious healing forces effective over thousands of miles, and a visionary who listened to spirit voices. We know too that the tsar and tsarina were not averse to listening to such voices, either indirectly through the advice of Rasputin or directly in their own experiments. In the early years of the tsar's reign, he constantly evoked the shade of his father for political advice, and a rumor persists that he actually went to war with Japan under the promptings of spirit messages.

14. DIRECT GUIDANCE

S O FAR, WE HAVE CONCENTRATED LARGELY ON INDIVIDUALS WHOSE SPIRIT contacts influenced the course of human history indirectly. But there have been others who took a much more central role. One example was a man seriously believed (by many English) to be the Antichrist predicted in the book of Revelation.

On August 22, 1779, Napoleon Bonaparte, who had been for a time a virtual prisoner in Egypt, slipped away by sea from that country. He was accompanied by a handful of his companions and, as one historian later put it, their two frigates "surprisingly" escaped interception by the British. The adjective is mild. Napoleon's escape, coming as it did at a crucial point in his career, was little short of miraculous. And there are aspects in the background of the adventure that were distinctly odd.

The Continent had been at war for five years when Napoleon concluded the peace treaty of Campo Formio with Austria. Only the sea war with Britain remained to be won. An invasion of England was planned and Bonaparte was appointed to command it. His army was assembled along the English Channel coast, but after a brief inspection in February 1798, Napoleon announced that the invasion could not take place. He reasoned that only command of the sea, which France patently did not have, could ensure success.

There are those who believe he did not reach this conclusion unaided, that he was, in fact, influenced by powers beyond his comprehension. According to a legend popular in wiccan circles, with the French poised to strike, witch covens gathered along the southeast English coast and engaged in a rite designed to raise a "cone of power." This carried into Napoleon's mind the utter conviction that his troops would be unable to cross the narrow strip of water. The experiment was repeated almost 150 years later when Hitler appeared poised to invade the British Isles. The source for this story, which has wide credence

Napoleon Bonaparte, who may have had an experience of the spirit world while visiting the Great Pyramid in Egypt

among the esoteric community in Britain, is the author and traditional witch Patricia (Paddy) Slade,[1] whose family had been involved in both the Hitler and Napoleon rituals. Mrs. Slade was twelve years old at the time of the threatened Nazi invasion and learned from her parents that a human sacrifice had been involved. The covens worked the rite "sky-clad" (i.e., naked) but greased themselves like Channel swimmers in order to keep warm. An elderly coven member volunteered to give his life force in order to lend power to the rite, refused to use grease, and died from exposure. Mrs. Slade heard about the ritual to stop Napoleon—unfortunately without details—from her grandmother, who claimed her great-grandmother in turn had actually taken part.

The idea that a mind might be influenced in this way is not without some foundation. Psychical investigators in the days of Queen Victoria were already claiming that it was possible to induce the hypnotic state telepathically—a fact more recently confirmed by the Russian scientist Dr. Leonid Vasiliev.[2]

It is a very short step from this discovery to the possibility that an occult group might indeed be able to influence someone at a distance.

But whether influenced by magic, or merely considerations of strategy, Napoleon decided against invasion. He suggested instead that France should strike at the heart of the British Empire by invading Egypt and threatening the route to India. The French Directory agreed, probably not because they thought the idea brilliant but because they were becoming wary of their little general's popularity and wanted him out of the way.

The Napoleonic genius and a measure of good luck made the expedition a striking success. Malta was taken on June 10, 1798, Alexandria stormed only weeks later, and the entire Nile delta rapidly overrun. Then, on August 1, disaster struck. Nelson's fleet engaged the French at anchor in Abu Qir Bay and destroyed every French ship. The myth of Napoleon's invincibility was shattered. Of more immediate importance, Napoleon found himself a prisoner in the land he had conquered. Turkey, which had a nominal suzerainty over Egypt, declared war on France in September. By February 1799, Bonaparte had marched into Syria in an attempt to prevent a Turkish invasion of Egypt. But his progress was halted by the British at Acre and by May he was forced to retreat.

On the broader front, Britain, Austria, Russia, and Turkey entered into a new alliance against France. One result was the defeat of the French armies in Italy, followed by almost total withdrawal from that country. The developments were far from popular in France and a coup d'état on June 18 pushed the moderates out of the ruling Directory, replacing them with Jacobins. A confused situation developed and it seemed possible that the Directory itself might fall. Cut off in Egypt, Napoleon remained in ignorance of the situation until, during an exchange of prisoners, the British commander in Palestine sent Napoleon a file of English newspapers as a courtesy. In them he discovered that a member of the Directory, Emmanuel Sieyes, had voiced the opinion that only a military dictatorship could prevent the restoration of the monarchy and commented, "I am looking for a sabre." Napoleon saw himself as that saber. With typical decisiveness, he made up his mind to return to France, even if it meant leaving his army behind.

The problem, however, was how to reach France. Nelson's blockade was solid and had remained so for months. But Napoleon, for reasons that have never been explained, began to act as if it did not exist at all. He gave orders for his frigates to prepare to sail, made all the necessary personal arrangements, and instructed that any change in the positions of the British warships be reported to him instantly. It was as if he was waiting for something he knew was about to happen. And happen it did. An inexplicable change in the British pattern gave him the opportunity he needed. Two fast ships slipped through the blockade and Bonaparte arrived in Paris on October 14.

Although the crisis in France had, in fact, diminished, Napoleon allied himself with Sieyes and successfully carried out a coup d'état on November 9 and 10. The Directory was disbanded and a consulate set up composed of Napoleon himself, Sieyes, and a former director, Pierre-Roger Ducos. In theory, each member had an equal share of power. In fact, Napoleon was master of the consulate and master of France.

The American author A. H. Z. Carr, intrigued by Napoleon's actions in face of the naval blockade, has put forward the theory that he was not acting blindly.[3] Carr felt he was, somehow, aware of undercurrents in the historical process that he could turn to personal advantage. This is an interesting suggestion and one that deserves to be taken seriously. Far too many turning points in history (as this one certainly was) seem to have come about through extraordinary manifestations of luck or chance, so many, in fact, that one begins to wonder if chance really is the explanation.

In 1894, for example, Guglielmo Marconi first began serious experimentation with radio waves on his father's estate near Bologna. Heinrich Hertz had already produced and transmitted such waves, but Marconi's tinkering enabled him to increase the range to about a mile and a half—enough to convince him the system had real potential as a means of communication. But he received no encouragement to continue his experiments in Italy, with the result that, in 1896, he went off to London where his first patent was filed a few months later. By the summer of 1897, the young physicist had shown it was possible to communicate at distances of up to twelve miles. By 1899, he had succeeded in pushing communication distance up to seventy-five miles. Some experts felt he was approaching the theoretical limit of his system. Marconi disagreed. In December 1901, he succeeded in transmitting signals from Cornwall in Britain to Newfoundland across the Atlantic Ocean. It was a staggering demonstration, not only because of the distance involved but because it was theoretically impossible.

Experts of the day were aware of two facts. The first was that radio waves traveled in straight lines. The second was that the surface of Earth was curved. Given this information, it was obvious that, pushed far enough, a radio wave would simply form a tangent to the planetary sphere and beam out into space. A simple calculation showed that, given these facts, the maximum effective range of radio was somewhere between one hundred and two hundred miles. Various physicists made this calculation and it is inconceivable that Marconi himself was unaware of it. Yet he continued with his experiments and succeeded not because of his genius, but because of his persistence. Unknown to Marconi or his fellow experts of 1901, there was in the upper atmosphere an electrically charged layer (now called the ionosphere) that bounced radio waves back to Earth instead of allowing them to stream off into space.

It is widely believed that the great scientific and technological achievements of our age came about through patient inquiry and the careful application of scientific logic. In fact, many breakthroughs have been a matter of luck—or something suspiciously like the process our ancestors called divine revelation. Most students are aware that Darwin's ideas on the origin of species were anticipated by the English naturalist, Alfred Russel Wallace. It is far less well known that the idea of natural selection came to Wallace in feverish inspiration while he was raving through a malarial attack. August Kekule hit on his structure of the benzene molecule through a dream he had in 1865. He saw a snake biting its tail while in whirling motion. Adrenaline was discovered when Dr. K. Oliver was attempting to test a device he had invented for measuring the diameter of an artery. During the course of his tests, he injected his son with an extract from the adrenal glands of a calf and thought he detected a decrease in the size of the artery. Today we know this could not have been the case. Nevertheless, he convinced a fellow scientist to examine his findings. The glandular extract was injected into a dog and a measurable increase in blood pressure took place. Medical science took another immense step forward through luck.

Sometimes the element of luck intertwines with itself in a fascinating mosaic. Marconi could never have made his discovery of the long-distance potential of radio waves without the discovery of these waves in the first place. The man who made it was Heinrich Hertz, who was lucky enough to notice a tiny spark emitted by a piece of apparatus across the room from the equipment he was currently using. The development of photography, a vital element in our culture, came about through a lucky chance. A silver spoon left lying on an iodized metal surface produced an image that was noticed by Louis-Jacques-Mande Daguerre. The discovery of X-rays was equally accidental. Wilhelm Conrad Roentgen forgot to remove a fluorescent screen from a table on which he was using a cathode ray tube. Louis Pasteur freely acknowledged the part played by chance in a number of his most important discoveries. The whole apparatus of immunization sprang from carelessness on the part of one of his assistants. The man neglected a culture of chicken cholera and it lost its virulence. But Pasteur noticed that it prevented chickens from becoming infected by the more powerful strain. Alexander Fleming searched for an antibacterial agent since his discovery during World War I that existing disinfectants damaged tissue. An airborne mold contaminated one of his culture plates and he noticed that bacterial growth around it had been stopped. The mold was *Penicillium notatum.* The cyclotron, an essential piece of equipment in the history of atomic energy development, worked by accident. Theoretically, it should have been grossly inefficient, but an unexpected effect of a magnetic field enabled it to become a practical proposition.

Taken singly, any one of these developments has had a revolutionary effect on our culture. Taken together, they have produced a profound change in the course of history. One must wonder how far the arm of coincidence can reach in such important matters, especially as the list is far from exhaustive. One is almost struck by the feeling that those involved were somehow *guided.*

Napoleon certainly believed he was guided. Among the discoveries of his savants during his occupation of Egypt was an oracular text found in the Valley of the Kings that he had translated into French for his own use. Following Napoleon's defeat at Leipzig in 1813, the work was discovered by a Prussian officer in a cabinet of curiosities and subsequently rendered into German. In 1835 it was issued in book form and became a publishing phenomenon, remaining in print throughout the entire nineteenth century and republished by the astrologer Judy Hall in 2003.[4] The oracle, which generates more than a thousand answers to a limited set of general questions, shows certain similarities to other ancient systems of divination, notably the *I Ching*, which, as we have seen, appears to have been spirit driven. The oracle may not have been Napoleon's only brush with Egyptian spirits. There is a speculative possibility of direct contact during his visit to the Great Pyramid.

The Great Pyramid has long been considered a repository of occult mysteries—or, alternatively, of scientific knowledge bequeathed by a high civilization now vanished from the face of the earth. Investigators have been particularly interested in the King's Chamber, a bare, flat-ceilinged room of polished red granite, some thirty-four by seventeen by nineteen feet high. This chamber, set deep in the heart of the pyramid, is empty except for a large, open sarcophagus of polished, chocolate-colored granite. When Napoleon entered it with a small group of advisers in 1798, he insisted that he be left alone for a time. His colleagues reluctantly agreed and filed out, leaving their leader to meditate on the mysteries of the ancient edifice. Napoleon subsequently emerged, white and shaken, but flatly refused to discuss what had frightened him. Years later, nearing death in exile on the small Atlantic island of Saint Helena, he recalled the experience again and seemed, momentarily, to be about to describe it. But he changed his mind and died with the mystery unexplained.

In the absence of facts, we may only speculate. But our speculations might be guided by the experience of Dr. Paul Brunton, a British author who, in the early 1930s, was one of the last men to receive permission to spend a night in the King's Chamber. In his record of the adventure,[5] Brunton describes a visionary experience in which he appeared to leave his body and learn the message of the pyramid (that men must turn their attention inward for salvation) from the spirit of a high priest of ancient Egypt.

Brunton's experience is in line with an esoteric doctrine that the Great Pyramid was originally built as a device for separating the soul from the body of a living initiate, thus allowing a foretaste of life after death—the essential shamanic experience. Whether Brunton's vision was subjective or a hallucination is almost beside the point. It is an observable reality that certain environments react on specific people in very similar ways and the sensation of leaving one's body is far more commonplace than most people imagine—surveys in Britain and the United States show that anywhere between 25 percent and 46 percent of people claim to have had an out-of-body experience at least once in their lives. We are entitled to wonder if Napoleon, an intensely religious man once quoted as saying that a state without religion was like a ship without a rudder, also believed that he left his body and conversed with a spirit.

Here again, the objective reality of his experience is beside the point, for a vivid, subjective vision would have been quite enough to produce a profound effect on his mind. It may have imbued him with a sense of destiny or a sense of history. Certainly he possessed both in his later days and could scarcely have done what he did without them. He was, like Hitler and Churchill in a later age, very aware of the contribution he was capable of making to the fate of nations. His answer to the British announcement of his exile in 1815 was typical: "I appeal to history!" In the light of all we have so far discovered, it would seem to be a history profoundly influenced by spirit intervention.

15. AN AMERICAN EXPERIENCE

SPIRIT INTERVENTION IN HUMAN AFFAIRS WAS NOT, OF COURSE, CONFINED to the Old World. Shamanism has existed in South America since time immemorial, as it has among the native North Americans. But by the time the nineteenth century rolled around, there was an intriguing coexistence between ancient spirit practices among the indigenous peoples and more recently developed contacts and techniques among the white settlers. As in the Old World, some contacts had profound implications for the cultural and political future of the continent. Among these were the experiences of a strikingly handsome young man named Joseph Smith Jr.

Smith was the product of a family that had seen hard times. His grandfather, Asael Smith, came from Topsfield, Massachusetts, but lost much of his property in America's economic downturn in the 1780s and moved to Vermont. His son, Joseph Smith Sr., managed to establish himself as a farmer, but a series of crop failures in the early years of the new century forced him to move with his growing family to Palmyra, New York. Joseph Smith Sr.'s third son, Joseph Jr., grew to maturity within a confused, and doubtless confusing, religious background. His mother, Lucy Mack, came from a family that espoused Seekerism, a movement searching for a new revelation to restore true Christianity, but she herself attended Presbyterian services. His father, Joseph Sr., seemed to have no religion at all—he declined to attend any church and kept his son at home with him on Sundays. The whole family believed in visions and prophecies, however, and tended to engage in the more superstitious practices of folk religion. Meanwhile Palmyra was constantly swept by a series of revivals generated by the Second Great Awakening, an evangelical Christian movement that had been gaining momentum since 1800.

Against this background, the adolescent Joseph Jr. developed into a

Joseph Smith, the young American whose meetings with spirits led to the establishment of the Mormon Church

likeable young man with romantic inclinations and an interest in such oddities as treasure hunting. He took to claiming he could locate buried gold by means of a crystal "peep-stone," and even managed to convince a few people he was endowed with supernatural powers. Unlike his father, the younger Joseph, now fourteen, seemed to feel the need of a church, but was confused about which one to join. Mindful of the New Testament advice that anyone lacking wisdom should ask God,[1] he went off to the woods to pray and was rewarded by a vision of the Almighty accompanied by Jesus Christ, both of whom told him, face-to-face, not to join any of the available churches, which were all in error. He went to break the news to a local minister who, predictably, dismissed the spirit encounter as delusional.

Smith continued to believe, however. He took the divine advice about churches but retained both his interest in religion and his practice of prayer. In 1823, he was rewarded with another spirit revelation. While praying in his bedroom for forgiveness, an angel named Moroni appeared to instruct him on the whereabouts of a set of gold plates inscribed with the history of the ancient peoples of America. Smith was to learn that this text was originally written by many ancient scribes inspired by the spirit of prophecy and revelation, then abridged and edited into its final form by a prophet-historian named Mormon. When he completed the work, Mormon gave the account

An artist's impression of Joseph Smith's first contact with the angel Moroni

to his son Moroni for safekeeping. It was this same Moroni, transformed into a glorified, resurrected being, who stood shining before Smith now.

The plates, claimed the angel, were buried in a hill not far from Smith's father's farm in Wayne County. Smith followed the directions and discovered the plates in a stone box, along with a breastplate and mysterious pair of silver-rimmed spectacles with crystal peep-stone lenses.

For four years the angel refused Smith permission to move the gold plates, then suddenly relented. Not only was he allowed to take them home, but he was charged with the task of translating them into English from the original "reformed Egyptian."[2] When Smith demurred, he was offered divine guidance and told to use the magical spectacles he had found in the stone box. With their aid, tradition has it that he completed the job within three months—an impressive feat for what turned out to be a 588-page volume. Other sources suggest a more reasonable time span of two years,[3] during which two of Smith's followers were visited by the spirit of John the Baptist and ordained into a priesthood.

The plates described the thousand-year history of Israelites led by God from Jerusalem to a promised land in the Western Hemisphere some centuries before the birth of Christ. Their descendants split into two warring tribes, the Nephites and the renegade red-skinned Lamanites. Hostilities were briefly interrupted by the appearance of Christ to the Nephites following their conversion to Christianity, but resumed apace until the Nephites were eventually overwhelmed. But before they were wiped out completely, one of their generals, by the name of Mormon, assembled the records of his people and abridged them into a single text that he engraved on the golden plates. This Book of Mormon was then hidden by his son, Moroni—the same Moroni who was now appearing in angelic form to reveal its existence to Smith.

The style of the book is reminiscent of the Old Testament, with names borrowed from or similar to those of the Bible. Some biblical chapters are closely paraphrased. The suspicion naturally arises that Smith composed the whole thing as a creative work of fiction, with the "gold plates" the most fictional element of all. Furthermore, the original plates disappeared once they had been translated, taken back, according to Smith, by Moroni. Nonetheless, no fewer than eleven witnesses were prepared to testify to having seen them, in some cases touched them and examined the engraving on them. Today, every printed copy of the Book of Mormon begins with a statement of their testimony in two uneven groupings:

THE TESTIMONY OF THREE WITNESSES

BE IT KNOWN unto all nations, kindreds, tongues, and people, unto whom this work shall come: That we, through the grace of God the Father, and our Lord Jesus Christ, have seen the plates which contain this record, which is a record of the people of Nephi, and also of the Lamanites, their brethren, and also of the people of Jared, who came from the tower of which hath been spoken. And we also know that they have been translated by the gift and power of God, for his voice hath declared it unto us; wherefore we know of a surety that the work is true. And we also testify that we have seen the engravings which are upon the plates; and they have been shown unto us by the power of God, and not of man. And we declare with words of soberness, that an angel of God came down from heaven, and he brought and laid before our eyes, that we beheld and saw the plates, and the engravings thereon; and we know that it is by the grace of God the Father, and our Lord Jesus Christ, that we beheld and bear record that these things are true. And it is marvelous in our eyes. Nevertheless, the voice of the Lord commanded us that we should bear record of it; wherefore, to be obedient unto the commandments of God, we bear testimony of these things. And we know that if we are faithful in Christ, we shall rid our garments of the blood of all men, and be found spotless before the judgmentseat of Christ, and shall dwell with him eternally in the heavens. And the honor be to the Father, and to the Son, and to the Holy Ghost, which is one God. Amen.

Oliver Cowdery
David Whitmer
Martin Harris.

THE TESTIMONY OF EIGHT WITNESSES

BE IT KNOWN unto all nations, kindreds, tongues, and people, unto whom this work shall come: That Joseph Smith, Jun., the translator of this work, has shown unto us the plates of which hath been spoken, which have the appearance of gold; and as many of the leaves as the said Smith has translated we did handle with our hands; and we also saw the engravings thereon, all of which has the appearance of ancient work, and of curious workmanship. And this we bear record with words of soberness, that the said Smith has shown unto us, for we have seen and hefted, and know of a surety that the said Smith has got the plates of which we have spoken. And we give our names unto the world, to witness unto the world that which we have seen. And we lie not, God bearing witness of it.

Christian Whitmer
Jacob Whitmer
Peter Whitmer, Jun.
John Whitmer
Hiram Page
Joseph Smith, Sen.
Hyrum Smith
Samuel H. Smith.

The signatory Martin Harris, whose name is appended to the first of these two testimonies, was a wealthy neighbor of Smith's and, despite some initial doubts, one of his earliest followers. He assisted in the translation and, when it was complete, mortgaged his farm in order to fund publication in book form. Date of first issue was March 26, 1830. Just eleven days later, Smith and a handful of followers formally organized themselves into a legal entity they called the Church of Christ. One of its more important teachings was the imminent return of Christ to Earth, a tenet that led Smith to an important project—the establishment of settlements known as Cities of Zion where followers could find refuge from the tribulations of the Last Days. In accordance with this plan, there was a general migration westward.

In Kirkland, Ohio, Smith acted on a further revelation to set up the United Order of Enoch, which introduced collective ownership among Mormons under the overall direction of the Church. Divine guidance failed him, however, when he opened his own bank to facilitate land purchases. The bank soon collapsed, leaving the Church itself in substantial difficulties. A warrant was issued for Smith's arrest on charges of banking fraud. Smith responded by leading his followers to Missouri where another Mormon community had already been established.

Missouri proved to be a less than peaceful environment. There was conflict between members of the new religion and their more orthodox neighbors. Mormon property was burned, women and children murdered. Eventually the Mormons lost patience and began to arm themselves. A group known as the Danites was formed to protect the community and avenge wrongs done to members of the Church. The situation degenerated into open warfare. It was clearly a war the Mormons could never win. After an ignominious surrender to some twenty-five hundred state troops, Smith was taken into custody and charged with treason. After several months in prison and a grand jury hearing, Smith managed to escape while being escorted to Boone County. His authority over his followers was by now at a low ebb, with many convinced he was a fallen prophet. His leadership was sliding slowly into the hands of his former defender, Brigham Young. When the governor of Missouri threatened to exterminate the entire community of some fourteen thousand souls, Young led them en masse to Illinois.

At first this seemed like a good move. For the next few years, things quieted down considerably and the Mormons were permitted to build their own city, Nauvoo, on the site of an abandoned town. But as their numbers and influence grew—Smith had long since instituted a missionary program to spread the word of his revelation—so did the resentment of their neighbors. To make matters worse, there was dissension within the Mormon community itself. Smith's popularity had further diminished following a revelatory ordinance issued by the Church permitting plural marriage for a limited elect . . . which naturally included Smith himself. He was also suspected of furthering his personal interests in Mormon land purchases.

By the middle of 1842, popular opinion in Illinois was noticeably turning against the burgeoning Mormon community. There was criticism in the press of their political and military aspirations and a massive scandal when Smith's bodyguard was accused of shooting at the Missouri governor. Although the bodyguard was subsequently acquitted, anti-Mormon elements in Illinois lost no time in spreading rumors that Smith had predicted the governor's death. Unsuccessful attempts were made to extradite Smith to Missouri, but his final downfall was not due to external enemies but to a split in his own ranks.

By the spring of 1844, a rift had developed between Smith and several of his closest followers, two of whom accused him of proposing marriage to their own wives. This led to the formation of a competing church and grand jury indictments against Smith for a series of alleged crimes, including polygamy. Smith retaliated by ordering the closure of a rebel newspaper, a poorly judged move that led directly to increasing opposition and eventually to a military confrontation with the Illinois governor. Smith and his brother Hyrum were arrested on charges of inciting a riot and treason against the state of Illinois. While they were awaiting trial, a mob stormed the jail. Hyrum was killed at once and Joseph Smith was shot several times before falling to his death from a window.

Joseph Smith's short, eventful life was marked by frequent—one might even say constant—spirit communications. Although the most important of these were undoubtedly the exchanges with the angel Moroni that led to the discovery of the golden plates, the early structure of the Mormon church was based on a continuing series of "revelations" during which spirit voices guided Smith on the way his organization should function. Although some of the advice was controversial—the polygamy edict is an obvious example—the fact remains that a church that had exactly six members on the day of its foundation in 1830 now boasts more than 14.1 million worldwide.[4] And, impressive though the growth may be, it does little justice to the financial power of the Mormon church (now officially the Church of Jesus Christ of Latter-day Saints), particularly in America. Although the church body issues no fiscal statements, one source claims that were it a corporate entity, it would rank approximately halfway down the Fortune 500 list of the country's top-earning companies.[5] Financial and voting power inevitably reflects on political influence. In 2012, Mitt Romney, a follower of Joseph Smith, became the Republican Party nominee for the presidency of the United States and missed election by the narrowest of margins.

PART THREE

SPIRITS IN THE MODERN WORLD

I T IS BY NOW EASY TO SEE HOW THE COURSE OF HUMAN HISTORY has been influenced, directly and indirectly, by spirit contacts. But it is equally easy to forget that history is a continuing process. Just as incidents and actions in the distant past continue to reverberate down the centuries, so incidents and actions in the modern era contribute, sometimes dramatically, to the unfolding of our future.

Spirit intervention cannot be dismissed as the product of earlier, superstitious eras. Nor, whatever its essential nature, has it succumbed to the materialistic rationalism of post-Enlightenment culture. As we shall see in this section, spirit contact, influence, and even intervention have all continued into modern times. Some might even make the case that, in the age of mass communications, spirit influence has actually increased.

16. IS *EVERYBODY* THERE?

T HE FOUNDER OF MORMONISM, JOSEPH SMITH, LIKE MOST PROPHETS, was and is considered by his followers to be an unusual, uniquely talented individual because of his spirit contacts. Yet four years after his death, the spirits were again making their presence known, this time to ordinary people right across America. Stranger still, the unlikely development was anticipated by the spirits themselves in a prophecy by the famous "Seer of Poughkeepsie," Andrew Jackson Davis.

Davis, who was born in rural New York State in 1826, seemed set for a life of obscurity—he was apprenticed to a shoemaker—when a tailor named William Levingston asked him to take part in some mesmerism experiments. Although Levingston had learned minimal technique from a traveling lecturer, the seventeen-year-old Davis turned out to be a dream subject. Soon he was exhibiting paranormal powers, like remote viewing, the ability to read a book blindfolded, and, most important, a talent for conversing with spirits. The experiments were a turning point in Davis's life. In 1844, he made visionary contact with the spirits of Swedenborg and the ancient Greek physician Galen. The latter engaged in a little propaganda for his own medical system, then told Davis he was destined to become a clairvoyant healer. Swedenborg went even further. He proclaimed Davis would be the instrument for a forthcoming revelation of wisdom and truth to the whole of humanity. Levingston and David promptly opened a clinic where David made trance diagnoses and prescriptions for sick clients.

A year later, Davis embarked on a series of public demonstrations in New York that resulted in some 157 channeled lectures. These so impressed a wealthy patron named Silone Dodge that he arranged to have them published in book form. Davis's career as a seer and clairvoyant was well and truly launched. He continued to write books, pamphlets, and articles throughout the remainder of his life and continued his work as a healer. Later in life, when a New York law banned mesmeric healers, he reacted by enrolling in the United States Medical College where he earned himself degrees in both anthropology and medicine—a move that allowed him to continue his practice.

Davis's prediction about widespread spirit contact came much earlier in his career, some four years after his initial vision of Galen and Swedenborg. Following information from his spirit contacts, he announced that soon everyone would be able to do what he did and converse with spirits directly. At the time it seemed highly unlikely, but before long, the new craze of Spiritualism was spreading through the country.

Modern Spiritualism, as a technique of spirit contact and a minority religion, owes its origins to raps that occurred in a two-room cottage at Hydesville, New York, in 1848.[1] The Fox family from Canada, who owned the cottage, were, like its previous residents,[2] frequently disturbed by noises in the night, until eventually Kate Fox, the youngest daughter, established communication with the source of the sounds, which subsequently claimed to be the spirit of a peddler who had been murdered in the house. But even before this open identification, Mrs. Fox suspected she was dealing with spirits and called in her neighbors to witness the phenomena. One of them wrote:

> There were some twelve or fourteen persons there . . . Some were so frightened that they did not want to go into the room . . . Mrs. Fox asked questions and I heard the rapping which they had spoken of distinctly. I felt the bedstead jar when the sound was produced.[3]

The few friendly neighbors soon turned into curious crowds, as word of the phenomena spread. Excitement increased when excavation of the cottage cellar produced some bones and teeth, promptly claimed as the remains of the murdered peddler.

Kate Fox and her sister Lizzie went to live with an elder sister, Leah, in Rochester, New York, and the phenomena—now considerably expanded from the original raps—went with them. The sound of coagulated blood poured on the floor was followed by the cold touch of spirit hands. A group of Methodists called round to speak in tongues, encouraging more spirit noises still. Tables moved of their own accord. Coded messages arrived from the Beyond.[4] Within a year, others began to discover they could move tables and produce spirit raps as well as, if not better than, the Fox girls. The practice of what became known as Spiritualism began to spread.

Davis took the Rochester phenomena to be fulfillment of his prophecy.[5] He already had a substantial following and his imprimatur added further impetus to the emerging movement. Soon Spiritualism was sweeping through America. In 1852, the wife of a New England journalist brought it to Britain.[6]

Although no longer the fad it once was, Spiritualist-style mediumship remains to this day the most popular method of spirit contact within Western culture. There are frequent television demonstrations on the satellite-based Paranormal Channel, Spiritualist churches represent a minor but tenacious religion in many capital cities, and even the traditional séance with its associated phenomena has been deemed worthy of a three-year investigation by the Society for Psychical Research.[7]

Where the main thrust of Spiritualism has always been communication with spirits of the dead, it is not unusual for mediums to become "channels" for "higher beings" who may or may not themselves be human. Historically, the founder of modern Theosophy, Madame Helena Petrovna Blavatsky, followed this pattern, beginning her New York mission by contacting "John King," the spirit of a dead buccaneer, but later transforming herself into a channel for the teachings of her highly evolved Secret Masters. More recently, the Spiritualist medium Grace Cooke (1892–1979) began her career with emphasis on postmortem communications but went on to found the White Eagle Lodge to promote the spiritual teachings of her "guide," White Eagle, who was once incarnated as a Native American.[8] Occasionally, individuals like Fran Rosen-Bizberg ("Parvati"), with no Spiritualist background or training, begin to operate as channels. Rosen-Bizberg is an American now living in Poland who followed a career path as an educationalist until, in 1997, she began to receive "transmissions" from an extraterrestrial "higher intelligence" originating in the constellation of Orion.[9]

While Spiritualism was still in its infancy among the white population of the nineteenth-century United States, a whole different form of intervention was developing among the Native American population, an intervention that would ultimately lead to disaster. The first indication of things to come arose among the Northern Paiute prophet-dreamers (medicine men or shamans) in western Nevada. Their visits to the spirit worlds convinced them that the Native American dead were about to return to earth. When they did, this would lead to an ousting of the whites and the restoration of native lands, food supplies, and the traditional way of life. In delivering the message, the prophet-dreamers mentioned one telling detail: this desirable situation would be hastened by the performance of special dances and songs revealed to the medicine men in their visions. Among these was a variation of a circle dance performed by Native Americans from prehistoric times. The new form was known as a Ghost Dance, since it was designed to encourage the protection of spirit ancestors.

The first Ghost Dance appears to have developed out of visions by a Paiute healer named Hawthorne Wodziwob (Gray Hair) in 1869. Wodziwob announced that he had traveled to the land of the dead where souls of the recently deceased promised to return to their loved ones in a few years' time. Circle dances were held within his community to celebrate the revelation. Wodziwob continued to preach his message for three years with the help of a fellow shaman named Tavibo. Tavibo in turn was the father of a boy named Wovoka, who later became better known under his English name of Jack Wilson.

Wilson was a particularly interesting individual. In his early years, he had visions and heard voices he attributed to God, but he experienced such difficulty in interpreting them that his family arranged shamanic help and training for him. During a solar eclipse on January 1, 1889, he had a particularly potent vision in which he stood before God and watched many of his tribal ancestors engage in the pursuits they had most enjoyed during their lifetimes. God then showed him a promised land teeming with game and told him how the red man might attain it. God's central message was one of love. The tribespeople were urged to love one another, stop intertribal warfare and, tellingly, live at peace with the whites. They were forbidden to lie or steal and had to abandon the age-old self-mutilation practices traditionally associated with mourning. Following these rules would reunite them with their loved ones in a new and better world where there would be no disease or old age. The message was essentially that already channeled through various other medicine men. There was even mention of a circle dance, a five-day ceremonial that, if performed at the proper intervals, would hasten the blissful reunion.

Wilson returned to normal consciousness convinced that with the aid of the dance, all evil would soon be dismissed from the world and the earth would be filled with love, food, and faith. He began at once to preach the message of his vision and was soon attracting the attention not only of his own people but of neighboring tribes. The power of his words was underpinned by the appearance of stigmata on his hands and feet. Gradually the revelation and its attendant ceremonial spread to the Missouri River, the Canadian border, the Sierra Nevada, and northern Texas. As it did so, it took on all the trappings of a religious movement and attracted a fast-growing number of converts, not only

A ghost dance, painted from life, one of many such spirit-inspired ceremonies that proved such a disaster for the Native American peoples

among the Native Americans but among a few of the white settlers as well.[10] By 1890, Wilson's words reached the Sioux, a tribe on the edge of rebellion.

Although Wilson's essential message was clearly one of peace and love, some listeners managed to misunderstand it. Among them was Chief Kicking Bear of the Lakota Sioux, who elected to focus on the concept of "ghost shirts," which were rumoured to repel bullets by means of spiritual power.[11] At the time, the Sioux were on a collision course with the American government, which had broken a treaty and embarked on a course of action that left the Native Americans close to starvation. Troops were sent in and when the Sioux began to celebrate the Ghost Dance, a nervous government, with no real understanding of what was going on, refused to withdraw the soldiers. The situation went from bad to worse until its culmination in the massacre at Wounded Knee, when the Ghost Shirts failed to protect the Sioux.

Changing conditions eventually made the Ghost Dance obsolete, although a few tribes kept it going into the twentieth century. The overall effect of the movement, however, was to prepare the Native Americans for further accommodation with the white population and, to some extent, an acceleration of native conversions to Christianity—developments with an extraordinary influence on the course of American history.

17. THE SPIRITS GO
TO WAR

THE VICTORIAN YEARS IN BRITAIN WERE AN AGE OF CONTRASTS. THESE were most obvious in the sexual sphere. Englishwomen of the eighteenth century were described by one shocked Continental historian as "much given to sensuality, to carnal inclinations, to gambling, to drink and to idleness." But by the time Victoria was firmly established on the throne, the image had changed. Respectability was the order of the day. A woman's place was in the home and the highest expression of her femininity was motherhood. Despite this, she was simultaneously desexualized, as if childbirth were unconnected to intercourse. Every effort was made to hide the fact that women had legs. They might, for all that was apparent from the fashions of the day, have moved on wheels from the waist down. Necklines rose until they clung modestly around the throat.

The contrast was even stronger in other spheres. The Victorian age saw science emerge from its beginnings as a plaything of the aristocracy to become the system of human thought that would eventually encompass the universe. By the time Darwin published his evolutionary thesis, the world was ready for it. There was, of course, great controversy and opposition. But this in itself was an indication of interest—a really unpopular theory is simply ignored.

Victorian science was essentially materialistic, a mechanistic discipline with both feet firmly planted on the ground. Some scientists actually saw an end to their work. Everything could be weighed, measured and categorized; and it had to be only a matter of time before everything actually was. Within this image of the sober Victorian scientist (an image just as strong as that of the sober Victorian puritan), questions of spirituality were considered superstitious and handed over to those bumbling bishops so often lampooned in *Punch*.

*Spiritualism, based on séances of this type, became a worldwide
movement during the Victorian era.*

Yet underneath the rationalism, there was a feeling of unease. God had
been dismissed from his universe and left a yawning chasm. It was a chasm
that was destined to be filled, at least partly, by the spirit world. The first
Spiritualist medium arrived in Britain in 1852 and excited enormous interest.
A year earlier, Cambridge University's Ghost Club had been formed to investigate supernatural phenomena. In 1882, an even more respectable investigatory body came into being with the formation of the Society for Psychical
Research. Fascination with the occult spread like an epidemic. In 1855, the
most spectacular medium of all time, Daniel Dunglas Home, arrived in
Britain from America and dominated the spiritualistic scene for fifteen years.
During this era too, the remarkable Russian Helena Petrovna Blavatsky first
set foot on British soil. At first she too dabbled in Spiritualism but soon began
to preach her own brand of occultism, Theosophy. She claimed to have
learned forbidden arts at the feet of Tibetan masters, whom she still served.

Some of the most popular books of the day were concerned with the
occult—a barometer of public interest. Blavatsky's *Isis Unveiled* and later

her *Secret Doctrine* were snapped up by enthusiastic readers, despite the difficulties of their content.[1] Dickens published his famous *Christmas Carol*, dealing with the return of Marley's Ghost. Bulwer Lytton, the aristocratic occultist, produced *The Haunters and the Haunted*, followed by his even odder *The Coming Race*, which introduced *vril* power to the world and influenced Nazi philosophy a century later. Eliphas Levi, the French magus, visited London and was persuaded to perform an evocation of the shade of Appolonius.[2] With such a floodtide running in the country, it was not surprising that the queen herself grew interested.

Victoria was eighteen years old on her accession to the throne in 1837, a young lady with so simple an upbringing that she had never had a room of her own. But she was obstinate and strong-willed, two characteristics that were to remain with her until the day she died. Prince Albert of Saxe-Coburg-Gotha, the man she later married, noted at the time that she "delighted in Court ceremonies, etiquette and trivial formalities." It was an accurate observation and here again the characteristic remained in evidence throughout her long reign. No one ever approached the queen lightly. No one, that is, except John Brown.

Brown, a dour, bearded Scot, made his mark in the British court after the death of Albert, the queen's beloved Prince Consort. On the face of it, Brown seemed an unlikely character to wield influence over Victoria, yet wield it he did. He had the run of the palace and, unlike prime ministers and heads of state, had instant access to the royal presence. Brown appalled the courtiers by his rough-and-ready manners; and laid claim to a minor place in history by the way he spoke to the queen. He seldom used the term "Your Majesty," but instead would address her simply as "Woman"—"Get on that horse, Woman" . . . "Mind your step, Woman" . . . and so on. The mystery was that Victoria, who laid enormous stress on formality, should put up with this treatment for an instant. She would certainly never have accepted it from her favorite prime minister, Benjamin Disraeli, who had to manipulate her with oily flattery. Nor would she have accepted it from members of her own family. To the queen, decorum was everything and the person of the monarch sacrosanct. Yet Brown was permitted his familiarities; and when he died, a few years before Victoria herself, she claimed she had lost her only real friend in the world. She even ordered a statue to be erected in his memory.

Brown was not popular at court. The Prince of Wales, Victoria's eldest son Edward, nursed a particular loathing for him and on his own accession to the throne had the statue torn down. The dislike may have been a matter of jealousy, for Edward's relations with his mother were often strained, but if Edward's reaction is easily explained, the nature of the relationship between John Brown and the queen was more mysterious. Contemporary gossips were so intrigued that they concluded Brown must have made Victoria his mistress—she was referred to behind her back as "Mrs. Brown"—but this is unlikely in view of her character and the enormous love she had for her husband, which if anything actually increased after his death. More to the point, there is no real evidence to support the view. A more likely explanation is that Brown's hold over Victoria may have been rooted, like the hold of Rasputin over his tsarina, in the shadow world of spirit contact.

Like so many of her subjects, Victoria was caught up in the wave of Spiritualistic practice that swept over her country during the early years of her reign. Buckingham Palace was the setting for a number of séances, and both the queen and her consort engaged in table-turning and similar experiments. Psychics and mediums were presented to Victoria, who showed an enthusiastic interest in their talents. One such individual was the clairvoyant Georgiana Eagle, who demonstrated her powers before the queen at Osborne House, on the Isle of Wight, in July 1846. The queen was so impressed that she had a watch inscribed to Miss Eagle for "meritorious and extraordinary clairvoyance." But the psychic died before the gift could be presented and the watch later went to Etta Wriedt, the American direct voice medium. Against this background, the greatest tragedy of Victoria's life occurred. Her husband died on December 14, 1861.

Victoria proposed to the dashing Prince Albert in October 1839 and married him on February 10 of the following year. At first she was determined that he should play no part in the government of the country (although a constitutional monarchy, royal influence in politics was considerably greater during the nineteenth century than it is today) but gradually relented. Within six months, Albert had access to the parliamentary dispatches. During Victoria's first pregnancy, he was given his own key to the boxes containing information on affairs of State usually reserved for the eyes of the reigning monarch.

Despite the image that has come down through the years, Victoria was far from puritanical—especially in her younger days. Albert, on the other hand, was described by the Duke of Wellington as "extremely straight-laced and a great stickler for morality." He had a strong, dominant personality and the influence of his attitudes on Victoria, though gradual, was profound. It is not overstating the case to say that he embarked on a training program for the queen. He taught her the virtues of hard work and orderly business methods, he taught her to insist on a say in ministerial appointments, and he taught her decorum. From his original position, which seems to have been almost that of a plaything, he became a towering power behind the throne—so much so, in fact, that historians refer to the period as the "Albertine Monarchy." Victoria adored him, asked his advice, and frequently followed it, on almost every important decision. Then, when the habits had been firmly established over a period of twenty-one years, it all ended. Albert contracted typhoid fever and died after a brief illness on December 13, 1861. Victoria's greatest influence was gone. She had no one to turn to. In the shock of her bereavement, she plunged into the horrors of a nervous breakdown that lasted two years.

Victoria withdrew during that time, temporarily relaxing her grip on the machinery of British politics, but even when she emerged from the worst of her emotional illness, she was unable to accept the change that had taken place. Instead of learning to stand on her own feet, to use her undoubted powers of judgment, she continued to behave as if Albert were still alive. When decisions had to be taken, she attempted to guess what Albert would have done and used this as her yardstick. At least such was the situation as seen by orthodox historians, but there may well have been more to it than that. Shortly after Albert's death, a thirteen-year-old medium, Robert James Lees, held a séance in Birmingham during which, it was claimed, the spirit of the prince consort came through with the message that he wished to speak with his wife, the queen. The development received a measure of publicity—one of the sitters was a professional editor. His published account of the séance was subsequently brought to Victoria's attention.

Despite her earlier interest in Spiritualism, the queen was by no means credulous. She was aware how often spurious communications followed the death of a public figure. Besides, her position dictated a discreet, low-key approach. She instructed two courtiers to attend the next Lees séance but warned them they were not to use their own names nor reveal their standing as emissaries from the court. If the courtiers were concerned, but not themselves believers in life after death, the séance must have come as something of a shock. The voice phenomenon produced by Lees was instantly recognizable as that of the late consort. More surprising still, the spirit addressed the courtiers by their real names. Eventually, reluctantly, they were forced to admit they had been sent by the queen.

It seems there followed a great deal of evidential material, including intimate details of life at the palace that only Albert could have known. The courtiers were impressed. But before the queen could take action, she received a letter from the schoolboy Lees. This letter was an example of automatic writing. According to Spiritualist theory, the shade of the deceased takes over the body—or at least the hand—of the medium long enough to pen a message. The message in this case was signed by a pet name used only between Albert and his wife and was packed with personal details. Victoria was utterly convinced that it represented a genuine spirit communication. She sent at once for Lees and a séance was held in the palace. The voice of Albert came through the medium and spoke to his delighted widow. Lees paid nine visits in all to Buckingham Palace and his séances impressed the queen so much that she asked him to join the royal household as resident medium. Lees refused the offer, apparently on the advice of his spirit guides, but did not leave the queen without solace. Albert's final message through him assured her that another medium had been chosen to keep the line of communication intact. This medium was "the boy who used to carry my (Albert's) gun at Balmoral."

Albert had always disliked cities, especially London. Since Victoria's first railway journey in 1842, the couple made a point of getting away from the capital whenever possible. After three visits to Scotland, which they both adored, a lease was taken out on Balmoral House near Ballater. In 1852, the estate was purchased outright and four years later, Balmoral Castle was completed. Victoria had always loved Scotland and a few periods of residence at Balmoral taught her to love the Scots as well. She and her consort lived in the Highlands "with the greatest simplicity and ease," as Lord Grenville wrote. Albert went shooting. The boy who carried his gun was John Brown.

After Lees's revelations, Brown was sent for and subsequently took up residence in Balmoral. He remained there, as Victoria's constant companion and medium, for more than thirty years. It seemed that when she wished to find out how Albert would have viewed a particular issue, she did not, as historians suppose, have to use her imagination. Brown would mount a séance and the dead prince would speak for himself. Victoria kept a detailed record of these séances and after Brown's death wrote a monograph about him that she wanted to publish. But her proposals were thwarted by her private secretary, Sir Henry Ponsonby, and by the then dean of Windsor, Dr. Randal Davidson, who was so disturbed by the prospect that he threatened to resign as court chaplain. Rather than risk scandal, Victoria abandoned the idea. Ponsonby got hold of Brown's private dairies and destroyed them. But the massive cover-up operation was not as thorough as it might have been. Years later, George VI happened on a detailed record of a John Brown séance that had somehow managed to survive. He read it with great interest and mentioned the fact to his speech therapist, Lionel Logue. Eventually the story leaked out until it was made public by the popular British journalist, Hannen Swaffer, who was also a Spiritualist. Despite Swaffer's revelations, Queen Victoria's interest in spirit contact failed to make much impression on the public mind, and less still on the minds of those historians and biographers dealing with the Victorian period. Thus background material on the whole fascinating story is difficult to come by.

Victoria's Spiritualistic interests reach down to the present day to produce a curious addendum to the tale. The most recent dramatic portrayal of the relationship between the queen and her servant is the movie *Mrs. Brown* starring Billy Connolly and Judy Dench. It contains no hint at all of the Spiritualist connection. But earlier, in 1975, Britain's Independent Television screened a dramatized documentary series based on the life of Edward VII. The actor who played Brown in the series was William Dysart, a man with enormous interest in psychical research and mediumship. In May 1973, a friend of Dysart's attended a séance held by the British direct voice medium Leslie Flint and there recorded a voice that claimed to be that of Brown. When Dysart heard the recording, he was intrigued enough to make his own copy. Some months later, when offered the part of Brown in the television series, he used the recording as a basis for his interpretation of the character and carefully copied the voice during his screen appearances.

But the importance of people like Brown, Lees, and Eagle far outstrips their entertainment value. The political life of France, Russia, and now Britain seems, within the last century or so, to have been profoundly influenced by spirit voices. Nor does the story end there.

Seventeen years after the death of Queen Victoria, the Armistice document ending the greatest military conflict the world had ever seen was signed in a railway carriage at Rethondes in France on November 11, 1918. Just two days earlier, the German emperor, Kaiser Wilhelm II, had been persuaded to seek asylum in the Netherlands, saving himself from capture and possible execution but assuring the collapse of the monarchy in Germany.

Wilhelm took up residence at Doorn, swiftly faded from the international limelight, and slipped with apparent ease into the lifestyle of a country gentleman. He died on June 4, 1941, his passing somewhat obscured by more important news. His native Germany was once again at war—and doing rather well, it seemed—under the guidance of a new leader. It was a curiously anticlimactic ending to the career of a man who was then universally held to have been personally, and almost solely, responsible for the eruption of World War I.

Today, however, historians increasingly tend toward the opinion that Wilhelm was an accomplice to war rather than its instigator. The kaiser himself may have shared this opinion if the description of his exile penned by Lewis Spence is to be believed. Writing just before the kaiser's death, Spence claimed Wilhelm was "known to spend the greater part of his time in the privacy of his princely library." But not, as one might suppose, studying politics, history, or military affairs. Spence claims the library was entirely comprised of books on the occult. Many of these works were on Freemasonry (a fringe aspect of the occult in most of its modern manifestations), but there was also volume after volume of works on less appetizing and more arcane societies like the Illuminati and the Cult of Lucifer.

The retired kaiser was, in Spence's view, perplexed:

> In advanced old age, the ex-Emperor of Germany seeks tirelessly in the pages of mystical books for those clues and traces which may guide him to a more precise understanding of the forces which not only seduced him into war, but, by reason of their own inherent defects and furious irrationalities, betrayed him into defeat and exile. Every work published which might seem to aid him in his quest is studiously scanned in the hope that it will cast some light, however vague, upon the identity of those hidden leaders of a secret and occult junta, who, he is convinced, were responsible for the calamity of 1914 and the debacle of 1918.[3]

The quotation is taken from a rare little work, now out of print, entitled *The Occult Causes of the Present War*—the "present war" being the 1939–45 conflict. Despite its florid style and a scarcity of evidence to back up its central thesis, Spence's intuitions are worthy of respect. For the kaiser was indeed involved in the occult during his days of power, and there is no reason to suppose he abandoned his interest after his abdication.

Wilhelm was born on January 27, 1859, in Potsdam, to Victoria (the eldest daughter of the British queen Victoria) and the crown prince Frederick, who later became Germany's Emperor Frederick III. The child had a withered left arm, and even in adulthood the limb never grew to full size—a fact often quoted in psychological analyses of his behavior. The boy grew into a man of stressed, restless, irresolute character, with a sense of duty, inculcated by a Calvinist tutor, that was often locked in conflict with his natural inclinations. In 1881 he married Princess Augusta Victoria of Schleswig-Holstein, who subsequently presented him with six sons and a daughter. Emperor Wilhelm I, the kaiser's grandfather, died in 1888. Frederick came to the throne, but was dying of cancer. Wilhelm became kaiser at the age of twenty-nine.

It was quickly apparent that the new emperor did not see eye to eye with his chancellor, Otto von Bismarck. Bismarck had, of course, been largely responsible for the policies that created the German Empire in the first place, but he was aging. Wilhelm may have felt he was losing his grip. In any case, the kaiser drove Bismarck into resigning as chancellor in the early months of 1890. His successor, Leo Graf von Caprivi, tried unsuccessfully to find a policy that would be at once acceptable to the Reichstag and the aristocracy, personified in Wilhelm. Prince Chlodwig von Hohenlohe-Schillingsfurst, next in line for the job, was equally unsuccessful. By 1900, the former foreign secretary, Bernard Furst von Bulow, had become chancellor. He was very much the kaiser's man and produced little of any real importance in solving Germany's internal problems (which sprang largely from the country's rapid industrialization). But he did abet the kaiser in a policy well tried by many other leaders faced with problems on the home front—the diversion of public attention toward more exciting matters abroad.

Wilhelm's performance in foreign policy was tactless and blundering. He developed a habit of interfering in international disputes that had little bearing on the welfare of the German nation. In 1911, this almost led to war by way of the Agadir Crisis. In 1914, he finally pushed things over the edge.

During the first world conflict, Kaiser Wilhelm was supreme commander of the Armed Forces, and though he seems to have left most of the work to his generals, he did nothing to discourage their grandiose plans, which ruled out any chance of a compromise peace. Today, historians speculate on his motivation and occasionally supply psychological answers like compensation activity for his withered arm, or the acting out of inner conflicts occasioned by a dominant mother and passive father. Doubtless all these factors played some part in the international drama that cost so many lives. But historians who do not, by and large, believe in demons, tend to underrate the influence exercised on the kaiser by a man who for years had felt himself a channel for demonic forces.

Houston Stewart Chamberlain, as one might guess from his name, was not a German. His father was a British admiral, but he was brought up by relatives and educated in France and Geneva, with the result that French became his first language. At the age of fifteen, a Prussian named Otto Kuntze was appointed his tutor and promptly set about filling the boy's head with the glories of the German race. In his twenties, Chamberlain, having already proven himself a brilliant pupil, was studying more edifying subjects like philosophy, natural history, medicine, physics, and chemistry. But the instilled love of things Germanic proved overpowering and he left Geneva at the age of twenty-seven for Bayreuth, where he was fortunate enough to meet the great German composer Richard Wagner, whose daughter he eventually married. In 1885 he moved with his first wife to Dresden, where his personal process of Germanization was completed. From 1889 he dwelt in Vienna, and in 1909 he returned to Bayreuth, where he lived until his death in 1927. His marriage to Wagner's daughter Eva took place in 1908, following the divorce of his first wife three years earlier.

On April 1, 1897, Chamberlain began work on a book entitled *Gundlagen des Neunzehnten Jahrhunderts* (*Foundations of the Nineteenth Century*). By October 31, 1898, the massive manuscript was finished. When it was published the following year, it ran to some twelve hundred pages. Despite this formidable length, it went through no less than eight editions in the next decade. Chamberlain found himself famous in his adopted Germany. He was still famous in the Hitler era, long after his death. By 1938, his magnum opus had sold more than a quarter million copies.

Foundations of the Nineteenth Century is a book that purports to hold the key to history, and the key is an understanding of race. Any grasp of contemporary events, Chamberlain argued, could only be obtained by studying the historical legacy that influenced them. He saw this legacy as Roman law, the personality of Christ, and Greek philosophy and art. He maintained that the peoples who carried this legacy were the Jews, the Germans, and the Mediterranean Latins. But only the first two were pure races and only the Germans were worthy of their heritage. In Chamberlain's eyes, it was the Teuton who saved humanity from the dark night of the Middle Ages and it was the Teuton who was the only real hope of the contemporary world. But he used the term broadly, taking in both Celts and Slavs and even those, of any race, who were philosophically Teutonic in their outlook. Nonetheless, he felt the importance of each nation was directly dependent on the proportion of Teutonic blood in its population. Chamberlain took some pains to insist he was not anti-Semitic and condemned this commonplace German attitude as "stupid and revolting." But he took even more pains to insist that Christ was not a Jew, arguing that his Galilean origins and his inability to pronounce Aramaic correctly were at least indicative of a high proportion of non-Semitic blood if not a full Aryan pedigree.[4]

Chamberlain's book also drew up a racial history of Judaism, tracing the mixture of Semite, Hittite, and Amorite blood. It was this final interbreeding that brought the Aryan strain into the bloodline. According to Chamberlain, the Amorites were "tall, blond and magnificent" but their racial intermingling came too late to do much good. The Jews were a bastard race—Chamberlain uses the curious word *negative* in this connection—lamentably lacking in true religion. In sharp contrast to this sorry picture was his portrait of the Germans, who had inherited the best qualities of the Greeks and Indo-Aryans and who were the foundation stone of God's plan for the future of the world.

Among Chamberlain's most avid readers was the leader of the German nation, Kaiser Wilhelm. The American historian William Shirer says it sent him into ecstasies.[5] An invitation to visit the palace was dispatched and the two became firm friends. That there was a mystical element to the friendship is beyond question. Much of their subsequent correspondence has survived, filled with phrases like, "It was God who sent your book to the German people and you personally to me" and "Your Majesty and your subjects have been born in a holy shrine."

As the friendship deepened, Chamberlain continually fed the kaiser's visions of glory, encouraging him to take an increasingly extreme stance, particularly in matters of foreign policy. The kaiser, after all, was the living embodiment of a race destined to become masters of the world. This cause, to Chamberlain, was "holy," as he reminded Wilhelm at the outbreak of the First World War. Germany, he said, would conquer the world "by inner superiority." It appears on the face of it to be little more than the rantings of a racialist crank, but it is a curious fact that Chamberlain did not believe himself to be the author of *Foundations of the Nineteenth Century*. He felt it was written *through him* by a demon. Nor was the conclusion metaphorical. He saw the process as identical to that whereby Spiritualist mediums produce messages from the Beyond by permitting their bodies to be taken over by incorporeal entities.

Chamberlain was aware of demons for most of his life. They drove him relentlessly to study and write. Their promptings explained the butterfly approach to his student career as he hopped from music to philosophy to botany to history. In 1896, a demon assailed him while he was traveling on a train, so that he was forced to cut his journey short, shut himself up for eight days in a hotel room in Gardone, and produce a thesis on biology. Most of his major works were written in this way. He would fall into trance and work feverishly, with little attention to his own comfort or surroundings. Afterward he would read the material with a sensation of surprise, unable to recognize it as his own. *Foundations* was written like this, the result of a demonic possession that lasted nineteen months.

If this was a work of fiction and our natural disbelief in demons had been suspended, we might by now be waiting with some impatience for the hero of our story, who would surely be a mystic representative of the Powers of Light. In reality, such a figure did indeed appear in the form of the quartermaster general, Helmuth von Moltke, chief of the Imperial General Staff of the German Army.

Von Moltke was a student of medieval mysticism, with particular reference to the history of the Holy Grail. He was also a close personal friend of Rudolph Steiner, an occultist of genius, who taught that individual evolution could be hastened by means of esoteric exercises and techniques. Whether von Moltke actually practiced these mystic disciplines we do not know, for like most occultists he was more reticent about the application of his studies than about the studies themselves. But it is likely that he did; and it is known that his insights were deep enough to leave him profoundly disturbed by the influence of Chamberlain on his kaiser.

As Europe moved inexorably into war, von Moltke, in his capacity of chief of staff, supervised the complex mobilization of the German forces. He was at his desk in the Konigsplatz Headquarters when he was swept away by one of the most dramatic esoteric experiences of his career. He plunged into a spontaneous nine-minute trance, which army doctors afterward dismissed as the result of strain and exhaustion. Von Moltke interpreted the experience differently and bequeathed to future generations the description of an intriguing and impressive vision.

It seemed as if his mind was swept back through time to the ninth century, where he found himself observing incidents in the life of the medieval pontiff, Pope Nicholas I. Interwoven with this scene was a curious under-standing of the historical process and a recognition that the world of centuries past had not obeyed the same hard rules of physics as governed our planet in 1914. In the days of Pope Nicholas, it was apparent that mankind was blessed with an expanded awareness, an extended conscious experience of spiritual realms and transcendental realities.[6] But it was also apparent that such a state of consciousness would not last. In order that men should develop an analyt-ical intellect and the scientific method take its proper place in the evolution of our species, a narrowing of attention became necessary. Pope Nicholas himself foresaw this development and privately predicted a time when the people of Europe would have only an awareness of three-dimensional reality. Direct experience of the spirit worlds would become the prerogative of a very few. For the masses, the only sustenance would be *revealed* religion; but even here, the activities of the Infernal Hierarchies would go a long way toward convincing men that the physical world was the only reality. Although the time scale of this grim development was measured in centuries, it was seen ultimately as a temporary necessity. The day would come when evolution reopened the psychic centers of mankind and once again allowed direct per-ception of spirit worlds.

In the course of his vision, von Moltke perceived something even more intriguing. He became aware of the effect of reincarnation on the historical process. It seemed to him that certain personalities reappeared on Earth at certain times, often grouped together to act out parallel dramas at different historical periods. In Pope Nicholas he recognized an early incarnation of himself, while his cardinals and bishops included members of the German General Staff. Later, in waking consciousness, all this struck him as unlikely, but the concept proved too disturbing to dismiss. Years of careful analysis showed him there were indeed parallels between the two situations. For example, both the medieval popes and the German General Staff were with-drawn from the mundane world, and, more important, both were vitally con-cerned with the future of Europe.

Perhaps the most disturbing aspect of the vision was the graphic pre-diction of mankind's impending plunge into materialism. It was as if human-ity were gradually falling asleep. Spiritual origins were forgotten. The once-empirical reality of higher planes and dimensions became nebulous and was eventually denied altogether. Blind chance was evoked to explain both the historical and evolutionary processes. In the forthcoming First World War, whole nations of sleepwalkers prepared to slaughter one another. This development was, perhaps, a spiritual necessity, designed to reawaken mankind through the medium of suffering, but it was an unpalatable necessity just the same. Von Moltke emerged from his vision a very troubled man.

The experience must have had a profound effect on von Moltke's outlook. Yet despite the revelation that a long, hard war was necessary, history shows he did his utmost to shorten the duration of the conflict. But his efforts were fruitless in the face of circumstance. The German master plan failed miserably and swiftly, and the war settled into the horrific stalemate typified by Flanders Fields. The failure led to the dismissal of von Moltke and his replacement as chief of staff by General Eric von Falkenhayne. By 1916, von Moltke was dead.

His story did not, however, end with his death. His widow, Eliza, was convinced she could still communicate with him and brought through a lengthy series of messages that, some occultists maintain, still circulate in photocopies through several of Germany's many modern secret societies. The messages were in the nature of prophecies: a defeat for Germany in the 1914–18 war, the fall of the Romanovs and the establishment of a Communist regime in Russia, the rise of fascism as an international creed, and the establishment of Adolf Hitler (whom he named) as the führer of Germany. There was, too, a reference to a familiar figure in these communications. Von Moltke predicted that his occult archenemy, Houston Stewart Chamberlain, would be among the first influential figures in Germany to welcome Hitler as the new messiah. In this, as in his other predictions, the spirit of von Moltke was all too accurate. None of these predictions was made in a vacuum. They were presented as essential outcomes of an unorthodox view of history, the long-term results of processes that began centuries earlier, hastened by the multiple reincarnations of personalities who had been intimately involved in the earlier dramas. They resulted from the communications of a disembodied spirit.

Within two decades, the disembodied spirits were at their war work again.

18. THE SPIRITS AND THE FÜHRER

THE FIRST WORLD WAR, WHICH BEGAN IN 1914, ENDED FOUR YEARS later with the signing of an armistice in a disused railway carriage in the forest of Compiègne. Months later, in 1919, the position was formalized in the Treaty of Versailles which demanded from Germany its old colonial possessions, massive financial reparations, and an admission of guilt for the whole sorry affair. That same year, a thirty-year-old war veteran named Adolf Hitler joined the tiny, obscure German Workers Party. Two years later, he became its leader. By then, the party had been reorganized, expanded, and renamed. It was now the National Socialist German Workers Party or, more concisely, the Nazis. In 1923, the party welcomed a new recruit named Heinrich Himmler.

Himmler's appearance on Germany's political stage—he was already head of an embryo SS when elected to the Reichstag in 1930—shows that spirit influence was still evident in European politics during the Nazi period and throughout the Second World War. There is evidence it may not have been confined to Himmler.

By the early 1930s, clubs devoted to all manner of esoteric matters had sprung up across the whole of Germany—there were fifty-two of them in Berlin alone.[1] They attracted a wide range of influential people from various walks of life, including the military, medicine, business, finance, and the arts. Among their activities were séances that attempted to contact spirit beings. An indication of their potential influence may be drawn from the fact that the host of one such series of séances was a wealthy aristocrat who sat on the board of I. G. Farben, the massive chemical conglomerate.

There is no doubt at all about the popularity of spirit communication and other occult practices in Germany before the First World War. In the devastation of the immediate postwar period and throughout the long, inflation-ridden economic crisis that followed, interest in such matters actually increased as people sought to escape from their everyday problems and find a deeper meaning to their lives. The country swarmed with psychics and mediums—one estimate puts their number at more than twenty thousand—keen to meet the demand. An example of the breed was Hermann Steinschneider, who achieved fame in Berlin as a stage mentalist under the name of Erik Jan Hanussen.

In the early stages of his career, Hanussen made no assertions beyond an ability to fool audiences using clever stagecraft, but by the late 1920s all that had changed. Hanussen now claimed a genuine psychism that led to communication with spirit forces and a consequent ability to prophesy. On one occasion, shortly after he moved to Berlin from his native Vienna, he fell into a trance in a museum and established contact with the spirit of a drowned woman whose glove was one of the objects on display. On another occasion, he was visited by the shade of his mistress, Betty Schostak, who had just died in a hospital. Whether Hanussen's mediumship was genuine or simply a ruse to enhance his stage reputation has proven a matter of considerable controversy. His most recent biographer, Arthur J. Magida, appears convinced his psychism was nothing more than a mix of cold reading and trickery. But trickery has always been a part of traditional shamanic techniques and the scientific investigation of mediums[2] has on several occasions led to the conclusion that genuine psychics will sometimes resort to fraud when their powers fail them. Certainly Hanussen's second wife, Therese, was convinced by four intimate years of marriage that her husband really did have paranormal abilities. She witnessed his healing the sick, claimed he used clairvoyance to help the police solve crimes, and believed he saved her life by insisting she move to a different seat in a café. Just moments later, another patron attempted suicide by shooting himself. The bullet went astray and struck the place where Therese had been sitting.[3]

Despite the fact that he was Jewish, Hanussen became a firm supporter of the Nazis, both before and after their bid to take control of Germany in the early 1930s. A report prepared by the American Office of Strategic Services in 1943 claimed he not only met regularly with Hitler, but actually tutored him in the art of effective public speaking.[4] There is no evidence to suggest Hanussen attempted to influence the führer directly with spirit messages, but he certainly attempted to influence other high-ranking Nazis, notably Count Wolf-Heinrich von Helldorf, the head of Berlin's storm troopers. On February 26, 1933, he packed his home with Nazi notables for a midnight séance during which an entranced medium—the actress Maria Paudler—predicted the Reichstag fire that occurred the following day. It proved an ominous portent. Since the Reichstag fire was almost certainly a "false flag operation" set by the Nazis themselves, historians speculate that Hanussen was suspected of betraying their secret. In any case, a month after the séance, three men, almost certainly members of Helldorf's SA, took him to a woods some twenty miles outside Berlin, shot him a total of twelve times, and buried his body in a shallow grave.[5]

Hitler's own brushes with spirits were attested to by a former Nazi president of the Danzig Senate, Hermann Rauschning. In 1939, Rauschning, now no longer a Nazi, published *Gespräche mit Hitler* ("Conversations with Hitler"), which subsequently appeared in English translation as *Voice of Destruction* (US) and *Hitler Speaks* (UK). In it, he claimed numerous conversations with Hitler and had this to say about the führer:

> Hitler was abandoning himself to forces which were carrying him away—forces of dark and destructive violence. He imagined that he still had freedom of choice, but he had long been in bondage to a magic which might well have been described, not only in metaphor but in literal fact, as that of evil spirits.[6]

Rauschning went on to chronicle Hitler's expressed interest in magic and the occult, even going so far as to suggest that the führer had a degree of personal mediumship: one story had it that Hitler awoke in the night screaming, having been awakened by an apparition in the corner of his room.

Certainly Rauschning's picture of Hitler as a mediumistic personality with profound occult interests is borne out by other sources. At age eighteen in October 1907, Hitler applied to enter the Viennese Academy of the Arts and was turned down on the basis that his test drawings were unsatisfactory. But instead of returning home, he stayed in Vienna and, as his money dwindled, gradually sank to the level of a tramp. During this period he shared a room with a student named August Kubizek, who later had this to say about the youthful Adolf:

> I was struck by something strange which I had never noticed before, even when he talked to me in moments of great excitement. It was as if another being spoke out of his body and moved him as much as it did me.[7]

This is a classic description of a mediumistic personality. Hitler's occult interests were confirmed by Otto Wagener, a prominent Nazi official who became a close confidant of Hitler's from 1929 to 1933. Wagener introduced the führer to the theory of Odic force developed by Baron Karl von Reichenbach in the mid-nineteenth century. Von Reichenbach taught that everyone had a source of power (usually quite unsuspected by themselves) that radiated outward in the form of invisible rays to create a sort of auric force field around the body. Hitler became infatuated with the idea and quickly adopted it for his own:

> Wagener, it's as though scales fall from one's eyes when one hears this theory for the first time. I must read the writings of this Reichenbach.[8]

The British author Trevor Ravenscroft claimed as his source Dr. Walter Johannes Stein, a Viennese scientist and follower of Rudolf Steiner. According to Stein, as reported by Ravenscroft, Hitler attained higher states of consciousness through the use of drugs and studied medieval occultism and ritual magic.[9] If this was true, it is worth noting that any working of medieval magic would almost certainly have involved the evocation of spirits, since the grimoires of the time dealt with little else. Stein was also alleged to have said that Hitler was initiated into a secret form of Western occultism based on Arthurian legends.

Ravenscroft claimed that Dr. Stein knew Hitler intimately in Vienna and often discussed esoteric matters with him, but critics like the investigative journalist Eric Wynants have since cast doubts on the source, suggesting that Ravenscroft never met Stein in the flesh but only communicated with him through a medium after his death—tantamount to dismissing any information obtained as fantasy.[10] But wherever the material originated, the fact remains that this pointer toward Hitler's early magical training is consistent with the reality of esoteric practice. Whole generations of Western occultists, up to the present day, have trained using secret techniques hidden in the Grail Cycle.[11]

For Hitler to have discovered these techniques without help would have been remarkable indeed. But he may have been guided by an occultist of greater experience. According to Ravenscroft, his esoteric mentor at the time was an unsavory, hunchbacked bookseller named Ernst Pretzsche, who claimed to have assisted various students along the troubled road to occult knowledge. At one point on Hitler's personal journey, Pretzsche seems to have suggested a dangerous shortcut—the peyote cactus. Peyote is an hallucinogenic plant containing some twenty-eight alkaloids, the principal of which is mescaline. Today, peyote and mescaline tend to be seen as part of modern society's drug problem. This view, while largely accurate, is nevertheless unfortunate. An ancient tradition suggests some psychedelics can, if properly used, open valid windows onto other dimensions of reality. Proper use involves physical and psychological preparation, plus the ingestion of the drug in controlled—usually ritualistic—circumstances. The tradition was well known to the Indians of Mexico, where Ernst Pretzsche spent a good deal of his life. Peyote was venerated as the manifestation of a god and used as a practical aspect of religion.

When Hitler came to take peyote, Ravenscroft claimed, his mind had been prepared by graded meditations and imaginal exercises directed by Pretzsche. As a result, it might be a mistake to dismiss his experience as a recreational drug trip. It is likely that he believed the cactus rendered him able to sense something beneath the surface of reality and divine his personal relationship with the universe. Details of Hitler's peyote experience are not known except for a few hints made to Dr. Stein. From them Ravenscroft pieced together a dramatic reconstruction and concluded that Hitler discovered himself to be "the chalice for the Spirit of the Anti-Christ."

Such overblown phraseology positively commands disbelief, yet more recent developments have finally brought absolute confirmation of Adolf Hitler's interest in the occult.

In the spring of 2001, France's deputy-secretary general of the Académie Diplomatique International, Timothy W. Ryback, had his first sight of the remnants of Hitler's personal library. Some twelve hundred volumes had been seized by American troops from the führer's private residences in Munich, Berlin, and Obersalzberg immediately after the war and transported across the Atlantic to the safekeeping of the Rare Book Division of the Library of Congress . . . where they languished unnoticed and largely unexamined for more than half a century. Ryback discovered that less than half the works stored in Washington's Thomas Jefferson Building had even been cataloged and of those only two hundred were searchable online. Further investigation unearthed another eighty Hitler books stored in Brown University in Providence, Rhode Island, which had received them as a donation toward the end of the 1970s. Among these were a number of occult works acquired by Hitler in Munich during the 1920s.[12]

Ryback made a thorough examination of the entire collection. Among other interesting works he discovered *Foundations of the Nineteenth Century* by Houston Stewart Chamberlain, the same demonically inspired author whose ideas profoundly influenced the kaiser. But perhaps more significant, he also found that certain of the volumes had been annotated by Hitler himself, a clear indication of his specific sixty-six interests. The most heavily annotated, with a total of sixty-six marginal markings, was a curious work by a Dr. Ernst Schertel, signed and dedicated to Hitler by its author. The name of the work that so fascinated Hitler was *Magische: Geschichte/Theorie/ Praxis*, or, in translation, *Magic: History/Theory/Practice*. In it, Dr. Schertel wrote: "Only by doing magic, through practice and gaining experience, will we recognize divinity and learn to be one with her." And earlier on the final page of his book: "The first and only important thing is communion with the demon."[13]

19. A MUSEUM OF
SPIRIT CONTACT

T HE MORE CLOSELY WE EXAMINE THE PHENOMENON OF SPIRIT INFLU-
ence, the more dramatic—and at times almost unbelievable—the
picture becomes. In what we like to term more credulous ages,
occultism was everywhere and nowhere more apparent than in the halls
of the mighty. The examples already cited scarcely skim the surface. A
hypothetical Museum of Spirit Contact might also contain the case of the
seventeenth-century alchemist and wizard, Dr. Lamb. On one occasion, contemporary documents record, Lamb entertained Sir Miles Sands and a Mr.
Barbor by making a tree appear in his rooms, then magically conjuring three
little spirits with axes to cut it down. This sounds like a trick or hypnotism
but Mr. Barbor—against instructions—pocketed a chip of wood from the
tree. That night he and his wife were plagued by poltergeist manifestations
until he threw the chip away, at which point the house became quiet.

Dr. Lamb was an influential occultist. He was personal physician to
the powerful Duke of Buckingham and a close friend of the king. In 1640,
his sinister reputation provoked a riot and, having pursued him across London
to St. Paul's Cross, the mob stoned him to death. When news of the incident
reached King Charles I, he rode out personally to help but arrived too late.
He was, however, so incensed that he fined the city £600 for failing to punish
the ringleaders.

Like his predecessor, Charles II came under esoteric influence. His
chaplain was Joseph Glanvill, an Oxford scholar and occultist whose interest
in the paranormal was so profound that he is sometimes called the father of
psychical research. He took part in numerous séances at Ragley Castle, the
home of Lady Anne Conway and, one must assume, carried messages from
the Otherworld back to the king.

Charles II of England, one of many monarchs who fell under spirit influence

Two centuries earlier, in 1441, a witchcraft trial unearthed further evidence of occultism in high places. Among the accused were the Duchess of Gloucester and Roger Bolingbroke, a world-famous scholar of his day. Bolingbroke was an alchemist and astronomer (which almost certainly means he was an astrologer as well). He enjoyed considerable personal influence with the Duke of Gloucester and his reputation assured a more diffuse influence over a far wider field. Although the judicial procedures of witchcraft trials have made the evidence they present notoriously unreliable, Bolingbroke does seem to have been a practicing magician, for his ritual implements were discovered. The courts did not take kindly to his activities, which, it was claimed, were designed to murder the king at a distance. Bolingbroke was hanged, beheaded, and quartered. The Duchess, charged with necromancy, witchcraft or sorcery, heresy, and treason, got off comparatively lightly. After public penance in London, she was jailed for life.

Nor, as we have seen, was occult influence confined to England. Close at hand, Ireland's first witch was a member of the aristocracy. Lady Alice Kyteler was charged on a variety of counts in 1324. She escaped the scandal by sailing for England, but her maid, Petronilla de Meath, was flogged, then burned alive. Further afield, the king of Sweden hired four sorcerers in 1563 to march with his army against the Danes. Their job was to raise storms that would confuse the enemy.

Our hypothetical museum would certainly feature an amazing magical scandal that erupted in France in 1398, when the Duke of Orleans was accused of sealing a pact with the Devil in order to murder the king. The monarch, who was in any case three-quarters mad, attempted to fight fire with fire and called in witches to cure his illness. When their arts failed, two magicians, who happened also to be Augustinian monks, were required to try their skill. They too failed and were subsequently beheaded.

The museum would also include the lives of the early popes, for several were enthusiastic magical practitioners. Among them was Benedict Caetini who was elevated to the papacy in 1294. Caetani's first act was to intern his predecessor, the elderly Pope Celestine V, in the Castle of Fumone. The old man died soon after and there was talk Caetini had him murdered. As Pope Boniface VIII, Caetini soon found his enemies multiplying. Large numbers of Franciscans turned against him. The poet Iacopone da Todi opposed him (and was jailed for his pains). When he issued a bull forbidding the taxation of clergy, he found himself in bad odor with the kings of England and France. Philip IV of France was particularly active in his opposition. He struck to the heart of papal revenues by banning the export of money from France and expelling foreign merchants. The Colonnas, an influential Roman family that included two cardinals, added to his problems with an insurrection that culminated in the armed robbery of papal treasures. Boniface went to war, but it took a year of bitter conflict to force the Colonnas into submission. Although not excommunicated, their possessions were seized and the pope bluntly refused to reinstate the cardinals to their former offices. The Colonnas promptly rebelled again and, unable to withstand Boniface militarily, fled Italy for France where they continued to conspire with the disaffected king.

In 1301, Philip imprisoned the French bishop, Bernard Saisset of Pamiers, to the fury of Boniface who issued another bull (delightfully entitled "Listen Son") that rebuked the king and demanded the bishop's release. Philip remained defiant. A secret meeting was held at the Louvre in Paris, during which Philip's councillor, Guillaume de Nogaret, demanded Boniface be denounced by a general council of the Church, then went off to Italy to try to stir up a rebellion. Although the rebellion never happened, Nogaret nonetheless became embroiled in an operation to undermine the pope. When he discovered that Boniface was about to issue a bull announcing Philip's excommunication, he decided on a kidnap attempt. He enlisted the help of some cardinals, one of the Colonnas—Sciarra—and several civic dignitaries of Anagni, the city where Boniface was spending the summer. None of them liked the pope very much and the kidnapping went off like clockwork. Unfortunately for Nogaret, however, the Anagni burghers had second thoughts and mounted a successful rescue mission just two days later. But Boniface had been badly beaten and abused by Sciarra Colonna (who wanted to kill him), and died on October 11, 1303, shortly after his return to Rome.

Incredibly, death failed to put an end to his problems. In 1310, seven years after Boniface was laid to rest, Philip convened a trial at Avignon. The defendant was the dead pope who now faced charges of murder, sodomy, and, most serious of all, consorting with devils. Witness after witness paraded into the courtroom to testify to these crimes. Even during his lifetime there had been rumors of the pope's sorcery. He was widely believed to have installed a demon as his personal adviser and consulted it on both spiritual and political questions. Now it was claimed that he had been in contact with not just one demon, but three. One had been given to him by an unnamed woman, another by a Hungarian, and the third by his namesake Boniface of Vincenza. Witnesses claimed the pope named this third demon "Boniface" because it amused him to think that Boniface had been given to Boniface by Boniface. Other accusers told how Boniface carried around a spirit in a finger ring.

All this, of course, sounds utterly preposterous to modern ears—the sort of medieval nonsense, rooted in naïveté and superstition, that fueled the Inquisition and triggered Europe's witch hunts. Nor is there any doubt that the trial was a politically inspired sham. King Philip, whose financial problems later persuaded him to move against the Knights Templar, was trying to put pressure on the current pope, Clement V, who was resident at Avignon. He wanted Clement's support for a lunatic scheme that would have placed him (Philip) at the head of a vast Christian empire centered on Jerusalem. When Clement finally gave in after a year, the trial was promptly abandoned. Most modern historians leave it at that. They accept that the charges against Boniface were fabricated and fantastic. While murder might be a possibility and Boniface would not be the first (nor, indeed, the last) pope to be suspected of sodomy, no one now takes the demonic accusations seriously. Yet there are elements in the evidence that might lead one to wonder if we should not give just a little more credence to his accusers. These elements concern the pope's alleged consultation with a spirit. When he needed its advice, witnesses claimed he would lock himself in his room. Soon there would emerge hissing sounds, followed by noises like the stampeding of cattle. Those waiting outside would feel the ground shake violently beneath their feet.

Incredible though it seems, early settlers in North America reported essentially the same phenomena when they witnessed the Shaking Tent Ceremony of Canada's Algonquin Indians. Sober anthropological studies later confirmed what had initially appeared to be wildly exaggerated or fictitious claims. When an Algonquin medicine man wished to consult with his spirits, he was first tied up securely by members of his tribe, then wrapped in a cloak, and placed, apparently helpless, in a large, barrel-shaped tent reserved for ceremonial purposes. The tent was not a flimsy structure. It was built around uprights as thick as tree trunks, lashed together to form a solid frame. Yet only minutes after the medicine man was placed inside, the tent would begin to tremble. The first signs of movement were usually accompanied by hissing noises, followed by a low, ominous rumbling like the stampeding of buffalo. After this, the tent would begin to shake with increasing violence until the very ground around it started to tremble. The spirit would then take possession of the medicine man inside and answer questions put to it by the tribe. A medieval pope seems to have been caught up in the same type of shamanic spirit experience. He was not the only one.

By the time Maffeo Barberini became pope in 1623, he had proved as astute at making friends as his predecessor Boniface was at making enemies. The new pope, Urban—the eighth to take that name—came from an aristocratic Florentine family and had followed a distinguished church career. He had learned the skills of diplomacy and knew how to make people like him. As pope, he supported France, engaged in building programs, strengthened the papacy's military capabilities, and acquired the Duchy of Urbino. Before long, the papal states came to dominate central Italy. He was a patron of the arts who was to succeed quite brilliantly in everything he attempted, until he made the mistake of declaring war on the Duke of Parma in 1642. But long before that, Urban was consorting with spirits

The interest arose out of a curious set of circumstances. In 1626 some-

*The 17th Century Pope Urban VIII, who employed a magician
to call up spirits whose advice he sought*

one leaked (or possibly forged) an important document—the pope's horoscope. Suspicion must fall on the Spanish, for Spain thoroughly disapproved of the pontiff's support for France. But whoever was responsible, the leak was potentially damaging. The horoscope predicted Urban would die sometime early in 1628. Spanish cardinals began, ostentatiously, to make preparations to elect a successor. As the predicted date of death approached, Urban appears to have become increasingly uneasy. With death hanging over him, he hired himself a magician.

The magician's name was Tommaso Campanella. He was born in Naples (then a kingdom) and became a Dominican monk at the age of fourteen. Seven years later he was imprisoned for heresy. It was just the beginning of a colorful career. He was no sooner released from prison than he found himself back again, having only just had time to make the acquaintance of Galileo, the great astronomer. From the comfort of his cell in Padua, he set about writing books so infuriating to Pope Clement VIII that Campanella was transferred to the prisons of the Holy Inquisition in Rome. It was the equivalent of a death sentence, but he hurriedly penned another book that argued that Clement should be made leader of the entire world and the pope released him in 1595. He then wandered the country stirring up trouble and predicting massive social changes for the year 1600. The doctrine attracted followers, many of them Dominicans like himself, but the authorities moved with ruthless efficiency so that by 1599 Campanella was back in jail, this time under torture. He escaped by pretending he was mad.

Campanella was to spend most of his remaining life in and out of jail. But his conviction that popes would make excellent world leaders attracted the interest of Urban, who had now acceded to the papal throne. By then, Campanella's association with astrologers and mystics had given him a reputation as something of a magician. Soon the rumors began to spread. The pope and the disreputable heretic of a Dominican were meeting secretly. But for what? Some far-fetched political plot? A homosexual liaison? The speculation grew wilder and wilder, but none of it matched what was actually happening. Urban and Campanella were engaged in midnight rites of evocation. They were calling up spirits.

The spirits apparently took the impending astrological threat to the pope quite seriously for they recommended the performance of a planetary ritual—an act of ceremonial magic designed to influence a forthcoming eclipse of the moon and substitute favorable conjunctions for those that had appeared in Urban's horoscope. Urban himself doubtless believed the operation was a success for he lived long beyond the predicted year and died peacefully in Rome in the summer of 1644. Like Boniface's "spirit-in-a-ring," the idea of using "planetary magic" to influence a horoscope seems quaint today. But this is hardly the point. A seventeenth-century pope was not just a spiritual leader. He was a man of immense political power—in today's terms, a cross between an American president and an Iranian ayatollah. His actions influenced the fates of nations. It is astonishing to think that such a man would base what he saw to be a life-and-death decision on spirit advice.

Astonishing or not, many other popes followed his example. One, Honorius III, was actually reputed to have written a grimoire, a magical textbook, that taught how to evoke evil spirits. The Borgia dynasty in particular showed signs of occult interest, closely related to their skills with poisons. Poisoning and the darker reaches of esoteric practice often went hand in hand, as shown by the Chambre Ardente affair in the reign of Louis XIV, which deserves an honored place in the museum. This began as an investigation into the wide-spread use of poison among the French nobility. In 1673, two Notre Dame priests told the police that they had learned through the confessional how large numbers of their flock were finding murder an efficient escape route from matrimonial difficulties. True to the ethics of the confessional, no names were mentioned, but four years later, Nicholas de la Reynie, then the Parisian police commissioner, discovered an international poison ring. This organization, which had structural parallels with modern dope rings, was headed by the aristocratic François Calaup de Chasteuil, who ran it along with a lawyer, a banker, and several of his friends among the nobility. Poisons were smuggled in from England, Portugal, and Italy, then distributed across France through a network of middlemen.

When the police swooped, vast stores of poison were uncovered. But de Chasteuil escaped. Rigorous questioning of his colleagues failed to bring out the full extent of their organization. Then, in 1679, a policewoman acting incognito discovered that a fortune-teller called Marie Bosse was not only marketing poison but that all her clients were members of the aristocracy. Investigations extending over several months soon showed that literally hundreds of courtiers had been making use of poisons. An appalled King Louis XIV agreed to set up a star chamber (the Chambre Ardente) to look into the allegations. One of its first witnesses was another psychic, Catherine Deshayes, Widow Montvoison, who has gone down in history as "La Voisin."

The cross-examination of La Voisin extended the net further and unearthed the information that abortion had been a major preoccupation of those involved —one witness claimed La Voisin had terminated twenty-five hundred unwanted pregnancies. By May 1678, the Chambre Ardente had condemned Marie Bosse and another fortune-teller, La Dame Vigoreux, to death by burning. Marie Bosse's son, François, was hanged. Judgment was reserved in the case of La Voisin and yet another professional psychic, La Lepere. Inquiries continued and more testimony was heard. As the months went by, it became increasingly obvious that the Royal Court had been thoroughly infiltrated by poison dealers, among them several ladies-in-waiting to the king's various mistresses. On January 23, 1680, the Chambre Ardente moved vigorously to arrest no fewer than eight aristocrats, including the king's favorite, Madame de Polignac. But poison was not the whole story. A witness named Lesage extended the inquiry to more esoteric realms when he accused three priests of conducting the notorious Black Mass—a rite designed to make contact

A highly imaginative depiction of the notorious Black Mass,
a ceremony designed to make contact with demonic spirits

with the Devil—over the bodies of naked girls. Then in February 1680, the
Abbe Mariette was arrested, accused of making wax figurines and sacrificing
pigeons. Yet another psychic was involved, a fortune-teller name La Filastre.
She told of a rite in which she sacrificed a child, then went on to admit participation in a Black Mass. She implicated two further priests, Abbe Cotton
and Abbe Deshayes. Her own newborn baby was sacrificed during a magical
ceremony and Mass said over the placenta.

The evidence grew more and more weird as more and more people
were arrested. The judges heard how Madame de Lusignan masturbated in
the woods at Fontainbleau with the aid of an Easter candle—all part of a
magical operation with a naked priest. Three amatory masses were described,
during one of which Father Tournet engaged in public intercourse with a girl
on the altar. Father Davot was accused of ceremonially kissing a naked
woman's genitals during the course of a Mass he was celebrating. Abbe Guibourg called on the demons of lust, Astaroth and Asmodeus, at the elevation
of the host. Sometimes these ceremonies were designed only to slaughter
babies in a magical manner so that their bodies might be used in various

esoteric potions and powders. But others, it appears, had been commissioned by aristocratic ladies in order to influence the king. A peculiarly detailed description of one of them has come down to us. The ceremony, conducted by the Abbe Guibourg, was designed to make a love charm to be used on the king by Mademoiselle des Oeillets, one of his mistresses.

Mademoiselle des Oeillets attended the rite in company with an occultist who was apparently instructing the abbe what to do. In the operation, it was necessary to collect and intermingle the sexual fluids of a man and a woman. While Mademoiselle des Oeillets seemed willing enough to contribute, she was having her period at the time and thus contributed a measure of menstrual blood to the chalice. Guibourg masturbated her friend and directed his semen into the cup. A powder made from bats' blood was then added and the mixture thickened with flour. Abbe Guibourg recited a conjuration to Astaroth, then bottled the mixture and gave it to Mademoiselle des Oeillets to take away. Presumably she then fed it to the unsuspecting Louis.

A nauseated king suspended the Chambre Ardent in August 1680. Its findings were becoming altogether too embarrassing. Secret investigations continued for a while, notably into the activities of the king's former mistress, Madame de Montespan, who, it transpired, was the central figure in the whole affair. Years afterward, in 1709, the Chambre records were burned on Louis XIV's orders. But some copies escaped the flames, leaving us today with yet more evidence of the part played by spirits in history.

A special section of the Museum of Spirit Contact would, of course, be devoted to exhibits from the modern era. During the summer of 1904, for example, an Altai Turk named Chot Chelpan heard the voice of a white-robed spirit riding a white horse. The spirit spoke an unfamiliar language, but other spirits translated. The spirit had promised a time of change was approaching and his orders to the Altai people would shortly be communicated to Chelpan's daughter. The girl soon confirmed that she had heard spirit voices and Chelpan began to preach a new religio-political creed among his people. One of its tenets was that all available money be spent on guns and ammunition to be used in the overthrow of Siberia's Russian overlords. The Russians eventually arrested Chelpan, but the move came too late: by that time, he had attracted literally thousands of followers who simply melted into the fastnesses of Mongolia and conducted guerrilla warfare against the authorities up to the Russian Revolution.

The Russian Revolution failed, for a time, to dampen enthusiasm for the rich tradition of occult thought and spiritist practice that had characterized the country for centuries, but by the second decade of Communist rule, ruthless prohibition and political repression made any overt expression of this tradition impossible. The Soviet Union presented, and continued to present, an atheistic-materialist face to the world that had little room for the supernatural. But despite official denials of spirit realities, there are clear indications that occult influence was not wiped out but merely driven underground. For every theosophist and anthroposophist who left the country following the ban on their beliefs, many others remained at home, simply electing to hide their beliefs and maintaining contact with those who left. Cultural science professor, Birgit Menzel reveals[1] that according to KGB records, the secret order of the Rosicrucian Templars in Moscow and St. Petersburg, with its spirit-based doctrines, remained active as late as 1937. Nor was it the only occult order to brave official Soviet wrath. Their influence proved so troublesome that the Kremlin established a host of "special agents for occult matters" in an attempt to root them out. The attempt was unsuccessful. By the 1970s there was an open revival of Qabalistic and various other spirit-inspired occult doctrines among Soviet intellectuals, writers, artists, poets, and musicians. Whether this renaissance reached into the political establishment and influenced the Cold War remains impossible to say.

A small but important exhibit of the museum would be the dairies of W. L. Mackenzie King, published in 1980 and showing that for decades he had been listening to spirit voices, including those purporting to be his dead mother and Franklin D. Roosevelt. King was prime minister of Canada between 1921 and 1930 and between 1935 and 1948. During the latter term, the dead Roosevelt told King he was wiser than Britain's wartime prime minister, Winston Churchill, and that Churchill should listen to King's advice. Churchill was infuriated when King, in his newly confirmed wisdom, sent him the text of the message. Also on display would be the newspapers that reported that the Italian president of the European Commission, Romano Prodi, used a Ouija board in 1978 to make contact with a fellow politician who had died a year previously.[2]

The newest exhibit would display a fascinating potpourri of media reports indicating that in the United States, President Obama felt compelled to apologize personally to Mrs. Nancy Regan, widow of the late president Ronald Regan, for claiming she had been involved in séances. Media reports also asserted Obama's secretary of state, Hillary Clinton, had been involved (during her husband's presidency) in channeling the spirit of Eleanor Roosevelt. There seemed to be no truth at all in the former allegation: Mrs. Regan's interest in astrology and psychism had apparently tempted the president into making an unwise joke. But the claims about Mrs. Clinton had a far less clear-cut provenance. The Clinton office was swift to issue an official denial of the media reports, claiming that Mrs. Clinton had merely been engaged in an "intellectual exercise" of the visual imagination. But it transpired that her guide in this exercise was Jean Houston, one of the most respected spiritual practitioners at work in America today. Houston holds doctorates in both psychology and religion and is deeply involved in the Human Potential Movement. In 1984 she began to teach seminars modeled on the ancient Mystery Schools, which some authorities believe taught techniques of spirit contact. The exercises developed by Dr. Houston have somewhat similar aims, although they involve neither narcotics, sleeping dreams, nor trance, but rather, as Mrs. Clinton rightly claimed, the use of the visual imagination. However, anyone well versed in the techniques of occultism might hesitate to dismiss such use of the imagination as merely an "intellectual exercise." There are modern Mystery Schools that hold that controlled use of the imagination is a valid method of contacting spirits.[3]

On display too would be an online jihad manual reportedly authored by Samir Khan, a US citizen killed in a drone strike in Yemen in 2011 and published under the auspices of al-Qaeda.[4] Alongside predictable advice on living outdoors and maintaining secrecy, the writer devotes an entire segment to a discussion of spirits known in the Arab world as *jinn* (sometimes *djinn*).

> Before I came to jihad, I knew the importance of *adhkar* [a remembrance of
> Allah through certain sayings and supplications] but not anything in relation
> to experience. On the first day I met with the mujahidin, before sunset ar-
> rived, a mujahid told me to make *adhkar*; he went on to explain that the
> Apostate Government of Saudi Arabia has individuals that work alongside
> evil jinns that spy on the mujahidin and give away their position. I was
> shocked and couldn't believe it. Later, other mujahidin confirmed the same
> thing to me, including some *shuyookh*, who would say that the same thing
> happens with the Apostates of Yemen. They will use *sihr* (magic) in order
> to fight the mujahidin. However, by Allah's grace, there are many good jinns
> that protect the mujahidin and defend us. This is the world of the unseen
> and Allah knows best. Therefore, it is imperative that you start memorizing

the *adhkar* for the morning and evening and start practicing it on a daily basis, not giving yourself an excuse to miss a single day. You need to do this in order to protect yourself from *shaytan* and the evil jinns that work for the *shayatin* among men.[5]

This ready, indeed casual, acceptance of spirits in the present day should surprise no one. Any careful reading of history presents a panorama of men and women in positions of power who have been influenced by, or actively practiced, the occult arts, almost always including communication with spirits. Are we to suppose that they kept their esoteric interests compartmentalized? Or is it more likely that voices from the Beyond guided their political decisions and hence the fate of nations?

On the face of it, the fundamental question posed in the Introduction—to what extent has contact with a "spirit world" influenced the course of human history?—has been answered. It is now clear that, whatever spirits may be, their influence has certainly been far-reaching. Yet so far we have concentrated exclusively on the social, political, and religious consequences of spirit contact. To understand the implications fully, it will be necessary to examine the personal impact of such communications.

PART FOUR

CONTACT—THEORETICAL AND PERSONAL

W HO ARE THE WHISPERERS? WHERE DO THEY COME from? What do they want? Where are they leading us? In the light of history, these are clearly important questions, yet they are almost never asked, let alone answered. When it comes to the nature of spirits, the world may be divided into two contrasting camps: the True Believers, who accept spirits as independent entities, and the Devout Skeptics, who prefer to claim spirits simply do not exist.

Yet it is clear that spirits *do* exist, at least as a recurring experiential phenomenon. Thus the fundamental question becomes: *what is their actual nature?* In this section we concentrate initially on the experience of contact as a foundation for evaluating various theories in a search for the answer that leads to a wholly unexpected and far-reaching conclusion.

20. CLOSE ENCOUNTERS OF THE SPIRIT KIND

I N THE SUMMER OF 1912, AN AMERICAN HOUSEWIFE NAMED EMILY G. Hutchings suggested to her neighbor, Pearl Curran, that it might be fun to try their hand at working a Ouija board. Today the name Ouija is a registered trademark of the game publishers Parker Brothers, but the board itself is a far cry from Monopoly or Risk. In its classical design, it features the letters of the alphabet, the numbers 0 to 9, and the words *Yes* and *No*. It is the first of these words that gives the board its name: Ouija is a combination of the French *oui* and the German *ja*, both meaning "yes." With the board comes a heart-shaped pointer set on universal rollers. If you rest your hand lightly on this pointer, the theory is that it will move of its own accord. When it does, it will sometimes spell out messages by moving to the relevant letters. In other words, a Ouija board is a device designed to contact spirits.

Neither Emily nor Pearl had a Ouija of their own, but they managed to borrow one from a friend. A little to their surprise, it worked and Emily received what purported to be a message from a dead relative. Encouraged by the communication, she bought a board of her own and she and Pearl embarked on a series of fairly lighthearted séances.

Although results were less than spectacular at first, the two friends persevered and after a time began to receive messages from Emily's mother and Pearl's father, both dead. Their interest in the board did not meet with the approval of their husbands. Mr. Hutchings, an agnostic, teased them both unmercifully. Pearl's husband was a committed Christian and wholly disagreed with what he saw as necromancy. Nonetheless the women continued to use the board and about a year after the experiments began, Pearl received a message that was to prove a major turning point in her life. It came from a spirit who introduced herself as Patience Worth.

Patience claimed to have been a poor country girl, born in Dorset, England, in 1649. In later life she emigrated to America where she was killed in an Indian raid in 1694. Although virtually uneducated, she had ambitions to become a writer and, as it turned out, more than enough talent to achieve them. The spirit of Patience began the painstaking process of dictating a vast literary output to Pearl Curran, letter by letter via the board. Within five years, the total volume of the communication had reached an astonishing four million words and included poems, short stories, plays, and novels. By the time she had finished, her body of work was sufficient to fill twenty-nine bound volumes—the equivalent of a major encyclopaedia.

Nor was the material mediocre. A three-hundred-thousand-word novel on the early life of Christ became a best seller and attracted a review in the *New York Times* as "a wonderful, beautiful and noble book." Another, set in seventeenth-century England, was described by the *Los Angeles Times* as a "masterpiece." Several of her poems were accepted by prestigious anthologies and one of them won a national poetry contest. This was all the more astonishing when set against the fact that Pearl Curran herself had no writing skills, little interest in literature, and only a minimal eight-year education.

Although the Patience Worth contacts were clearly of a far higher literary standard than most séance-room messages, they remain in a category typical of nineteenth- and early twentieth-century Spiritualism. While Pearl Curran never believed herself to be a medium and had nothing to do with the Spiritualist movement, the communicating entity claimed to be a spirit of the dead. Since the Fox Sisters produced their first raps in New Hampshire, virtually all attempts at spirit communication were aimed at establishing contact with dead relatives or individuals like Patience who, while not related, at least claimed to have once been ordinary living human beings. But in more recent years, that pattern has begun to change.

There were hints of an approaching change even in Victorian times. When Madame Helena Petrovna Blavatsky founded the Theosophical Society in 1875, she claimed her authority ultimately derived from "Secret Masters," highly evolved individuals who communicated to her a body of esoteric wisdom. These masters were magical and spiritual adepts who watched over the progress of humanity as a whole and, occasionally, tinkered with the mechanism of evolution by occult means. These claims were taken seriously by some of the finest minds of her day. Even a highly unfavorable report on her psychical abilities by the Society for Psychical Research in 1885 did little to stem the interest in Blavatsky's doctrines—an interest that continues, embodied in a flourishing Theosophical Society, to this day.

Blavatsky was a Russian who turned to spiritualism after a narrow escape from drowning. She claimed psychic powers and demonstrated mediumistic abilities. Despite this, her Secret Masters were not spirits in the conventional sense of the term. Although they occasionally communicated telepathically, they were also capable of sending her letters from India, sometimes by ordinary post, sometimes by *apport*.[1] While Blavatsky did not believe the Secret Masters were discarnate, other occultists were not so sure. The Hermetic Students of the Golden Dawn was a Victorian occult order traditionally held to have been founded on the basis of a charter issued by a German adept. But its early leaders—notably the colorful S. L. MacGregor Mathers—believed themselves guided by Secret Chiefs who were wholly equivalent to Blavatsky's Secret Masters except that they existed in another, spiritual reality and only rarely took on material form.

The Golden Dawn was the first example in recent historical times of what is called a "contacted" Mystery School—an esoteric teaching or training organization ultimately directed by a spirit entity or entities. It was certainly not the last: a number of occult organizations at work today claim the same provenance. But serious occult work is, almost by definition, a minority interest and it was not really until the 1930s that the doctrines of humanity's secret guardians began to disseminate more widely. One of the better-known vehicles for this dissemination was the medium Grace Cooke. Grace was the ninth child of a large Victorian family who lost her mother at the age of seven. Although the family was Nonconformist, Grace's father attended a séance after his wife's death where the medium, Mrs. Annie Boddington, brought through such a convincing message from Grace's mother that he converted forthwith to Spiritualism. Grace and the remainder of the family followed suit. Even as a girl, Grace began to demonstrate psychic and mediumistic gifts—she gave her first spirit reading to a stranger at the age of thirteen—and through what appears to have been a lonely childhood was visited by a comforting presence she called simply the "old man."

It is an article of Spiritualist faith that every medium is accompanied by a "guide," a sort of psychic bodyguard who acts as a gatekeeper, vetting, organizing, and sifting those of the dead who clamor to communicate with the living. Such guides are usually seen as powerful and evolved entities. Grace Cooke's husband Ivan remarked[2] that they require "that gentle wisdom which comes by living close to God." When Grace began her own career as a public medium in her late teens, it became clear that the "old man" who had been visiting her was in fact a visionary manifestation of her guide, an entity named White Eagle.

From this relatively modest beginning as a psychic gatekeeper, White Eagle evolved over a period of years into something much more like one of Blavatsky's Secret Masters. He claimed to be in contact with, or possibly even a member of, a Brotherhood of Adepts resident in the Himalayas and began to use Grace Cooke as the vehicle for a body of teaching designed to assist the welfare of humanity. By the 1930s, the focus of Grace Cooke's life had shifted. She concentrated less and less on the Spiritualist preoccupation with postmortem survival and more and more on the spiritual teachings that originated from White Eagle. In 1936, she and her husband Ivan established the White Eagle Lodge, described as an "undenominational Christian church founded to give practical expression to the White Eagle teaching."

The church was later followed by the White Eagle Publishing Trust, designed primarily to commit the words of White Eagle to print. Through these twin vehicles, the esoteric doctrines of the "Brotherhood of Adepts" today reach out to hundreds of thousands, if not millions, of people worldwide. It is probably fair to say that many, perhaps even most, of these people consider White Eagle to be a disembodied spirit, but according to Ivan Cooke:

> White Eagle's contact with his medium is always by a process of projection. He lives . . . in the mountains of the East and he can project either himself or his influence half across the world to her by functioning, like other initiates, in the ethereal body. So while he lives in a physical body . . . he is able . . . to function in the ethereal world which pervades this physical globe.[3]

Grace Cooke is now dead, but the communications from White Eagle continue through the mediumship of her immediate family. Whether White Eagle himself still inhabits a body in the Himalayas is not altogether clear. What is clear is that this form of "spirit message" is now being disseminated to more people than at any other time since the days of the *Iliad*. And the phenomenon continues to grow.

In the 1960s, a young American author named Jane Roberts decided that with the emergence of flower power and renewed interest in things spiritual, there might be a market for a book on the development of ESP. In order to research the work, she bought a Ouija board, and in December 1963 she embarked on a series of experiments with the help of her artist husband, Robert F. Butts Jr.

Their initial contact was with the spirit of an English teacher named Frank Withers, who had lived with his wife Ursula in Elmira, New York, and died in 1940. On the face of it, this appeared to be a straightforward post-mortem communication of the Spiritualist type, but in the next Ouija session, Withers expanded the picture by revealing that the American schoolteacher was only one of his incarnations. In a much earlier life as a soldier in sixth-century Turkey, he had known both Jane and her husband. The three of them had also been friends during incarnations in Denmark.

This interesting development took a further step forward with the third Ouija session. Frank Withers told them he would prefer to be known as "Seth" which was more appropriate to the totality of his being than the name he happened to have been given in his last earthly incarnation. At the same time, he suggested new names for both Jane and her husband. These names—"Ruburt" for Jane and "Joseph" for Robert—were, he claimed, more closely associated with their spiritual essence than the ones they used in their mundane existence. This renaming is not at all unusual in occult circles where there is a wide-spread belief that the individual should seek out a name that more fully expresses his or her innermost essence. It is less common in the wider context, although some religious groupings have it as part of their conventions.

Seth, it quickly transpired, was much more than a teacher of English. If anything, he was a Teacher (with a firmly placed capital "T") in the tradition of White Eagle and Madame Blavatsky's Secret Masters. The Seth doctrines are generally founded on the concept that human beings come into physical incarnation in order to learn and evolve, but that there are even greater opportunities for personal development in other higher levels of existence. Emphasis is laid on ethics and karma.

Jane and her husband embarked on regular Ouija sessions. As they did, a curious thing happened. Jane discovered that instead of having to wait for answers to be spelled out letter by letter, they had begun to formulate in her mind almost as soon as the question was asked. Since she was certain she was not generating the answers herself, it occurred to her that they were being implanted telepathically by Seth. The idea panicked her. She had never thought of herself as any sort of medium and was not at all sure she wanted to become one. Robert reassured her. He felt she should go along with what was happening. Eventually Jane relaxed. From using the Ouija it was a short, but important, step to automatic writing—a much more efficient and satisfying method than Ouija. Eventually she agreed to hold séances and before long direct voice channeling was taking place.

Direct voice mediumship is one of the more spectacular esoteric pursuits, harking back to the days of the great prophets and sibyls. The medium allows a benign possession by the spirit entity, who then uses her vocal cords to converse directly with sitters or to dictate, and sometimes to record, specific messages. Typically the possession is marked by changes in posture, facial expression, body language, and voice. Witnesses will occasionally, albeit rarely, report what is called an "overshadowing" in which the relevant spirit form appears to be mistily superimposed on the physical channel.

Like most individuals caught up in this form of communication, Jane underwent periods of doubt—a pattern often repeated in other mediums—but overcame them, often with the help of Seth himself. The result, within two months, was a 230-page typewritten manuscript of Seth material. It was the first example of an outpouring that continues to this day. Like Patience Worth, the writings were subsequently published and attracted substantial interest—so much so that several of the Seth books have become best sellers and brought both Seth and Jane Roberts international fame.

Blavatsky and MacGregor Mathers were enthusiastic occultists. Grace Cooke practiced for years as a Spiritualist medium. Pearl Curran and Jane Roberts experimented with Ouija boards. But sometimes spirit contact can arise, wholly unexpectedly, without the presence of any of these factors. A case in point was what happened to a young Londoner, Ian Graham, in the early 1980s.

Although mildly interested in subjects like astrology, and a meditation practitioner, Ian saw himself as neither an occultist nor a medium. His religious background was conventional—his family were members of the Church of Scotland. But at the age of twenty-nine, the name "White Bull" popped into his mind during a meditation session. Years before, the pop singer Tommy Steele had recorded a novelty song called "Little White Bull." Ian owned a copy as a child and now could not get the song out of his head. It was a bizarre beginning to what proved to be a life-changing event.

A few weeks after the meditation session, he first heard of the term "channeling," a new buzzword coined to describe the type of teaching contact experienced by people like Grace Cooke and Jane Roberts. This contact was now becoming so prevalent that it needed to be differentiated from the familiar phenomenon of mediumship, which sought a much more straightforward communication with the dead. A friend had visited one of the new "channelers" and proceeded to tell Ian all about it. Ian was frankly skeptical—he thought the whole thing smacked of a con game—but was sufficiently intrigued to organize a channeled reading for himself. The communicating entity told him he was wanted as a member of the entity's group.

It was too good an opportunity to miss and Ian went along a week later. The session began with a meditation and the moment he closed his eyes, he found himself in a North American Indian encampment. It struck him as a corny vision, an opinion that solidified as he seemed to be shown around the encampment by the communicating entity. He had just decided it was all his own imagination when the entity suddenly pointed to a tall Indian holding his horse beside a tree. "That's my friend White Bull," the communicating entity said. "He's going to work with you."

The final breakthrough came less than a month later while Ian was meditating. He had the sensation of his hands growing and his body filling out. The bone structure of his face seemed to be changing as well. Then a voice that was not his own used his mouth to announce, "I am White Bull."

With an exclusive public school background, Ian Graham might easily have become a stockbroker or surgeon. Instead he found himself embarking on a career as a channeler. For a long time he could hardly believe it was happening. In the first two years he was wracked with self-doubt, more than half convinced that White Bull was some sort of self-created fiction and the act of channeling was sheer delusion. But he quickly discovered that the advice White Bull gave to clients was helpful and sometimes carried them through serious crises. He also discovered that the advice was not always what he himself would have given. It became increasingly difficult to hold on to his skepticism.

It is clear from all this that something extraordinary had happened to Ian Graham, something that went well beyond his early doubts. In many ways, he was like the early Greeks of Julian Jaynes's study. His life became increasingly focused on a specific and very personal spirit contact prepared to give advice and guidance when required. Where Ian—and others like him—differed from those early Greeks was in his ability to resist the voice. Where the heroes of the *Iliad* seem incapable of denying their "gods," even when divine orders led them into destructive situations, modern channels retain their autonomy.

After initial doubts, Ian Graham settled into a career as a professional channeler and became, if anything, too successful. A constant stream of callers to his London flat meant he had less and less time for himself. At this point, skepticism was the least of his problems. He grew increasingly resentful of White Bull. The spirit had in many ways taken over his life. Friends would turn up demanding to talk with White Bull when Ian wanted them for himself. For someone who was meeting different people every week, it was a lonely existence. It was also a curiously absent existence. He was spending a great deal of his time in trance. There were days when, on his own admission, he threw tantrums and had furious arguments with White Bull. Sometimes he refused to channel altogether.

But Ian Graham and White Bull eventually reached a mutually beneficial compromise. Ian had decided he wanted to forge a career for himself as a teacher and lecturer, but the decision was reached that this would be in addition to, not instead of, his work as a channeler. He moved to France and began to organize workshops and seminars on spiritual topics.

Although the lectures and workshops have now taken something of a backseat, Ian Graham is today an internationally known and respected channeler with a particularly enthusiastic following in Belgium, Germany, and the Netherlands. White Bull's influence is even more far-reaching. There is a valley named after him in New Zealand and a White Bull record label in Belgium. His advice on creative themes has been sought by an American moviemaker and he has contributed to the choreography of a ballet presented at the Paris Opéra. The first dictated book of White Bull's wisdom, now published in eight languages, has become a bible for his international followers.

Grace Cooke had a Spiritualist background, so it is perhaps not entirely surprising that she developed a spirit contact. Blavatsky and Mathers were practicing occultists whose techniques might be expected to generate such experiences. But Jane Roberts, Ian Graham, and even Pearl Curran—just three of many who might have been studied—seem to represent a different trend. They are all people who, in a sense, had spirit contact thrust upon them. More important, today's media technology means that the words of each spirit can potentially reach a wider audience than at any time in human history. If the trend continues, we may yet see spirit influence in human affairs comparable to that of ancient times. In such circumstances, it is useful to examine both the details of some spirit contacts and what spirits can and cannot do, again drawing on the experiences of those in closest contact with them—

Aleister Crowley, the modern English magician whose contact with the spirit Aiwass led him to proclaim a 'New Aeon' and establish a new religion

mediums and magicians. An interesting place to begin might perhaps be the most notorious magician of them all, the "wickedest man in the world," Aleister Crowley.

In 1906, while the British poet Victor Neuburg was an undergraduate at Cambridge, he fell under the influence of Crowley, an initiate of the Hermetic Order of the Golden Dawn. Neuburg was enormously attracted to Crowley, and not alone because of his magical erudition. Crowley was bisexual and had initiated the young writer into a homosexual relationship. By 1908, he was composing poems to his "sweet wizard" that left little doubt as to the depths of his feelings.[4]

Three weeks before his finals, Neuburg traveled to London and took initiation into Crowley's magical order, the Astrum Argentinum, vowing "in the presence of this assembly to take a great and solemn obligation to keep inviolate the secrets and mysteries of this Order." In the summer of 1909 he was at Crowley's house on the shores of Lough Ness, practicing ritual magic and having his bottom flogged with stinging nettles. In late autumn of the same year, the two lovers set sail for North Africa and docked at Algiers on November 17. They took a tram to Arba, then walked south. By November 21, they were in Aumale where Crowley bought Neuburg several notebooks.

His plan was that Neuburg should use them to record the results of an operation in Enochian magic.

Crowley carried in his rucksack a copy of the Enochian Calls he had made from Dr. John Dee's manuscripts in the British Museum—lengthy incantations in an obscure language claimed to call up certain energies and spirits. He had already experimented with two of them and was now determined to find out what would happen if he used the rest. Over a period of days and nights they worked their way through the Calls until, by December 6, they had reached what was technically known as the Tenth Aethyr, an area of magical reality inhabited by the "mighty Devil" Choronzon, Lord of the Powers of Chaos.

In the early afternoon they walked a considerable distance from the town of Bou Saada to reach a valley of fine sand. There, in the desert, they traced a magic circle of protection, sealed with the words *Tetragrammaton, Ararita*, and *Shadai el Chai*. The first of these is a reference to the four-lettered name of God (JHVH), which, according to magical tradition, must not be spoken aloud. *Ararita* is a magical formula associated with skin problems according to Crowley's own writings,[5] while *Shadai el Chai* is a Hebrew godname the magicians associated with the *mudra chakra*, a subtle sexual center of the human body. Beyond the circle, Crowley and Neuburg traced a triangle in the fine sand of the valley floor and fortified this too with divine names. This figure was designed to contain any spirit entity that might appear. Crowley then sacrificed three pigeons he had brought so that the released energy would give Choronzon something with which to manifest.

Neuburg moved into the circle. Crowley, acting on an impulse that most experienced magicians would find bizarre, entered the triangle. It is possible that Crowley, as eccentric in his magical practice as he was in most other aspects of his life, wanted to find out what it felt like to be possessed by a demon. Jean Overton Fuller, who wrote a biography of Neuburg, considered that Crowley had "ceased to be completely sane" by this stage.

Neuburg began the ceremony by chanting aloud the following oath:

> I Omnia Vincam, a Probationer of the Argentinum Astrum, hereby solemnly promise upon my magical honour and swear by Adonai the angel that guardeth me, that I will defend this magic circle of Art with thoughts and words and deeds. I promise to threaten with the dagger and command back into the triangle the spirit incontinent if he should strive to escape from it;

and to strike with the dagger anything that may seek to enter this Circle, were it in appearance the body of the Seer himself. And I will be exceedingly wary, armed against force and cunning; and I will preserve with my life the inviolability of this circle. Amen. And I summon mine Holy Guardian Angel to witness this mine oath, the which if I break, may I perish, forsaken of him. Amen and Amen.[6]

Neuburg then performed the Lesser Banishing Ritual of the Pentagram. This short ceremony, which he presumably learned from Crowley, who in turn had it from the Golden Dawn, is a method of preparing a place for magical working. It performs essentially the same function as disinfecting an operating theater prior to surgery. With the place suitably prepared, Crowley, wearing a black magician's robe, made the Enochian Call in his high-pitched, rather nasal voice:

The thunders of judgment and wrath are numbered and are harboured in the North in the likeness of an oak whose branches are nests of lamentation and weeping, laid up for the Earth which burn night and day: and vomit out the heads of scorpions and live sulphur, mingled with poison. These be the thunders that 5678 Times (in ye 24th part) of a moment roar with an hundred mighty earthquakes and a thousand times as many surges which rest not neither know any echoing time herein. One rock bringeth forth a thousand even as the heart of man does his thoughts. Woe! Woe! Woe! Woe! Woe! Woe! Yea Woe! Be on the Earth, for her iniquity is, was and shall be great. Come away! But not your mighty sounds.[7]

Neuburg heard Crowley's voice call out "Zazas, Zazas, Nasatanda Zazas" followed by a string of blasphemies. Neuburg glanced toward the triangle and there discovered a beautiful woman, somewhat similar in appearance to a prostitute he had known in Paris. She began to call softly to him and make seductive gestures. Neuburg ignored her. The woman then apologized for trying to seduce him and offered instead to lay her head beneath his feet as a token of her willingness to serve him. Neuburg ignored this too.

The demon—for so Neuburg considered the women to be—promptly changed into an old man, then a snake that, in Crowley's voice, asked for water. Unmoved, Neuburg demanded "in the name of the Most High" that the demon reveal its true nature. The thing replied that it was Master of the

Triangle and its name was 333. This is a reference to Gematria, an aspect of Qabalah in which numbers are substituted for letters in an individual name, then added to provide a final code. The best-known example appears in the biblical book of Revelation where the Antichrist is numbered as "six hundred, three score and six"—double the number of Neuburg's demon.

A curious argument developed between Neuburg and the creature. Neuburg called on his own and Crowley's Holy Guardian Angels. The demon claimed it knew them both and had power over them. Neuburg firmly demanded that it reveal its nature and the demon finally admitted that its name was Dispersion and it could not be bested in rational argument.

Equipped with the exercise book Crowley had given him, Neuburg was trying to write all of this down when the demon cunningly swept sand over the boundary of the circle and leaped upon him in the form of a naked man. An extraordinary scene ensued. The two, now locked together, rolled over and over on the sand. Neuburg tried desperately to stab the demon with his magic dagger. The creature in turn attempted to bite him in the back of the neck. Eventually Neuburg got the upper hand and drove the demon back to its triangle. He then retraced the part of the circle that had been obliterated with the sand. After remarking that the tenth Aethyr was a "world of adjectives" without substance, the demon asked permission to leave the triangle to get its clothes. Neuburg refused and threatened it with the dagger. After some further argument, the demon finally disappeared and the black-robed Crowley took its place. They lit a fire to purify the place, then obliterated both circle and triangle. The total ceremony had lasted two hours and exhausted both of them.

Since this account was extracted by Jean Overton Fuller from Neuburg's original notes, here we have a full, eye-witness description of what happens when a magical evocation is undertaken. But Crowley had an earlier, more important experience of spirit contact that seems a little easier to accept and indicates how far-reaching the consequences of such contact may be.

In 1903, the distinguished painter Gerald Kelly introduced his sister to Crowley. The pair took to each other at once. Rose, aged twenty-nine, was widowed but no longer in mourning: she was engaged to an American named Howell, flirting with a solicitor called Hill, and planning an affair with a third admirer by the name of Frank Summers. According to Tobias Churton, "Crowley maintained she was highly intelligent *and* an empty-headed woman: just his type."[8] Never one to miss an opportunity for scandal, Crowley proposed she marry him—purely as a matter of form—in order to get rid of the inconvenient Howell and Hill, after which she could then have her planned affair with Summers. Rose agreed and, following a nineteen-hour engagement, the pair were married in Dingwall on August 12. At once they fell in love with each other and all plans for Rose's affair were abandoned. Instead, they left on a tour of Paris, Marseilles, Naples, and, eventually, Cairo. Here they visited the Great Pyramid and on November 23, Crowley used his connections in the Anglo-Egyptian administration to secure them a private viewing of the King's Chamber. Determined to liven up the honeymoon, Crowley performed an evocation of air elementals and the chamber filled with a bluish light. They extinguished the solitary candle but the light persisted until dawn. It was Rose's first brush with spirits, but not, as it transpired, her last.

By March 1904, the couple was still in Cairo, having abandoned their hotel for an apartment near the city center. On the sixteenth of the month, Crowley attempted to recapture the magic of the King's Chamber by evoking a spirit considerably more impressive than the air elementals—God Himself. Rose, by now pregnant, saw nothing, but she did get the feeling of something "waiting for her."[9] Crowley decided to carry on his rituals day and night for a week. It appears to have been a good decision, for the following day Thoth, the ancient Egyptian god of magic and writing, appeared. The entity filled Rose with such inspiration that she produced a psychical message for Aleister revealing that he had offended the Egyptian god Horus and ought now to invoke him. Successful results were promised for the weekend.

Crowley was astonished that Rose had even heard of Horus and determined to find out how deeply her knowledge ran. The results of his questioning were impressive:

> Rose knew Horus's nature was "force and fire"; knew his presence was characterized by a deep blue light. She recognized his name is hieroglyphics. She knew Crowley's past "relations" with Horus in the Golden Dawn . . . She knew his lineal figure, colors, knew "his place in the temple," knew his weapons, knew his connection with the sun, knew his number was five, and picked him out of first three, and then five different and arbitrary symbols . . . The odds against passing all the tests were enormous.[10]

Enormous or not, Crowley decided on one more. He turned Rose loose in the Bulak Museum with instructions to identify the god among the various exhibits. She passed several images of Horus without comment, then suddenly exclaimed, "There he is!" She was pointing to the display of an ancient funerary stele that featured a seated Horus surmounted by a sun disc, itself a Horus symbol. To Crowley the double Horus symbolism was significant, but not nearly so significant as the stele's catalog number—666, the number of the Great Beast in the biblical book of Revelation, with whom Crowley totally identified. From that point on, he began to take Rose very seriously as a psychic. So too did Rose. She began advising Crowley on how best to evoke Horus and, while his magical experience sometimes ran contrary to what she said, she insisted the rituals follow her exact instructions, again promising results by the weekend.

The next day was Saturday, the start of the weekend, but while Crowley followed orders the ritual produced no results at all. Sunday, however, was a different matter. As Crowley completed the evocation, Rose brought through a message revealing that this was the Equinox of the Gods, the starting point of a new age, the Age of Horus, replacing the old age associated with Jesus Christ and Christianity. Crowley, said the entranced Rose, had been chosen as the link with the new gods. This heady message did not originate from Horus himself but from an entity named Aiwass. Crowley was unsure whether this was a spirit being or not:

> The only point undetermined is whether He is a discarnate Being or . . . a human being, presumably Assyrian, of that name. And that I simply do not know and cannot reasonably surmise because I do not know the limits of the powers of such an One.[11]

It was not long before he found the answer for himself. Just over two weeks later, Rose delivered another, remarkably straightforward trance message: for the next three days, Aleister was instructed to enter the temple in their flat precisely at noon, write down what he heard, and stop precisely at 1:00 p.m.

Once again, Crowley did what he was told. On April 8, 1904, he entered the temple[12] and sat down at the desk, equipped with his Swan fountain pen and several sheets of quarto paper. What happened next is perhaps best described in his own words:

> The voice of Aiwass came apparently from over my left shoulder from the furthest corner of the room. It seemed to echo itself in my physical heart in a very strange manner, hard to describe . . . The voice was of deep timbre,

musical and expressive, its tones solemn, voluptuous, tender, fierce or ought else as suited the moods of the message. Not bass—perhaps a rich tenor or baritone.

The English was free of either native or foreign accent, perfectly pure of local or caste mannerisms, thus startling and even uncanny at first hearing.

I had the strong impression that the speaker was actually in the corner where he seemed to be, in a body of "fine matter," transparent as a veil of gauze, or a cloud of incense smoke. He seemed to be a tall, dark man in his thirties, well-knit, active and strong, with the face of a savage king, and eyes veiled lest their gaze should destroy what they saw. The dress was not Arab; it suggested Assyria or Persia, but very vaguely.[13]

Crowley hastily began to scribble down the words the figure dictated: "Had! The manifestation of Nuit. The unveiling of the company of heaven. Every man and every woman is a star. Every number is infinite; there is no difference. Help me, o warrior lord of Thebes, in my unveiling before the Children of men!"[14]

As the warrior lord struggled to keep up, the message became a little more obscure. "Be thou Hadit, my secret centre, my heart & my tongue! Behold! it is revealed by Aiwass the minister of Hoor-paar-kraat. The Khabs is in the Khu, not the Khu in the Khabs.Worship then the Khabs, and behold my light shed over you!"[15] To Crowley himself, this was more understandable than it might be to the average reader. He knew, for example that the *khu* was the spirit-soul of Egyptian mythology, while *khabs* translated as the "starry sky."

Crowley, apparently of his own volition, broke the message down into numbered verses, rather like those of a Bible, so he may have had some intuition of what the whole operation was all about. But in any case, Aiwass brought the truth home to him during their very first session together. Verse 35 of Chapter 1 explained, "This that thou writest is the threefold Book of Law."

As instructed by Rose, Crowley finished his work promptly at 1:00 p.m., but returned at noon the following day and the day after to continue with the task. The result was a 6,235-word manuscript, broken into three chapters, that literally changed his life. It pronounced that the "word of the Law" was *thelema* (Greek for "will") and the essence of a spiritual life was "do what thou wilt": "Do what thou wilt shall be the whole of the Law." The phrase has echoes of Rabelais, who also advocated do what thou wilt, John Dee whose angels told him "do that which most pleaseth you," and even Saint Augustine who preached "Love and do what you will." Crowley, who would certainly have approved of Rabelais and believed himself to be the reincarnation of Dee's medium, Kelley, worked hard to make the doctrine his own, both in his personal behavior and as a teaching to his students. Like so many spirit-inspired doctrines, it is followed to this day by Thelemites who admire Crowley and members of the magical Order of the Silver Star, cofounded by Crowley in 1907.

21. THREE CONJURATIONS

I N ANY EXAMINATION OF PERSONAL CONTACTS WITH SPIRIT BEINGS, WE NEED to be particularly careful not to allow our postmodern prejudices to color any reaction we might have to the evidence presented. It is relatively easy to accept Crowley's account of the voice of Aiwass as something he genuinely experienced. Mediumistic communications of this type are so commonplace, they are even demonstrated on television. But Neuburg's report of the demonic conjuration in the Egyptian desert may prove a step too far for rationalists. These are no longer the Middle Ages. Surely demons and their ilk have long ago been banished as primitive superstitions?

The point is not whether demons exist in their own right as sentient entities, but whether the *phenomenon* of demonic encounter forms part of human experience, and whether this phenomenon can be induced by, for example, ritual evocation. Historically, of course, there can be little doubt that it does and it can. Consider, for example, the account that appears in the papers of Benvenuto Cellini (1500–1571), Italy's master Renaissance sculptor.[1]

In 1533 or 1534 (the exact date is uncertain), Cellini met with a Sicilian priest versed in the art of ritual magic who agreed to show him an evocation, having first voiced a few dire warnings about the dangers. The site chosen was the ruins of the Roman Coliseum. Cellini brought his friend Vincentio Romoli, while the priest was accompanied by a second magician from Pistoia. The equipment laid out included ceremonial robes, a wand, several grimoires, a pentacle, incense, kindling, and a supply of assafœtida grass. While the others watched, the Sicilian drew circles on the Coliseum floor and fortified them ceremonially. One of the circles was left incomplete. The magician led his companions through the gap before closing it and concluding his ritual preparations. Cellini and Romoli were given the job of lighting a fire in the circle. When they got it going, they were instructed to burn quantities of incense. While the man from Pistoia held the pentacle, the priest began a conjuration ritual. An hour and a half later it bore fruit. According to Cellini's own account, the Coliseum was filled with "several legions" of spirits.

Cellini expressed himself satisfied with the demonstration, but the Sicilian undertook to perform the ceremony again in the hope of obtaining more spectacular results. To this end, he made a fresh stipulation: he wanted a virgin boy to attend. Cellini brought a young servant with him, a twelve-year-old named Cenci.

Romoli returned to the Coliseum for the second operation, but the magician from Pistoia did not. His place was taken by another of Cellini's friends, Agnolino Gaddi. Once again the circles were drawn and consecrated, the fire lit, and the incense burned. Cellini himself held the pentacle this time as the Sicilian priest began the evocation. It is plain from Cellini's account that the conjuration—spoken in a mixture of Hebrew, Greek, and Latin—was directed toward demons who controlled legions of infernal spirits. Much sooner than before, the Coliseum was packed with entities. Cellini asked them to bring him a woman with whom he was in love, a Sicilian girl named Angelica. The spirits replied through the mouth of the magician that Cellini and she would be together within a month.

Although all seemed well at this point, the operation quickly began to go wrong. The magician himself was the first to notice. There were, he said, too many spirits present—possibly as many as a thousand times more than he had called up. Worse, they had begun to misbehave. Twelve-year-old Cenci screamed that they were all being menaced by a million of the fiercest "men" he had ever seen. Four giants, fully armed, were trying to enter the fortified circle. The priest launched into a formula of dismissal. The little boy began to moan and buried his head between his knees, convinced they were all as good as dead.

Cellini tried to reassure him but failed, possibly because he himself was shaking like a leaf. The child cried out that the Coliseum was on fire and that flames were rolling toward them. He covered his eyes with his hands in a paroxysm of terror. The magician broke off his chanted license to depart in favor of stronger means. He instructed Cellini to have his assistants pile assafœtida on the fire. But Cellini's assistants were by now too paralyzed with terror to comply. Cellini lost his temper and shouted at them. It had the desired effect and soon the foul-smelling grass was burning merrily. The spirits began to depart "in great fury."

None of the experimenters felt like leaving the protection of their magic circle. They stayed huddled together until morning when only a few spirits remained "and these at a distance." With the sound of Matins bells ringing in their ears, the sorry group left the circle and headed home, with little Cenci clinging desperately to Cellini and the Sicilian. Two spirits accompanied them, racing over the rooftops and along the road.

The last word on this remarkable experience goes, some centuries later, to Madam Blavatsky, who wrote, "The subsequent meeting of Cellini with his mistress, as predicted and brought about by the conjurer, at the precise time fixed by him, is to be considered, as a matter of course, a 'curious coincidence.'"[2]

Another historical record that may point toward an even more dramatic encounter with demonic forces is contained in *A True Account of the Jena Tragedy of Christmas Eve*, a German judicial inquiry issued 1716. The story it told was one of the most interesting and frightening in the annals of magical practice, although the inquiry itself was investigating not magic, but violent death.[3]

The affair began about a year before the inquiry itself. A peasant named Gessner was working in his vineyard when he discovered a coin. The inquiry did not record what it was, but it proved sufficiently valuable to persuade Gessner to hunt for more. One or two more coins turned up. Gessner concluded they were an indication of a buried hoard that would make him rich and wondered where he could get a grimoire to help him find it. Many German grimoires of the day contained advice on how to persuade spirits to reveal treasure. Gessner had actually owned one, a collection of conjurations entitled *Theosophia Pneumatica*, but lost it prior to his discovery of the coins.

Gessner discussed the problem with a friend, a tailor named Heichler, bemoaning the fact that he no longer had a grimoire that would enable him to find the rest of the treasure by magical means. Heichler was sympathetic. More important, he was able to introduce Gessner to a practicing magician, a student named Weber. Weber was reputed to be the owner of various ritual implements and such rare grimoires as the *Clavicula Salomonis* and the *Key to Faust's Threefold Harrowing of Hell*.

The meeting took place in Weber's rooms, which he shared with a youth named Reche. Gessner asked for the magician's help, but Weber was hesitant. Conjurations were lengthy, tiresome operations, and he had no intention of undertaking one unless he was sure it would prove worth his while. Gessner told Weber he had taken part in conjurations before (which may have been true) and claimed he had seen the treasure hoard in the vineyard; or at least seen its guardian spirit. He produced the coins, claiming he had managed to steal them despite the guardian's attempts to stop him, then went on to describe other spirits he had seen in the locality.

Weber was impressed. He agreed to lend his magical talents to the search and the two men worked out an arrangement by which Weber was to receive a portion of the treasure when it was found.

At this point, an individual named Zenner entered the story. He was, like Gessner, a peasant and seems to have bought his way into the conspiracy with the aid of a mandragore. A mandragore is the specially prepared root of a mandrake plant. The tuber contains a toxic narcotic that, if it fails to kill, may produce visions. In the eighteenth century, it had a fearsome reputation among magicians, who believed it shrieked in agony when uprooted. Since the plant is inedible, it was harvested only for magical purposes. By an accident of nature, mandrake roots often take humanoid shape: two arms, two legs, and an abundant leafy growth taking the place of hair. To create a mandragore, the effect was often heightened by carving, after which the root was cured in vervain smoke to accompanying incantations. A mandragore was considered a talisman of enormous potency. Zenner, who had stolen his from the husband of his mis-

Two mandragores, magical instruments for opening treasure locks and circumventing their spirit guardians

tress, told Gessner, Weber, and Heichler that it could open locks at a distance.

The four began their preparations. Working on the basis of Gessner's description, Weber concluded that the guardian of the hoard was the spirit Nathael, apparently a Hebrew demon. Christmas Eve, only days away, was considered propitious for a conjuration. Weber consulted his textbooks and discovered an odd number of participants was specified. Heichler, the tailor, was busy during the pre-Christmas rush and readily agreed to drop out. Finding a site for the operation proved more controversial. Heichler offered an empty room in his house, but Gessner objected. He was convinced demons were deceitful and he was afraid they might try to fool their conjurers by taking on the appearance of inhabitants of the house. It would be safer, he argued, to hold the conjuration in some remote spot. After considerable discussion, their final choice fell on a little hut owned by Heichler, situated in the same vineyard where the treasure was buried.

The conspirators then fell to discussing luck pennies, which were supposed to reproduce themselves when the relevant ceremony was performed over them. Was there, they wondered, a chance that the spirit might exchange luck pennies for ordinary pennies if they brought a few along? They decided it would be worth a try despite the fact that, according to Weber's grimoires, each participant had to have a specific number of coins, carried in a bag of a particular material, purchased at a given price. Heichler agreed to make the bags, which he gave to his wife who, in turn, sold them back to him and his three colleagues at the specified price.

In the afternoon of Christmas Eve, Gessner and Weber called to collect Zenner. But now that the ordeal was close at hand, Zenner was beginning to take fright. He urged his companions to change the venue to somewhere less isolated and suggested using an empty house of which he was the caretaker. The three men went off to inspect the premises, but quickly discovered it unsuitable. There were no shutters on the windows; besides which, Zenner had mislaid his key. Consequently, armed with lanterns and protective amulets, they set out for the vineyard hut. Before entering, Weber penciled the word *Tetragrammaton* on the door.

The three men went inside to discover that Heichler had left them some coals for their brazier and a tallow candle. The brazier itself was makeshift: they used a flowerpot and the fire gave off so much fumes that they were forced to open the door. Weber drew a magical circle on the ceiling, then began to read the conjuration from *The Key to Faust's Threefold Harrowing of Hell.* After a time he began to feel dizzy, then fell unconscious across the table. His last memory was of his two companions regarding him curiously.

The following day, Christmas, the tailor Heichler made his way to the hut to find out what the other three were doing. Gessner and Zenner were both dead. Weber was alive, but apparently insane. He could not speak. When aroused from his torpor, the best he could produce was grunts and gibbering. Heichler called in the authorities, who stationed three watchmen at the hut to guard the corpses until they could be fully examined. The next morning, one of the watchmen was dead and the other two were unconscious.

The judicial inquiry from which this account is drawn centered on the fate of Weber and his associates, so there is little information about the death of the watchman. But the record had a great deal to say about the would-be magicians. The body of the unconscious Weber was covered with marks and bruises. Zenner's corpse was in an even more appalling state: it was covered in huge weals and scratches. His tongue protruded horribly and there were many individual burns on his face and neck. No instrument was found in or near the hut that could have explained such injuries. The only source of fire was the flowerpot brazier, but this was undisturbed and the corpse nowhere near it.

Accounts like these raise the question of how conjurations are actually carried out, a problematic investigation since, while instructive grimoires abound, there are very few detailed first-person accounts of what really happens when the instructions are put into practice. Nonetheless, the record of one such operation has come down to us, made especially interesting since it was written by a Victorian magician whose works remain required reading for Western occultists to the present day. More interesting still, Alphonse Louis Constant, the French author better known by his pseudonym Eliphas Lévi, was, for most of his life, a theoretical magician only. His account of the evocation of Apollonius of Tyana is the only recorded instance of his ever having undertaken a practical magical experiment:

> In the spring of the year 1854 I had undertaken a journey to London, that I might escape from internal disquietude and devote myself, without interruption, to science. I had letters of introduction to persons of eminence who were anxious for revelations from the supernatural world. I made the acquaintance of several and discovered in them, amidst much that was courteous, a depth of indifference or trifling. They asked me forthwith to work

wonders, as if I were a charlatan, and I was somewhat discouraged, for, to speak frankly, far from being inclined to initiate others into the mysteries of Ceremonial Magic, I had shrunk all along from its illusions and weariness. Moreover, such ceremonies necessitated an equipment which would be expensive and hard to collect. I buried myself therefore in the study of the transcendent Kabalah, and troubled no further about English adepts, when, returning one day to my hotel, I found a note awaiting me. This note contained half of a card, divided transversely, on which I recognized at once the seal of Solomon. It was accompanied by a small sheet of paper, on which these words were penciled: "Tomorrow, at three o'clock, in front of Westminster Abbey, the second half of this card will be given you." I kept this curious assignation. At the appointed spot I found a carriage drawn up, and as I held unaffectedly the fragment of card in my hand, a footman approached, making a sign as he did so, and then opened the door of the equipage. It contained a lady in black, wearing a thick veil; she motioned to me to take a seat beside her, showing me at the same time the other half of the card. The door closed, the carriage drove off, and the lady raising her veil I saw that my appointment was with an elderly person, having grey eyebrows and black eyes of unusual brilliance, strangely fixed in expression. "Sir," she began, with a strongly marked English accent, "I am aware that the law of secrecy is rigorous amongst adepts; a friend of Sir B—L—[4] who has seen you, knows that you have been asked for phenomena, and that you have refused to gratify such curiosity. You are possibly without the materials; I should like to show you a complete magical cabinet, but I must exact beforehand the most inviolable silence. If you will not give me this pledge upon your honour, I shall give orders for you to be driven to your hotel." I made the required promise and keep it faithfully by not divulging the name, position or abode of this lady, whom I soon recognized as an initiate, not exactly of the first order, but still of a most exalted grade. We had a number of long conversations, in the course of which she insisted always upon the necessity of practical experience to complete initiation. She showed me a collection of magical vestments and instruments, lent me some rare books which I needed; in short, she determined me to attempt at her house the experiment of a complete evocation, for which I prepared during a period of twenty-one days, scrupulously observing the rules laid down in the thirteenth chapter of the "Ritual."

The preliminaries terminated on 2nd July; it was proposed to evoke the phantom of the divine Apollonius and interrogate it upon two secrets, one which concerned myself and one which interested the lady. She had counted on taking part in the evocation with a trustworthy person, who, however, proved nervous at the last moment, and, as the triad or unity is indispensable for Magical Rites, I was left to my own resources. The cabinet prepared for the evocation was situated in a turret; it contained four concave mirrors and a species of altar having a white marble top, encircled by a chain of magnetized iron. The Sign of the Pentagram, as given in the fifth chapter of this work, was graven and gilded on the white marble surface; it was inscribed also in various colours upon a new white lambskin stretched beneath the altar. In the middle of the marble table there was a small copper chafing-dish, containing charcoal of alder and laurel wood; another chafing-dish was set before me on a tripod. I was clothed in a white garment, very similar to the alb of our catholic priests, but longer and wider, and I wore upon my head a crown of vervain leaves, intertwined with a golden chain. I held a new sword in one hand, and in the other the "Ritual." I kindled two fires with the requisite prepared substances, and began reading the evocations of the "Ritual" in a voice at first low, but rising by degrees. The smoke spread, the flame caused the objects upon which it fell to waver, then it went out, the smoke still floating white and slow about the marble altar; I seemed to feel a quaking of the earth, my ears tingled, my heart beat quickly. I heaped more twigs and perfumes on the chafing-dishes, and as the flame again burst up, I beheld distinctly, before the altar, the figure of a man of more than normal size, which dissolved and vanished away. I recommenced the evocations and placed myself within a circle which I had drawn previously between the tripod and the altar. Thereupon the mirror which was behind the altar seemed to brighten in its depth, a wan form was outlined therein, which increased and seemed to approach by degrees. Three times, and with closed eyes, I invoked Apollonius. When I again looked forth there was a man in front of me, wrapped from head to foot in a species of shroud, which seemed more grey than white. He was lean, melancholy and beardless, and did not altogether correspond to my preconceived notion of Apollonius. I experienced an abnormally cold sensation, and when I endeavoured to question the phantom I could not articulate a syllable. I therefore placed my hand upon the Sign of the Pentagram, and pointed the sword at the figure, commanding it mentally to obey and not alarm me, in virtue of the said sign. The form thereupon became vague, and suddenly disappeared. I directed it to return, and presently felt, as it were, a breath close by me; something touched my hand which was holding the sword, and the arm became immediately benumbed as far as the elbow. I divined that the sword displeased the spirit, and I therefore placed it point downwards, close by me, within the circle. The human figure reappeared immediately, but I experienced such an intense weakness in all my limbs, and a swooning sensation came so quickly over me, that I made two steps to sit down, whereupon I fell into a profound lethargy, accompanied by dreams, of which I had only a confused recollection when I came again to myself. For several subsequent days my arm remained benumbed and painful. The apparition did not speak to me, but it seemed that the questions I had designed to ask answered themselves in my mind. To that of the lady an interior voice replied—Death!—it was concerning a man about whom she desired information. As for myself, I sought to know whether reconciliation and forgiveness were possible between two persons who occupied my thoughts, and the same inexorable echo within me answered—Dead!

I am stating facts as they occurred, but I would impose faith on no one. The consequence of this experience on myself must be called inexplicable. I was no longer the same man; something of another world had passed into me; I was no longer either sad or cheerful, but I felt a singular attraction towards death, unaccompanied, however, by any suicidal tendency. I analysed my experience carefully, and, notwithstanding a lively nervous repugnance, I repeated the same experiment on two further occasions, allowing some days to elapse between each. There was not, however, sufficient difference between the phenomena to warrant me in protracting a narrative which is perhaps already too long. But the net result of these two additional evocations was for me the revelation of two kabalistic secrets which might change, in a short space of time, the foundations and laws of society at large, if they came to be known generally.[5]

Cellini's story of the Coliseum conjuration was not written for publication, nor for any form of personal aggrandizement. It formed a part of his private papers and was only discovered after his death. The tragedy at Jena was recorded in a judicial inquiry that had no agenda other than to establish the truth behind some bizarre deaths. Dr. E. M. Butler, formerly Schröder Professor of German at the University of Cambridge, went on record with the statement that:

The circumstantial evidence is so realistic, even including a diagram of the scene; the account is so sober; the admissions of the one remaining witness ring so true; the judicial procedure was so meticulous; the strict adherence to known facts so close; that, together with the absence of torture, they positively command belief.[6]

Although Lévi did publish an account of his experiences, there seems little indication of self-aggrandizement here either. By that time, his reputation was already well-established, as was his extreme reluctance to involve himself in demonstrations of the magical arts. He once said, "To practice magic is to be a quack; to know magic is to be a sage." On this occasion, he seems to have been persuaded to "quackery" by the mysteriously romantic circumstances of the unnamed lady's invitation.

In all three cases, there is no reason to conclude the reports are anything other than accurate accounts of unusual human experiences, although how we should interpret these experiences remains for the moment an open question. Crowley's demon in the desert, Cellini's frightening encounter, and the Jena tragedy all raise the question of whether infernal experiences are still possible in the modern era, again with essentially the same answer. The reports of America's Ed and Lorraine Warren, whose investigations of more than three thousand paranormal disturbances included the case that subsequently became famous as the *Amityville Horror*, are only some among many that attest to demonic experiences up to the present day.[7] Crowley was not above producing fiction designed to inflate his reputation as a magician, but we must remember that the description of what happened in the Egyptian desert was penned by Victor Neuburg, an altogether more modest and more reliable character.

We need also to examine our own preconceptions of what spirits can and cannot do, preconceptions that can be alive and well even in those who do not actually believe in spirits. They arise from a consensus picture formed by the particular emphases given by the authors of various contact reports. But the consensus is not the whole of the picture. Sometimes spirits prove capable of things seldom mentioned in the literature that has accrued around them. They may, for example, do more than make contact; they may elect to share, more or less permanently, the same mind-space of those they wish to speak to. More peculiar still, they may actually be donated by one contact to another.

22. SPIRIT TRANSFERS, SPIRIT POWERS

DOLORES ASHCROFT-NOWICKI WAS BORN IN JERSEY, ONE OF BRITAIN'S Channel Islands, into a family with a marked interest in Spiritualism and the occult. She had early ambitions to become an actress and took RADA (Royal Academy of Dramatic Art) training, but her professional career was destined to follow a very different course. The turning point came when she joined an esoteric organization called the Society of the Inner Light and there became acquainted with the man who was to be her spiritual mentor, Walter Ernest Butler.

Butler was elderly when Dolores met him, but a career in the Far East had presented him with the opportunity of studying Oriental occultism, which he combined with training in the Western Esoteric Tradition, a body of doctrines and techniques rooted in Alexandrian hermeticism and the Jewish Qabalah.

In the mid-1960s internal disagreements in the Society of the Inner Light led to the resignation of several members, some of whom went on to establish organizations of their own. Among them was a couple named John and Mary Hall who ran a secondhand book service in Toddington, near Cheltenham, England. In tandem with the author Gareth Knight, another member of the Inner Light, the Halls launched a mail-order course in psychospiritual and magical training that they distributed as part of their business. With the exception of the first six lessons written by Gareth Knight, the course was penned by Butler, who eventually took over the course administration when it became so popular that it was interfering with the Halls' other business. In the early 1970s, copyright was reassigned to him and he gradually began to transform it into a loosely knit esoteric school. The designation was changed from Helios, named originally for the Halls' book service, to Servants of the

Light. In later life Butler went on to write several books[1] on magic and psychism, some of which became classics of their genre. One of these works was dedicated to his own teacher. He gave no clue to his readers that the teacher was not human.

It was some time into their relationship before Dolores learned this either. Butler was cautious about discussing something that, as the general mindset of the day, would likely mark him as a lunatic. But the time came when he told Dolores that the Helios course had been dictated to him by someone he called the Opener. He repeated that the Opener was a spirit contact, but declined further information. Butler believed the Opener to be ancient Egypt's Opener of the Ways, the deity Upuaut. Although some scholars describe Upuaut as a wolf-god, others believe him to be identical to Anubis, the jackal-headed Egyptian god of the dead. Butler was among the latter. He used the names Opener, Upuaut, and Anubis interchangeably.

Ernest Butler was diabetic—a surprisingly common condition among psychics—and in later life the condition worsened to such an extent that he lost circulation in one leg and had to have an amputation.[2] But even before then he worried about who was going to take over his developing school when he was gone. He asked his spirit contact about it and was told that a successor would be brought to him. He would know it was the right person because he or she would give Butler the secret name of his spirit contact—which Butler knew—and also that he or she would tell Butler they would take over his work when he died.

By what must seem a long-odds coincidence, around the time this was happening, Dolores Ashcroft-Nowicki found herself bombarded by references to the Egyptian god Anubis. She would open a book at random and there would be a picture or a reference. She would see his image as a decorative motif. She even began to dream about him. It happened so often, she began to wonder what on earth was going on and determined to ask her spiritual mentor about it at the first available opportunity.

Dolores and her husband, Michael, flew to Southampton where they collected Butler and took him to London for a meeting of the Inner Light Society. All three of them lunched together in an Indian restaurant at the top of Haverstock Hill. It was a fine day and afterward they sat outside on a bench. The two men were engaged in conversation when Dolores—who had had experiences of psychism since childhood—became aware she had been joined by an Anubis figure. At first it was no more than a feeling and she tried to ignore it, but the feeling intensified, then became a vivid inner vision, almost a waking dream. Eventually she broke into the conversation and asked Butler if he knew anything about Anubis. He was so startled that he dropped his pipe, which shattered on the pavement.

The entity began to talk to Dolores. "Give him my name," it instructed. "Tell him you are here to take over his work after he dies!" Dolores wanted none of it. Ernest Butler was a frail, old man suffering from a chronic illness. As a well-brought-up young woman, she had no intention of talking to him about his death. Butler for his part did not seem to want to talk about Anubis. He suggested they might be running late for their meeting and should go. They stood up and move off down the road. The entity followed. It kept repeating the same message: "Tell him my name. Tell him you will take over his work after he dies."

They reached Steele's Road where their meeting was due to take place. The entity was now so insistent that Dolores's nerve finally broke. She stopped Butler with a hand on his arm and told him the message. He shrugged and told her, "You took your time coming. I expected you before this."

After the meeting, Dolores and Michael put Butler on the train to Southampton. As he was leaving, he told her she would be the next Director of Studies of the Servants of the Light. It did not strike her as good news and she resisted for much of the following week. The Anubis entity reappeared and she berated it about her predicament. Specifically she was at the start of her career and did not feel herself qualified to teach. The entity told her not to worry—he would be the one doing the teaching. It was the beginning of an increasingly strange time for Dolores. She continued to see Ernest Butler regularly and absorbed a great deal of theory from him. But more important, he taught her trance techniques for reaching the spirit world. Her contacts with Anubis become more frequent. Sometime before Butler's death in 1978, the spirit brought up the question of becoming her indweller. The term was new to Dolores, but she quickly learned that an indweller is an entity—itself not necessarily human—that forms a permanent link with a human being, occupying essentially the same mental "space" and sharing the same physical body. The relationship is one of mutual benefit. The indwelling entity gains experience of physical reality and is enabled, within limits, to interact with it. The host gains information, companionship, guidance and, usually, a sense of purpose.[3]

Dolores had not read Julian Jaynes's book on the bicameral mind when she first heard about indwellers, but there seems little doubt that what her spirit contact was suggesting was similar, if not identical, to the historical phenomena Jaynes describes. As we have seen, Jaynes suggested that in ancient times people were commonly guided by spirit voices they accepted as gods. Here was a potential repeat of the experience in a twentieth-century context. Dolores did not hesitate, did not even ask questions. The moment she agreed, the indweller entered her. It happened so quickly she did not even shiver. As the entity began their new relationship, she felt the arrival of something that took up residence in her mind and has shared the space inside her head ever since. As had happened in the contact with Butler, the presence described itself as the Opener of the Ways and claimed a provenance that reached back to ancient Egypt. Although mainly aware of the Opener as an inner dialogue, Dolores sometimes heard an "external" voice or, more rarely, saw an objective figure. Here again, the parallels with Jaynes's historical descriptions are obvious.

Prompted in part by her own desires, in part by the indwelling Opener, Dolores Ashcroft-Nowicki embarked on a career that has to some extent paralleled those of figures like Blavatsky. She became a world traveler as a professional teacher of esoteric doctrines, ritual magic, and other occult techniques. She and her husband, Michael, continued to run the Servants of the Light and Dolores began to write books on esoteric subjects. She embarked on an extensive program of workshops, lectures, and seminars. More than a quarter of a century after she received her indweller, she found herself involved in the transfer of another entity.

Among Dolores's closest friends at the time was an American teacher of spiritual practice named Shakmah Winddrum (Anna Branche), who had an extensive following and an international reputation as a charismatic and compelling speaker.[4] They met at one of Dolores's lectures and hit it off at once. Sometime after the event, the indweller who was now as much a part of Dolores's life as her husband and children, asked if she would be prepared temporarily to "carry" a second spirit contact who was destined to indwell Shakmah. Unlike the Opener, the newcomer was not a member of the Egyptian pantheon, nor a "god" of any sort. But he was an historical personage.

Old Testament scriptures briefly tell the story of a visit to King Solomon by the Queen of Sheba:

> And she came to Jerusalem with a very great train, with camels that bare spices, and very much gold, and precious stones: and when she was come to Solomon, she communed with him of all that was in her heart. And Solomon told her all

her questions: there was not any thing hid from the king, which he told her not
... And she gave the king an hundred and twenty talents of gold, and of spices
very great store, and precious stones: there came no more such abundance of
spices as these which the queen of Sheba gave to king Solomon. And the navy
also of Hiram, that brought gold from Ophir, brought in from Ophir great plenty
of almug trees, and precious stones. And the king made of the almug trees pillars for the house of the Lord, and for the king's house, harps also and psalteries
for singers: there came no such almug trees, nor were seen unto this day. And
king Solomon gave unto the queen of Sheba all her desire, whatsoever she
asked, beside that which Solomon gave her of his royal bounty.[5]

But that was not, apparently, all he gave her. The visit of the Queen of
Sheba is described in First Kings and again, virtually word for word, in Second
Chronicles. In the poetic Song of Solomon, however, are two passages that schol-
ars believe throw a little more light on the historic encounter. The first reads:

Let him kiss me with the kisses of his mouth: for thy love is better than wine
... the king hath brought me into his chambers: we will be glad and rejoice
in thee, we will remember thy love more than wine.[6]

A long-standing oral tradition insists that Solomon and the Queen of
Sheba not only met formally as heads of their respective states, but were so
instantly enamored with each other that they had a brief, passionate affair.
When the queen returned to her native land, she was pregnant with
Solomon's child. The location of her native land remains the subject of controversy, but most experts believe it was somewhere in Africa. This too is
supported by a sentence in the Song of Solomon of such intensity and beauty
that it continues to resonate down the years:

I am black, but comely, O ye daughters of Jerusalem, as the tents of Kedar,
as the curtains of Solomon.[7]

In Ethiopia there is no controversy. The Queen of Sheba is not only
believed to have originated in that country, but her son by King Solomon,
Menelyk, became the founder of a royal dynasty that ruled Ethiopia until
September 1974, when the last of the line, Emperor Haile Selassie, was forcefully deposed in a mutiny of the police and armed forces.

It was the spirit of Menelyk that the Opener wanted Dolores to carry to Shakmah Winddrum. There was no advance warning of the development. Dolores was in the United States for a workshop, taking a shower in the house where she was staying. Her Opener asked if she was prepared to "carry" a second spirit for a short time and when, in some confusion, she agreed, the new entity moved in at once. The experience of sharing her mind with two indwellers was so overwhelming that she burst into tears. She was still noticeably upset when she went downstairs and when her host wondered what was wrong, she asked him for a drink. The only alcohol in the house was a bottle of Amaretto liqueur and Dolores, although normally moderate in her drinking habits, finished most of it. The following day she flew to Philadelphia to meet the proposed recipient.

Shakmah was no stranger to spirit contact. After a conventional education and career, she became embroiled in esoteric pursuits after she was initiated into the Voodoo priesthood in Haiti in 1963. Voodoo is a religion that originated in Haiti but is also practiced in Cuba, Trinidad, Brazil, and the southern United States, notably Louisiana. Its roots go back to the tribal religions of western Africa, particularly Benin, but it contains elements of Roman Catholicism and representations of Christian saints share the altar with more ancient gods. The main focus of worship is a high god, Bon Dieu, but respect is paid to one's ancestors, the dead in general, and spirits called Loa. The Loa are African tribal gods and it is they who are usually identified with Roman Catholic saints. (The snake god, for example, is seen as much the same being as Ireland's patron saint, Saint Patrick, credited with banishing all snakes from the island.) Rituals, led by a priest called a houngan or a priestess called a mambo, involve the invocation of the Loa by drumming, dancing, singing, and feasting. In such ceremonies, ecstatic trance frequently occurs and the Loa typically take possession of the dancers in order to perform cures and give advice. The new initiate mambo experiences the ecstatic trance and the spirit possession. But the possession is strictly temporary—it never outlives the ceremony itself.

On her return to the United States, Shakmah evolved her own form of esoteric practice, which blended Qabalistic, African, Christian, and even some French medieval spiritual elements. In private ceremonies she would frequently enter into trance in order to communicate with ancestor spirits and pass on a body of doctrines to her followers. For all this, she had no specific experience of indwelling.

When Dolores and Shakmah met, Dolores told her she was "carrying something for her." With a finely tuned intuition, Shakmah guessed at once what she meant—Dolores had told her about Anubis—but did not want it. An indweller was fine in theory, but it suddenly seemed she was about to give away every semblance of privacy she possessed. In spite of this, Dolores laid a hand on her shoulder. At that point Dolores felt the Menelyk entity flow out of her. Shakmah felt another presence in her mind.

Spirit possession, as practiced in ecstatic religions like Voodoo, is a different—and in a sense easier—experience than indwelling. As trance intervenes, host consciousness moves aside and the possessing spirit takes over. When, later, the spirit withdraws, the host emerges from trance with little or no memory of what has occurred, rather like waking from a deep sleep. With indwelling there is a sharing of consciousness, an altogether different phenomenon that requires a host's long-term dedication. The result is something similar to the biblical idea of a "familiar spirit." The discovery that such "familiars" can be transferred consciously to a different host is a surprise that calls into question the common preconceptions about the contact experience.

One of the strangest eyewitness accounts of spirit contact ever written was penned by a barrister named Henry D. Jencken and appeared in the February 1867 edition of *Human Nature*. It described what happened at a séance he had attended along with the Earl of Dunraven, Lord Lindsay, a Captain Wynne, and the prominent scientist William Crookes. The relevant part read, verbatim:

> Mr. Home had passed into the trance still so often witnessed; rising from his seat, he laid hold of an arm-chair, which he held at arm's length, and was then lifted about three feet clear of the ground; travelling thus suspended in space, he placed the chair next Lord Adare, and made a circuit round those in the room, being lowered and raised as he passed each of us. One of those present measured the elevation and passed his leg and arm underneath Mr. Home's feet. The elevation lasted from four to five minutes. On resuming his seat, Mr. Home addressed Captain Wynne, communicating news to him of which the departed alone could have been cognisant.
>
> The spirit form that had been seen reclining on the sofa now stepped up to Mr. Home and mesmerised him; a hand was then seen luminously visible over his head, about 18 inches in a vertical line from his head. The trance state of Mr. Home now assumed a different character; gently rising he spoke a few words to those present and then opening the door proceeded into the

corridor; a voice then said—"He will go out of this window and come in at that window." The only one who heard the voice was the Master of Lindsay and a cold shudder seized upon him as he contemplated the possibility of this occurring, a feat which the great height of the third floor windows in Ashley Place rendered more than ordinarily perilous. The others present, however, having closely questioned him as to what he had heard, he at first replied, "I dare not tell you"; when, to the amazement of all, a voice said, "You must tell; tell directly." The Master then said, "Yes; yes, terrible to say, he will go out at that window and come in at this; do not be frightened, be quiet." Mr. Home now re-entered the room, and opening the drawing-room window, was pushed out semi-horizontally into space, and carried from one window of the drawing-room to the farthermost window of the adjoining room. This feat being performed at a height of about 60 feet from the ground, naturally caused a shudder in all present. The body of Mr. Home, when it appeared at the window of the adjoining room, was shunted into the room feet foremost—the window being only 18 inches open. As soon as he had recovered his footing he laughed and said, "I wonder what a policeman would have said had he seen me go round and round like a teetotum!" The scene was, however, too terrible—too strange, to elicit a smile; cold beads of perspiration stood on every brow, while a feeling pervaded all as if some great danger had passed; the nerves of those present had been kept in a state of tension that refused to respond to a joke. A change now passed over Mr. Home, one often observable during the trance states, indicative, no doubt, of some other power operating on his system. Lord Adare had in the meantime stepped up to the open window in the adjoining room to close it—the cold air, as it came pouring in, chilling the room; when, to his surprise, he only found the window 18 to 24 inches open! This puzzled him, for how could Mr. Home have passed outside through a window only 18 to 24 inches open. Mr. Home, however, soon set his doubts to rest; stepping up to Lord Adare, he said, "No, no; I did not close the window; I passed thus into the air outside." An invisible power then supported Mr. Home all but horizontally in space, and thrust his body into space through the open window, head foremost, bringing him back again feet foremost into the room, shunted not unlike a shutter into a basement below. The circle around the table having reformed, a cold current of air passed over those present, like the rushing of winds. This repeated itself several times. The cold blast of air, or electric fluid, or call it what you may, was accompanied by a loud whistle like a gust of wind on the mountain top, or through the leaves of the forest in late autumn; the sound was deep, sonorous, and powerful in the extreme, and a shudder kept passing over those present, who all heard and felt it. This rushing sound lasted quite ten minutes, in broken intervals of one or two minutes. All present were much surprised; and the interest became intensified by the unknown tongues in which Mr. Home now conversed. Passing from one language to another in rapid succession, he spoke for ten minutes in unknown languages.

A spirit form now became distinctly visible; it stood next to the Master of Lindsay, clad, as seen on former occasions, in a long robe with a girdle, the feet scarcely touching the ground, the outline of the face only clear, and the tones of the voice, though sufficiently distinct to be understood, whispered rather than spoken. Other voices were now heard, and large globes of phosphorescent lights passed slowly through the room.[8]

The "Mr. Home" referred to in this account was Daniel Dunglas Home, a young Scot born March 20, 1833, to parents so impoverished that they gave him up at birth to the care of his aunt, Mary Cook. By Home's own account, his contact with spirits began early: his cradle rocked of its own accord in the home of his adoptive parents. While he was still a small boy, the Crooks emigrated to America and settled in Greeneville, near Norwich, Connecticut. In his early teens, he had a vision of a school friend who apparently indicated that he had died three days earlier. A letter subsequently arrived, confirming the death. A few years later, Home's birth mother, Elizabeth, also emigrated to America, but died shortly thereafter. Once again Home had a spirit vision informing him of the time of death.

Home began to attract poltergeist phenomena, with raps sounding in his home similar to those produced by the Fox sisters. Three ministers of different religious denominations were called in to witness what was happening and all concluded the boy, now eighteen years of age, was possessed by the Devil. A table moved of its own accord and the raps continued. Neighbors began to complain and Home's aunt, at her wit's end, threw him out of the house.

Ruth Brandon, a writer clearly not enamored with Home, suggests he was an opportunist who jumped aboard the Fox Sisters' bandwagon, but instead of accepting money for his demonstrations, used them instead to get himself free bed and board.[9] Whatever the motivation, Home held his first formal séance in 1851. A local newspaper reported that a table had moved despite attempts to stop it and Home's reputation quickly spread. He began to travel around New England working (without charge) as a healer and communicating with the spirits of the dead. He felt he was "on a mission to demonstrate immortality."[10]

A year later, his fame had spread dramatically. He sometimes gave six or seven séances a day, often attracting prominent people. Not all of them were believers. The distinguished scientist Professor Robert Hare investigated his claims, as did Supreme Court Judge John Worth Edmonds. Both decided he was genuine.

Home had never been a particularly healthy man and in early 1854 he was diagnosed as having tuberculosis. His doctors recommended a change of climate and in March of the following year he set sail for England. He quickly became something of a darling of London society, although reaction to his abilities was mixed. Robert Browning lampooned him in the poem *Mr. Sludge the Medium* and the psychical researcher Frank Podmore accused him of cheating while William Crookes claimed that Home had levitated five to seven feet above the floor in good light more than fifty times. It was while he was in London that Home began to demonstrate an even more unusual ability—the power to elongate his body parts. Henry Jencken left the following account:

> I caused Mr. Home to place his hand firmly on a piece of paper and then carefully traced an outline of the hand. At the wrist joint I placed a pencil against the "trapezium," a small bone at the end of the phalange of the thumb. The hand gradually widened and elongated about an inch, then contracted and shortened about an inch. At each stage I made a tracing of the hand, causing the pencil point to be kept firmly at the wrist. The fact of the elongating and contracting of the hand I unmistakably established, and, be the cause what it may, the fact remains; and in giving the result of my measurements and the method adopted to satisfy myself that I had not been self-deceived, I am, I believe, rendering the first positive measurement of the extension and contraction of a human organism.
>
> The phenomenon of elongation I am aware has been questioned and I do not quarrel with those who maintain their doubt despite all that may be affirmed. In my own experience I have gone through the same phases of doubt and uttered disbelief in what I was seeing. The first time I witnessed an elongation, although I measured the extension of the wrist, I would not,

could not, credit my senses; but having witnessed the fact some ten or twelve times, and that in the presence of fifty witnesses, from first to last, who have been present at these séances where those elongations occurred, all doubts have been removed; and that the capacity to extend is not confined to Mr. Home, was shown some months ago at Mr. Hall's, where, at the séance held in his house, both Mr. Home and Miss Bertolacci became elongated. The stretching out and contracting of the limbs, hands, fingers above described, I have only witnessed on this one occasion and I am much pleased to have a steady Oxonian to aid me in making the measurements above detailed.[11]

Although Jencken only saw it once, Home's ability to elongate and contract was witnessed by a great many others, as was his apparent ability to control the effects of fire. On several occasions he laid his head on burning coals without injury and persuaded various sitters to handle the coals for themselves, again without harm. He was also capable of manifesting a halo of flames around his head and persuading an accordion to play of its own accord. The latter trick was commonplace among mediums of the day; Crookes undertook to investigate Home's version scientifically. In one experiment, Crookes showed in a laboratory situation that Home could influence the weight of a board resting on a balance scale merely by placing his fingers in a glass of water resting on the end of the board. In another, an accordion purchased by Crookes played by itself in Home's presence. During this experiment Home's hands and feet were restrained and the accordion placed inside a wire cage through which an electrical current was passed. Crookes and two other witnesses stated that they distinctly saw the accordion "floating about on the inside of the cage with no visible support."[12] Crookes concluded that, having satisfied himself by careful experiment, the phenomena observed were genuine.[13]

These paranormal powers, spectacular though some of them appear to be, seem unimportant when set against the observable fact that when a spirit makes contact with a human being, some factor of the experience is almost preternaturally persuasive. In other words, when a spirit requests or commands, the contacted human feels an almost overwhelming urge to obey. This goes some way to explain the astonishing influence spirit contact has had on the course of human history, but opens up another vital, fundamental question: what *are* these creatures who have whispered in the ear of humanity throughout the generations?

We know broadly what they claim to be and the context in which they claim to live. Historical analysis shows that several themes recur across a broad range of spirit communications. Perhaps the most common is the concept of a primal, ongoing, cosmic conflict between the Powers of Light and the Powers of Darkness. This, of course, is a common motif in world religions. The New Testament book of Revelation, itself a visionary document, states:

> And there was war in heaven: Michael and his angels fought against the dragon; and the dragon fought and his angels, And prevailed not; neither was their place found any more in heaven. And the great dragon was cast out, that old serpent, called the Devil, and Satan, which deceiveth the whole world: he was cast out into the earth, and his angels were cast out with him.[14]

In the apocryphal Book of Enoch, the war is associated with the biblical Flood. The story begins when rebel angels teach humanity military skills, a development that leads to much suffering:

> And then Michael, Uriel, Raphael, and Gabriel looked down from heaven and saw much blood being shed upon the earth, and all lawlessness being wrought upon the earth. And they said one to another: "The earth made without inhabitant cries the voice of their cryings up to the gates of heaven. And now to you, the holy ones of heaven, the souls of men make their suit, saying, 'Bring our cause before the Most High.'"[15]

When the Archangels do just that:

> Then said the Most High, the Holy and Great One spake, and sent Uriel to the son of Lamech, and said to him: "Go to Noah and tell him in my name 'Hide thyself!' and reveal to him the end that is approaching: that the whole earth will be destroyed, and a deluge is about to come upon the whole earth, and will destroy all that is on it. And now instruct him that he may escape and his seed may be preserved for all the generations of the world." And again the Lord said to Raphael: "Bind Azazel hand and foot, and cast him into the darkness: and make an opening in the desert, which is in Dudael, and cast him therein. And place upon him rough and jagged rocks, and cover him with darkness, and let him abide there for ever, and cover his face that he may not see light. And on the day of the great judgment he shall be cast into the fire."[16]

The same broad theme is echoed in the Koran when God banishes the angel Eblis from heaven for his refusal to worship the newly created Adam. In banishment, Eblis becomes the Devil or Satan and stands against God thereafter as the representative of evil. The conflict of light and darkness arises again in the Hindu religion, in the benign and wrathful deities of Tibetan Buddhism, in the Ohrmazd-Ahriman conflict of Zoroastrianism, in Mormonism, in the Norse sagas, in the Jewish Qabalah, and in the opposition of Osiris and Set in ancient Egypt.

As an archetypal theme, it has lost none of its appeal today. In America, it provides a basis for the entire Wild West mythos. It forms the plotline of movies like George Lucas's *Star Wars*. It appears again and again in works of literature from the most banal thrillers to the literary epics of great authors. But the spirit communications tend to take the theme further than either its religious or literary statements. The primal conflict is often linked with human evolution and the idea that those on a spiritual path may be called on to take sides and fight . . . or at very least, stand up and be counted. But the conflict itself tends to be seen in more sophisticated terms than simple Good versus Evil. It is often presented as a need for increased consciousness, personal responsibility, spiritual growth, and a developed—as opposed to imposed—ethical base. All this, by definition, requires change from the individual and from society as a whole. This, in turn, highlights two doctrines that run like luminous threads through many spirit communications.

One is the idea that the evolution of humanity is being helped, guided, and perhaps even directed by individuals and entities who stand higher on the evolutionary ladder than the rest of us. These beings are the Guides of Spiritualism, the Hidden Masters of Theosophy, the Secret Chiefs of the Western Esoteric Tradition, the Polar Brotherhood of the White Eagle Lodge. Time and time again, these communities claim to be in touch with the voices.

The second is the notion that individual evolution—and hence the evolution of our species as a whole—is intimately linked with the processes of reincarnation and karma. The expression "karma" derives from Hindu philosophy. It is rooted in a Sanskrit term that translates as "activity" and is broad enough to encompass any type of human action, thought, or feeling. The doctrine of karma suggests that thoughts and deeds are seeds that produce fruit according to their nature. Good thoughts and deeds generate beneficial circumstances for the individual, while bad thoughts and deeds generate misery. On the face of it, this seems naive. It is a matter of observation that sinners often flourish while the greatest saints are sometimes forced to endure lives of poverty and pain. To meet this problem, exponents of karmic doctrine suggest that the rewards (or punishments) of karma are not always harvested in this life, but in later incarnations. Thus the doctrines of karma and reincarnation are inextricably linked.

A rather more profound exposition of karma describes it as the mechanism that conditions the evolution of the human soul. Thoughts and deeds determine who and what you are, influencing character, your level of spiritual evolution, and how far you are a prey to old, unconscious patterns of thought, emotion, and behavior. Since beliefs, desires, and habits all influence actions and actions in turn influence circumstances, the mechanism of karma is seen as a wholly rational process that can be clearly traced in, for example, psychoanalysis. From this viewpoint, the problem of the comfortable sinner disappears. Appearances are no longer important. It is the interior life that counts; the prince in his palace may be brutally unhappy despite his wealth and power, and may indeed be so locked into unconscious behavior patterns that he is barely alive. Thus, at this level, karma and reincarnation are no longer necessarily linked. Exponents simply state that *if* reincarnation is a fact, then the inheritance of old patterns could very well carry the karmic process from life to life.

Both karma and reincarnation are widely accepted in the belief systems of Asia. In the industrialized West, however, they are associated only with the minority tradition of occult, hermetic beliefs.[17] The same can be said for the vast body of spirit communication. While it is often expressed in religious terms, its essential nature is almost always occult. The association is so close that one school of thought actually holds that most hermetic teachings originate in the spirit world. As seminal a text as the *Poemandres* begins with the words "Methought a Being more than vast, in size beyond all bounds, called out my name and saith: What wouldst thou hear and see, and what hast thou in mind to learn and know?"[18] Another Hermetic text, *The Secret Sermon on the Mountain*, is presented as a discourse between Hermes Trismegistus and his son Tat as they return together from a mountain. But it quickly becomes clear that Hermes is present only in spirit form: "I have passed through myself into a Body that can never die. And now I am not as I was before; but I am born in Mind."[19] Hermes explains that his original form has been dismembered, purged of the "brutish torments" of matter, leaving him in a colorless, immortal body that cannot be touched or measured, although it can still be seen—almost the classical description of a spirit. The transformation, which is recommended to Tat, was accompanied by the arrival of ten benevolent spirits (called "powers" in Mead's translation).[20]

Within the spirit messages, there are several interesting subtexts. One is the idea that each of us somehow *elects* to be born into the world in order to learn. Another is that personal evolution not only involves multiple incarnations but incarnations outside this planet. A third is that the Spirit Masters have sometimes taken on physical bodies as well—and in so doing often formed relationships with the very people who act as their mediums today. Although conveniently thought of as a Native American, Grace Cooke's White Eagle claimed to have incarnated as a Tibetan, an Egyptian priest-pharaoh, a monk, and an alchemist . . . and that some of these lives were shared with previous incarnations of Grace herself. Jane Roberts's Seth has dictated a body of teachings that include the idea that the individual develops spiritually over a series of incarnations until (s)he reaches sufficient ethical heights to gain access to "higher planes" where godlike powers await. White Bull remarks, "The first purpose of your presence in a physical body is to evolve spiritually" and indicates that the evolution involves reincarnation.

In summation, then, the worldview propounded by many spirit voices suggests that we are all of us involved in a cosmic conflict between good and evil. As spirit entities ourselves, we make a decision to incarnate in order to learn, evolve, become increasingly conscious, and thus more fully play our part in the grand design. In the process we are helped by entities, human or otherwise, still in the spirit world. Their influence works at a cultural level and may account for the peculiar patterns in history and equally peculiar coincidences. It also works specifically in the lives of many individuals, some of whom become aware of the influence and decide to cooperate with it consciously. Alongside these benign helpers are their adversaries who do not wish well for the human race. Their influence is also felt both culturally and individually, as the archetypal possession of politicians like Adolf Hitler ably attests.

There is, however, a second level to the spirit teachings. The entire range of doctrines just outlined, all the way up to the cosmic conflict between Good and Evil, relates only to the world of phenomena. Beyond there is a reconciliation of opposites in absolute Unity. This concept, which is characteristic of all mystical doctrines, appears time and again in spirit communications. "You really exist in a fog that screens you from this extraordinary beauty, this complete oneness," says the spirit collective "Mark" in a communication with the British therapist and author Jacquie Burgess. "All is one. All is one, darlings. This is our song." The same message emanates from Up-uaut: "In reality every particle of intelligent life is a God. You who read this, I who teach it, your neighbor, your friend, your employer, your enemy, all are a living part of the Creator, therefore all is God without exception." White Eagle, White Bull, Seth, and scores of other communicators are united in their belief that All is One.

Is there any justification for believing them? In other words, are spirits what they claim to be?

23. A SKEPTICAL INQUIRY

JAMES RANDI DOUBTS THE SPIRITS. HE SAYS CATEGORICALLY, "NO REALLY good evidence for spirits is currently available."[1] His online *Encyclopedia of Claims, Frauds, and Hoaxes of the Occult and Supernatural*[2] repeats the quote and makes short work of Daniel Dunglas Home, claiming he controlled all aspects of his "séance performances" and was "discovered cheating several times." The same entry suggests that trickery was the driving force behind Home's spirit accordion—his sitters were fooled by his playing a mouth organ hidden in his mustache.

Randi, a Canadian/American stage conjurer who has made a lifetime career out of investigating reports of the paranormal, represents the tip of an

James Randi, a leading debunker of spirits and the paranormal

iceberg. He has been, for many years, the most recognizable public face of a movement that began, in its modern manifestation, with a book published in 1952—*Fads and Fallacies in the Name of Science* by Martin Gardner. The book was, according to its own subtitle, a study of human gullibility, investigating "the curious theories of modern pseudoscientists and the strange, amusing and alarming cults that surround them." Subjects covered included UFOs, orgone therapy, Dianetics, phrenology, reincarnation, and vegetarianism. Gardner followed up with more books and many essays on similar themes, stimulating public interest in the process. For a time he seemed to be fighting a losing battle—there was a significant upsurge of interest in the paranormal in the United States and Britain during the early 1970s—but then, in 1976, a philosophy professor named Paul Kurtz used a conference of the American Humanist Association as the launching pad of a new organization originally called The Committee for the Scientific Investigation of Claims of the Paranormal (CSICOP for short) and later changed to The Committee for Skeptical Inquiry or CSI. The organization was—and is—dedicated to the critical examination of a wide range of claims about the validity of the paranormal. Its official organ is the *Skeptical Inquirer*, an international bimonthly "magazine for science and reason." At about the same time as this was going on, James Randi was getting into his stride with public challenges to psychics, personal investigations, and numerous media appearances. Dozens of skeptical groups sprang up throughout the United States and abroad. The science writer Dr. Michael Shermer founded the Skeptics Society and launched the magazine *Skeptic*. On the face of it, these developments were very welcome, some might even suggest overdue. But experience suggests the Skeptical movement quickly showed itself less interested in evenhanded scientific examination of the paranormal than in debunking the paranormal at any cost, often with ridicule and innuendos of fraud. Randi clearly expressed one of the most common suspicions underlying skeptical thought:

> Replication by [stage] conjurers of such wonders as spoon-bending, clairvoyance, precognition and levitation (long established as items in the conjuring repertoire) cannot prove anything about claims of real paranormal performance—except that it can easily be done by trickery.[3]

He was by no means the first to promote the theory that spirits (and most other paranormal phenomena) might be explained by trickery. In 1854, as word of the strange occurrences at Hydesville was spreading throughout America, Ira and William Davenport, two brothers from Buffalo, New York, announced they were experiencing similar marvels and went on tour to prove it. They were accompanied and introduced by Dr. J. B. Ferguson, a Restoration Movement minister, who assured audiences that everything they saw was the result of spirit power. What they did see was vividly described to his grandson by the Victorian illusionist John Nevil Maskelyne who, as a young man in 1865, witnessed a Davenport performance in Cheltenham, England:

> The Davenports, clad in black . . . walked on to the stage amid enormous applause and sat down. They were bound hand and foot to their bench . . . townsmen assisting in the tying and thoroughly examining all the knots; the skeleton wardrobe was wheeled on to the stage and examined; and the musical instruments placed in position. Then the lights were turned out. Almost immediately bells began to ring, music was played, hands were seen apparently floating about the wardrobe.[4]

Maskelyne, however, arranged for a friend to draw aside a window blind and in the sudden shaft of afternoon sunlight "clearly saw Ira Davenport throwing the instruments out of the wardrobe." It was neither the first nor the last time the Davenports were exposed, but "they just moved on, in dignified sorrow, going to as many English towns as they could while the going was good."[5] In essence, the Davenports were escapologists, masquerading as mediums, and in 1910 Ira demonstrated some of his techniques to Harry Houdini.[6] In the latter half of his career, Houdini devoted much time and energy to exposing fraudulent mediumistic practice and frequently gave stage demonstrations of how their supposed powers could be produced by mechanical means. John Gordon Melton comments: "The exposure of widespread fraud within the spiritualist movement severely damaged its reputation and pushed it to the fringes of society in the United States."[7] How widespread the fraud became is illustrated by the fact that it was possible to purchase "séance kits" with all the equipment necessary to fake spirit phenomena. Today, such kits are still available and have grown, if anything, more sophisticated. The Box of Delights Séance Kit, for example, includes gimmicked bottles that can be made to move around and topple as if controlled by invisible hands.[8]

But the fact that mediumistic and other spirit phenomena can be—and frequently has been—duplicated by trickery does not constitute proof of uni-

Harry Houdini, the escapologist and stage magician,
who spent the latter part of his career exposing fraudulent mediums

versal fraud, which is why scientific investigation is of such importance. There are, of course, some who would argue that such investigation has been under way since 1882 when the Society for Psychical Research was founded in London to "conduct organised scholarly research into human experiences that challenge contemporary scientific models."[9] In the century since then, the society has indeed reported that some apparent spirit phenomena were the result of trickery, deception, lies, misrepresentation, natural causes, misinterpretation, and fraud. But it has also reported others that appeared to be genuine. It is this latter category that has attracted the attention of the Skeptical movement, members of which are concerned that supposedly scientific investigations may not have been carried out properly. In a great many cases, the skeptics have conducted investigations of their own, often on phenomena declared genuine following earlier examinations. In no case so far[10] publicized by the Skeptical movement has *any* paranormal phenomenon been found genuine. The result has been a general debunking of the work of those scientists and academics who have taken a practical interest in psychical research.

One important example of debunking, frequently mentioned in skeptical literature, is the confession of fraud made by Margaret Fox in 1888. An entry in Randi's encyclopedia on the Fox sisters, whose experiences were the foundation of modern Spiritualism, points out that they confessed to faking the raps by cracking their toe joints and bouncing an apple on the floor. The entry concludes:

> The public confessions had done nothing to dampen the belief in the Fox
> sisters or the movement they had started. The believers expressed their regret
> at the fact that the sisters had been forced into lying, and spiritualism con-
> tinued as if the confessions of the Fox sisters had never happened.[11]

There is a small error in this entry, which gives the impression that more than one Fox sister confessed—an error unfortunately repeated in much of the skeptical literature. The context of the confession is as follows:

Following the outbreak of raps in their home at Hydesville, the two younger Fox sisters, Kate and Margaret, persuaded their older sister, Leah, that the phenomena were genuine. Almost immediately, Kate and Margaret embarked on a career as mediums, with Leah as their manager. For a time, the two younger girls were extraordinarily successful and their séances were attended by the rich and famous, but both developed serious drinking problems. In later years, they quarreled bitterly with Leah, continued to drink heavily, experienced severe personal problems, and watched their careers— and their income—dwindle. Margaret began to contemplate suicide.

In 1888, Margaret walked onstage at the New York Academy of Music to announce that she and Kate had produced the raps at Hydesville by cracking their toe joints, after which Leah had forced them into a career of mediumship. According to contemporary press reports, she vigorously denounced the whole Spiritualist movement, calling it an "absolute falsehood from beginning to end . . . the flimsiest of superstitions [and] the most wicked blasphemy known to the world." She demonstrated toe cracking while under observation by doctors called out of the audience and the noises were sufficiently audible to be heard "throughout the theater." Her sister Kate sat in a box overlooking the stage throughout the performance. Kate's silence has been taken by skeptics as an affirmation of agreement with her sister's words, hence the mistaken idea that both confessed. The error—if it was an error—was a small one. For the skeptics, Margaret's solitary confession was enough to mark the case closed on the Fox sisters and the whole Spiritualist movement.

But as any experienced police officer will confirm, a confession is not necessarily proof of guilt. The confessor may be an attention-seeker, or mentally unstable, or attempting to protect or hurt someone else. The confession may have been the result of coercion, torture, or bribery. It is also necessary to take into consideration any attempt made by the suspect to withdraw the confession at a later stage. (One estimate[12] places the number of false confessions leading to criminal convictions in the United States as high as 25 percent.) More than one of these factors was present in the case of Margaret Fox. She was a lonely, suicidal alcoholic, who had spent a lifetime seeking attention as a medium. A New York City reporter had advanced her $1,500— a very substantial sum in the day—to give him an exclusive on a confession of fraud. The denunciation of Spiritualism generally might be expected to hurt Leah, who by this stage had made a small fortune from the movement. Furthermore, the silence of younger sister Kate did not appear to signify assent, as the skeptics insist. Her letters home following the confession expressed dismay and shock at the attack on Spiritualism. Margaret herself withdrew her confession, in writing, the year after she made it. Rather than tackling these factors, skeptical literature tends to dismiss some or all of them as "excuses."[13]

Elements of the confession itself present their own difficulties. We know nothing of the "doctors" who appeared from the audience to supervise Margaret's toe-cracking demonstration; and while she certainly managed to produce audible sounds, it is difficult to reconcile the cracking of a toe joint with William Crooke's description of the séance room sounds produced by Kate Fox under test conditions:

> These sounds are noticed with almost every medium . . . but for power and certainty I have met with no one who at all approached Miss Kate Fox. For several months I enjoyed almost unlimited opportunity of testing the various phenomena occurring in the presence of this lady, and I especially examined the phenomena of these sounds. With mediums, generally it is necessary to sit for a formal *séance* before anything is heard; but in the case of Miss Fox

it seems only necessary for her to place her hand on any substance for loud thuds to be heard in it, like a triple pulsation, sometimes loud enough to be heard several rooms off. In this manner I have heard them in a living tree —on a sheet of glass—on a stretched iron wire—on a stretched membrane—a tambourine—on the roof of a cab—and on the floor of a theatre. Moreover, actual contact is not always necessary; I have had these sounds proceeding from the floor, walls, etc., when the medium's hands and feet were held—when she was standing on a chair—when she was suspended in a swing from the ceiling—when she was enclosed in a wire cage—and when she had fallen fainting on a sofa. I have heard them on a glass harmonicon—I have felt them on my own shoulder and under my own hands. I have heard them on a sheet of paper, held between the fingers by a piece of thread passed through one corner. With a full knowledge of the numerous theories which have been started, chiefly in America, to explain these sounds, I have tested them in every way that I could devise, until there has been no escape from the conviction that they were true objective occurrences not produced by trickery or mechanical means.[14]

A more subtle problem was unearthed by the academic Robert McLuhan, who took the trouble to examine the details of the confession itself. In it Margaret Fox claimed that when the raps began at Hydesville, she was eight years old, while her sister Kate was six and a half. This was simply untrue. A statement by the girls' mother made just two weeks after the start of the disturbances in 1848 describes Margaret as fourteen years old and Kate as twelve. McLuhan found it implausible that Margaret could have misremembered her age—there is a huge emotional distance between an eight-year-old and a fourteen-year-old—and tried to work out why she might have lied about it. He came to the following conclusion:

What struck me about Maggie's statement . . . is that she took great pains to persuade her audience that she and her sister were capable of fooling their mother. Mrs. Fox did not understand it, Maggie said, "and didn't suspect us of being capable of a trick because we were so young . . . no one suspected us of any trick because we were such young children."

Maggie also suggested that being so young they were supple enough to manage the necessary physical contortions: "Such perfect control is only possible when a child is taken at an early age and carefully and continually taught to practice the muscles which grow still in later years. A child of twelve is almost too old" . . . The fact that she was anxious about it suggests to me that she had not actually experienced the scenario she was referring to. In short, she was making it all up, and changing her and her sister's ages was a ploy designed to make it sound plausible.[15]

One might also wonder why the skeptics who accepted Margaret's confession so readily failed to question who it was who took the little girls at an early age and "continually taught them to practice the muscles which grow still in later years" in order to prepare them for a career faking ghostly noises.

McLuhan did not stop with the Fox confession when he decided to investigate paranormal phenomena. As a skeptic himself, he was naturally sympathetic toward the investigative work undertaken by the Skeptical movement and the criticisms it made of those scientists prepared to accept some phenomena as genuine. But closer examination led to disillusionment. His turning point came with the examination of an historical account of a poltergeist outbreak in 1772. The brief facts of the case, described in painstaking detail in a contemporary pamphlet signed by six witnesses, were these:

A Londoner by the name of Mrs. Golding was in her parlor on January 6 when she heard the sound of china breaking in the kitchen. Her maid, twenty-year-old Ann Robinson, came in to tell her plates were falling from a shelf. Mrs. Golding went to investigate and found herself in a veritable maelstrom of poltergeist activity: violent noises sounded all over the house, various objects were hurled about as if by invisible hands, a clock tumbled over and broke, as did an earthenware pan of salted beef. Mrs. Golding and Ann fled from the house to take refuge with a neighbor, but the violence followed them. They escaped it temporarily by going to the home of Mrs. Golding's niece, but it started up again at eight o'clock that evening. Dishes fell from shelves and turned themselves upside down. When replaced, they fell off all over again. A cat was pelted with eggs. A pestle and mortar jumped six feet onto the floor. Buckets of liquid suddenly bubbled and frothed over. Various other items were flung about and Ann was struck on the foot by a teapot.

McLuhan discovered that, according to the skeptical stage magician Milbourne Christopher, a rational explanation was put forward some years later by a magazine editor named William Hone, who published an article claiming that the maid Robinson had confessed to faking the whole thing. She had thrown the eggs at the cat. She had hung joints of ham in such a way that they would fall down under their own weight. She had strung wire behind the plates so she could make them jump from the shelves. She had tied horsehairs to various objects so they could be made to move as if of their own accord. She had added chemicals to the liquid in the buckets to make it froth over.

McLuhan found all this difficult to accept but was initially persuaded by Christopher who, as a professional illusionist, stated that such tricks were by no means impossible. But doubts began to creep in.

> The more I thought about it, the more I wondered. This business of attaching horsehairs to objects sounds rather difficult. Would the maid have wrapped the hairs right round and tied knots to keep them in place? Just how long were they? Or did she use glue? You'd think it would require some time and absolute privacy to prepare such things unobserved . . . Even if she had had the opportunity to prepare the disturbances at Mrs. Golding's house, would she have had the same chance to do so at the neighbor's house? And the niece's house too?
>
> It's risky arguing with an expert, a point that the conjurer-sceptics themselves are keen to nurture. But Christopher is trading heavily on his privileged status: his scenario is unrealistic. Whole shelves of plates falling down, being replaced and falling down again, and other objects throughout the house coming alive at the same time, causing serious damage—this suggests not conjuring but somebody running amok.[16]

In rejecting the stage magician's explanation, McLuhan felt he had crossed some sort of Rubicon but was unable to rid himself of the conviction that if anyone was being credulous here, it was the skeptic himself. Later, he discovered that a characteristic of most skeptical investigations was that "explanations of paranormal claims don't have to be coherent . . . *as long as they restore normality*."[17] Says McLuhan:

> The idea that a young servant girl might choose to spend her limited leisure time and meagre wages procuring a chemical that would make the liquid bubble in her employer's bucket, along with all the other curious conjuring tricks, helps resolve an awkward problem but leaves appalling new ones in its wake. Why go to such lengths? How did she acquire the skills to do all this without being observed? In any other circumstances it's hard to think that the girl would entertain such bizarre notions for a minute. Yet here it

seems the alternative is so unthinkable that just about any idea will do, no matter how intrinsically implausible it may be in itself. How is it possible not to be sceptical about the sceptic's view?[18]

To judge from the examples given in his book on the subject, skeptics claim that all paranormal phenomena and spirit communications are the result of fraud. Furthermore, the skeptical position frequently predicates two unspoken assumptions: (1) that a rational examination of "spirits" must necessarily involve examination of "spirit phenomena" and (2) that the concept of spirits must be susceptible to physical proof. Neither assumption is correct. Many apparent spirit communications generate no physical phenomena, nor are they capable of being proven or disproven in any way likely to satisfy a skeptical materialist.

Prior to the emergence of Spiritualism in the nineteenth century, much of humanity's "spirit encounters" were like that—personal experiences that led to theories of postmortem survival or the existence of immaterial intelligences and entities. Even within Spiritualism itself, communications need have no accompanying paranormal activity: many, perhaps even most, involve only the spoken words of an entranced medium. Thus, many of the skeptical objections are irrelevant. In particular, the question has never been whether spirit encounters are "real"—they clearly *are* real as experiential phenomena—but whether the theories that purport to explain them are actually correct.

24. THE BICAMERAL THEORY

Julian Jaynes believed he could provide a convincing theory of spirits. As noted earlier, his researches led him to the conclusion that prior to about 1250 BCE, spirit contact with mankind was almost universal. But there came a point in human evolution when things began to change. The gods, for reasons that must have been incomprehensible at the time, began gradually to withdraw. Fewer and fewer of them walked visibly among humanity. They took to communicating from a distance so that only the divine voice could be heard. But even this voice faded with time. Jaynes charted these changes over an approximate thousand-year period by examining what happened to mankind's oracles.

The first oracles, he believed, were no more than specific locations where anyone could go to listen to the voice of their gods. The surroundings might be impressive, perhaps a little frightening, and natural sounds like running water or whispering winds would be conducive to hearing voices. But there was no priest, no sibyl. If the gods declined to be present in the home, oracles were areas of holy ground where the deity might be persuaded to speak more freely.

But as time went on, the nature of these sacred places underwent a subtle change. Increasingly, the voices declined to converse with just anybody. Their words were reserved for priests or priestesses who attended at the locale. It was not that the spirits were reticent about giving advice—far from it. But their voices could only be heard by an elite who conveyed the gods' instructions to the general public.

With the passage of the years, even the priests and priestesses could no longer hear the spirits unless they underwent a prolonged period of training and embarked on special ceremonies to persuade the discarnate entities to speak. At this point, however, the priesthood still listened to the gods and passed on their words.

Somewhere around the fifth century BCE, Jaynes believed, the situation changed again. The priests and priestesses could no longer simply listen. They had to allow themselves to be possessed by the spirit in order for communication to take place. This involved even more elaborate training and was hard on the medium, who would often foam and convulse under the strain. The process did, however, have the benefit of allowing people once again to hear the words of the god directly, albeit spoken through the mouth of a human host.

Unfortunately this benefit eventually disappeared as the words of the god became more and more garbled so that the utterings of a possessed medium had to be interpreted by a skilled expert and experienced in the process. This marked the split between priest and prophet, priestess and sibyl. In essence, some people trained as mediums and entered on careers as convulsive ecstatics while others became interpreters of the divine word. With the split came a shift in the power structure, giving the (interpretative) priest a special authority still claimed to the present day.

Jaynes believed the final step in this six-stage process came when the abilities of the sibyl grew so erratic that interpretation became impossible. At this point, the ancient oracles died out altogether. Delphi survived longer than most, but only, in Jaynes's view, because of a cultural nostalgia for the good old days when the gods walked and talked with men.

But who or what were these "gods" who were responsible for the establishment of our earliest civilizations? The descriptions that have come down to us make it quite clear they were not the high moral and spiritual beings associated with our modern ideas of divinity. As many scholars have pointed out, the antics of the Olympians were a catalog of lust, greed, envy, and aggression—characteristics depressingly comparable to the worst traits of humanity.

Even more striking from our present-day viewpoint is that they were described as beings who walked and talked with humanity like physical kings. This has led to conjecture among less orthodox students of ancient history that the gods might not have been gods at all, but visiting aliens from some distant planet whose advanced technology was mistaken for magic and miracles. Jaynes too believed the gods were not real gods, but he has no time for the extraterrestrial hypothesis. Instead, he stated bluntly:

The gods are what we now call hallucinations. Usually they are only seen and heard by the particular heroes they are speaking to. Sometimes they come in mists . . . suggesting visual auras preceding them. But at other times they simply occur. Usually they come as themselves, commonly as mere voices, but sometimes as other people closely related to the hero.[1]

The idea that spirit voices were hallucinations is intimately associated in Jaynes's thesis with another premise. Jaynes was convinced that human consciousness is a relatively recent acquisition. It is, he believed, an evolutionary development not much more than three thousand years old.

On the face of it, this seems unlikely. The earliest known civilization—the Sumerian—dates back to around 4500 BCE. Dynastic Egypt was established around 2925 BCE. The middle of the third millennium BCE saw flourishing metal-using cultures in Crete, the Cycladic islands, and the southern part of the Aegean mainland. Even the relatively recent civilizations of South America, generally dated no earlier than 1500 BCE, still arose at a time when, according to Jaynes, no human on the planet was capable of conscious thought. But Jaynes, a professor of psychology, argues that consciousness is not necessary even for the most complex of tasks. Although consciousness often plays a part in such activities as perception, judgment, thinking, reasoning, learning, and the assimilation of experience, it is not actually necessary for any of them.

If, for example, you close your left eye and focus with your right on the left-hand, left page margin of this book, you will still be fully conscious of the sweep of type across the two open pages. But if you then place your index finger at the start of any line and move it slowly right across the open pages, you will discover that there is an area in which the fingertip vanishes, only to reappear again a little farther on. This conjuring trick is related to the physical structure of the human eye, which has a blind spot in its field of vision. Since we dislike blind spots, we fill it in where it occurs, through a process analogous to a computer filling in a missing part of a picture by deduction from the rest. Once "filled in," the former blank spot becomes part of your perception. Nor is it illusionary. While the perception does not come about through the usual process of light striking the retina, it is still a valid analogy of what is there on the printed page. Sweep your eye across and you will be able to read it, without having to worry about any blank. But while valid, this is a perception in which consciousness plays no part at all. You do not, in other words, notice the blank spot and think to yourself that it is something you must fill in. The process is entirely unconscious. So consciousness is not always necessary for perception.

The notion that judgment is a conscious function was demolished by the psychologist Karl Marbe as long ago as 1901, using a simple experiment. Marbe had an assistant hand him two small objects, and handed back the lighter of the two after carefully examining how he made the judgment. He realized he was aware of a great many things about the two objects: their feel against his skin, the downward pressure on his hands as they reacted to gravity, any irregularities in their shape, and so on. But when it came to making the judgment, he found that the answer was simply there, apparently inherent in the objects themselves. Actually, the judgment was made by the central nervous system at a wholly unconscious level.

It was an attempt by another scientist, H. J. Watt, to punch holes in Marbe's experiment that led to the truly astonishing discovery that thinking, apparently the most obviously conscious of all human activities, is not a conscious process either. Watt suspected that the whole business of weight judgment was not actually unconscious but a conscious decision that happened so quickly that Marbe's subjects simply forgot what they had done.

To try to prove this theory, he set up a series of word-association experiments that allowed the process to be broken down and examined in four constituent parts. The results of these experiments showed that, provided the subject understood in advance what was required, thinking became entirely automatic. It arose, of its own accord, once the stimulus word was given. As Jaynes says, one thinks before knowing what they're supposed to think about. In other words, thoughts are not conscious. Consequently, in this instance, as in many others, consciousness is not necessary for one to think.

It is apparently unnecessary for reasoning also. The celebrated French mathematician Jules-Henri Poincaré told the Société de Psychologie of Paris how, on a trip, he had solved one of his most difficult problems:

> The incidents of the journey made me forget my mathematical work. Having reached Coutances, we entered an omnibus . . . At the moment when I put my foot on the step, the idea came to me, without anything in my former thoughts seeming to have paved the way for it, that the transformation I had used to define the Fuchsian functions were identical with those of non-Euclidian geometry.[2]

The process by which Poincaré reached this conclusion did not require consciousness. Nor did the processes by which the structures of the atom and the benzene molecule were discovered or the solution to the mechanical problem of how to construct a viable sewing machine. In all three instances the solutions came through dreams.

Learning does not require consciousness either. Indeed, in some types of learning, the intrusion of consciousness actually blocks the process. This is particularly true of what is called "signal learning," sometimes referred to as conditioning or, less pejoratively, learning by experience. When a puff of air is blown into someone's eye, they blink—the reflex is involuntary. If a light is shone into the eye immediately before blowing and the process is repeated several times, the eye begins to blink at the light, before the puff of air. The subject's body has learned that the stimulus is about to come and anticipates it by blinking. But there is no consciousness involved in this learning process. So far as the subject is concerned, it simply happens. Furthermore, if the subjects tries to speed up the process by blinking consciously after every flash of the light, the reflex will arise much more slowly, if at all.

A great deal more than reflex actions can be learned without the intervention of consciousness. A charming case study reported by Lambert Gardiner in *Psychology: A Study of a Search* tells of a psychology class that decided to teach their professor that they preferred him to stand at the right of the lecture hall. Each time he moved to the right, they paid closer attention to what he was saying and laughed more heartily at his jokes. While he remained completely unconscious of what was going on, he was soon delivering his lectures so far to the right of the hall that he was almost out the door.

Assimilation of experience is often associated with consciousness—indeed there was a time when psychologists *defined* consciousness as the assimilation of experience. That time has long gone. It is fairly likely that you use a telephone frequently and apply the full light of consciousness to the various numbers you dial. But could you say now, without looking, what letters are associated with what figures on the dial? You brush your teeth each morning: how many are on view in the bathroom mirror as you do so? Could you list, again without looking, the ornaments on your mantelpiece? A few attempts like these quickly indicate how poor a vehicle consciousness is in assimilating your daily experiences.

Most people will notice instantly when a familiar clock stops, even though the sound if its tick may not have impinged on their consciousness for years. Not hearing the clock tick until it stops is a familiar cliché, but one that demonstrates clearly that assimilation of experience (the clock stopping) can be carried out very efficiently without consciousness. This is even more clearly demonstrated by the use of hypnosis in situations like the loss of car keys. In a trance, people can often be persuaded to recall where they left them, even though consciously they have no awareness of their location whatsoever. The experience of leaving the keys was not consciously recorded, but it was accurately recorded all the same.

It is now clear that consciousness is unnecessary to survive even the busiest day. Indeed, it is observable that consciousness is not only unnecessary in daily life, but also unexpectedly absent from much of it. When driving a car, for example, the driver is no longer aware of the various complexities involved. He or she does not think consciously of applying the brake, changing the gear, or moving the wheel so many inches clockwise. These things, so far as consciousness is concerned, simply happen—although consciousness can override any one or all of them at will. The same applies to activities like riding a bicycle, skiing, using a typewriter, or operating machinery, however complex, with which one is really familiar. It is as if, during waking hours, we are accompanied by an invisible robot to whom we can hand over control of those functions with which we do not personally wish to be bothered.

There is strong survival pressure toward handing over as much as possible to the robot, since it can often do the job a great deal better than the individual concerned. Anyone may cast their mind back to the time when they were learning to drive a car. Every operation had to be carried out consciously, at a substantial investment of memory and attention. One had to remember to depress the clutch before engaging a gear. One had to estimate (or read off a dial) the precise engine revs that would allow this to be done comfortably. One had to judge distances and the width of the vehicle accurately and continuously. The whole process was a nightmare; and while it remained conscious, one drove badly and with difficulty.

The same process is evident in a baby learning how to walk. It is a pitiful process, full of stumbling and heavy falls. But every adult was like that once, a bipedal animal who could crawl but not walk. With instinct and encouragement we learned, but learning—in this, as in so many things—meant turning over control to the robot. When it came to walking, we manage this so effectively that, unlike car driving, consciousness no longer has a veto over how it is done. The curious fact is that adults no longer have the least idea how to walk. They decide where you want to go, of course, and when, but the process that establishes their balance, contracts their muscles, and initiates subtle, continuous feedback controls is as far beyond reach as the surface of the moon.

Clearly, if there are things like driving a car that the robot can do better, there are also things like walking that the robot can do perfectly and the individual cannot do at all. This fact encourages us to hand over more and more tasks to robot control. Sometimes this is done quite consciously. Zen Buddhism, when applied to tasks like archery, is a case in point. The Zen practitioner is encouraged not to aim at the target but to "become one with it" and allow the target to "attract the arrow."[3] This is really a process of giving the bow to the robot, which shoots a great deal more accurately than the archer. More modern sports systems, such as Inner Tennis—which allows players to rehearse their technique imaginally before putting it into physical practice—aim at substantially the same result. Athletes everywhere readily accept that they reach their peak when they cease to think—and worry—about their game.

So long as we are discussing motor skills, this situation is acceptable. Indeed, it is absolutely necessary. But the trouble arises when the robot starts to do the thinking. Robotic thinking is by no means uncommon. Crass examples abound in the oratory of politics and religion, where enthusiastic practitioners chant slogans at one another, under the comfortable impression that they are engaging in a debate. They are, in fact, merely sitting on the sidelines of a robot war.

Other examples are more subtle, consequently more dangerous. How often have any of us found ourselves parroting an opinion that actually belonged to the newspaper read that morning? How often have words reflected a mindless reaction to some stimulus that effected individuals in ways they did not really begin to comprehend? How often has one passed the time of day with a neighbor, discussing the weather, or even the garden, with no more conscious input than pressing the playback button of a tape recorder? In all of these familiar situations, it is the robot that is actually speaking.

Sad to say, the robot is an eminently helpful creature, eager to take more and more of the burden from conscious shoulders. It will breathe, walk, drive, speak, even think for us, and, unless we are very, very careful, psychoanalysts claim, it will live our lives for us. But to Professor Jaynes, this slipping back into unconscious, robotic living is an evolutionary regression, a personal mirroring of the way things used to be for the whole of humanity. Prior to about 1000 BCE, everyone left their lives *entirely* to the robot and had no hope at all of waking up and taking charge. Consciousness as we know it simply did not exist.

In this curious psychological state, humanity moved from its primitive hunter-gatherer existence to develop agriculture, establish villages, then towns, and, eventually, city civilizations . . . all without a single conscious thought. But not without help. According to Jaynes:

> Volition, planning, initiative (was) organised with no consciousness whatsoever and then "told" to the individual in his familiar language, sometimes with the visual aura of a familiar friend or authority figure or "god" or sometimes as a voice alone. The individual obeyed these hallucinated voices because he could not "see" what to do himself.[4]

This is an exciting concept and one that might go some way toward solving the dilemma of the voices heard by so many people across the sweep of history. But is there really evidence to underpin it?

Jaynes used the 1959 excavation of a Mesolithic site at Eynan, twelve miles north of the Sea of Galilee in Israel, as an important foundation of his conclusions. The remains discovered belonged to the Natufian culture (itself named for another Israeli site) but were like nothing ever seen before. The Natufians were hunter-gatherers who up to then were believed to have used flint weapons and lived in cave mouths. But the excavations unearthed evidence that changed the picture completely. What the archaeologists found was no nomadic site but a permanent town—the first of three to be discovered—of circular stone-built houses. Among the structures in this primeval community was what Jaynes believed to be the earliest known example of a king's tomb. There are suspicions that this structure may have been constructed in stages, with each stage marking some form of religious development. Within the innermost, hence earliest, chamber were two skeletons. One was of a woman wearing a shell headdress. The other was of an adult male. Archaeologists looked to the elaborate nature of the tomb and decided the individuals buried inside must have been the world's first king and his consort.

Jaynes himself went further. He argued this was not simply the world's first king, but the world's first *god*-king. To understand why he reached this conclusion, we must put it into the context of his theory that at the time the Natufian culture flourished, humanity did not possess consciousness.

What was such a state actually like? We have already examined how easily any one of us might slip back into robotic function, but today this is always a temporary condition. We wake up often enough to accept wakefulness as our natural state. Indeed for many of us it seems to be our only state since the bouts of robotic behavior tend to get forgotten. Furthermore, a robot take-over does not rob us of consciousness completely—only of a consciousness of the task the robot happens to be performing. The searchlight inside our head simply turns elsewhere, to think about a different problem, plan our day at the office, fantasize about a loved one. It does not switch off altogether. But when the robot took over completely, as Jaynes believed it did for most of human history, things were very different.

Jaynes claimed that these people lived with no sense of ego whatsoever, no Joycean "stream of consciousness" maintaining an inner dialogue. The unconscious state influenced their experience of memory. There was obviously no such thing as conscious recall, no decision to remember, no struggle for the word on the tip of the tongue. Function was always and forever a matter of stimulus-response. And when in a new situation they were instructed by a voice of authority.

This is one of the most interesting aspects of Jaynes' theory. Today, "hearing things" or "seeing things" generally suggests the need of treatment in a mental hospital, but such symptoms are only indicative of insanity in acutely distressed people—and sometimes not even then. Although there has been very little formal research on the subject, one survey across a population base of more than 15,000 showed 7.8 percent reported hallucinations among healthy men and 12 percent among healthy women. Visual hallucinations were twice as common as auditory and the highest frequency was reported between the ages of 20 and 29. National differences emerged with Russians and Brazilians experiencing many more hallucinations than the overall average. In all cases, the people involved were physically and mentally healthy.

The discovery that it was possible to remove parts of the right brain without influencing the patient's well-being led early psychiatrists to conclude that much of the right brain was simply unnecessary. Jaynes believed that the right brain mirror of Wernicke's Area once functioned to organize experience—including interactions with authority figures like tribal chieftains —and code it into admonitory "voices." These were then transferred across the *corpus collosum* to be picked up, hence "heard," by the Wernicke's Area in the left brain. In essence, the right brain "Wernicke" was an hallucination generator, but the hallucinations themselves were beneficial and survival oriented.

It is easy to understand the necessity for a coding mechanism that will allow the individual to benefit from experience. Without it, we could not possibly survive. But once we understand the nature of the two hemispheres, it is easy to see how this particular coding mechanism led to belief in the gods. From our present perspective, we can appreciate that the messages passed across the *corpus collosum* were an amalgamation of personal life experience and the instructions of one's tribal or family superiors. But that, of course, is not how they were experienced. The transfer to the Wernicke Area ensured they were heard as spoken orders and mistaken for objective speech. The "voice" might occasionally be the voice of a relative, living or dead, sage, chief, king or other authority figure, but however presented it would always carry the additional numinousity of the right brain. Even today, right brain contact—in the form of inspiration, for example—will often elicit a feeling of awe. The poor, pedestrian left brain simply is not used to the creative fireworks. How much more striking must the sensation have been when the contact came in the form of hallucinatory orders. No wonder our ancestors concluded they were listening to a god. That conclusion was reached, Jaynes theorized, if not at Eynan in 9000 BCE, then at some time and place very close. But it is Eynan that provides us with the evidence. In the king's tomb, the bones of the woman indicate that she was laid out more or less as you might expect, lying on her back to take her eternal rest. But the man was not. He was buried in a raised position, propped in place with stones.

On the face of things, it is difficult to see why any tribe should take the trouble to do this with the body of their dead king. But Jaynes thought he knew. While the king lived, his voice—the voice of immediate authority—was incorporated into the hallucinations of his followers. When he died, the voice remained. To the followers the conclusion was obvious. The king was not dead at all. They propped him up so he could continue to give them orders. And at some point, their intellectual evolution was sufficiently far advanced to allow them to draw an even more important conclusion. Since the hallucinated voice carried the numinousity associated with the right brain, it eventually dawned on the tribe that a dead king was a god-king.

From this primitive beginning, sprang virtually the whole religious edifice of human thought. Belief in postmortem survival, ancestral spirits, and the reality of a divinity or divinities, all rests on this hallucinatory foundation, itself firmly rooted in the very structure of our brains. Our ancestors had no need of faith. They knew these things from personal experience.

The physiological foundation of Jaynes's theory is based partly on the discovery that the human brain is divided into two hemispheres, each with a specific function and a particular mode of mentation. In essence, there are two identities inside the skull. They normally cooperate seamlessly. The left hemisphere, in 95 percent of the population, is associated with logical thought, reasoning, speech and consciousness. The right hemisphere is the creative half of the partnership, providing such functions as intuition, aesthetic values, visions and dreams—the stuff of the unconscious. It is important to realize that the "entities" who "inhabit" *both* hemispheres are capable of thought and rational function, but the one that humans are most aware of and think of as their identity is personified in the left hemisphere.

In the left hemisphere, there are three areas related to the function of speech. The most important is Wernicke's Area, a portion of the left temporal lobe above and to the rear of the left ear. It stores and processes vocabulary, syntax, meaning and understanding. Destroy it in an adult and he or she will be rendered incapable of meaningful speech. But if the entire portion of the right brain corresponding to Wernicke's Area is removed—as has been done surgically to treat certain conditions—nothing much happens. The ability to speak and verbal thinking are unaffected.

This then was Jaynes's explanation of what spirits are and where they come from. In simple summary, the whisperers are self-generated hallucinations and the spirit world is firmly located in the soft gray matter of the right brain. But rational though it sounds, it is an explanation that does not hold water.

Julian Jaynes first summarized his ideas on humanity's emerging consciousness at an invited address to the American Psychological Association in Washington in 1969. His reception was sufficiently positive to encourage him to publish a much fuller account in 1976. Despite a sober, unmemorable title, *The Origin of Consciousness in the Breakdown of the Bicameral Mind* generated such widespread interest that it was issued in paperback. Critical reaction was, to say the least, generous. One reviewer suggested his theory might become the most influential idea presented in the second half of the Twentieth century. Another found his evidence "compelling." A third compared him with Freud in his ability to generate a new view of human behavior. But impressive though it was, there are weaknesses in Jaynes's case.

Although it was his reading of the *Iliad* that first made him wonder about the provenance of human consciousness, Jaynes chose to begin his historical evidence with the Mesolithic burial at Eynan. Here was his first mistake. During the 1960s, when Jaynes began to examine the evidence, the archaeological consensus of prehistory was based on the assumption that political structures and religious beliefs were more or less similar to those of historical times. Specifically, it was assumed that rulers, be they tribal chiefs or primitive kings, were male.

This assumption ran so deep that when archaeologists reported on their study of Minoan Crete, they referred constantly to a line of kings despite the fact that not one single representation of a male ruler was ever found. When the evidence for female involvement in political life became too strong to ignore, it was explained away by the suggestion that the women may have taken temporary charge while their men were at sea. Here too the conclusion was unsupported by any evidence. This sort of pervasive, if largely unconscious, chauvinism remains a feature of archaeology to this day. It is certainly a feature of Jaynes's analysis of the Eynan burial.

In the tomb, the excavating archaeologists found two human skeletons, one male, one female. Given the elaborate nature of the structure, it was obvious these had been important personages. Jaynes assumed it was equally obvious that the male was the more important of the two. It was the male who was identified as a king and, since he had been buried in an unusual way, the foundation of the hallucinatory voice theory was neatly laid down. As king, he represented the ultimate authority figure in life. His bicameral (unconscious) subjects functioned on the instructions of their leader and when he died, the stress of the loss caused them to hallucinate his voice. In fact there is absolutely no evidence to suggest the male really was the more important of the two. Rather the reverse—it was the female who wore the headdress. The only significant thing about the male—and it seems of very small significance when stripped of Jaynes's elaborate speculations—was that he was not buried lying flat. His head was propped on a pillow of stones while more stones were piled on top of his lower body.

Since Eynan was first excavated, substantial evidence has accumulated that our earliest ancestors believed, almost exclusively, in a female deity. At Çatal Hüyük, for example, James Mellaart discovered remains of Neolithic shrines dated to about 6500-5800 BCE. Huge figures of goddesses are modeled in high relief on the walls. A series of stone and terra-cotta statuettes found in these shrines represent a female figure, sometimes accompanied by leopards. The main deity of these Neolithic people was clearly a goddess, a mistress of animals. Her character was vividly depicted on a schist plaque carved to represent two scenes, a sacred marriage and a mother with child. At Hacilar, near Lake Burdur, a somewhat later culture revealed further statuettes of goddesses associated with felines.

The idea that our forefathers believed God to be female proved a bitter pill for archaeologists. They have typically fought a rearguard action from the position that female deities represented a local aberration, to the idea that there may once have been a goddess cult, and finally, with enormous reluctance, to their present position that prehistory was characterized by a near worldwide worship of the Great Goddess. Since political structures are an outgrowth of human thought and human thought is an outgrowth of human belief, it is likely that at a time of Goddess worship, temporal authority was mainly vested in women. This means that in the Eynan burial, the recumbent female with the shell headdress is far more likely to have been queen of her community than the male was to have been king. At best he may have been a consort with some associated prestige but probably little-enough real authority. He could equally well have been the woman's son or the Natufian equivalent of a boy toy. In such circumstances, the propping of the head may be of no importance whatsoever.

But this is not the only weakness in Jaynes's case. The psychological aspect of his overall thesis is based on the assumption that the breakdown of the bicameral mind was largely triggered by the invention of writing. At the time he developed his ideas, the orthodox consensus held that writing was invented in Sumaria sometime in the third millennium BCE. This tied in rather neatly with the remainder of his evidence, which appears to show a gradual shift in human mentation from that time until 1300 BCE when the bicameral breakdown became widespread and very evident. By 1979, however, there were indications that writing was actually invented far earlier than the orthodox consensus allowed. American academics Allan Forbes Jr. and T. R. Crowder found a hitherto unrecognized script incorporated in Upper Palaeolithic cave art. Nor was this unexpected discovery a series of crude glyphs. It carried all the indications of a developed alphabet. The implication is that the earliest writing must have predated the Upper Palaeolithic by a substantial margin.

These American findings were supported by an increasing volume of evidence from other fields. As long ago as 1956, another American academic, Professor Charles Hapgood, put his students to work on the analysis of sev-

Bolivia's Tiahuanaco ruins, believed by some to be more than 17,000 years old

eral ancient maps that seemed to show some curious and anomalous features. Although he published the results of this work in 1966, they were not well received—or indeed widely discussed—by his fellow academics. Nor was this surprising. Hapgood concluded, against the rock-solid consensus of his day, that the maps contained evidence of an advanced civilization (unequaled in Europe before the second half of the eighteenth century) that had flourished in the Ice Age.

Conventional wisdom has it that the last Ice Age ended about ten thousand years ago. To have flourished during this era, Hapgood's lost civilization must logically have been established at a far earlier date. This too seems to be borne out by a wealth of supporting evidence.

High in the Bolivian Andes, for example, lie the cyclopean ruins of Tiahuanaco, an ancient city built using earthquake-proof architectural and engineering techniques we would find difficult to match today. Because of the sophistication of the buildings, archaeologists initially assumed Tiahuanaco had to be of recent origin and dated its foundation around 150 BCE with a growth pattern that ended as late as 900 CE. However, this dating has failed to withstand serious scrutiny. The problem is that an extensive area of Tiahuanaco—called the Kalasasaya—functioned as an astronomical observatory. Most modern archaeologists accept this without question, but one, Arthur Posnansky, decided to use the ancient observations recorded in the stonework to date the site itself. His initial figures indicated the city was functioning in 15,000 BCE.

Although his findings were accepted by the Bolivian government, Posnansky's academic colleagues were not so sure. One of them, a German astronomer named Rolf Muller, pointed out that the figures could easily point to a date of 9300 BCE. Even this calculation indicates the existence of a sophisticated urban culture with advanced building techniques in the Ice Age, exactly as Hapgood predicted from his maps. But Muller himself decided that the evidence *could* be interpreted to support Posnansky's earlier date. The only real reason for questioning it was that it seemed incredible.

Incredible or not, Posnansky's 15,000 BCE dating of Tiahuanaco is actually superseded by a very curious dating of the ancient Egyptian civilization given by the Ptolemaic priest Manetho. Contrary to the beliefs of modern Egyptology, which dates the unification of Egypt and the foundation of dynastic rule to about 3100 BCE, Manetho maintained that prior to the pharaohs we know about, a line of predynastic monarchs ruled for a period not far short of fourteen thousand years. If the figure is correct, it would date Egyptian civilization to an era some two thousand years earlier than the "fantastic" date calculated by Posnansky for Tiahuanaco—once again in the depths of the Ice Age.

Since Hapgood's lost civilization has not been precisely dated, it is worth noting that Manetho claimed the prehistoric rulers were preceded by a dynasty of "Horus-Kings" dating back a further 15,000 years. But even these extraordinary figures are conservative when compared to those given in a much older source, the Turin Papyrus. The papyrus, which appears to have been written around 1400 BCE, agrees with Manetho, more or less, by allocating a 13,400-year reign to the predynastic pharaohs. However, the Horus-Kings were said to have begun their reign some 23,000 years earlier, giving a foundation date for ancient Egypt in the region of 36,400 BCE. It perhaps goes without saying that while orthodox Egyptology is happy to accept both these sources as reliable guides to the kings of dynastic Egypt, the earlier figures are dismissed as fantasy.

In recent years, however, the orthodox view has come under increasingly violent attack. Critics have pointed to the long recognized—and long ignored—mystery surrounding the development of Egyptian culture. The archaeology of the Nile Valley does not indicate the expected stage-by-stage developments from primitive hunter-gatherers to sophisticated urban dwellers. Instead, the entire edifice—including the engineering skills that built the pyramids—seemed to spring up out of nowhere. Since this is manifestly impossible, the suggestion has been made that the civilization evolved elsewhere and migrated to the valley around 3100 BCE. If this suggestion is correct, it follows that the civilization itself is older—possibly far older—than the orthodox consensus allows.

Support for this view comes not from an Egyptologist but from a geologist. Professor Robert Schoch of Boston was asked to date the Great Sphinx at Giza on the basis of its weathering patterns, and he came up with a minimum figure of 5000 BCE. He thought there was a distinct possibility it could be anything up to two thousand years older. These dates may seem conservative when compared with those in the Turin Papyrus, but they are still thousands of years earlier than the orthodox consensus allows.

Although figures like the Sphinx and mysterious ruins like Tiahuanaco have gripped the public imagination, they represent only a small tip in an iceberg of evidence that now points to the existence of a far more sophisticated prehistoric culture than has generally been believed. This evidence is examined in considerable detail in two of my previous books.[5]

Copper was mined before flint in Serbia. There are prehistoric copper mines on Lake Superior and in California, Arkansas, New Mexico, Missouri, Illinois, Indiana, Georgia, New Jersey, and Ohio. Prehistoric iron-smelting furnaces have also been found. Manganese was mined near Broken Hill in Zambia 28,130 years ago.

In 1987, Birmingham University archaeologists Lawrence Barfield and Mike Hodder excavated a prehistoric sauna. Another was discovered in the Orkney Islands.

There is evidence that the horse was domesticated in Europe sometime before 15,000 BCE. A cave drawing at La Marche in France shows one wearing a bridle, as do prehistoric engravings found at the Grotte de Marsoulas and St. Michel d'Arudy.

Tumuli on New Caledonia and the Isle of Pines in the southwest Pacific contained more than four hundred man-made *cement* cylinders thirteen thousand years old. There are paved prehistoric roads in Yucatan, New Zealand,

Kenya, and Malta. There is a water tank in Sri Lanka with a surface area equivalent to Lake Geneva. There are 170,000 miles of underground aqueducts, thousands of years old, in Iran.

Not alone does the evidence point to a high-level prehistoric civilization with substantial technical skills, but there are clear indications that our species has had a much longer history on the planet than orthodox science currently allows. In 1969, for example, twelve fossil footprints dated to 1,000,000 years BP were discovered between Woolongong and Gerringong, Australia. A year later, construction workers on a dam near Demirkopru, in Turkey, discovered a set of human footprints pressed into volcanic ash. They are 250,000 years old. In 1997, human artifacts 116,000 and 176,000 years old were found at the Jinmium site in Australia's Northern Territories. Finds in Siberia, England, France, and Italy indicate human habitation of those countries prior to 1,000,000 BP, the time most orthodox scientists believe the first hominids (*Homo erectus*) were only just beginning to leave Africa. England, Belgium, India, Pakistan, and Italy are just a few of the countries that have yielded up weapons and other implements in strata older than the 2 million years commonly assigned to the evolution of *Homo habilis*, the first tool-user.

All this—and I would stress again that the foregoing finds represent only a very few examples selected from a vast body of evidence—would appear to put paid to the simplistic linear progression of human evolution on which Jaynes developed his theories. If you accept the orthodox picture of prehistory, it is easy to understand how he came to believe the primitive hunter-gatherer communities—assumed to represent the highest development of humanity prior to about 7000 BCE—were characterized by a bicameral mind. It is also easy to trace the threads of evidence that led him to conclude that the introduction of large-scale urban communities (about 5000 BCE) began to put pressure on the ancient bicameral structures while the development of writing led to their eventual breakdown.

Once you realize that the orthodox picture of this linear progression is in error, what appeared to be evidence supporting Jaynes's theory quickly falls away. If urban civilization and the invention of writing were key factors in the development of consciousness, then consciousness developed not between 3000 and 1300 BCE but with the emergence of an advanced—and, according to Hapgood, global—civilization in the distant depths of the Ice Age.

But the new ideas about prehistory only throw into doubt Jaynes's notions about the emergence of consciousness. They leave untouched his whole body of research into humanity's widespread experience of voices and visions. This is distinctly weird, for it means that Jaynes's examination of ancient history has unearthed something quite extraordinary. He has shown, from an analysis of inscriptions and texts, that there was a time within recorded history when virtually everyone could hear "spirit" voices and sometimes see "spirit" visions. He has also shown that the ability gradually atrophied—or, if you prefer, that the "spirits" gradually withdrew. His analysis suggests they disappeared altogether with the last of the great oracles. But we know this was not the case. Throughout human history, for good or ill, the voices have never ceased. In such circumstances, we may be justified in asking if the human race is mad, for our objections to Jaynes's theory refer only to his postulate of the bicameral mind. They leave open the possibility of hallucinations stemming from some other source.

25. SPIRITS OF THE DEEP MIND

I N 1895, CARL GUSTAV JUNG, THEN AGED TWENTY, BEGAN HIS MEDICAL studies at the University of Basel, but events in his early life had already directed his attention to the possibility of a career in psychiatry, a somewhat disreputable profession at the time. Five years later, he was working in the Burghölzli, a psychiatric hospital in Zurich, and researching his doctoral dissertation, later published under the title *On the Psychology and Pathology of So-Called Occult Phenomena*. The object of his research was his fifteen-year-old cousin, Helene Preiswerk, who had begun to experiment with table-turning in July 1899 and only one month later was already showing signs of mediumistic somnambulism. Jung attended her séances almost from the beginning and made careful note of the phenomena she produced.

Helene's first spirit contact was with Samuel Preiswerk, her grandfather, whom she had never known during his lifetime. Witnesses who had known him remarked on how accurately she conveyed his voice and manner. She was, it appears, what the Spiritualist movement calls a "direct voice medium"—that is to say, the spirits would take control of her vocal cords while she was in trance and speak directly to sitters through her. In this way, she "brought through" various deceased family members, several of whom spoke flawless High German, in stark contrast to Helene's customary Basel dialect. The sittings were impressive, so much so that people began to come to her for advice, an unlikely development considering her age. Soon she began to exhibit a different kind of mediumship in which she remained aware of her surroundings but took on a new persona called Ivenes, a quiet, dignified, more mature character altogether.

In September 1899, someone presented her with a copy of Kerner's *The Seeress of Prevorst* and her manifestations changed again. She took to

The young C. G. Jung, who earned his doctorate
with a thesis on spirit mediumship

magnetizing herself using mesmeric passes during her sessions and, possibly as a consequence, began to exhibit the ability to speak in a wholly unknown language.[1] In her Ivenes persona she claimed to visit Mars, where she saw firsthand its great canals and the flying machines of its advanced civilization.[2] She claimed interstellar journeys as well and visited spirit worlds to receive instruction from "clear spirits" while she herself gave instruction to "black spirits." Jung noted that the spirits manifested in her tended toward two distinct types—the dour and the exuberant—corresponding with the mood swings of Helene's own somewhat volatile personality.

Helene meanwhile began to produce detailed memories of what purported to be past lives. She had been a Christian martyr at the time of Nero, a thirteenth-century French noblewoman named Madame de Valours who was burned as a witch, a young girl seduced by Goethe, and a host of others. In many of these incarnations she had borne children, who produced their own descendants, so that over a period of only a few weeks, she constructed an elaborate network of genealogies that often stretched down to her present day. Sometimes these became complex indeed. As the mother of Goethe's love child, for example, she became Jung's great-grandmother.[3] As Madame de Valours, she was the mother of Jung in a previous incarnation. More complexities were to follow. By March 1900 she had begun to elaborate her own cosmology. Jung stopped attending her séances at about this time, but some six months later Helene was discovered engaging in fraud when she began to produce *apports*, small objects alleged to be mystically transported into the séance room by spirit helpers.

Jung interpreted the totality of the phenomena produced by Helene in the light of current German and French psychiatric theory, based on developments and experiments dating back more than a hundred years to the time when Franz Anton Mesmer believed he effected his cures through the medium of an invisible fluid. His star pupil, Amand-Marie-Jacques de Chastenet, Marquis de Puységur, came to think differently. By the summer of 1785, when a Strasbourg Masonic Lodge asked him to teach its members the principles of animal magnetism, he summed up the entire doctrine in two words: *belief* and *want*. "I believe that I have the power to set into action the vital principle of my fellow men; I want to make use of it; this is all my science and all my means."[4] He had come to see certain conditions and their cures in terms of psychological rather than physical processes. In so doing, although the fact is seldom acknowledged, he laid the foundation of modern psychiatric theory.

Puységur donated a practical technique as well. Mesmeric healing was based largely on the production of a series of crises in the patient, who would typically convulse violently for a time, then emerge improved in health and finally cured. While Puységur was attempting to induce a convulsive crisis in a twenty-three-year-old peasant named Victor Race, whom he was treating for a minor respiratory complaint, the patient exhibited a very peculiar reaction. Instead of convulsing, he fell into a strange kind of sleep in which he appeared to be aware of everything going on around him, was capable of answering questions, and actually seemed more alert and intelligent than in his normal waking state. When Mesmer was consulted about the development, he proved less than impressed and dismissed the new state as a "sleep crisis"—just one of various mesmeric crises, and not even a particularly important one. He proved wrong on all counts. The new state had nothing to do with sleep. It was not just one of various mesmeric crises; in fact, it was not a mesmeric crisis at all. And it ultimately proved more important than mesmerism itself. Puységur had inadvertently discovered the art of hypnosis.

His experiments with the technique quickly convinced him that the real curative agent was not some mysterious magnetic fluid but the exercise of the magnetizer's will.

It was not the only presage of things to come. Toward the end of his life, in the latter half of the nineteenth century, Justinus Kerner, the parapsychologist who investigated the famous Seeress of Prevorst, fell into a depression. To divert himself, he took to making inkblots on a sheet of paper, which he would then fold in half. He elaborated on the resultant shapes, referring to the final figures as *klecksographien*, which he said were ghosts and monsters, each assigned to its own place in Hades. His book on the subject, posthumously published and also called *Klecksographien*, became in later years the inspiration of Hermann Rorschach in his development of modern psychology's inkblot test.

At much the same time, the French neurologist Jean-Martin Charcot was making an international name for himself for his work in the Salpêtrière Hospital in Paris. His most spectacular achievements were the success of his efforts to have hypnotism accepted by the French Académie des Sciences and his investigation of traumatic paralysis,[5] which he showed often to have psychological roots that lay outside the patient's awareness. Hypnotism itself was investigated and the discovery of aspects like somnambulism and posthypnotic suggestion implied the existence of an area of the mind of which the individual was normally unaware. Before long, Charcot was postulating the existence of unconscious "fixed ideas" that acted as the nuclei of neuroses. Although there was no developed theory of the unconscious as a whole, there was certainly a growing acceptance that certain mental areas and aspects lay outside individual consciousness.

An important factor that influenced emerging psychological theories was the wave of Spiritualism that crossed the Atlantic from America to sweep nineteenth-century Europe. Techniques like automatic writing, seen by mediums as a method of communication with spirits, were increasingly investigated by neurologists for their insights into the workings of the human mind. Other practices, traditionally associated with spirit contact, included the use of black mirrors, crystal balls, and even bowls of water. One experiment involved the drawing of a white circle on a black floor, then having patients stare at it until they produced a variety of visions and hallucinations. The combination of hypnosis with such techniques virtually guaranteed results, so that by the 1880s, even the founders of the Society for Psychical Research were coming to the conclusion that these methods were more likely to detect hidden contents of a subject's mind than to communicate with spirits. It was only a matter of time before the new psychology began to investigate mediumship itself.

Among the very first to do so was Theodore Flournoy, a physician, philosopher, and psychologist who held the post of professor of psychology at the University of Geneva in Switzerland. He was a man somewhat interested in psychical research, but he approached the subject from the standpoint of an experimental psychologist. His guiding principle, derived from *Hamlet*, was "Everything is possible" . . . but he was careful to add a modification: "The weight of evidence must be in proportion to the strangeness of the fact." In December 1894, Flournoy was invited by a fellow professor at the university to attended a private séance held by a Swiss medium named Catherine Muller. She was, by all accounts, an impressive figure, a tall, beautiful, thirty-year-old with black hair and eyes, who was so convinced of the truth of Spiritualism that she made no charge for her demonstrations. At the first of these sittings, she certainly impressed Flournoy by telling him accurately of events that had happened in his own family prior to his birth. This seemed, on the face of it, to be information she could not possibly know, but Flournoy was far from satisfied that there could not be a rational explanation. He launched an exhaustive inquiry into Muller's background and discovered that there had once been a brief connection between her parents and his own. He concluded that she might consequently have heard of the events she mentioned in a wholly explicable way.

Flournoy did not, however, suspect fraud. As a psychologist he thought the more likely explanation was that she had long forgotten the events but somehow accessed the memories in the peculiar atmosphere of the séance. He decided to continue his investigation and became a regular sitter at Muller's mediumistic demonstrations. Coincident with this decision, Muller's mediumship underwent a change. In her original sitting, she had remained awake while she described psychic visions of spirits as they arrived and produced raps by which they conveyed messages. Now, however, she fell into a deep trance state and began to recall scenes from previous lives, manifesting personality changes as she did so. Flournoy continued his investigation for five years and subsequently published his findings in a book called *From India to the Planet Mars*,[6] which contained an exhaustive account of Muller's experiences and an analysis of their content.

What emerged from their collaboration was strange indeed. Muller made contact with a spirit guide named Leopold, an apparent reincarnation of the eighteenth-century Italian magician Cagliostro. The entity frequently possessed her completely during séances and took to advising Flournoy on how he should respond to her revelations. The revelations themselves fell into three distinct cycles. In the first of these, Muller recalled details of a past life in fifteenth-century India where she had lived as an Arab princess Simandini, married to Sivrouka, a Hindu potentate. The life ended when Sivrouka died and Simandini was obliged to commit suttee on his funeral pyre. Muller claimed Flournoy was the reincarnation of Sivrouka and reminded him of several incidents from their life together. The second cycle had an equally unhappy ending: Muller became possessed by the reincarnatory personality of the French queen Marie Antoinette who was executed for treason by guillotine on October 16, 1793. The third cycle was bizarre. It involved life on Mars. Muller claimed to travel there in spirit and knew the planet intimately. She offered proof by describing its terrain and inhabitants: carriages without horses or wheels, emitting sparks as they glided by; houses with fountains on the roof; a cradle having for curtains an angel made of iron with outstretched wings. Its inhabitants were exactly like the people of Earth, apart from the fact—somewhat shocking in Flournoy's era—that both sexes wore the same costume, formed of ample trousers and a long blouse, drawn tight about the waist and decorated with various designs.

It was a rich vein for analysis and Flournoy mined it thoroughly. He discovered that the main verifiable details of Muller's Indian incarnation were drawn from a published *History of India*. Sources for her supposed life as Marie Antoinette were also easy to find. It quickly became apparent that much of the information Muller gave originated in books she had read as a child—and had in all probability forgotten. The vivid landscapes of Mars, he decided, were "romances of the subliminal imagination"[7] generated by wish fulfillment and forgotten memories. His investigation further suggested that each "past incarnation" was built upon what he called a "reversion"—an involuntary regression to an earlier stage of life. Her Martian fantasies originated in early childhood, her Indian "incarnation" was built on her personality at the age of twelve, while Marie Antoinette arose out of the girl she was at age sixteen. Flournoy's analysis of the Martian language that Muller could write as well as speak convinced him that it was structured on French. After his book was published, an expert linguist attested that the content was actually a distorted form of Hungarian, the mother tongue of Muller's father. The medium's spirit guide, Leopold, was, Flournoy decided, an unconscious subpersonality of Muller that emerged from its subliminal state, freed by her experience of trance. He concluded that her visions began as "simple entoptical phenomena" produced naturally by the retina and later transformed into full-blown hallucinations under the influence of suggestion. The raps and table movements were, Flournoy thought, probably produced by Muller herself through involuntary muscle movements. He was even more dismissive of Muller's apparently paranormal abilities such as speaking Sanskrit while manifesting details of her Indian incarnation:

> No one dares tell her that her great invisible protector [Leopold] is only an illusionary apparition, another part of herself, a product of her subconscious imagination; nor that the strange peculiarities of her mediumistic communications—the Sanscrit, the recognizable signatures of deceased persons, the thousand correct revelations of facts unknown to her—are but old forgotten memories of things which she saw or heard in childhood.[8]

Flournoy used this and other investigations to draw far-reaching conclusions about the subliminal mind, mediumship, and spirit contact in general. He was convinced of the extraordinary creativity vested in the subliminal mind: one of his patients was a young mother who proved capable of dictating philosophical fragments far more sophisticated than her apparent level of knowledge would allow. He believed the subliminal mind acted as a compensatory mechanism, pointing to Muller as a well-educated, ambitious woman who, frustrated by her social and economic status, created her elaborate fantasies as a form of wish fulfillment. He believed too that such fantasies often had a playful element. One interpreter of Flournoy's insights put the case succinctly: "Most mediums do not wish to deceive, they just wish to play, like little girls with their dolls, but sometimes fantasy life gains control."[9]

While Flournoy was investigating mediumship in Geneva, Sigmund Freud was beginning to develop his own concept of the unconscious mind in Vienna. Freud himself loathed anything that smacked of the occult, but Jung had no such misgivings and threw himself into the investigation of his cousin's mediumship with enthusiasm. But it was an enthusiasm tempered by the doctrines of his mentor, Flournoy. Consequently, Jung classified Helene Preiswerk's mediumistic abilities under four categories: somnambulism, semi-somnambulism, automatic writing, and hallucinations. He attempted to discover the sources of her fantasies and decided one must be Kerner's work on the Seeress of Prevorst while another was overheard conversations about Kant's cosmology. Like Flournoy, he attributed table tipping at the séances to the medium herself, thorough "involuntary muscle movements." One of his more intriguing conclusions was that the Ivenes persona represented Helene as a grown-up and emerged due to an intuition that she would die young. She did, in fact, die prematurely in 1911, from tuberculosis.

Jung's final conclusions closely mirrored those of Flournoy. His dissertation made frequent use of terms like *hysteria* and *epileptoid.* He often referred to the subjects of his study as "patients." He cited alcohol as a possible factor in one example of the mediumistic phenomenon[10] and summed up the entire mediumistic process in the following words: "The impressions received in somnambulism go on working in the subconscious to form independent growths and finally reach perception as hallucinations."[11]

The findings of Flournoy and later Jung were accepted almost without question by the emerging discipline of analytical psychology, conventional psychology, and modern scientific thought. Although Jung changed his mind about spirits in later life, the consensus opinion to this day still considers spirits in the same light as Jung and Flournoy did more than a century ago. They are hallucinations of the deep mind. Variations on the theme abound. When the academic Elizabeth M. Butler came to analyze Cellini's Coliseum conjuration, she reached the conclusion that everything took place exactly as Cellini had described it . . . but only with qualifications. Her published account of the conjuration begins with the observation that there was a strong visionary element in Cellini's nature[12]—and one that did not necessarily represent a clairvoyant perception of spirits. For example, she came to the conclusion that the Ferryman Cellini saw during a life-threatening illness "certainly derived" from Dante's description of Charon in the *Inferno.*[13] Furthermore, she is happy to call into question the genuineness of the manifestations and the magician involved. In this latter respect she suggested nothing so crude as the magic lantern theory put forward by other commentators[14] but rather pointed out that nowhere in the account did Cellini categorically state that he saw or heard the demons personally. If he did not, then, since his companions Romoli and Gaddi were silent on the matter, we rely only on the statements of the magician and, more particularly, the boy Cenci.

Although Butler is fair-minded enough to leave open any question of deliberate fraud, there is little doubt where her sympathies lie when it comes to an explanation:

> What are we to think of the good faith of the magician? . . . He must . . . have believed in . . . magic and therefore presumably in his own performances and powers. It seems to me clear that he did; and like many another was hallucinated by his own invocations and the incense.[15]

It appears, though, that the term *hallucinated* is not to be taken in the sense it is used by Flournoy and Jung. Cenci's account is dismissed on the grounds that he was "highly impressionable" and visual imagination is much more vivid in childhood than in later years. Butler suggests that this is the precise reason why children are so often associated with magical experiments of this type. "And it was from Cenci that the panic spread throughout the circle; the magician himself was obviously affected by the terror-stricken boyish voice."[16] So, spectacular though it might appear in Cellini's account, the Coliseum conjuration really took place only in the imagination of the participants, perhaps with a little mass hysteria thrown in. Views of this type are so deeply embedded that few modern commentators stop to consider those instances of spirit "hallucinations" seen simultaneously by more than one person or recurringly associated with a particular place. An example would be the widely reported "Grey Lady" hauntings of ancient sites throughout the world.

26. PERSONAL ENCOUNTERS

THE MORNING OF MY THIRTY-SECOND BIRTHDAY WAS A CLOUDLESS JULY day, unusual for Ireland. I was living alone at the time in the rented gate lodge of the Hamwood Estate in Dunboyne, County Meath. A perk of the tenancy was the use of a delightful walled garden, first planted in the fifteenth century but renovated extensively in Victorian times. I decided to take time off work and do a little reading in the sunshine. At around 11:00 a.m., I equipped myself with a paperback, a flask of chilled fruit juice, and a rug, which I spread on the lawn. Twenty minutes later, I was reading my book when a young woman appeared from the direction of the main house. She looked to be in her thirties, dark-haired and pretty. She was also dressed quite formally, in a manner rather more suited to the evening than a sunny summer's morning. I remember thinking there might be a party arranged at the main house and she was a houseguest trying out her outfit. She walked across the lawn and as she came closer, I called out a greeting but, to my surprise, she ignored me. I watched as she walked past and continued across the lawn until she reached a low box hedge some ten to twelve feet from where I was lying. Then, while I continued to watch her, she vanished. It was almost exactly like the transporter effect in *Star Trek*: she shimmered, then faded, and eventually disappeared completely, leaving a momentary sparkle in the air.

I was shocked—hairs literally stood up on the back of my neck. For a moment I simply stared, then scrambled to my feet and ran across the lawn with some mindless idea that she must have fallen down behind the little hedge. But there was no one there. After a moment, with thumping heart, I was prepared to accept that I had seen a ghost.

Almost forty years later, I had another paranormal experience. I awoke in the early hours of the morning to find a tall figure standing at the foot of my bed. For some reason, I felt no fear. I believed myself to be fully awake:

I was in bed with my wife beside me and there was no question in my mind that I was dreaming. But at the same time, I was aware that I was not in my normal state of consciousness: the creature staring down at me was not physically present, at least not in the way I would usually define "physical." A form of nonverbal communication began between us. I would be tempted to describe it as telepathic, except that it was not telepathy as I would normally imagine it. There was no voice in my head. I simply knew, all of a piece, what the entity wanted me to do and why. The bed in my room is aligned north-south. There are two windows in the eastern wall. To the northeast of my home, some fifteen miles away, is a megalithic site known as Castleruddery Stone Circle, an untidy layout of forty stones about a hundred yards in diameter with two enormous (fifteen-ton) quartz boulders acting as portal stones at the entrance. The circle is surrounded by a low earthwork and several thornbushes. Beyond is a ditch, no longer visible from the ground. Official estimates date the site to about 2500 BCE. To reach the circle in physical reality, it would be necessary to drive for approximately half an hour, then turn off the N81 some five miles northeast of Baltinglass and follow the signs. But now it seemed to me that the entire eastern wall of my bedroom had become transparent. I could see the intervening countryside stretched out like an open plain and the circle itself luminous in the moonlight. The entity carried me across the landscape until I found myself standing inside the circle. In this location, I had visionary encounters with tall, silver-skinned creatures and what appeared to be the "little people" of Irish mythology before the entity carried me back to my home.

Whatever the explanation for either of these experiences, it is clear they were essentially *different*. In my first sighting, the woman appeared solid, physical, and, apart from the anomaly of her dress, completely normal. But she failed to communicate, even when spoken to. It was as if she was completely unaware of my presence. In my second sighting, the entity, although objectively standing in my bedroom, appeared neither solid nor normal. It was not only aware of my presence, but skillfully communicated mind to mind in a manner that I was capable of understanding without difficulty. Both encounters could reasonably be thought of as involving spirits, but did they? Was it possible that certain "spirit sightings" do not involve spirits at all?

I subsequently asked the owners of the Hamwood estate if there had been any previous reports of ghostly sightings in the garden. There had not, but apart from this fact, my experience had hallmarks of what psychical researchers informally refer to as a "Grey Lady."

Grey Ladies do not have to be ladies at all but can take the form of male apparitions, phantom animals, and sometimes even inanimate objects like carriages or cars. They are far and away the most commonly reported form of ghostly encounter. More than two hundred of them are listed on a single Internet site devoted to haunted places in the United Kingdom alone,[1] and this record is far from exhaustive. Such sightings vary enormously and are typically seen by more than one person at more than one time. The Grey Lady in the Willard Library of Evansville, Indiana, for example, was first reported by a custodian in the late 1930s but has continued to be seen at intervals by library staff and visitors up to modern times. (The last recorded instance was in August 2010.) A more typical instance involves the Grey Lady of Levens Hall, an English stately home south of Kendal in Westmoreland. Levens Hall is an Elizabethan mansion built ca. 1586, and reported sightings of its Grey Lady go back several centuries: in the days when a coach and four was the standard form of aristocratic transport, her sudden appearances often startled the horses. Today, she startles motorists who have reportedly braked sharply to avoid collision with a figure who simply fades away.

A prime characteristic of the Grey Lady phantoms is that, like my young woman in the garden, they never speak even when spoken to, never communicate in any way, and never show awareness of the carriages, cars, and human beings who frequently bear down on them. A member of the Bagot family who own Levens Hall once cycled through the phantom without disturbing her walk. Another common characteristic is that they tend to appear in exactly the same place, often at a given time of day or on a given date. At Levens Hall, the ghost always appears on the driveway. In the Church of Saint Michael and All Angels at Rycote in Oxfordshire, the apparition invariably glides from a pew to vanish into a stone wall.

A clue to what might be going on here lies in the experience of the psychical investigator and author Sheila St. Clair. Ms. St. Clair reported[2] a Grey Lady sighting while staying in an Irish manor house. The phantom in this instance was actually male but behaved in characteristic Grey Lady fashion by ignoring Sheila as he strolled in his nightgown from one side of her bedroom to the other before making an exit through the wall. The case had some interesting, and possibly significant, details. One was that the ghost walked in midair an estimated two and a half feet above the floor level of the room. Another was that the owners of the manor later confirmed there had once been a doorway in the wall at the spot where the phantom disappeared, but it had been bricked up for more than fifty years. Yet another was that the original floor of the room had once been at a substantially higher level but had been lowered in Victorian times during renovations to get rid of dry rot. The impression left with Sheila was that the ghost was not haunting the bedroom in which she was trying to sleep but seems to have been walking across the chamber as it used to be in the Victorian era, with its feet firmly planted on the original floor and its exit made through a door that was then visible.

Cases of this type—and there are a great many of them—have led psychical researchers to develop a theory that Grey Lady ghosts are not ghosts at all (in the sense of being spirits of the dead) but rather some hitherto unsuspected form of natural data recording imprinted on some aspect of the haunt scene and capable of being "played back" when conditions are right. What the recording medium might be remains an open question. A particular type of rock has been put forward as a possibility, as have a range of natural and man-made materials such as brick, mortar, and wood. The British archaeologist and dowser Tom Lethbridge, who investigated the subject thoroughly, suggested that since many such sightings are reported near water—lakes, rivers, marshes, and the like—the carrier might be an electrical field generated by dampness.

The theory remains to be proven, although it has gained widespread acceptance among psychical researchers, but there is substantial suggestive evidence to support it. One historical example concerns the Battle of Edgehill, the first major clash between Cavaliers and Roundheads in the English Civil War. The battle, which involved some fourteen thousand[3] men at arms, was fought on October 24, 1642. Fierce fighting went on for three hours and both the Royalist and Parliamentarian armies suffered heavy losses. Two months later, a group of travelers, guided by some local shepherds, were approaching the site of the battle shortly after midnight when they heard the sound of drums, followed by moans of pain. Phantom armies abruptly appeared,[4] carrying the familiar standards of Royalist and Parliamentarian forces, and proceeded to duplicate the action of their earlier clash.

The witnesses hastened to the nearby town of Kineton where they woke a justice of the peace named William Wood, who in turn awakened his neighbor, the Reverend Samuel Marshal, and together both men took sworn statements. The following night (a Sunday) a large party from the town and neighboring parishes went to Edgehill to investigate. About half an hour after they arrived, the phantom armies reappeared to reenact the battle. The next night an even larger audience turned up, but nothing happened. The following weekend, however, the phantom battle was refought on both Saturday and Sunday nights. The phenomenon continued each weekend for several weeks.

In early 1643, a printer named Thomas Jackson published the story, which then came to the attention of the king at Oxford, who was sufficiently intrigued to dispatch six trusted investigators under the command of Colonel Lewis Kirke. After interviewing a broad cross section of eyewitnesses, the king's men set out to see for themselves. They not only reported back that the stories had been true, but actually recognized the faces of individuals, like Sir Edmund Varney, who had been killed in the original battle. But clearly we are not dealing with spirits of the dead in this instance, if only for the fact that while many men were killed at Edgehill, many more survived and were alive and well elsewhere in England while their phantoms fought on the old battle site.

The theory of "natural recording" would appear to receive support from the curious fact that there seems to be a limit on the age of ghosts sighted in the British Isles. In 1709, the Reverend Thomas Josiah Penston was walking on the Norfolk Broads when a spectral Roman army marched past him and disappeared. In 1988, a workman carrying out repairs on a subterranean chamber in the English city of Bath saw a Roman cross the room and disappear through a wall. But the Roman era appears to mark a demarcation point for British ghosts. The Roman invasion began in 43 CE, with the legions entering a country already heavily populated since prehistoric times. Yet reports of ghostly Picts, Angles, Saxons, and the rest are virtually nonexistent, while Paleolithic hunting bands are never reported at all. One is tempted to think less in terms of spirits and more of a recording wearing out. The psychical researchers Eric Maple and Lynn Myring record—unfortunately without specific location or reference details—a case that reinforces this perception. The first reported sighting, in the eighteenth century, was of a woman wearing a red dress and shoes. The next, which occurred some seventy years later, found her wearing pink. By the nineteenth century she had become a typical Grey Lady, dressed in white. In 1939 there was a report of phantom footsteps and the rustle of a dress, but no visual sighting. When the house was demolished in 1971, all that remained was a faint sense of her presence.[5]

An alternative theory to the postulate of natural recording was put forward by the American author Whitley Strieber while discussing my sighting of the phantom in the walled garden. During his radio program *Dreamland*, he suggested that the young woman was neither a natural recording nor a spirit, but an example of a "time slip." He envisioned a Victorian lady walking in her garden when a glitch in the fabric of time permitted me a brief glimpse of her before the "rift" closed again. Curiously, there are well-documented, if little known, examples of this sort of thing happening. In January 1912, for example, while still a young man, the distinguished historian Arnold Toynbee climbed one of the twin summits of Pharsalus, in Greece. There he "slipped into a time pocket" (his words) and found himself back in the days when the forces of Philip of Macedon faced the Roman legions at this spot in 197 BCE. The weather had changed: in place of the bright sunshine, there was now a heavy mist that parted to allow him a view of the downhill Macedonian charge. As he watched, the Romans spotted a weakness in the Macedonian flank, wheeled their men, and attacked with such ferocity that Toynbee had to turn his face away from the slaughter. Almost at once the scene disappeared and he was back in a peaceful, sunlit present. Toynbee had several similar experiences in the coming months—on Crete, in Ephesus, in Laconia, at the ruins of Mistrà in Sparta. The experience was so profound that it inspired him to write his monumental twelve-volume *Study of History*.[6]

Despite Toynbee's subjective reaction, it might be possible to classify at least some of these experiences in the same category as the Edgehill battle, but other reports seem to point much more conclusively toward Strieber's suggestion about time slips. One concerned an Englishman named P. J. Chase of Wallington in Surrey who was strolling down a road in 1968 when he came across two picturesque thatched cottages with hollyhocks in their gardens. One of them bore the date 1837. The next day Chase mentioned the cottages to a friend, who insisted they did not exist. When Chase returned to the spot where he had seen the cottages, he found his friend was right: the only buildings there were two brick houses. An elderly resident of the locality confirmed, however, that the cottages *had* existed but had been torn down to make room for the houses some years previously.

The author Colin Wilson describes[7] an even more specific time-slip at Fotheringhay Church in Northamptonshire that involved a Cambridge schoolteacher named Mrs. Jane O'Neill, when she visited the church in the early winter of 1973. There she spent time admiring a picture of the Crucifixion behind the altar on the left side of the church. The work had an arched top featuring a dove with outstretched wings. Later in her hotel room she mentioned the picture to a friend named Shirley, who claimed she had never seen it, although she had visited the church often. Concerned by Shirley's reaction, Mrs. O'Neill rang the local postmistress, who confirmed there was no picture of the Crucifixion, although there *was* a board behind the altar with a painting of a dove.

A year later, Jane O'Neill returned to Fotheringhay Church to find the outside as she remembered it, but the inside was a different building, much smaller than she recalled. There was, as the postmistress said, no painting of the Crucifixion, and the dove behind the altar was totally different from the one she had seen. Mrs. O'Neill then contacted a Northamptonshire historian, who told her that the original Fotheringhay Church had been torn down in 1553 and the present building erected on the site. Further research confirmed that the church Mrs. O'Neill entered in 1973 was the one that had been demolished more than four hundred years previously.

Other examples of the "time slip" phenomenon include the experiences of two late Victorian schoolteachers, who apparently walked into a different time-stream while visiting the former palace of Marie Antoinette in Versailles, near Paris, France, and of Air Marshal Sir Victor Goddard who appears to have flown his biplane some four years into the future.[8] But whether "time slip" or "natural recording," the only concern of our present investigation is to show that a certain type of experience, often classified as an encounter with a spirit, may be nothing of the sort within our present definition of the term. Whatever else one might say about them, it is clear that the Grey Lady phenomenon has had little or no impact on the course of human history, if only for the fact that Grey Lady specters never communicate. But the situation is a little less clear-cut in another apparent spirit manifestation.

27. THE GEIST THAT POLTERS

W HEN I WORKED IN JOURNALISM AS A YOUNG MAN, I WAS DIS-
patched to investigate an attack on a remote farmhouse in
County Armagh, Northern Ireland. As reported to my editor,
someone had thrown a volley of stones onto the farm roof during the night
and broken a window. The farmer suspected a neighboring family with whom
he had a grudge. On the face of it, this sounded like one of those pointless
feuds that sometimes break out among neighbors, but when I arrived on the
scene, it turned out to be something very different. There had been, in the interim,
a second attack of stones, but this time during daylight. The farmer and his
son were in the building at the time and both rushed out to catch the perpe-
trator. But though they reached the farmyard while the attack was still going
on, there was no one in sight, nor anywhere obvious where someone might
hide. The stones that thundered down—it was a corrugated iron roof—
appeared to fall from nowhere. During my interview with the farmer, he
added a telling detail. When the stones stopped falling and they went back
into the house, several cups fell off a dresser in the kitchen for no apparent
reason. There was one further incident of the same type a week or so later,
but with a much lighter fall of stones and no disturbances inside the house.
After that, the phenomenon stopped completely. Brief though the whole thing
had been, enough had happened to establish that the "attacker" was not a
neighbor but a poltergeist.

Colin Wilson, who has devoted an entire book to the subject, estimates
that there are more than a thousand recorded cases of poltergeist activity.
Perhaps the earliest, which occurred toward the end of the ninth century CE,
bore a passing resemblance to the case I investigated as a reporter. According
to the account handed down in the *Annales Fuldenses*,[1] the phenomenon

began on a farm—this time near Bingen on the Rhine—and involved the throwing of stones by an invisible hand. But events did not end there. The stone throwing was followed by raps on the walls, so violent at times that the entire house shook, while shortly after harvest, the farmer's crops mysteriously caught fire. Word of the outbreak reached the bishop of Mainz, who concluded that evil spirits were at work and dispatched a team of exorcist priests to get rid of them. When the ritual began, the priests were pelted with stones.

In subsequent years, many came to share the bishop's conclusion about poltergeist phenomena. The very term *poltergeist* derives from the German and translates as "noisy ghost or spirit," and while it has not always been seen as outright evil, it is frequently described as "troublesome" or "mischievous." Typical of poltergeist activities are rains of stones, mud, dirt, and various small objects; raps and other noises; the movement of furniture; the displacement and in some instances levitation of ornaments, cutlery, kitchen china, and the like; and the setting of small fires. In the late 1970s, the British parapsychologists Alan Gauld and A. D. Cornell conducted a computer analysis of cases from 1800 to the present day. Some sixty-three typical poltergeist characteristics were identified, including the movement of small objects (64 percent), nocturnal activity (58 percent), raps (48 percent), the movement of large objects (36 percent), and the opening and shutting of doors and windows (12 percent). In only a quarter of all cases did activity last for more than a year.[2]

The dry statistics give little impression of the violence and variety of many poltergeist outbreaks. In a relatively modern case, a poltergeist announced its presence to the McGrath farming family of County Westmeath in Ireland during August 1981 by making noises on the roof. This was followed by electric lights switching on and off and small household objects mysteriously moving from their normal places. The phenomena died down at Christmas but started up again in the New Year. Like the County Armagh case I investigated, stones cascaded onto the roof. Buckets and churn lids were thrown around the farmyard by invisible hands. The McGraths called in a priest who blessed the house, but while activity ceased for a time, it started up again after two weeks. A brother of the owner was "chased" by a plastic bucket and saw a cable swinging violently while there was no wind to move it. Doors opened of their own accord, shoes were taken from the house and left outside, a window was smashed in, logs for the fire were moved about, and a kitchen brush somehow found its way onto the roof—as a daughter of the house discovered when it fell on her head.

An even more extreme example—and a case that has become a classic of poltergeist literature—was recorded by the Reverend Joseph Glanvil in 1666. Glanvil described how he went to a house in Wiltshire[3] and there found "two modest little girls in bed between seven and eleven years old." There was a mysterious scratching sound coming from behind the bolster. Glanvil was certain the noise could not have been made by the girls—their hands were in view. He searched the room without finding the cause, but later discovered a linen bag with something moving about inside it, like a rat or a mouse. He drew the bag inside out, but it was empty.

Glanvil investigated the background to the mysterious sounds he had heard. Five years previously, in March 1661, a magistrate named John Mompesson was trying cases in the village of Ludgershall, East Wiltshire, when court proceedings were disturbed by the sound of drumming. He sent the local constable to investigate and quickly discovered that the noise was caused by a tinker named William Drury, who had arrived in the village a few days earlier. Drury had requested public assistance on the strength of papers signed by eminent magistrates, but so far the request had been refused. Mompesson ordered the tinker be brought before him, examined the papers, and pronounced them forgeries. Consequently he committed Drury to jail until the next sitting of the Assizes and confiscated his drum.

Within a few days, the tinker escaped. For want of anything better to do with the drum, the court bailiff sent it off to Magistrate Mompesson. It arrived at Mompesson's home in Tidworth while he was away in London. When he came home, terrified servants told him there had been knocks and raps in the house for three nights running. The magistrate suspected intruders and went to bed with a loaded pistol. When the sounds started up, Mompesson leaped out of bed brandishing his pistol. He rushed into the room where the noises came from, only to find they had moved to another room. The magistrate followed. The noises moved again. Soon he was chasing them all over the house. Eventually they moved outside. Mompesson gave up and went back to bed and lay listening as the noises continued. Among them he could clearly hear the sound of drumming.

The noises returned night after night, often continuing for hours on end; then suddenly they stopped. For three weeks there was silence; then the noises started up again, worse than ever, often seeming to follow Mompesson's children around. At this point, other poltergeist phenomena began to manifest. Small articles moved of their own accord. Invisible hands tugged a breadboard away from a manservant. When a minister arrived to pray, the noises increased in volume and were accompanied by the smell of burning sulfur. Soon the Mompesson house was filled with knocks, raps, bangs, slamming doors, and mysterious lights. One morning the magistrate's horse was found on its back with a hind hoof jammed in its mouth. A visitor had his sword snatched away. Another found that the coins in his pocket had turned black. The local blacksmith was attacked with pincers. The spirit developed a voice. Witnesses claimed it shouted, "A witch! A witch!" at least a hundred times. The contents of ash cans and chamber pots were emptied into the children's beds. The phenomena, somewhat abated, were still manifesting five years later when the Reverend Glanvil paid his call.

A case in modern-day Pontefract, an historic West Yorkshire market town in England, produced some unusual features. When Colin Wilson investigated in 1980, he discovered that the disturbances, some fourteen years earlier, had begun with a drop in temperature, a rattling window, and an extraordinary drizzle of fine white dust inside the house at 30 East Drive. The dust did not fall from the ceiling but appeared to manifest out of nowhere some distance below it, so that when residents stood up their heads protruded beyond the top of the dust cloud. At much the same time, pools of water began to form on the floor, re-forming each time they were wiped up. Investigation showed the floor beneath the linoleum was dry and the pools continued to appear even after the main water was cut off. Before that happened, another water effect occurred when green foam rushed from taps and flushing toilets. A button-operated tea dispenser near the sink began to operate of its own accord. As the button went in and out as if pressed by an invisible finger, tea leaves cascaded onto the draining board until the container was empty. Sugar was also strewn across kitchen work surfaces. Alongside these oddities came more typical examples of poltergeist activity: a loud crash in a hallway, a light switching on of its own accord, a plant separated from its pot and moved halfway up a flight of stairs while the pot was flung onto the landing above. There were also banging noises, a vibrating kitchen cupboard, and a wardrobe that swayed and tottered for no apparent reason.

After this brief, violent burst over a matter of days, the manifestations stopped for a period of two years, then started up again with the movement of a bedspread from a bedroom to the bottom of the stairs. This was followed by plant pots upending themselves in the hallway with a loud crash. A paint-brush and bucket of paste were flung across a room, a roll of wallpaper reared up like a cobra, a carpet sweeper flew up into the air, a wooden pelmet was ripped from the wall and tossed out of the window. After these and even more violent phenomena, the Pritchard family who lived in the house understand-ably concluded, like many other victims of the noisy ghost, that they were dealing with a spirit—they called it Mr. Nobody. But was a spirit really involved?

Another well-attested poltergeist "haunting" challenges any facile con-clusion. Rosenheim is a small town southwest of Munich. In November 1967, the lighting system in the local office of a German lawyer named Sigmund Adam began to show serious faults. Strip lights failed explosively and with such consistency that he installed a special meter. It showed sudden, inex-plicable surges of current. The local electrical company, the Stadtwerke, were called to investigate and came to the conclusion that there was something wrong with the power lines. They installed a direct cable, but still the lights exploded. Sigmund Adam then had his own generator installed and changed the strip lights for ordinary bulbs, but the problem remained. The mystery deepened when he tested his meter on a 1.5 volt battery. It showed an impos-sible output of 3 volts. He was still wondering what to do when his phone bill arrived, showing a massive increase over his usual level of calls. Phone company technicians installed a monitor that showed someone was dialing the speaking clock for hours on end, four, five, and even six times a minute—faster than it was physically possible to make the connection.

A local reporter arrived to investigate. When a lightbulb fell out of its socket as he was leaving, he decided a spirit was involved and wrote up a report on the Rosenheim ghost. When the story was taken up by the national press, it attracted the attention of one of Europe's leading parapsychologists, Professor Hans Bender of the Institute of Paranormal Research in Freiburg. Bender mounted an investigation during which lights swung for no apparent reason, pictures turned on the wall, and a heavy filing cabinet was moved by unseen hands. But the spirit proved not to be a spirit. Bender noticed that all the phenomena seemed to be associated with a teenage girl, Anne-Marie Schaberl, who had joined the company direct from school two years previ-ously. The connection was not subtle. The surges of current occurred only when she was in the building. When she walked along a corridor, the over-head lights would begin to swing back and forth. Adam responded to the dis-covery by firing the girl. There seems no doubt that Schaberl, a tense, unhappy, suspicious, and aggressive teenager, was the ultimate cause of all the problems. The phenomena stopped at once when she left but broke out in another office once she found employment there. When she went ten-pin bowling with her fiancé, the electronic equipment ceased to function properly. She took a mill job but left when a machinery malfunction led to the death of a coworker.

This was not the only case of its type. At much the same time as the Rosenheim poltergeist in Germany, there was an outbreak in a wholesale novelty store in Miami, Florida. Some two hundred separate incidents were reported, involving the movement of items from shelves and multiple breakages. When parapsychologists J. G. Pratt and W. G. Roff investigated, they quickly narrowed down the focus of the disturbances to a nineteen-year-old shipping clerk named Julio. Like Schaberl, he was a frustrated individual with strong feelings of hostility for which he had limited outlet. Another American case a few years later showed the same essential pattern. An elderly couple living in Olive Hill, Kentucky, had so many of their possessions smashed by a poltergeist that they were forced to move. The *geist* moved with them and under professional investigation was found to be associated with the couple's twelve-year-old grandson, Roger. The boy generated some 179 incidents, including the levitation of a heavy kitchen table, which not only jumped into the air but rotated some forty-five degrees before settling down on the backs of nearby chairs. Investigators noted that the number of incidents decreased in inverse proportion to their distance from the boy.

Cases like these led to the theory that poltergeist outbreaks had little to do with spirits. The historian and academic Richard Cavendish sums up the position:

> Because poltergeist incidents usually occur in close proximity to a living person, parapsychologists tend to regard them as instances of psychokinesis or PK. Since poltergeist incidents are recurrent and arise unexpectedly and spontaneously, they are commonly referred to as instances of "recurrent spontaneous psychokinesis" or RSPK. They appear to be unconscious cases of PK since the person who seems to bring them about is usually unaware of his involvement. Some persons remain convinced that RSPK phenomena are due to the agency of an incorporeal entity such as the spirit of a deceased entity or a "demon" which has attached itself to some living person and which causes the incidents by PK. However, since there is no evidence for

such spirits apart from the phenomena themselves, most parapsychologists are of the opinion that poltergeist phenomena are examples of unconscious PK exercised by the person around whom they occur.[4]

While Cavendish is correct in his assertion that a majority of psychical investigators subscribe to the "unconscious PK" theory, there is evidence that the theory itself may not hold for every case. PK is defined as "movement of physical objects by the mind without use of physical means." The fact that the talent is recurrent, spontaneous, or unconscious does not change this. So how does "the movement of physical objects by the mind" account for these reports:

- In 1877, disturbances at a farm in Derrygonnelly, Ireland, were investigated by the physicist and Society for Psychical Research founder Sir William Barrett, who reported: "I mentally asked it, no word being spoken, to knock a certain number of times and it did so. To avoid any error or delusion on my part, I put my hands in the side pockets of my overcoat and asked it to knock the number of fingers I had open. It correctly did so." Barrett repeated the experiment four times without error. The focus of the poltergeist activity in this case was the twenty-year-old daughter of the house, Maggie, but if she was using unconscious PK to produce the raps, she must also have been using something else—presumably telepathy—to answer Barrett's silent questions.

- In 1952, Hans Bender, the parapsychologist who handled the Rosenheim case, was called in to investigate a poltergeist outbreak in the home of the mayor of Neudorf, in Baden, Germany. In this instance, three witnesses watched as a collection of nails appeared eight inches below a bedroom ceiling before falling to the floor. The origin of the nails was a locked cupboard in the kitchen. The problem was obvious: how did the nails move out of the cupboard without damage to its structure or themselves? How did they pass through intervening walls and ceiling without leaving holes? Bender became particularly interested in this phenomenon—which is quite frequent in poltergeist cases—and eventually postulated the existence of a "higher space," or fourth dimension of matter, which would allow "freedom of movement" and account for the apparent penetration of matter by matter. Whatever the validity of this postulate, one can say with confidence something more than PK was involved.

Some years ago, I personally investigated a brief poltergeist incident involving a Dublin woman who complained of an "invisible presence" in her home. At first this was merely an impression without specific phenomena, but when she went upstairs to take a bath, she felt something furry, like a small animal, brush against her as she climbed into the tub. She told herself she was imagining things, but while she was in the bath, the creature burned her arm and bit her on the leg. When she ran from the bathroom, it pushed her so violently that she fell downstairs, fortunately without injuring herself beyond some bruising. She showed me the bite mark and the burn. The former was a smallish wound on the inner thigh like the bite of a cat or similarly sized animal. The latter was circular, as if someone had stubbed out a lighted cigarette on her arm. Although the injuries could certainly have been self-inflicted and no one actually witnessed her fall downstairs (although I confirmed that two of her children found her in a heap at the bottom), I could see no reason then or now why she should have decided to fabricate such a preposterous story. Besides, similar phenomena have been reported across a broad cross section of cases, including one in Indianapolis, Indiana, where the grandmother of the house was "bitten" invisibly fourteen times and a daughter bitten once.

Poltergeist activity continues to be reported to the present day. In 2004, one set a series of fires along a railway line in Canneto, Italy. Although a rational explanation was subsequently proposed, part of the village had to be evacuated. In 2007, videos of alleged poltergeist activity in Barnsley, England, were uploaded to YouTube. The following year, Easington Council in County Durham, England, paid part of the fee demanded by a medium to exorcise a poltergeist from a housing estate in Peterlee. In 2011, the *Sun* newspaper carried a series of articles on another council house poltergeist that produced a gamut of typical phenomena including thrown pots and pans, flying chairs, lights switched on and off, and cupboard doors ripped off their hinges.[5]

It is difficult to see how the simple movement of physical objects by the mind could produce more than a fraction of the phenomena described in this chapter. There is also the problem of those poltergeists that develop a voice. The phantom drummer of Tidworth continually shouted "Witch!" while witnesses of numerous other cases have mentioned hearing obscenities from "entities" presenting themselves as demonic. It is also true to say that in some, fortunately rare, instances, the focus of poltergeist activity has

331 | THE GEIST THAT POLTERS

actually been killed by his or her own supposed PK. Arguably the best-recorded example was the American case of the Bell Witch. The victim was a farmer named John Bell, who lived with his wife, Lucy, and their nine children in Robertson County, Tennessee.

The disturbances began in 1817 with small knocking and scratching sounds the family put down to the activity of rats in the walls of their home. These tended to occur at night and gradually increased in volume until members of the family began to get out of bed and light lamps to investigate. When they did so, the noises stopped. After a time, more overtly paranormal phenomena began. Bedclothes were dragged from beds by invisible hands, chairs were turned upside down, stones were mysteriously thrown. After about a year, the activity had become so constant and so extreme that everyone in the family was losing sleep. The whole house would shake under the impact of the noises and family members would have their hair pulled violently.

A neighbor, James Johnson, discovered that the poltergeist seemed to be aware of being spoken to, but attempts to persuade it to cease its activities only made things worse. The Bell children were pelted with stones when they came home from school, and both they and visitors to the house suffered resounding, but nonetheless invisible, slaps to the face. Mysterious gasping sounds eventually developed into a low whispering voice capable of passing random remarks. Betsy, the twelve-year-old daughter of Bell, began to suffer shortness of breath and fainting spells while her father's tongue swelled and his jaw stiffened so badly that he was often unable to eat.

The poltergeist's original low whisper transformed itself into several different, highly audible voices. All claimed to be spirits; one identified itself as an Indian whose bones had not received a proper burial, another as a witch named Old Kate Batts. Four members of Old Kate's family manifested their own individual voices and introduced themselves as Blackdog, Mathematics, Cypocryphy, and Jerusalem. These entities sometimes sounded drunk, at which times the room would be filled with the smell of whiskey. Old Kate herself seemed to have a particular dislike of John Bell, whom she promised would be tormented for the rest of his life.

The Bells called in a local cunning man, who prescribed an emetic for Betsy. The child promptly vomited brass pins and needles while the voice of the witch mocked that she would soon have enough to open a shop. The phenomena continued to grow more and more extreme. A household slave's head was covered in spittle. A sledge was dragged three times around the house.

John Bell had his shoes jerked off repeatedly and was stunned by a heavy blow to the face. The witch sang derisive songs and raved and cursed at him. After three years of this ill-treatment, Bell suffered a nervous breakdown and took to his bed. On the morning of December 19, 1820, the family found him in a coma. When his son, also named John, discovered an unusual bottle in the medicine cupboard, the witch boasted that she had given Bell Sr. medicine in the night that had "fixed him." He died the following day.

It is difficult to square much of the Bell Witch phenomena with current PK theory either. The entity certainly manifested as a spirit, and later as several spirits. Each spoke in a different voice and displayed an individual persona. While actual communication between the Bell family and the entities was limited—the "witch" mostly confined herself to hurling threats, curses, and abuse—some 16 percent of cases surveyed by Alan Gauld and A. D. Cornell featured intelligent communication between the poltergeist and agent, sometimes including data the agent does not have. It is perhaps worth recalling that the raps heard in the home of the Fox sisters, which gave rise to the Spiritualist movement, eventually imparted the information that the "spirit" involved was that of a murdered peddler whose body had been buried in the cellar. In the summer of 1848, the girls' elder brother David organized a dig in the Hydesville cellar, which unearthed human bones and teeth. All this is far beyond any known, or even theoretical, PK effect, unless we broaden the definition of PK to include an apparent ability to work miracles. Any dispassionate examination of the evidence must suggest that the phenomenon is far more complex than the PK theory would imply. While the Rosenheim case appears entirely explicable in terms of unconscious PK, other poltergeists certainly do not. They manifest as independent entities, quite separate from the unfortunate individuals they haunt.

In those cases where we can rule out fraud, time slips, right-brain hallucinations, deep mind hallucinations, and recurrent, spontaneous, unconscious PK, is it possible the spirits are simply spirits after all?

28. THE BOGGLE THRESHOLD

B Y NOW IT IS ABUNDANTLY CLEAR THAT THE TERM *SPIRIT* COVERS A RANGE of disparate phenomena. Also, many apparently impartial investigations into the subject have collided with something psychical researchers refer to as the "boggle threshold." *Boggle threshold* is defined as the point at which one ceases to be impartial or open-minded and instead discovers it is impossible to believe something, whatever the evidence. Indeed, the boggle threshold will often stop an individual considering the evidence in the first place. For many people, telepathy falls below their boggle threshold and may consequently be investigated thoroughly, while leprechauns do not and consequently fail to be investigated at all. In our postmodern culture spirits seem to straddle the threshold itself. Even those who suspect there might be something in the reports will unconsciously ignore evidence that lies beyond their boggle threshold.

One example is Dr. Elizabeth M. Butler, who concluded that Cellini's Coliseum conjuration took place only in the imagination of its participants. Interestingly, Butler unearthed (then subsequently ignored) the evidence that would mitigate against such a conclusion. From internal clues in Cellini's text, she deduced that the Sicilian magician may have used the *Lemegeton* as an instruction manual for his ceremony. The *Lemegeton Clavicula Salomonis* ("Lesser Key of Solomon") was certainly a popular grimoire in Cellini's day and, with portions of its content dating back to the fourteenth century or earlier,[1] it may be considered typical of the sorcerous handbooks of the time. In its most complete form, the work consists of five parts, the first of which, called *Geotia*, contains the formulas for binding evil spirits—precisely the sort of demons with which Cellini's sorcerer was trying to make contact.

After listing—and briefly describing—the seventy-two "mighty kings or princes" commanded by the legendary King Solomon, the book details the construction of a magical circle, a triangle of evocation, a magical ring, a brass vessel, and various parchment figures, all used to control the spirits. Then comes the first conjuration:

> I Invoke and conjure you spirit [NAME] . . . by him whome all creatures are obediant and by this ineffable name Tetragrammaton Jehovah . . . that you *visibly and affably* speak onto me with a Clear voice Intelligible, and without any ambiguity Therefore come ye in the Name Adonay Zebeoth.[2] [my italics]

Should the spirit prove intransigent, the book recommends a second conjuration, which includes the instructions, "therefore come you paecable, vissible and affable . . . to manifest what I desire speaking with a perfect and clear voice, Intelligible unto my understanding &c."[3] This might be followed up with a "constraint," which demands that the spirit come quickly from all parts and places of the world, wherever it may be, and appear before the circle "visible and affably speakeing with a voice Intelligible to my understanding."[4]

Such powerful conjurations are deemed sufficient to call a spirit unless it happens to be bound with chains in hell, in which case the magician is instructed to evoke its king and require him to "cause, enforce & compel NAME to come to me hear before this Circle in a fair and comely forme without doeing any harme to me or any other Creature."[5]

If the king is uncooperative, the magician might then resort to the magical equivalent of violence and begin to lay curses on the spirit, threatening it with fire, excommunication, and the destruction of its seal unless it "immediately comest & appearest visibly, affably, friendly & courteously hear unto me before this Circle in this Triangle in a faire and comly forme and in no wise terrible, hurtful or frightful to me or any other creatures whatever upon the face of the Earth and made rationel Answers to my requests and performe all my desires in all things that I shall make onto you."[6] When (at last!) the spirit does appear, it should be bound to "remaine affable and visibly hear before this circle."[7]

A somewhat different approach is taken to the evocation of angels who should, according to the *Art Pauline* section of the *Lemegeton*, be called into a crystal. But here too there is emphasis on *visible* appearance. The conjuration politely requests the angel to:

shew thy selfe visibly and plainly in his crystal stone to the sight of my Eyes speaking with a voice Intelligible and to my understanding . . . I invocate, adjure, command & most powerfully call you forth . . . to visible appirition . . . and commandeth you to Transmitt your Rayes visible and perfectly into my sight: and your voice to my Ears, in and threw this Crystall stone: That I may plainly see you and perfectly hear you speak unto me . . . Therefore . . . descend and shew your self visible and perfectly in a pleasant and comely form before me in this Crystall stone: to the sight of my Eyes speaking with a voice Intelligible and to my apprehension.[8]

In Part IV of the *Lemegeton* ("Salomon's Almadel Art") there is a rare description of what to expect when a spirit does appear: "And when he appeareth . . . he descends first upon the superscription of ye Almadel as if it were a Mist or Fogg."[9] In order for the mist to coalesce into visible appearance, the operator is required to burn three small grains of "masticke," the smell of which will persuade the spirit to begin speaking. Should this fail to make him appear fully, the magician must use a golden seal to make certain marks on the candles used in his ceremony, an action guaranteed to bring the evocation to a wholly successful conclusion. The text adds the interesting detail that when the spirit departs, "he will fill the whole place with a sweet and pleasant smell which will be smelt a long time."[10]

Two things are obvious from a study of the *Lemegeton*:

The first is that the evocation of spirits is no easy matter: alternative techniques are offered again and again, clearly predicated on the suspicion that each in turn might not work. The second is that the term *visible* sounds like a drumbeat through every evocation. What the operator wants and expects is *visible* appearance. Only seeing is believing, and if the spirit is not seen with the magician's physical eyes, then a second conjuration must be attempted—and a third or a fourth—until the spirit appears. The very location of the appearance is specified. In the case of the angels, the image floats up from the depths of a rock crystal. In the case of demons, they are conjured into the magical triangle from which they may not escape until released by the sorcerer. Nor is there the least suggestion that the creature in the triangle is in any way a vision. What arrives is a physical being that first appears nebulously, in the form of a fog or mist, then gradually solidifies.

For proof that the entity really does become solid, we can turn to the *Grimorium Verum*, which recommends giving it a piece of bread or a walnut before it disappears again.[11] Instructions for the discovery of treasure that appear in the same grimoire further underline the corporeal nature of the manifested demon, which has sufficient solidity to leave footprints when it walks. The operator is instructed that, when the spirit appears, "Then you will follow Lucifer, or the spirit that he will send in his place, planting your feet over his footprints and tracing his steps."[12] Even where angels are conjured into crystals, it is expected that they make an appearance discernible to the physical eye. Over and over, the *Lemegeton* insists on clarity and intelligibility: these divine spirits must be seen and heard when they occupy the shewstone.

From all this, it is quite clear that the author of the *Lemegeton* and, by extension, those who made use of it were unconcerned with the subjective imagination, even the vivid imagination of childhood evoked by Butler as an explanation. They aimed for *visible* appearance of the spirit and nothing less would do. This is further indicated by frequent references to the fact that the spirit (particularly demonic spirits) should manifest in fair form and do harm to no one. The operator had no wish to have the wits frightened out of him by an ugly devil, whose ability to cause physical harm was never for a moment in question.

Another factor comes into play when considering the nature of evoked spirits. Cellini's impulse to consult the Sicilian sorcerer seems to have been simple curiosity. He was interested in magic and wanted to see for himself what would happen if a spirit evocation was carried out by a professional. But this was not a typical motivation. Magicians who went to the trouble of calling up spirits usually wanted something tangible. Various grimoires, the *Lemegeton* among them, even listed specific spirits for specific jobs. Surgat, a demon associated with Sunday, was relied upon to bring a stone that would render the wearer invisible,[13] the angel Sophiel conferred a knowledge of herbs,[14] while Lucifuge Rofocale "has the control, with which Lucifer has invested him, over all the wealth and treasures of the world"—at least according to the *Grand Grimoire*.[15] The *Book of the Sacred Magic of Abra-Melin the Mage* has long catalogs of spirits, controllable by means of magic squares, for specifics such as visions, scientific information, predictions, drawing water from mines, the production of timber, weather control, the bringing of books, food, or wine, the secrets of love, and even the evocation of further spirits.[16]

Since instructions for spirit evocation appear in some of the earliest magical texts of medieval times[17] and the object of such a practice was almost always severely practical, the mind-set of the magician becomes clear. Far from the imaginary creatures suggested by Butler, the sorcerers of medieval and Renaissance times thought of spirits as objective entities, angelic or diabolic, which might be commanded and set to work by technical means or the assistance of God. The natural home of some entities was another level of reality (heaven or hell) while others—nature spirits and the like—had a terrestrial abode. But in either case, they had the ability, when summoned to the immediate environment of the magician, to take on material form in any shape they wished and engage in practical tasks, often aided by innate magical abilities.

The thought that spirits might have an objective reality seems to have lain beyond Dr. Flournoy's boggle threshold, not to mention that of many of his professional readers. Although sympathetic to his medium, Flournoy never for a moment considered that her spirits might be anything other than unconscious constructs. Like Butler, he unearthed evidence to the contrary but dismissed or ignored it. While discussing Muller's spirit guide Leopold, he mentions that the entity has been called upon by "cultivated people" *during the medium's absence.* Since Leopold is presented as an aspect of Muller's unconscious mind, one might reasonably expect this to be a futile exercise, but Flournoy blandly states, "Naturally they obtain responses, through the table or otherwise and that causes unseen complications."[18] But not for Flournoy's theories: the complications he notes amount to nothing more than a degree of jealousy on the part of the medium that her guide should communicate with others. On the question of raps, Flournoy's boggle threshold is also evident. He attributes the raps to involuntary muscle movements by the medium but fails to address the problem of raps when the medium is not present. Even more conspicuously, he describes one instance in which Muller's chair was pulled from under her by "invisible hands"— surely something well beyond the reach of "involuntary muscle movements." Elsewhere, Flournoy remarks on her ability to speak Sanskrit, produce recognizable signatures of deceased persons, and reveal a thousand correct facts unknown to her, then dismisses them all as "old forgotten memories of things which she saw or heard in her childhood." Flournoy offers no proof of his assertion, but the boggle threshold of generations of orthodox psychologists has ensured that it is now taken as established fact.

At the same time, criticism of orthodox psychological theory hardly constitutes proof that spirits actually exist. There seems little doubt that there is a psychological aspect to much spirit phenomena and there have been many cases in which simple hallucination provides the obvious explanation. But it is only possible to maintain that *all* aspects of spirit encounters and communications are hallucinatory by ignoring vast quantities of intrusive evidence. One psychologist who found he could no longer ignore the evidence was Carl Jung.

Jung began his psychiatric career in agreement with Flournoy that the spirit communications produced by mediumship were essentially the medium talking to herself, or, more accurately, to her own subconscious mind. But Jung had too much intellectual honesty to cling to outmoded opinions, even when they were his own, and in time, life experience led him to revise his early ideas about spirits.

In 1925 he visited what was then British East Africa on an expedition commissioned by the British government to conduct ethnographic interviews with the Bugishu people inhabiting the western and southern stretches of Mount Elgon. Jung, who was then fifty, had by this time developed a broad interest in the paranormal and lost no time in questioning his hosts about spirits. But when he raised the subject during a palaver, "a deathly silence fell on the assembly. The men glanced away, looked in all directions and some of them made off."[19] Jung's Somali headman and the tribal chief conferred together for a moment, then the headman returned to Jung's side to whisper furiously in his ear, "What did you say that for? Now you'll have to break up the palaver."[20] The incident was an object lesson for Jung, teaching him never to use the word *seleteni* ("ghosts" or "spirits") if it could possibly be avoided. A little later in his stay, he discovered why.

One morning while visiting the water hole near Jung's camp, a young native woman collapsed with a septic abortion and was carried back to her home in a high fever. Her tribespeople had little faith in any remedies their European visitors could offer, or indeed in their local medicine man. They decided to call in a witch doctor from another village. The man arrived and began to sniff around the woman's hut like a dog, moving in decreasing spirals until he stopped suddenly and announced that the trouble was caused by the girl's grandfather with whom she had lived since childhood. The grandfather had died recently and his spirit told the witch doctor that he was bored and lonely in ghost land so he had come down the trail at night to get the girl. This was what made her ill. Jung wrote:

The doctor prescribed building a ghost-house, so they made one very neatly of stone . . . and they put in a bed and food and water . . . And the next night the ghost looked in and thought it seemed very nice, so he went in and slept until very late . . . the girl's fever went down and in three days she had quite recovered.[21]

Despite the lighthearted tone of his account, Jung took spirits very seriously. It must have been clear to him that something was going on here that went beyond hallucinatory perceptions of the personal unconscious. The incident with the woman led him to conclude that the tribe's ancestral spirits lived in the bamboo zone high on Mount Elgon and he made a trip there in order to search for them. In the stillness of the bamboo groves, his guides began to behave strangely and clearly did not want to continue. When he confronted one of them, the ashen-faced man insisted there were "thousands and thousands" of ghosts in the groves.[22] On a different occasion, Jung saw one for himself, a creature with an enormous owl-like face and eyes at least a yard in diameter. During a hike he heard music and people talking when no one was actually there.[23]

Later in life he was visited, first in a dream, then as a full-blown waking vision, by a figure he called Philemon. He described the figure as an "old man with the horns of a bull . . . [and] . . . the wings of a kingfisher with its characteristic colours."[24] Although he believed Philemon had arisen out of his unconscious, he also concluded that the vision was not his personal creation. Such figures somehow *produced themselves* and had a life of their own.[25] Furthermore, Philemon often demonstrated superior insight to Jung himself.[26]

As Jung's thinking matured and his personal experiences expanded, he went on to develop a theory of the unconscious that gave a whole new perspective to the problem of spirits. Jung claimed he discovered a collective unconscious—a suprapersonal layer of the psyche—due to a dream he had while returning home from America. In his dream he found himself in the upper story of a house he knew to be his own, furnished in a comfortable modern style. When he descended to the ground floor, he found everything much older—dating back to the fifteenth or sixteenth century. Stone steps led to a cellar that clearly dated to Roman times, while a trapdoor and more steps brought him to a cave cut in the bedrock with a scattering of bones and broken pottery "like remains of a primitive culture."[27] Jung interpreted this dream as a model of the psyche and concluded that the primitive cave represented a sort of mental bedrock that was in no way generated by the individual's thoughts or experience but was common to the whole of humanity. He later found proof of his theory in an hallucination presented by one of his patients who experienced the sun as having an erect penis—a profound mythic symbol from a second-century CE Hellenistic magical text that was not published until four years after Jung had seen his patient.

This version of events is hotly disputed by Harvard psychologist Richard Noll, who argues that E. Schwyzer, the so-called Solar Phallus Man, had his hallucination much later than Jung claimed (so that it might well have been generated by something he read) and was not even Jung's patient in the first place.[28] For Noll, the roots of Jung's ideas are more suspect than scientific. In sharp contrast to Jung's own writings and those of his immediate followers, Noll's biography of Jung[29] portrays him as a practicing pagan,[30] who believed himself to be the reincarnation of Goethe[31] and Meister Eckhardt,[32] studied alchemy, the Hermetica, and Blavatsky's Theosophy, and, most important, took instruction from a spirit (the aforementioned Philemon). In short, Noll's conclusion is that Jung was a practicing Hermeticist. Such a portrait, of course, places Jung—despite his protestations of academic and scientific respectability—firmly within the Western esoteric tradition and is particularly interesting in the light of similarities between his theory of a collective unconscious and esoteric ideas about a so-called Astral Plane.

Jung defined the collective unconscious in the following words:

> The collective unconscious is a part of the psyche which can be negatively distinguished from a personal unconscious by the fact that it does not, like the latter, owe its existence to personal experience and consequently is not a personal acquisition. While the personal unconscious is made up essentially of contents which have at one time been conscious, but which have disappeared from consciousness through having been forgotten or repressed, the contents of the collective unconscious have never been in consciousness and therefore have never been individually acquired, but owe their existence exclusively to heredity. Whereas the personal unconscious consists for the most part of complexes, the content of the collective unconscious is made up essentially of archetypes. The concept of the archetype, which is

an indispensable correlate of the idea of the collective unconscious, indicates the existence of definite forms in the psyche which seem to be present always and everywhere . . .

My thesis, then, is as follows: In addition to our immediate conscious-ness, which is of a thoroughly personal nature and which we believe to be the only empirical psyche (even if we tack on the personal unconscious as an appendix), there exists a second psychic system of a collective, universal and impersonal nature which is identical in all individuals. This collective unconscious does not develop individually but is inherited. It consists of pre-existent forms, the archetypes, which can only become conscious secondar-ily and which give definite form to certain psychic contents.[33]

Despite the careful formulation of his theory, Jung was well aware that it left him open to charges of mysticism, and he went to some pains to defend himself by insisting it contained no more mysticism than the concept of instincts.[34] Nonetheless, when he came to give examples of his postulated archetypes, it became clear that some corresponded to the gods of ancient mythology. Others were capable of demanding worship or of possessing individuals and groups, sometimes to negative effect: "There is no lunacy people under the domination of an archetype will not fall a prey to."[35] Archetypal figures appeared in dreams,[36] as visions and, as we have seen from his own experience of Philemon, as psychopompic projections—that is, apparent intrusions into day-to-day waking reality; all manifestations tra-ditionally attributed to spirits.

Thus, Jung's critics might be forgiven for assuming that his new theory was no more than a reformulation of some very old esoteric ideas: the arche-types were spirits and the collective unconscious was the spirit world visited by shamans and mediums. If there was any difference at all, it lay in the fact that for centuries, the spirit world was believed to be "out there" or "up there," while Jung's insight was that it was actually "*in* there."

This closely mirrors an idea central to occult practice from the nine-teenth century to the present day—the concept of an Astral Plane that runs parallel to and is accessible from our world. The starry terminology seems to have originated with the French magus Eliphas Lévi, who postulated a force of nature "more powerful than steam" that magnetized the stars and transformed into "astral light" therein.[37] In human beings, the same energy formed a subtle body that acted as a mediator between the individual and the astral light, enabling him or her to act on the whole of nature by an application of will. Tellingly, Lévi also taught that the astral light was the "common mirror of all thoughts and forms."[38]

Lévi's ideas were taken up by the Golden Dawn, a pseudo-Masonic Victorian magical society. They taught the use of technical aids like tattva cards to enable the projection of the astral body into another level of reality, the Astral Plane.[39] Golden Dawn initiates followed Lévi in their belief that their training enabled them to view this parallel reality, as one might today use a television set to view the actions of individuals in a distant studio. But by the time Dion Fortune founded her Society of the Inner Light in 1922, the expression "Astral Plane" was increasingly seen as an archaic term for the visual imagination itself.[40] The distinction, however, is not so clear-cut. Imagination was no longer accepted by occultists as a subjective function of the mind but rather a perceptible world in its own right, particularly when it manifested in dreams and visions. Lévi went some way toward marrying the two viewpoints in the Introduction to his *History of Magic* when he stated:

> A particular phenomenon occurs when the brain is congested or overcharged by Astral Light; sight is turned inward instead of outward; night falls on the external and real world, while fantastic brilliance shines on the world of dreams . . . The soul then perceives by means of images the reflection of its impressions and thoughts. This is to say that the analogy subsisting between idea and form attracts in the Astral Light a reflection representing that form, configuration being the essence of the vital light; it is the universal imagination, of which each of us appropriates a lesser or greater part according to our grade of sensibility and memory.[41]

Lévi's use of the term *universal imagination* brings the concept of the Astral Plane closer still to Jung's idea of a collective unconscious, and it is significant that the Astral Plane is believed by modern occultists to be the home of spirits. Perhaps more to the point, they also believe it to be part of a grouping of "Inner Planes," seen as objective realities that are nonetheless accessible by turning the attention inward. For Jung, the collective unconscious was also an objective aspect of the human psyche. Esoteric doctrine and Jungian psychology blend absolutely in the therapeutic technique of "active imagination" defined by Jung as a "sequence of fantasies produced by deliberate concentration," which he believed produced proof of a collective unconscious.[42] Active Imagination is identical to a modern esoteric technique known as "pathworking," which allows practitioners controlled access to the Astral Plane.[43]

But whether expressed in Jungian or esoteric terms, the concept of an objective aspect of the human psyche only goes partway toward an explanation of spirits. This becomes evident when spirit manifestations are accompanied by physical phenomena or seen by more than one person at the same time. Jung himself found it possible to accept that some physical events might have direct psychic causes, but many of his professional colleagues were not so sure. When Freud and Jung experienced what Jung called a "catalytic exteriorization phenomenon"—a loud report in a bookcase following a curious sensation in Jung's diaphragm—Freud dismissed the idea that it might have had a psychological cause as "sheer bosh" and remained unable to accept it even when the noise repeated.[44]

Most of us are a little like that. Cultural conditioning in Western society brings with it a tendency to view all psychological content as subjective. Thus we can readily accept that spirits might be the unconscious constructs of a medium or the personal hallucinations of a magician. We might even accept, in the light of Jung's theory of a collective unconscious, that some eruptions from the depths of the psyche have origins independent of our personal experience. But for most of us, the idea that psychic entities might become visible and even tangible, as the grimoires insist, or move tables and throw objects, as Spiritualism attests, is usually a step too far. Nonetheless, some experimental work has been done to suggest that a mechanism for such effects does exist.

In 1966, the British psychologist Kenneth J. Batcheldor published a report in the *Journal of the Society for Psychical Research* entitled "Report on a Case of Table Levitation and Associated Phenomena."

Batcheldor, an active member of the Society for Psychical Research, had become interested in Spiritualist reports of table-turning during the Victorian era. Table-turning is a specific type of Spiritualist séance during which participants sit, often in total darkness, with their hands placed on the surface of a table, which will then allegedly move of its own accord, due to the intervention of spirits. Batcheldor noted that the practice had become something of a rarity in the sixties and decided to carry out his own investigation. To this end, he set up a small group of sitters in Exeter and, on April 25, 1964, began what became a series of 200 experimental séances. None of the sitters laid claim to any mediumistic ability and Batcheldor himself did not accept the spirit hypothesis of séance room phenomena. Of the 200 sittings, 120 produced no paranormal results. Physical phenomena, not necessarily paranormal, occurred in the remaining 80.

Early sessions saw some movement of the table, but nothing that could not be explained by involuntary muscle action on the part of participants. On the eleventh sitting, however, Batcheldor reported that the table rose clear of the floor and floated in the air. Since sitters' hands were only in contact with the *top* of the table, this ruled out involuntary muscle action. It did not, however, rule out deliberate fraud, as the séance had been held in darkness. With the aid of one of his sitters, who was a professional engineer, Batcheldor began to introduce tighter controls. At this point, a curious pattern emerged. Batcheldor discovered that phenomena were relatively easy to produce (with a little patience) when no controls were imposed and the séance was held in total darkness. Once controls were introduced—tape recording the proceedings, attaching sensors to the feet of the table, and so on—the phenomena immediately stopped but gradually crept back over a series of séances. Any new set of controls would cause the pattern to repeat.

Batcheldor found that by introducing controls very gradually, in small increments, and allowing his sitters to get used to them, he could induce not only table movements up to and including total levitation but a whole range of "spirit" phenomena familiar from Victorian reports. These included raps, breezes, intense cold, lights, the sensation of being touched, the pulling back of sitters' chairs, movement of objects such as a rattle and a trumpet, the "gluing" of the table to the floor so that it could not be moved, and even apports (small objects apparently appearing out of nowhere).

Batcheldor's experimental technique proved repeatable. By 1979, he estimated that at least ten groups had produced paranormal phenomena using his methods. The leader of one of them, Batcheldor's colleague and collaborator, Colin Brookes-Smith, reported that given suitable procedures, paranormal forces could be made available "by the pound."[45]

The effect of these various experiments was to separate séance room phenomena from the automatic assumption of spirit intervention. It seemed clear to Batcheldor that what was behind the phenomena was not disembodied spirits but the (unconscious) minds of his sitters. Batcheldor theorized that "natural artifacts"—that is, unfamiliar occurrences like table movements caused by muscle contractions—gradually conditioned the sitters to accept the possibility of paranormal manifestations, thus clearing the way to produce them. It may be noted that Batcheldor's ability to create paranormal effects "by the pound" did not absolutely rule out spirit intervention, but if spirits were somehow inhabitants of "inner space," as postulated in Jung's model, then it did clearly demonstrate the existence of a mechanism whereby they might influence the physical world.

But while Batcheldor was conducting his experiments, a serious complication was on the horizon. In September 1972, members of a Canadian research group led by Dr. A. R. G. Owen, a former fellow at Trinity College, Cambridge, and a seasoned psychical researcher, decided to find out whether they could create a ghost.[46] To this end, they invented a fictional character named Philip, a well-born Cavalier officer who lived at the time of the English Civil War. Although married, Philip had an affair with a gypsy girl named Margo. When his wife, Dorothea, discovered what was going on, she denounced Margo as a witch. Margo was subsequently burned at the stake and a heartbroken Philip committed suicide by flinging himself off the battlements of Diddington Hall, his family home. The only factual element in this lurid tale was the family home. There really was a Diddington Hall (in Warwickshire) and group members found photographs of it to help them visualize the details of their story. They then began a series of séances designed to make contact with "Philip."[47]

For a year they were unsuccessful. Then one of the members stumbled on Batcheldor's work, reports of which suggested that a lighthearted approach tended to be more conducive to phenomena. They began to tell jokes and sing while seated around the séance table. Three or four sittings later, they heard their first rap after which the table began to slide across the floor. One member had the presence of mind to ask aloud if Philip was causing this and was answered by an extraordinarily loud knock. The group quickly established a one-knock-for-yes, two-knocks-for-no code and set up a line of communication. Over several subsequent séances, the communicating entity confirmed details of its life, which matched—and in some instances creatively embroidered on—Philip's fictional story. He also proved capable of providing apposite answers to questions that lay outside his story altogether.[48]

The communications were accompanied by spectacular physical phenomena. These included rolling knocks across the table, table movements such as tilts and slides, raps made to order at specified locations in the room, distortions rising like oranges out of the table surface, and the flickering of electric lights on demand. During the making of a documentary movie about the séances, witnesses reported that the table levitated fully, about half an inch from the floor (although the action was not captured on film). When the group later took part in a television discussion, Philip managed to persuade the table to climb a set of steps in order to join the panelists on the platform. This complex and highly entertaining maneuver *was* recorded on camera.[49]

As with Batcheldor's work, the Toronto experiment proved repeatable by different groups, including one that met at a hotel in the Malverns on September 24, 1995, and conjured a fictional Saxon priestess named Coventina using a modified form of Solomonic ritual. The "entity" answered questions for some twenty minutes, having spontaneously "possessed" one of the participants who passed into a mediumistic trance.[50]

Although the implications of these experiments have yet to find their way into mainstream thought, they establish beyond all doubt that if the human mind really is the ultimate home of spirits, it is a much more complex habitat than consensus psychology currently imagines—a conclusion confirmed by further experimental evidence.

29. A SCIENTIFIC
FOUNDATION

S TANISLAV GROF WAS BORN IN CZECHOSLOVAKIA IN 1932. HE TRAINED
as a physician and psychiatrist. In 1956, he graduated from medical
school and just months later presented himself at the Psychiatric
Department of the School of Medicine in Prague for an experiment that was
to change the course of his life. It was an experiment with LSD.

LSD is the common name for lysergic acid diethylamide, a potent psychoactive drug first synthesized in Switzerland in 1938. Its immediate physical effects can include drowsiness, dizziness, dilated pupils, numbness or
tingling, weakness, tremors, and nausea. But even the most pronounced of

*Stanislav Grof, the world-renowned psychiatrist whose investigation of
human consciousness led him to a belief in alternate realities*

these is insignificant when set against its mind-altering qualities. LSD evokes mood changes, thought changes, and an altered perception of time and space. Grof found its impact almost devastating:

> This experience profoundly influenced my personal and professional life and provided the inspiration for my lifelong commitment to consciousness research.[1]

LSD usage did not long remain confined to the laboratory. In the 1960s it was taken up as drug of choice by the Hippie movement where it was used to intensify emotional connections with others and achieve what were believed to be insights into nature and the universe. Championed by psychedelic gurus like Timothy Leary, its use became so widespread among students that some politicians began to see it as a national crisis. In tandem with this development, legitimate use declined markedly. In the United States, it came under the restrictions of the Drug Abuse Control Amendment of 1965. The following year, the only authorized manufacturer withdrew the drug from the market and transferred its supplies to the federal government. Leary responded with his famous advice:

> If you take the game of life seriously, if you take your nervous system seriously, if you take your sense organs seriously, if you take the energy process seriously, you must turn on, tune in and drop out.[2]

After the closure of legitimate supply sources, a flourishing black market in LSD quickly sprang up. In a predictable backlash, the medical profession decided there was no real clinical use for the drug and, by the early 1990s, had more or less abandoned serious research. Many reference sources now routinely cross-reference it and other psychoactive drugs with "substance abuse." All are said to induce hallucinogenic states.

There is, however, another viewpoint. It was put forward by the English intellectual Aldous Huxley in two essays combined to make a single book, i *The Doors of Perception and Heaven and Hell*.[3] After an experiment with mescaline—a natural derivative with similar affects to LSD—he outlined a theory that carried psychedelics into the realm of mysticism. Huxley, who was almost blind when he took the drug, experienced profound perceptual changes and vivid visions. But they were not, he decided, hallucinatory.

Broadly speaking, there have been two schools of thought about the human mind throughout most of the twentieth century. One suggests it is a thing in itself, operating the brain as a driver might operate a car. The other, which has the support of the orthodox scientific paradigm, believes "mind" to be no more than a collection of subjective impressions generated by the electrical activity of the brain. Huxley subscribed to the first of these two theories. He believed that mind was not only a thing in itself but substantially more far-reaching than most of us imagine. He used the term *mind at large* to describe it.

According to Huxley, mind at large is capable of a vastly extended perception of reality—so extended, in fact, that it is counterproductive in terms of survival. Simply put, if you are prey to constant visions, you are likely to end up underneath a bus. Thus the brain evolved as a sort of reducing valve, filtering out those impressions that are unnecessary for the job at hand. He believed that drugs like mescaline and LSD interfered with the efficiency of the brain in this respect and allowed extraneous information to come through. In the words of the poet William Blake, the "doors of perception were cleansed." Far from promoting hallucinations, the drugs actually permitted a more profound experience of reality.

This was a viewpoint with which Grof quickly came to agree. In 1956, he embarked on one of the most eccentric psychiatric careers of the century. Like his more orthodox colleagues, he treated patients suffering from various emotional and psychosomatic illnesses such as depression, neuroses, alcoholism, and drug addiction. But he also concerned himself with a substantial number of terminally ill patients—mostly cancer victims—with no specific psychiatric problems at all. In each case he used such drugs as LSD, psilocybin, mescaline, dipropyl-tryptamine, and methylene-dioxy-amphetamine—all extremely powerful mind-altering substances. After conducting more than four thousand such sessions, with peripheral involvement in another two thousand directed by colleagues, the legal and professional pressures on those who used such drugs, even in a medical context, became too great. Grof switched emphasis to a special breathing technique that he and his wife discovered triggered similar non-ordinary states of consciousness.

In 1992, he coined the name *holotropic* to describe such states. It was a combination of two Greek terms: *holos*, meaning "whole," and *trepein*, which translates as "moving toward." If, then, *holotropic* means "moving toward wholeness," the implication is that we are not whole in our everyday state of consciousness but identify only with a small fragment of what we really are. Grof's conviction in this respect stemmed directly from the experiences of his patients. Over and over they reported the *same sort* of changes in perception and worldview. This development was independent of intelligence, education, cultural background, or profession. In a holotropic state, *everybody* started to see the world in essentially the same way. Remarkably, the holotropic worldview includes direct experience of spirits. Says Grof:

> Holotropic states of consciousness can also provide deep insights into the worldview of cultures that believe that the cosmos is populated by mythological beings and that it is governed by various blissful and wrathful deities. In these states we can gain direct experiential access to the world of gods, demons, legendary heroes, suprahuman entities and spirit guides. We can visit the domain of mythological realities, fantastic landscapes and abodes of the Beyond. The imagery . . . can feature mythological figures and themes from any culture in the entire history of humanity. Deep personal experiences of this realm help us realise that the images of the cosmos found in pre-industrial societies are not based on superstition or primitive "magical thinking" but on direct experiences of alternate realities.[4]

Grof found his holotropic adventurers were also in agreement that beyond mundane perceptions of the phenomenal universe—and even beyond the alternate realities of the spirit worlds—the cosmos was a mystical unity. This typically presented itself in one of two forms. One was an experience of Absolute Consciousness, immanent in all there is and ever was. The other was an experience of Cosmic Void, a transcendent "emptiness" that somehow contained the potential of everything that is, will be, and ever was. Absolute Consciousness and Cosmic Void seem at opposite ends of a spectrum, if not actually contradictory. But the holotropic worldview agrees with the insights of mystics down the ages that both are one and the same thing. Grof summarizes his findings in the following words:

> In holotropic states . . . it is possible to transcend the boundaries of the embodied self. These experiences offer us the opportunity to become other people, groups of people, animals, plants and even inorganic elements of nature and of the cosmos. In this process, time does not seem to be an obstacle and past and future events can become as easily available as anything happening at present.

Experiences of this kind convey a very convincing insight that all boundaries in the material world are illusory and that the entire universe as we know it, in both spatial and temporal aspects, is a unified web of events in consciousness. It becomes very clear that the cosmos is not an ordinary material reality but a creation of intelligent cosmic energy or the Universal Mind . . .

While such transpersonal experiences dramatically change our understanding of the nature of everyday material reality, there are others that reveal dimensions of existence that are ordinarily completely hidden to our perception. This category includes discarnate entities, various deities and demons, mythological realms, suprahuman beings and the divine creative principle itself . . . Experiences of this kind demonstrate that cosmic creation is not limited to our material world, but manifests on many different levels and in many dimensions.[5]

Despite the uniformity of holotropic reports, there remained the problem of whether they represented an objective reality or some sort of shared hallucination. Even Jung balked at this hurdle. Although he frequently referred to an objective psyche, he was careful to explain it as arising out of our basic brain structure. The collective unconscious was collective in the sense of belonging to all humanity, not in the sense of being a single mental entity that each of us tapped into.[6] But Grof went the whole hog. He noted time and again that patients in the holotropic state were able to obtain verifiable information by means of extrasensory processes. That is to say, they learned things they did not already know as their minds expanded beyond the confines of the treatment room. Such observations went a long way to convince him that the holotropic experience was valid and something akin to Huxley's mind at large.

The whole question of extrasensory information is controversial. There is good reason to believe that the brain faithfully records every impression—including background noises and other inconsequential details—that reaches it. Every book you have ever read, every TV program you have ever seen, every snatch of conversation you have ever heard is in there and will remain in there, barring accidents, until the day you die. This is obviously not to say that the entire wealth of stored information is available to you. Clearly in your normal state of consciousness it is not. But in altered states, such as hypnotic trance, or under electrical stimulation of the brain, the most extraordinary details can be recalled. This means that information presenting itself as the result of extrasensory perception *may* sometimes actually be the stored memory of something you read or experienced years ago and have long since forgotten.

Skeptics argue that it is impossible to determine where any hypothetical ESP begins and memory ends and consequently invoke Occam's razor[7] to dismiss the extrasensory hypothesis altogether. But for Grof, the holotropic insights are something more than theory. He has personally witnessed at least one practical application.

The Esalen Institute was founded in California in 1962 to promote the exploration of human potential. It runs an extensive program of courses and workshops on subjects like consciousness expansion, holistic health, parapsychology, and even the mental aspect of sports training. After Grof took up residence in the United States, he was appointed a scholar in residence at the institute. One of the events he was involved in organizing was a month-long seminar on Buddhism and Western psychology. A guest facilitator at the seminar was a master swordsman from Korea. At one point during the event, the Korean offered a special demonstration of his skills. For this he required one of his pupils to lie down on his back on the grass. A napkin was then placed on his naked stomach and a watermelon placed on top of the napkin. The swordsman retreated to a distance of fifteen feet and had his head covered with a tightly fitting thick black velvet bag. He was then given an enormous sharp-bladed sword. He stood quite still for several minutes.

As Grof later described the incident, every dog in the area suddenly began to bark. The Korean immediately joined in with a wild howl, then— still blindfold—began to *cartwheel* furiously toward his pupil. As he reached him, he swung the giant sword viciously and cut the watermelon neatly in two. There was a slight trace of the sword blade on the napkin beneath, but the pupil's body was unharmed.

The assumption of most of those watching was that the swordsman must have carried a vivid, detailed mental picture of the scene that allowed him to perform the precision feat. But the Korean gave a different explanation: "You meditate and wait until all is one—the swordmaster, the sword, the grass, the melon, the disciple—and then there is no problem."[8]

This type of demonstration is by no means unique. But despite the anecdotal evidence, a majority of scientists still consider mind at large a nonsense since mind itself is no more than the passage of electrons through the synaptic gateways of the brain. The claim is repeated again and again in the reference sources of modern psychology, yet it can only be maintained by ignoring the result of an experiment carried out by the distinguished British neurophysiologist, Dr. W. Grey Walter, in the 1960s.

Grey Walter announced his findings in his 1969 Eddington Memorial Lecture. The procedure he had followed was based on the fact that the human brain generates small but measurable electrical signals. Electrodes were attached to his subjects' scalps over the area of the frontal cortex. These transmitted any brain electrical activity via an amplifier to a specially constructed machine. Set before the subject was a button that, when pressed, caused what Grey Walter described as an "interesting scene" to appear on a TV screen.

When one decides to take a particular physical action, such as pressing a button, a 20-microvolt electrical surge occurs across a large area of the cortex. This is technically known as a *readiness wave*. What Grey Walter did was amplify the readiness wave to such a degree that it could directly trigger the TV picture. This obviously happened a fraction of a second before the button was actually pressed. The subject decided to press the button and the readiness wave surged across the cortex. The electrodes detected and amplified it, sending a signal to the machine, which called up the TV picture before the subject could actually reach the button. He called the process "auto-start."

Subjects usually figured out what was happening fairly quickly and trained themselves to "will" the pictures onto the screen without touching the button at all. It soon became clear that subjective mental state was everything. For the trick to work, they had to duplicate exactly their mind-set in pressing the button. If their attention wandered or their minds locked themselves up by thinking of the need to concentrate, the readiness wave failed to rise and no picture was delivered. But once they got the knack, they could actually combine auto-start with auto-stop. They could will pictures onto the screen directly, then dismiss them with the relevant mind-set when finished.

Despite superficial appearances, none of this was the mind acting directly on matter since the switch was triggered by a perfectly ordinary electrical surge originating in the subject's brain. But once the subjects learned they could produce the pictures without pressing the button, their minds *were* directly influencing matter—the physical matter of their own brains. A decision of the mind, applied in a particular way, was all it took to change the electrical potential of the frontal cortex. There was no physical aspect to the cause: as the subjects got into their stride, the button was neither pressed nor attempted to be pressed.

A 20-microvolt surge is a small thing, but its implications here are enormous, for it settles once and for all the controversy about the independent reality of the mind. Grey Walter's findings have never been challenged, merely ignored, yet they show clearly that the prevailing scientific paradigm is just plain wrong. The mind is *not* simply the way we experience the electrical activity of the brain. It is a thing in its own right, separate and distinct from the body. This single fact leaves open the prospect of mind at large. It also lays down a scientific foundation for the possibility of postmortem survival and the reality of spirits.

If, as Grey Walter demonstrated, mind is a thing in itself, then it becomes reasonable to ask what it is made from and where it is located. Surprisingly, modern physics seems to provide answers to both these questions.

Wolfgang Pauli was born in Vienna in 1900. At the age of twenty, he produced a two-hundred-page encyclopedia article on Einstein's theory of relativity. Five years later, he had completed the work on electrons that was to win him a Nobel Prize. In 1930, he predicted the existence of a very peculiar subatomic particle called the neutrino. It was the most elusive of particles, having virtually no characteristics. It had neither mass, electric charge, nor magnetic field. It was not subject to gravity, nor influenced by electrical or magnetic fields, and it could pass through any solid body, even a planet, as if it were empty space. The only thing that could stop it was a head-on collision with another neutrino, and the chances against that happening were estimated at ten billion to one. Long though these odds might be, it seems there were enough neutrinos to make sure collisions did occur. In 1956, scientists F. Reines and C. Cowan eventually detected one at America's Atomic Energy Commission nuclear reactor on the Savannah River. But if neutrinos existed, they did not exist in the way many other particles exist. They resembled nothing more closely than the building blocks of ghosts. This resemblance was not lost on scientists, who began to speculate about the possibility of other particles that, if they did not actually define ghosts, might at least provide a more respectable "missing link" between matter and mind.

It was the eminent astronomer V. A. Firsoff who first suggested (in 1967) that mind was a "universal entity or interaction" of the same order as electricity or gravitation. Firsoff went on to speculate that "mind-stuff" could be equated with other structures of the physical world. As Pauli had done more than thirty years earlier, Firsoff predicted the existence of a new particle, the mindon, as the elementary aspect of "mind-stuff." Mindon properties would be very similar to those of the already-confirmed neutrino. To an entity composed of mindons, the physical universe would scarcely exist. At best it would be seen as thin patches of mist. Even massive bodies like suns would be barely visible, detectable only by their neutrino emissions. According to Firsoff, the brain of such an entity might deduce our existence but would have trouble confirming it with instruments that themselves were composed of neutrino/mindon particles. At least, the mindon entity would have problems confirming the existence of our *physical bodies*. The entity would be aware of the human psyche (itself composed of mindons, according to Firsoff's own theory) and might, if it managed to communicate, accept the psyche's perception of itself as having a physical body. At this level, it becomes possible to envisage the growth of a belief structure in which the "immaterial" bodies of humanity were one of the mysteries of existence.

Firsoff has pointed out that our physical universe is no "truer" than that of the neutrino, only rather more familiar. We now know that neutrinos exist, but exist in a different kind of space and are governed by different laws. Einstein's calculations show that the speed of light is an absolute in the physical universe. This is normally taken to mean that it is simply impossible for anything to travel faster. But what Einstein actually found was that nothing could be *accelerated* to a speed faster than that of light. The difference is subtle but real. It leaves room for naturally occurring particles that come into existence *already* traveling faster than light. For such particles, the speed of light is a barrier downward, not upward—they can never slow *below* 186,000 miles per second. Firsoff suggested that since neutrinos were not subject to electromagnetic or gravitational fields, they might not be bound by speed limits either. They might, in fact, have their own—different—time. Physicists have since gone on to speculate about the existence of another particle, the tachyon, which exceeds the speed of light and moves backward in time as a result.

Mental entities like Jung's archetypes or even the essence of identity have no definite location in physical space. One may imagine their essential self to be located just behind their eyes, but clearly this does not hold true for the self experienced in dreams or altered states of consciousness. It does not even hold true for certain racial groupings, notably the Celts, who had a tendency to experience themselves as living behind their navels. Although people are aware of an inner self, there is no instrument on Earth that can locate it directly. To Firsoff, this suggested that mindons inhabited a genuine mental "space" governed by different laws from those of the physical universe—in short, an alternate reality. Alternate realities used to be the stuff of science fiction, but that was before the emergence of quantum mechanics.

The foundation of quantum mechanics was laid down in 1900 by the German physicist Max Planck, who postulated that energy is composed of tiny, separate units he called quanta. Albert Einstein built on this insight and won a Nobel Prize for his work. In 1913, a Danish physicist named Niels Bohr applied the new rules of quantum theory to the basic structure of the atom and discovered they worked. By 1927, Germany's Werner Heisenberg had formulated his "uncertainty principle," which states that it is impossible to measure both the position and momentum of a subatomic particle. You can measure one or the other, but not both. Heisenberg went on to create a complete theory of quantum mechanics—he called it "matrix mechanics"— as did the Austrian physicist Erwin Schrödinger from a different viewpoint.

Quantum mechanics solved all of the great difficulties that troubled physicists in the early years of the twentieth century. Eventually, it became the most successful theory ever developed to describe the fundamental nature of the universe. It has been tested experimentally time and again and continues to provide the best explanation of a whole host of effects. But for all its successes, quantum mechanics describes an *Alice in Wonderland* world based on probabilities where nothing makes much sense anymore.

In a fundamental experiment of quantum mechanics, a beam of subatomic particles is directed toward a sensitized target that will register their impact. A screen with two slots—which can be opened and closed independently—is placed between the beam and the target. It seems obvious that if both the slits are opened, twice as many particles will get through compared to if you only open one. The reality is that more particles reach the target if only one slit is open. This finding runs contrary to common sense and scientists have wrestled with the dilemma since the 1930s when the experiment was first carried out. To make sense of their findings, they began to suspect that subatomic particles were not particles at all, but waves. A wave would pass through both slits simultaneously, recording no more hits on the target than would be the case with a single slit. Indeed, since a number of the waves might be expected to collide—thus canceling each other out—fewer would get through two slits than one. Unfortunately for this solution, the particles only behaved like waves while they were passing through the slits. When they hit the target, they behaved like particles again. A wave would be expected to strike all at once, like a sea wave breaking along the length of a beach, but this did not happen. The particles struck in specific locations like little cannonballs.

Physicists were forced to accept that these particles behaved like particles in certain circumstances and like waves in others. This made so little sense that they began to wonder if the "wave" might actually be a collection of possibilities that behaved in a wavelike manner. In other words, the basic particle was still a particle, but instead of simply observing its actual behavior, one must take into account everything that could happen to it—all its probabilities, in other words—and the mind must organize them into a wavelike structure. Quantum particles began to be seen increasingly as probability waves. As each particle approached the open slits, the probability wave (which really only exists in the mind of the observer) represents the different possibilities open to it—whether it passes through the top slit or the bottom slit, or strikes the screen and is absorbed or deflected. This probability wave could not predict exactly where the particle would go, only where it was most likely to go.

The theory of probability waves explained particle behavior up to a point but left physicists with the problem of explaining how probabilities somehow managed to interfere with one another exactly like physical waves. But in 1957, a young American physicist named Hugh Everett III came up with the answer in the course of his doctoral work at Princeton University. He suggested that if two probabilities can interfere with each other, each of them must have an actual existence. But since there is no way that conflicting probabilities can exist in our universe, it followed that there must be a second, parallel universe to house the second probability.

It has to be said that while Everett's theory has attracted a large number of supporters, a majority of physicists still hold to a different explanation. Rather than evoking a parallel universe, they believe our own universe actually splits briefly to accommodate the passage of a single particle through two different slits and re-forms again once it has done so. The determining factor here is not the particle or the slits but the fact that the particle is under observation. This idea seems unlikely, and even Einstein once remarked that he could not accept that the universe changed just because a mouse looked at it.

But then as it happens, Einstein's relativity theory (when applied to black holes) supports the idea of parallel universes as well.[9] The mathematics of rotating black holes suggest the existence of an infinite number of alternate realities. There is even a theoretical process, called quantum tunneling, by means of which it might be possible to pass from one parallel universe to another. The implications of these theories have not been lost on the more maverick of modern physicists. One of them, Fred Alan Wolf, has gone on record with the speculation that quantum tunneling may provide a rational explanation for ghosts and other psychic phenomena. For Wolf, a parallel reality may be the home of spirits.

Curiously enough, there are spirit contacts who agree. The idea of a parallel reality is echoed in the words of Dolores Ashcroft-Nowicki's Upuaut. Asked bluntly if he was real, he replied, "Yes, very, but on my plane of existence rather than yours." White Bull, the guide who uses Ian Graham as a channel, describes himself as "dangling at the end of a rope" held by friends in a "world of light." Although expressed in religious terms, the "world of light" is clearly another dimension of reality. "Mark," a collective of entities communicating through a British channel, enlarges on the theme: "We are a different expression of energy . . . we do have structure but it is more like patterns or like waves of sound and light. Both is correct in a sense but not really very complete as a description . . . We cannot be measured in the way that you would measure light or heat. We are existing in another reality altogether, another dimension you sometimes call it."

Interestingly, "Mark" believes humans do not exactly move into a different dimension of reality after death, but rather become more fully aware of a dimension into which they have always extended—and it is the same dimension, the same parallel reality, that nonhuman entities share:

> In a way you move closer to our reality then (after death) and sometimes humans who extend towards us consciously in their physical life will connect with us much more fully on what you term death, which is more truly a transformation of perception and consciousness.[10]

The comment neatly bridges the theories of Wolf and Firsoff and encompasses the findings of Grey Walter. A unified theory begins to emerge.

It starts with the discovery that the mind is a thing in itself, not simply an illusion created by the electrical activity of the brain. But even as a thing in itself, it is clearly not of the same order as, for example, a chair or the book. It exists in its own "space" and quite possibly its own "time." This gives us a wholly new concept of ourselves. The essence of a human being is actually an entity, composed of particles similar to neutrinos or Firsoff's mindons, that exists in a parallel reality. In order to experience the world as we know it, this entity links itself—at least temporarily—to a physical vehicle, the human body, as players link with their avatars in massive multiplayer online games. In so doing, it limits its perceptions of its own reality, narrowing focus for the sake of survival.

There is no longer any reason to believe death of the physical vehicle results in the destruction of the mindon entity. But nor, contrary to much religious thought, does it go anywhere. Rather it again expands its awareness of its own sphere of reality, the sphere it never actually ceased to inhabit. One could speculate that it might, at some stage, decide to link with another body for further experience of physical reality, thus providing a foundation for the widespread oriental theory of reincarnation.

It would appear that in the normal course of events, the mindon entity's link with matter is forged at a very early stage of development of the physical vehicle—perhaps at the moment of conception, perhaps in the womb and certainly no later than the moment of the infant's first breath. The formation of the link begins a process of growth and the storage of impressions that continues until physical death. Clearly if suitable vehicles exist, there is no reason why incarnation of the mindon entity should not take place on planets other than Earth.

Within this theory, "spirits" become mindon entities without permanent links to physical bodies. The difference between "human" and "nonhuman" entities is less clear-cut than it might seem from our usual perspective, as is the difference between "male" and "female" entities. A human may be simply a mindon creature, of whatever pedigree, that manages to make the physical link; or it may be that only certain mindon "species" are equipped for human body incarnation. Sex is dependent on the body selected, although there is the possibility of a preexistent gender structure that influences the body of choice. While contact with matter is usually achieved through the incarnation process, it seems there are rare circumstances in which two or more mindon entities may share the same physical vehicle (indwelling) or where one may oust the other (possession). The transfer of mindon entities, as reported by Ernest Butler, Dolores Ashcroft-Nowicki, and others, while still largely mysterious, becomes at least feasible.

This is a theory that accords with the history of spirit contact down the ages. It reconciles the conflict between the experience of spirit voices as an inner phenomenon and spirit claims to be separate, objective beings. But is there direct evidence to support it? Is there even evidence to back up Grey Walter's startling findings? Once again, the answer is yes.

In 1959, an amateur ornithologist named Friedrich Jürgenson went into the woods near his Swedish home to record birdsong. He had made similar recordings many times before, but on this occasion he found a faint, strange voice on the tape, calling his name. He ran the tape again and again, adjusting the volume, concentrating hard. The voice was definitely there and he eventually decided it belonged to his mother. It sounded as if she had been somewhere deep in the woods calling to him. Yet Jürgenson's mother had been dead for years. This was the beginning of a whole new chapter in the annals of psychical research. Jürgenson went on to produce many more mysterious recordings. In 1964, he went public and a Stockholm publisher brought out his book *Rösterna från Rymden* or *Voices from Space*. Among those who read it was a Latvian psychiatrist with a lifelong interest in the paranormal, Dr. Konstantin Raudive.

As Raudive began the book, he was not particularly impressed. He was familiar with most of the scientists engaged in psychical research at the time and Jürgenson was definitely an outsider. Perhaps more important, he came across as a highly imaginative man—perhaps even overimaginative—and Raudive suspected he might be capable of conjuring up visions in an empty room or voices out of the silence. But as he continued to read, Raudive found himself fascinated by the central theme of the book—that spirit voices, "voices from space," could actually be recorded.

Jürgenson's work contained no hint of how recording the dead might be done. Jürgenson confined himself to claims that he had recorded not only the voices of dead relatives and friends, but historical personages like Hitler and the recently executed Carl Chessman, an American who became a bestselling author while confined to death row for murder. It was all very frustrating for someone like Raudive whose whole instinct was to investigate such claims for himself. In April 1965, he contacted Jürgenson and asked to hear some of his tapes. Jürgenson agreed.

Raudive traveled to Sweden with a colleague, Dr. Zenta Maurina, and took a liking to Jürgenson at once. The Swede seemed sincere and deeply committed to his research. He allowed the visitors immediate access to his tapes. The voices were audible enough against a background hiss, but Raudive and his colleague found it impossible to make out what they were saying. They were faint and spoke very quickly with a peculiar rhythm. But as the tapes were repeated several times, their ears gradually attuned. At this point, they had only Jürgenson's word that the tapes were genuine. The man was a movie producer and might well have hired actors to pretend to be spirits. But Jürgenson agreed to make a new recording on the spot. When he played back the tape, there were voices on it that Raudive believed could not have come from anybody in the room. Nor did they seem to be glitches on the tape or sounds that Jürgenson had somehow prerecorded. The incident that ruled out both these possibilities arose when Dr. Maurina remarked she was under the impression that inhabitants of the Beyond led a happy, carefree existence. Her comment was duly recorded on the tape . . . as was the reply of *"Nonsense!"* from a wholly unknown voice. The spirits had become interactive.

All the same, Raudive was not entirely convinced. Although he was now certain Jürgenson was not faking the tapes, he thought there might be explanations of the phenomenon other than the spirit hypothesis. There was the obvious possibility of a freak pickup of radio transmissions, for example. Clearly more research was needed. In June 1965 Raudive joined Jürgenson on his Swedish estate at Nysund to carry it out.

At first they managed to produce only faint, scarcely audible voices, but at 9:30 p.m. on June 10, they got a clear, good-quality recording. Raudive later found that anyone who listened to it could make out the voices easily. First there was one that called, "Friedrich, Friedrich." Then a woman's voice said softly, "Heute pa nakti. Kennt ihr Margaret, Konstantin?" After a brief pause, the same voice sang, "Vi tálu! Runá!" Finally a different female voice said, "Va a dormir, Margarete!" Almost all these phrases are a mixture of languages. Raudive, himself a formidable linguist, identified German, Latvian, English, and French. Putting these together, the translation would be: "Fredrick, Fredrick! Tonight. Do you know Margaret, Konstantin? We are far away! Speak! Go to sleep, Margaret." The name "Margaret" struck Raudive forcefully. He had been deeply affected by the recent death of a friend named Margaret Petrautzki and the coincidence of the name gave him much food for thought. He decided to continue serious research on his own. It was a decision that was to influence the course of his entire career, for the voice phenomenon came to fill almost his whole life.

There are three ways of producing electronic voice recordings, two of them very simple indeed. All that is needed is patience and some basic equipment.

The method that gives the clearest voices requires a radio, a short aerial (somewhere between 6 and 10 centimeters [2 and 4 inches]), a recorder, and something called a diode, which is fairly readily available in any specialist radio or electronics outlet. The aerial is attached to the diode and the diode to the radio. You then turn on the medium waveband and tune the set to what is technically known as an inter-frequency—anywhere on the wave band where no station is broadcasting. This tuning produces "white noise," a constant hiss of static. The tape machine is set to record from the radio, either via a microphone or, better, using a cable input. If an open microphone is used, it will obviously pick up sounds made naturally within range, and these have to be carefully differentiated from any paranormal voices that might arise. As against that, open microphone recording allows the possibility of recorded interactions between the voices and the experimenter. The diode method is likely to give best results of any method unless the equipment is set up close to a strong radio transmitter, which can cause interference that is difficult to block out.

A second method is almost identical to the first except that no diode is used. The radio is joined to the tape recorder exactly as for recording a program and once again tuned to an interfrequency. The third and simplest method of all involves setting up a recorder and microphone in an empty, quiet room and recording the silence for half an hour or so. It was this method Raudive used initially in his solo experiments, and it took him three months of patient work before a taped voice answered one of his own spoken observations with the words, "Pareizi tá büs!"—Latvian for "That's right!"

Interestingly, while this was the first voice he heard, it was not the first he actually recorded. When he replayed earlier tapes, he discovered many others he had not noticed before. This is a commonplace in the electronic voice phenomenon. Most people are able to distinguish only seven levels of volume and seven levels of pitch in the ordinary course of events. Because of this, most of the voices remain inaudible until the ear is attuned through practice. It is only when the individual is experienced enough to distinguish single phonemes—the smallest individual units of sound—that it becomes possible to hear all the voices properly. Individuals with musical training typically experience far fewer problems in this type of research than others and it was Professor Atis Teichmanis of the College of Music in Freiburg, Germany, who was first able to confirm accurately that the electronic voices specifically differed in both pitch and volume from those of the average human voice.

But if the voices were so difficult to distinguish, how could anyone be certain they were more than psychological projections? The human nervous system is so well designed to distinguish patterns that it frequently discerns them where they are not really present. Hence we see faces in the clouds and pictures in the fire. More to the point, it is perfectly possible—especially when tired—to "hear" whispers in white noise that are nothing more than the listener's expectations.

In 1968, the Otto Reichl Verlag of Remagen published Raudive's account of his experiments in German under the title *Unhörbares Wird Hörbar* ("The Inaudible Becomes Audible"). On October 13 the following year, the British publisher Colin Smythe was handed a copy while at the Frankfurt Book Fair. In 1971, Smythe brought out an expanded version of the book under the rather more commercial title of *Breakthrough.*

Breakthrough is not a particularly readable book. Most of its 391 pages are devoted to an increasingly tedious transcript of Raudive's polyglot tapes. But it did contain an indication that scientists other than himself were working on the voice phenomenon and some were prepared to take a strictly nuts-and-bolts approach. The work was sufficiently successful to persuade one of Colin Smythe's executives, Peter Bander, to produce a book of his own on the subject. This offering, which was published by Colin Smythe in 1972, was much more superficial in its approach than the Raudive original but also far more readable. It dealt in part with the promotional activity that surrounded *Breakthrough* and the way in which the media dealt with the idea that ghosts might be recorded on tape. But more important, it detailed some of the work that had been done to establish the objective reality of the voices. Much of it was impressive.

First, tests were carried out to ensure that the voices were actually present as magnetic traces on the tape and not simply psychological projections into the white noise. Jochem Sotscheck, director of the Acoustics Research Group at the Central Office for Telegraphic Technology in Berlin, made use of a voice printer to show not only that the voices really existed but occurred in the same frequency range as human speech.

Once it was realized that *something* was impressing on the tape, the next stage was to rule out any question of freak electronic intrusions—radio broadcasts, high-frequency transmissions, or even, as one authority suggested, low-frequency communications used by the CIA. This was done by attempting a voice recording from inside a Faraday cage.

A Faraday cage is a device named for the nineteenth-century British pioneer of electromagnetism, Michael Faraday. It screens out all known forms of electromagnetic radiation and consequently creates a quarantine area into which no broadcast energy can penetrate. The recording device was set up inside the cage. Although a rational electronic explanation was now ruled out, the voices still appeared on the tape.

As the press became increasingly interested, more and more tightly controlled experiments took place. A typical example was one set up by a Sunday newspaper at the Pye Laboratories. Under the watchful eyes of twelve observers, Raudive was challenged to produce a voice while completely isolated from the machines and control devices set up by electronics engineers. In eighteen minutes there were two hundred voices on the tape, twenty-seven of them clear enough to be played back through a loudspeaker. Pye's chief engineer of the day, Ken Atwood, tried everything he knew to stop the voices or at least explain them within known electronics theory. He failed to do so and afterward commented philosophically, "I suppose we must learn to accept them."

Other experts came reluctantly to the same conclusion. The physicist and electronics engineer A. P. Hale examined tests carried out in a screened laboratory and could only say, "I cannot explain what happened in normal physical terms." Hans Bender of the University of Freiburg went on record with the statement that examination with high-quality technical equipment "made the paranormal hypothesis of the origin of the voice phenomena highly probable."

With the reality of the voice recordings—and their paranormal origin —established beyond all reasonable doubt, it becomes possible to embark on a logical analysis of their content. The picture that emerges is extremely interesting.

First, the voices are fragmentary. There are no lengthy messages on the tapes and little direct continuity. An entity will typically record a few words— a sentence or two at most—then disappear. Sometimes the same entity will return later but will seldom attempt to pick up where he left off. Where there are multiple voices on a tape, the impression one gets is of people jostling for attention while using a difficult and often faulty telephone connection. Even when a voice gets through solo, the messages are frequently clipped—"Here is Ivarits"—and sometimes nonsensical as in the bewildering: "Statowitz one man eight nought one inch rub off." It is also clear that the individual entities attempting to communicate all have their own agendas. One complains of being a slave. Another insists it is surrounded by scoundrels. A third cuts through the words of a fourth with the testy exclamation, "Oh you chatterbox!"

Despite this, certain of the entities appear willing, even anxious, to enter into a dialogue with the experimenter. Many are interested in the process of communication and will sometimes put forward their own theories as to how it works. (Raudive was once told he functioned like radar.) Others attempt to describe their current state, but such descriptions tend to be vague, confused, and often contradictory. Thus the importance of the electronic voices is not what they say but the fact that they exist.

Raudive recorded more than thirty thousand of them. At first they claimed to be dead relatives and friends. Later he discovered he had recorded what purported to be the voices of Tolstoy, Jung, Stalin, Hitler, Mussolini, and Churchill. Although Tolstoy and Stalin both spoke Russian, almost all the rest showed the now familiar mixture of languages. As other researchers began to work independently with the phenomenon, it became obvious that multilingual messages were very much a Raudive trademark—others either did not get them at all, or only rarely. This discovery led to the suspicion that Raudive somehow influenced the type of voices that came through. Although he remained cautious in his public pronouncements, Raudive himself came to believe there could be a mediumistic aspect to the whole phenomenon.[11] That is to say, the investigator is himself a channel that allows the voices to manifest. Several others have speculated along the same lines.

The entire electronic voice phenomenon is directly in line with all of the other findings. Discarnate mindon entities seem really only capable of contact with matter through the cooperation of another of their kind that has already forged a physical body. But by attempting to imprint directly on magnetic tape, in however confused and fragmentary a fashion, the voices have moved beyond the old, familiar controversy. What the recordings have done is show that they are really there.

CONCLUSION

S OMETIME IN THE DEPTHS OF PREHISTORY, A PRIMITIVE HUMAN WAS BORN
with a genetic mutation that allowed him or her to hear a voice, perhaps
even see a figure, that others could not. The development proved to
have survival potential—the voice might sometimes whisper the location of
game or warn of an impending landslide in a mountain pass—so that the
mutation began to spread slowly into the community. Not everyone carried
the gene, of course, but eventually the principles of Darwinian evolution
ensured the emergence of an elite group of people with the power to visit
what they thought of as a spirit world and return with information or abilities
of use to their tribe. With experience, these people—shamans, witch doctors
—came to discover techniques, often including fasting, physical ordeals, or
plant narcotics, that encouraged the development of powers of contact like
their own. The long association between humans and spirits had begun.

These origins are speculative and may well prove entirely fictional, but
the reality of spirit contact is not. Evidence of such contact is not remotely
controversial. Historians recognize the phenomenon as a fact of human
experience (without necessarily accepting the reality of spirits) from time
immemorial. The multitude of examples contained in this book have largely
been drawn from perfectly orthodox, well-respected academic sources. But
if the phenomenon is accepted, its implications are not. Indeed, its implications have scarcely been examined before now. Yet, as we have seen again
and again throughout the earlier sections of this book, spirit influence on
human history has been widespread, central, and profound.

It is important to emphasize that one does not have to believe in spirits
in order to recognize this reality. But it is equally important to recognize that
those who glibly dismiss spirits as hallucination or imagination are express-
ing opinions based more on assumptions or prejudice than any sound, rational

foundation. For the sad, surprising fact is that despite sterling efforts by bodies like the Society for Psychical Research, mainstream science lacks the will, interest, or funding to mount a serious, comprehensive investigation of the subject. Hence a phenomenon that has shaped the course of human history—and will continue to do so—has received ludicrously little attention. We know the Whisperers are here but have yet to discover, definitively, what they are.

I have attempted my own modest investigation of this vital question and the time has now come to draw some conclusions from the effort. But first a summary of the investigation itself:

Although a few rare individuals have achieved spontaneous interaction with spirits through visions and dreams, the two main avenues of contact in the West have been ritual conjuration and the séance room techniques of Spiritualism. The instruction manuals of the conjurers insist, almost without exception, that the spirits may, indeed must, be called to visible appearance. Within Spiritualism, the emphasis has typically been on the conveyance of verbal, or, less often, written, messages from beyond the grave; but even here there is a tradition of visible manifestation through the work of specially gifted "materializing mediums" and "spirit photography."[1]

Today's culture of rational materialism makes it difficult to accept the visible appearance of spirits. The discovery of an unconscious aspect of the human mind led to the theory that "spirit messages" were communications with the deep psyche, such as Flournoy's unconscious memories, wish fulfillment, and subliminal fantasies. In the case of the conjurer, the dialogue might take place via a full-blown hallucination, so that the "spirit" might become "visible" at least to himself. This is more or less the position of modern Solomonic magicians in America, who argue that the "demons" are, in fact, unconscious complexes (in the Freudian sense) that need to be personified and brought to the light of consciousness for the magician to reach his full potential.[2] One authority advocates the use of self-hypnosis to render the personifications visible.[3] In the case of the Spiritualist medium, the form of dialogue is often openly subjective to begin with—intuitions, impressions, voices in the head—and lends itself to the Flournoy theory even more readily.

Barbara Lex, associate in psychiatry at Harvard Medical School, has shown that patterned, repetitive acts, such as rhythmic drumming, chanting, or the invocations of a ceremonial conjurer, have an impact on the human brain and nervous system. This creates what she refers to as a state of "ritual trance" conducive to "extraordinary behaviors" like glossolalia, the handling of fire, and apparent contact with spirits.[4] In essence, lengthy prayers and the repetition of sonorous "names of power" monopolize the verbal-logical activities of the left cerebral hemisphere, leaving the right hemisphere to function freely.[5]

In her analysis of the poor right-hemisphere performance with regard to verbalization, Lex indicates she has little doubt that this hemisphere is the home of so-called mystical imageries and symbols.[6] Thus there is a psychophysical basis for the efficacy of ritual conjuration, and also a mechanism from which Flournoy's "subliminal fantasies" might emerge, perhaps in the form of culturally conditioned imagery. A similar mechanism exists within Spiritualism. Lex maintains that ritual trance "arises from manipulation of universal neurophysiological structures of the human body" and is consequently a potential behavior of all normal human beings,[7] where the grimoires promise successful conjurations to anyone prepared to follow the rituals diligently. Spiritualism relies, by and large, on the presence of specially gifted individuals—that is, mediums—who characteristically self-induce a trance state in order to achieve spirit contact. Here too there may be a question of cultural conditioning. Where the cultural expectation of the Middle Ages was of demonic or angelic visitation, the cultural expectation of the Victorian Spiritualist was of postmortem communication from a postulated, and surprisingly simplistic, "Summerland." In both cases, the individuals concerned got what they expected. In all cases it seems reasonable to assume we are dealing with right-brain imagery erupting from the personal subconscious.

But reasonable or not, there are problems with Flournoy's theory. The most obvious is the fact that "spirits" have shown themselves capable of presenting the conjurer/medium with data—like Dee and Kelley's Enochian language—that he does not already possess and seems incapable of fabricating. Jung's answer to this problem was his theory of a collective unconscious. Even as a student he noticed that his mediumistic cousin, Hélène Preiswerk, exhibited a "No. 2 personality" in trance that was distinctly more mature than her waking persona.[8] At the time, he dismissed this as a precocious development of the psyche occasioned by an unconscious understanding that she was destined to die young. Later, his experience with Philemon gave him personal proof that what he had thought of as "secondary personalities" were capable of greater insight and knowledge than the person who manifested them and thus could not be secondary personalities at all.

Yet Jung's eventual formulation of a collective unconscious remains unsatisfactory. To say there is a portion of the human psyche that manifests nonpersonal content and autonomous entities is really little different from the magician's assumption that there exists a spirit world from which spirits may be summoned. All Jung did was locate the spirit world inside the magician's head.

Neither Jung nor Flournoy went any distance toward solving the problem of the physical manifestations associated with spirit contact. Even if we dismiss as nonsense the *Grimoire Verum* suggestion that a manifested spirit might eat a walnut, we are still left with a mass of Spiritualist evidence for raps, levitations, apports, and the rest. Jung was aware of the problem but never achieved a solution. His attempt to interest Freud in the carefully worded "catalytic exteriorization phenomenon" was met with ridicule, and while Jung later approached the same problem obliquely by way of his theory of synchronicity, mainstream psychology still declined to recognize the possibility that the human mind could have a direct affect on its physical environment.

Jung died in 1961, three years before Batcheldor began the experiments that showed conclusively that exteriorization might be generated to order by groups who cared to use his methods. Six years before the Rosenheim poltergeist case, in which a nineteen-year-old girl was the unwitting cause of paranormal electrical and telephone disruptions, Batcheldor convinced psychical researchers that the same psychokinetic abilities might be vested in a single individual.[9] Had Jung lived another decade, one imagines he would have had a field day with the implications of Batcheldor's work. But no one else did. Today, Batcheldor's name is virtually unknown to professional psychologists, even those of the Jungian school. The implications of the Owens's experiments are even more profound. Novelists have long bemoaned the tendency for fictional characters to go their own way (thus ruining a perfectly good plot), but the fictional character Philip took this tendency to a whole new level. For Philip was an exteriorized entity, identical in every way to traditional manifestations in the séance room. Had the Owens group not known better, he would certainly have been accepted as a genuine spirit.

One is immediately moved to wonder how many other apparently genuine spirits have been the unconscious creations of Spiritualist groups or ceremonial conjurers, projected into the real world by a hitherto unsuspected mechanism of the human mind. The answer is almost certain to be some, perhaps even most, but it would be dangerous to assume it applies to all. The sticking point is Jung's observation, mirrored in the experience of practitioners throughout the entire history of the Western esoteric tradition, that his familiar spirit Philemon was capable of teaching him things he did not already know. Surely a creation is in no position to teach its creator? From a commonsense viewpoint, the answer is obvious, but the question contains a subtle trap: it assumes we know the real nature of the creator. Experimental work by the American neurobiologist Roger Sperry suggests we may not.

During the 1950s, Dr. Sperry, a professor of psychobiology at the California Institute of Technology, carried out a series of surgical experiments, at first on animals and later on human patients, during which he severed the corpus callosum, a band of nerve fibers connecting the two hemispheres of the brain. The result of his work, which earned him a Nobel Prize for Medicine in 1981, showed in summary that each hemisphere was capable of functioning independently of the other, each specialized in different tasks, but that one—the left—was normally dominant over the other. He concluded, however, that the right hemisphere (the activities of which we are normally unaware) was "a conscious system in its own right, perceiving, thinking, remembering, reasoning, willing and emoting, all at a characteristically human level."[10]

In other words, the human psyche contains not just one but two seats of consciousness, an insight confirmed by Sperry when he said, "Both the left and the right hemisphere may be conscious simultaneously in different, even in mutually conflicting, mental experiences that run along in parallel."[11] Thus, while we think of ourselves as a single consciousness, we are, in fact, dual. The British author Anthony Peake makes the intriguing suggestion[12] that right-brain consciousness may have a different perception of reality from that of the more familiar left brain, and consequently may be the root of such visitations as Socrates's *daemon* and the visionary experiences of Jakob Boehme.[13] For Peake, right-brain consciousness gave rise to the esoteric concept of a "higher self," while a whole range of spirits—angels, demons, shades of the dead—may represent its attempts at communication in any illusory form necessary to attract our attention.

Some aspects of Peake's theory were anticipated by Julian Jaynes, who was also intrigued by the implications of Sperry's split-brain experiments. But whether we accept these ideas or not, the very fact of a hidden right-brain consciousness clearly provides a possible mechanism for the creation of "spirits" that demonstrate knowledge and insights unknown to our familiar waking selves. Furthermore, even without this mechanism, it is important to recognize that the closest analogy to the creation of entities like Philip is the birth of a child: the infant may be created by its parents and to some extent molded by them, but over time it becomes an autonomous individual, potentially capable of learning more than those who gave it life.

In summary, then: spirit contact, for centuries, was widely taken at face value as communication with discarnate intelligences inhabiting a non-material reality. With the advent of Victorian materialism, however, this view of the phenomenon began to be questioned and alternative ideas put forward. Although some apparent spirit manifestations were shown to be fraudulent, fraud clearly could not account for them all and, increasingly, psychological explanations began to be advanced. Initially, these were confined to ideas like unconscious fabrication, self-deception, or pathological hallucination, but proved unsatisfactory in accounting for certain aspects of the phenomena.

Jung's concept of a collective unconscious went some way toward solving the dilemma—the idea of spirits as inner (i.e., psychological) yet objective entities was certainly in accord with major aspects of their nature—but failed to explain how they exerted an influence on the physical world. Batcheldor's work confirmed experimentally that a dependable mechanism for such influence actually existed. Owens's experiments showed it possible to evoke a fictional spirit that took on many of the aspects of traditional spirit manifestations and demonstrated an ability to acquire information outside of the data that comprised its original story. The experimental findings clearly point up the need for modification of Jung's collective unconscious theory—not to mention serious modification of the way in which spirits have been viewed historically. What emerges is the realization that the human mind has capabilities far beyond anything most of us would normally suspect.

The ancient world knew what spirits were. They were entities that shared our planet—fairies, elementals, ancestral ghosts, and even gods who lived in trees, streams, and sacred groves. Sometimes you saw them, sometimes not. They had the power of invisibility or else they simply hid themselves extremely well. Modern tribal communities know this too.

Victorian anthropologists knew what spirits were. They were delusions of the primitive mind, entertaining fictions humanity once needed to explain such mysteries as the hurricane or a lightning flash. They had no place in a universe where everything would soon be weighed and measured.

Julian Jaynes knew what spirits were. They were hallucinations generated by minds that had not achieved self-awareness and needed mock-ups of gods and similar authority figures to tell them what to do. Their usefulness diminished as the bicameral mind broke down. They were banished, more or less, by the developed light of consciousness.

Carl Jung knew what spirits were. They were inherited structures in the depths of the human psyche that sometimes contacted and often influenced the conscious mind. They were objective in the sense that they formed no part of personal consciousness or experience, nor were they in any way created by the individual.

All were theories attempting to explain a phenomenon that seems to have been part of human experience throughout recorded history. The phenomenon itself is real. It is with us still and can be studied to this day. But none of the popular theories so far advanced has proven entirely satisfactory. It is difficult to believe that we share the world with an invisible miscellany. But it is equally difficult to accept the Victorian conviction that spirits are nothing more than primitive personifications of natural forces or wish fulfillment for an afterlife. The problem is the one that Carl Jung discovered when he met Philemon. That spirit knew a great deal more than he did. How could such knowledge arise from the personification of a natural process or wish fulfillment? Jung attempted a solution with his postulate of a collective unconscious that contained structures reflecting the evolution of the race. No wonder Philemon knew more than he did. The "spirit" had the whole of human history to draw on.

But that was only Jung's public stance. In private he acknowledged that there were difficulties with his theory. Why, for example, did the "structures" of the collective unconscious present themselves as personalities? Why, in other words, did spirits stubbornly behave like spirits? And how was it that they were (sometimes) able to influence the material world? It is only since the Grey Walter experiment that we can come to grips with the real nature of spirits. It is only since the development of quantum physics that we can begin to understand the theoretical structure of spirit worlds.

Ironically, the spirit voices have tried to explain these realities all along. Among the Raudive tapes is a recording that contains the words "Raudive, antiwelten sind." The German phrase translates as, "Raudive, anti-worlds exist." In another, a voice complains, "There is no time," echoing Firsoff's suggestion that beings in a neutrino universe might exist outside the time flow we experience. Over and over, the taped voices insist that a bridge must be built between the two dimensions: "One must have the bridge . . . Konstantin, please the bridge . . . Build, build the bridge . . . Build the bridge now, Konstantin . . . Span the bridge . . . Build the bridge! Make the voice!"

The use of religious and occult terminology frequently conceals a bedrock rationality in many spirit communications, but the messages require a shift of viewpoint. This shift goes beyond the acceptance of a parallel universe and even beyond the idea that we somehow interact with it. We are also asked to believe that the parallel universe is inhabited not only by the souls of the human dead, but also by a variety of aliens with an interest in humanity. The communicating entity Upuaut maintains, for example, that the gods of ancient Egypt were not gods at all in the sense of all-knowing, all-powerful deities, but rather fallible beings who happened to be a little more evolved than those they were trying to assist.

Whatever we may think of this—and Upuaut, like several other spirit contacts, claims to be the product of an ancient evolution that was once as primitive as any human culture—there is no doubt spirits are typically the recipients of what psychologists term "projections." They become, in effect, the receptacle of their listeners' hopes and fears and are often credited with powers and insights they neither claim nor possess. The situation is further complicated by their numinous quality. This is something inherent in the experience of contact that causes humanity, instinctively, to treat spirits with respect, to give weight to their words, and to act on their instructions. Whether this is always a good thing remains open to question. Even a superficial reading of history indicates that spirit advice does not always benefit the recipient. These are all factors that make it extremely difficult to see the spirit voices for what they really are.

So long as we could pretend they were hallucinations, we could comfortably ignore them. But there is clear and mounting evidence that some of the voices are not and never have been hallucinations. They know things we don't. They can move from host to host. They leave traces on magnetic tape. The latest findings of physics allow the possibility that they are creatures from a parallel world. If we are to believe the spirit messages and the results of the Grey Walter experiment, then we have our own natural extension into that world, albeit with a limited awareness. In a very real sense we are as much citizens of the parallel dimension as the ghosts and gods we have associated with it for so long. It is this that allows mediums and channelers to reach between the dimensions and extract information from those beyond.

The real problem with investigating a spirit world is that throughout the twentieth century and into the twenty-first, we have been culturally conditioned to believe it could not possibly exist. Most scientists today "know" there are no such things as spirits and consequently decline to investigate the evidence. This attitude, reprehensible (and unscientific) though it is, extends to many of the rest of us. When we hear claims that spirits may be popped conveniently into a crystal, that evolved entities are looking after the welfare of humanity, that discarnate beings have interfered with human history, it all seems far too romantic, too "occult" to take seriously. It runs contrary to all we think we know about the world. But this is only to say it runs contrary to the current mind-set.

That mind-set is still largely conditioned by the superstition of Victorian materialism. No matter that the leading physicists today are convinced the universe is *maya* or illusion, that the observing mind interacts with reality and may, in some sense, actually create it. No matter that many of their theories have now been experimentally confirmed. We simply do not believe them. We cannot feel this new, strange world in the gut. It has nothing to do with our everyday lives.

Technology routinely delivers miracles. Who needs telepathy when there are mobile phones? Who needs a crystal ball to see things at a distance when we can switch on the TV news? Many of the old psychic marvels have been devalued, and with them the ease and wonder with which our ancestors met a spiritual creation. We live as if the material world was all there is. We armor ourselves with skepticism. But if this armoring sometimes protects us from mistakes, it also locks us in a mental prison. We are no longer open-minded enough to wonder if the world is *really* like that. If anybody challenges our beliefs, we write them off as "unrealistic," stupid, or incurably romantic.

Yet the evidence that has arisen—the evidence of history, the evidence of experience and observation, the evidence of modern physics—positively demands that we consider a new paradigm. It may be unfamiliar and uncomfortable, but that is the price routinely paid for progress. The new paradigm suggests humans are more than they realize. It is a matter of personal experience that they are more than their bodies. Each day we are perpetually aware of our inner processes—thoughts, emotions, imaginings. Each night we are aware of dreams. These processes are not physical, but they are real. Yet we have been taught to believe they are somehow less true, and less important, than physical phenomena. But for more than fifty years now our scientists have been studying the nonmaterial realities of the quantum field. Some have even begun to speculate about linkages between their findings and the world-view taught by mystics through the generations. Within the new paradigm, we become a continuum that extends from the physical world into an incredible nonmaterial universe. This is the universe Jung called the collective (or objective) unconscious, the universe the shamans call the "spirit world," the universe of the Summerland, the place where the Raudive voices live, the dimension inhabited by entities like Seth and Mark and Anubis. Non-material though it may be, it can no longer be dismissed as unreal. For the stuff of ghosts has now been detected in particle accelerators and quantum physics shows there are worlds upon worlds . . . beyond.

This is the reality to which history points us. This is the reality taught by every major religion. This is the reality of the mystic's vision and the shaman's quest. This is the quantum reality discovered by our scientists. How long will it take for us to grasp it?

BIBLIOGRAPHY

Acosta, Fr. Joseph de. *The Natural and Moral History of the Indies.* London: Hakluyt Society, 1880.

Agrippa, Henry Cornelius. *Three Books of Occult Philosophy.* St. Paul, MN: Llewellyn, 2000.

al-Halveti, Tosun Bayrak al-Jerrahi. *The Name & the Named: The Divine Attributes of God.* Louisville, KY: Fons Vitae, 2000.

Almedingen, E. M. *The Romanovs.* London: The Bodley Head, 1966.

Ashcroft-Nowicki, Dolores. *Highways of the Mind: The Art and History of Pathworking.* Wellingborough, UK: Aquarian Press, 1987.

Assagioli, Roberto. *Transpersonal Development.* Bath: Crucible, 1991.

Bander, Peter. *Carry On Talking.* London: Colin Smythe, 1972.

Benz, Ernst. *The Theology of Electricity.* Eugene: Pickwick, 1989.

Black, Jason, and Christopher S. Hyett. *Pacts with the Devil.* Las Vegas: New Falcon, 2002.

Blavatsky, H. P. *Isis Unveiled.* Pasadena, CA: Theosophical University Press, 1972.

Braden, Charles S. *Spirits in Rebellion.* Dallas: Southern Methodist University Press, 1987.

Brandon, Ruth. *The Spiritualists: The Passion for the Occult in the Nineteenth and Twentieth Centuries.* London: Weidenfeld and Nicolson, 1983.

Braude, Ann. *Radical Spirits.* Gibraltar: Beacon Press, 1989.

Breggin, Peter. *Toxic Psychiatry.* London: HarperCollins, 1993.

Brennan, Herbie. *The Atlantis Enigma.* London: Piatkus Books, 1999.

———. *The Secret History of Ancient Egypt.* London: Bedford Square Books, 2011.

Brennan, J. H. *Astral Doorways.* London: Aquarian Press, 1972.

———. *The Magical I Ching.* St. Paul, MN: Llewellyn Publications, 2000.

———. *Mindreach.* Wellingborough, UK: Aquarian Press, 1985.

———. *Nostradamus: Visions of the Future.* London: Thorsons, 1992.

———. *Time Travel: A New Perspective.* St. Paul, MN: Llewellyn Publications, 1997.

Brier, Bob. *Ancient Egyptian Magic.* New York: Perennial, 2001.

Britten, Emma Hardinge. *Modern American Spiritualism.* Carretera: University Books, 1970.

———. *Nineteenth Century Miracles.* London: William Britten, 1883.

Brittle, Gerald. *The Demonologist: The Extraordinary Career of Ed and Lorraine Warren.* Bloomington, IN: iUniverse, 2002.

Buhler, George. *The Laws of Manu.* Charleston, SC: BiblioLife, 2009.

Brunton, Paul. *A Search in Secret India.* London: Rider & Co., 1970.

Buranelli, Vincent. *The Wizard from Vienna.* London: Peter Owen, 1976.

Burleson, Blake W. *Jung in Africa.* London: Continuum, 2005.

Butler, Elizabeth M. *The Fortunes of Faust.* Cambridge: Cambridge University Press, 1952.

———. *Ritual Magic.* Stroud, UK: Sutton Publishing, 1998.

Carr, A. H. Z. *Napoleon Speaks.* New York: Viking Press, 1941.

Casaubon, Meric, ed. *A True & Faithful Relation of what Passed for many Yeers Between Dr. John Dee and Some Spirits.* London: T. Garthwait, 1659.

Cavendish, Richard, ed. *Man, Myth & Magic.* London: Purnell, 1970.

Charles, Canon H. R. *The Apocrypha and Pseudepigrapha of the Old Testament.* Oxford, UK: The Clarendon Press, 1913.

Churton, Tobias. *Aleister Crowley: The Biography.* London: Watkins Publishing, 2011.

Clark, J. Kent. *Goodwin Wharton.* Oxford, UK: Oxford University Press, 1984.

Cooke, Ivan. *The Return of Arthur Conan Doyle.* Hampshire, UK: White Eagle Publishing Trust, 1975.

Crowley, Aleister. *777 and Other Qabalistic Writings of Aleister Crowley.* New York: Red Wheel/Weiser, 1987.

Dalai Lama XIV Bstan-'dzin-rgya-mtsho. *Freedom in Exile: Autobiography of His Holiness the Dalai Lama of Tibet.* London: Abacus, 1998.

d'Aquili, Eugene G., Charles D. Laughlin Jr., and John McManus. *The Spectrum of Ritual: A Biogenic Structural Analysis.* New York: Columbia University Press, 1979.

Darnton, Robert. *Mesmerism and the End of the Enlightenment in France.* Cambridge, MA: Harvard University Press, 1968.

Dawkins, Richard. *The God Delusion.* London: Black Swan, 2007.

Dee, John. *A True and Faithful Relation of What Passed for Many Years between Dr. John Dee and Some Spirits.* Berkeley, CA: Golem, 2008.

Dempsey, T. *Delphic Oracle: Its Early History, Influence and Fall.* Whitefish, MT: Kessenger, 2003.

Dennett, Daniel C. *Consciousness Explained.* London: Penguin, 1992.

Dillon, Matthew. *Pilgrims and Pilgrimage in Ancient Greece.* London: Routledge, 1997.

DuQuette, Lon Milo. *My Life with the Spirits.* York Beach, ME: Weiser, 1999.

Eamon, William. *Science and the Secrets of Nature.* Princeton, NJ: Princeton University Press, 1996.

Ellenberger, Henri F. *The Discovery of the Unconscious: The History and Evolution of Dynamic Psychiatry.* New York: Basic Books, 1970.

Encyclopædia Britannica 2009 Ultimate Reference Suite. Chicago: Encyclopædia Britannica, 2009.

Englis, Brian. *Trance.* London: Paladin, 1990.

Eysenck, H. J. *Sense and Nonsense in Psychology.* London: Pelican, 1960.

Fanger, Claire. *Conjuring Spirits: Texts and Traditions of Medieval Ritual Magic.* Stroud, UK: Sutton Publishing, 1998.

Felton, D. *Haunted Greece and Rome: Ghost Stories from Classical Antiquity.* Austin: University of Texas Press, 1999.

Flournoy, Theodore. *From India to the Planet Mars*. Translated by Daniel B. Vermilye. New York: Harper & Brothers, 1900.

French, Peter. *John Dee: The World of an Elizabethan Magus*. London: Routledge, 2002.

Fuller, Jean Overton. *The Magical Dilemma of Victor Neuburg: Aleister Crowley's Magical Brother and Lover*. Oxford, UK: Mandrake of Oxford, 2005.

Gauld, Alan. *A History of Hypnotism*. Cambridge: Cambridge University Press, 1995.

Gettings, Fred. *Ghosts in Photographs: The Extraordinary Story of Spirit Photography*. New York: Harmony Books, 1978.

Goldsmith, Margaret. *Franz Anton Mesmer: The History of an Idea*. London: Arthur Baker, 1934.

Goodrick-Clarke, Nicholas. *Black Sun*. New York: New York University Press, 2003.

———. *The Occult Roots of Nazism*. London: Tauris Parke, 2005.

Grof, Stanislav. *The Cosmic Game*. Dublin: Newleaf, 1988.

———. *The Holotropic Mind*. San Fransisco: HarperSanFransisco, 1993.

Guinness, Ivor Grattan, ed. *Psychical Research: A Guide to Its History, Principles, and Practices*. Wellingborough: Aquarian Press, 1982.

Hall, Judy. *Napoleon's Oracle*. London: Cico Books, 2003.

Hanegraaff, Wouter J., et al., eds. *Dictionary of Gnosis and Western Esotericism*. Leiden: Brill, 2006.

Harper's Encyclopedia of Mystical and Paranormal Experience. San Francisco: Harper-SanFrancisco, 1991.

Herrigal, Eugen. *Zen in the Art of Archery*. London: Routledge & Kegan Paul, 1953.

Hogue, John. *Nostradamus and the Millennium*. London: Bloomsbury, 1987.

Höhne, Heinz. *The Order of the Death's Head: The Story of Hitler's SS*. Translated by Richard Barry. London: Classic Penguin, 2000.

Huxley, Aldous. *The Doors of Perception and Heaven and Hell*. London: Vintage Classics, 2008.

Hwa, Jou Tsung. *The Tao of I Ching*. Taiwan: Tai Chi Foundation, 1984.

Jacolliot, Louis. *Occult Science in India*. Translated by William L. Felt. London: William Rider & Son, 1919.

Jaynes, Julian. *The Origin of Consciousness in the Breakdown of the Bicameral Mind*. Boston: Houghton Mifflin, 1976.

Jung C. G. *The Archetypes and the Collective Unconscious*. London: Routledge, 2008.

———. *Memories, Dreams, Reflections*. London: Fontana, 1971.

———. *Psychology and the Occult*. London: Ark, 1987.

———. *The Undiscovered Self*. London: Routledge and Kegan Paul, 1977.

Kaczynski, Richard. *Perdurabo: The Life of Aleister Crowley*. Berkeley, CA: North Atlantic Books, 2010.

Kerner, Justinus. *The Seeress of Prevorst: Being Revelations Concerning the Inner-Life of Man, and the Inter-Diffusion of a World of Spirits in the One We Inhabit*. London: Unlisted Publisher, 1845.

Lachman, Gary. *Jung the Mystic: The Esoteric Dimensions of Carl Jung's Life and Teachings*. New York: Jeremy P. Tarcher/Penguin, 2010.

Laver, James. *Nostradamus; or, The Future Foretold*. Maidstone, UK: George Mann, 1973.

Leeming, David, and Jake Page. *God: Myths of the Male Divine*. New York: Oxford University Press, 1997.

Leoni, Edgar. *Nostradamus and His Prophecies*. New York: Wing Books, n.d.; retitled reprint of *Nostradamus: Life and Literature*, 1961.

Lévi, Eliphas. *The History of Magic*. Translated by Arthur Edward Waite. London: Rider & Son, 1922.

———. *Transcendental Magic: Its Doctrine and Ritual*. Translated by Arthur Edward Waite. Twickenham, UK: Senate, 1995.

Lings, Martin. *Muhammad: His Life Based on the Earliest Sources*. Santa Fe, NM: Inner Traditions, 1987.

Lisiewski, Joseph C. *Ceremonial Magic and the Power of Evocation*. Tempe, AZ: New Falcon Publications, 2006.

Livy. *The Early History of Rome*. Translated by Aubrey De Sélincourt. London: Penguin Classics, 2002.

Longford, Elizabeth. *Victoria R.I.* London: Weidenfeld & Nicolson, 1998.

Luck, Georg, trans. and ed. *Arcana Mundi: Magic and the Occult in the Greek and Roman Worlds*. Baltimore: John Hopkins University Press, 2006.

McLuhan, Robert. *Randi's Prize*. Kibworth Beauchamp, UK: Troubador, 2010.

Magida, Arthur J. *The Nazi Séance*. New York: Palgrave Macmillan, 2011.

Maple, Eric, and Lynn Myring. *Haunted Houses, Ghosts and Spectres*. London: Usborne, 1979.

Marcuse, F. L. *Hypnosis, Fact and Fiction*. London: Penguin, 1959.

Maskelyne, Jasper. *White Magic*. London: Stanley Paul & Co., n.d.; probably late 1930s.

Mathers, S. L. MacGregor, trans. *The Book of the Sacred Magic of Abra-Melin the Mage*. Chicago: de Laurence, 1948.

———. *The Key of Solomon the King*. York Beach, ME: Weiser, 2001.

Narby, Jeremy, and Francis Huxley, eds. *Shamans Through Time*. London: Thames and Hudson, 2001.

Naydler, Jeremy. *Shamanic Wisdom in the Pyramid Texts*. Rochester, VT: Inner Traditions, 2005.

Nelson, Geoffrey K. *Spiritualism and Society*. London: Routledge & Kegan Paul, 1969.

Noegel, Scott, et al., eds. *Prayer, Magic and the Stars in the Ancient and Late Antique World*. University Park: Pennsylvania State University Press, 2003.

Noll, Richard. *The Aryan Christ: The Secret Life of Carl Gustav Jung*. London: Macmillan, 1997.

———. *The Jung Cult: Origins of a Charismatic Movement*. London: Fontana, 1996.

O'Brien, Barbara. *Operators and Things*. New York: A. S. Barnes, 1975.

Oppenheimer, Janet. *The Other World*. Cambridge: Cambridge University Press, 1985.

Ostling, Richard N., and Joan K. Ostling. *Mormon America: The Power and the Promise*. New York: HarperOne, 2007.

Ostrander, Sheila, and Lynn Schroeder. *Psychic Discoveries Behind the Iron Curtain*. Upper Saddle River, NJ: Prentice Hall, 1984.

Pauwels, Louis, and Jacques Bergier. *The Morning of the Magicians.* Translated by Rollo Myers. London: Souvenir Press, 2007.

Peake, Anthony. *The Daemon.* London: Arcturus, 2008.

Pearsall, Ronald. *The Table-Rappers.* London: Michael Joseph, 1972.

Peterson, Joseph H., ed. and trans. *Grimorium Verum.* Scott's Valley, CA: CreativeSpace Publishing, 2007.

———. *John Dee's Five Books of Mystery.* York Beach, ME: Weiser, 2003.

———, ed. *The Lesser Key of Solomon.* York Beach, ME: Weiser Books, 2001.

Randi, James. *The Supernatural A-Z: The Truth and the Lies.* London: Headline, 1995.

Randolph, Paschal Beverly. *Seership: Guide to Soul Sight.* Quakertown, PA: Confederation of Initiates, 1930.

Raudive, Konstantin. *Breakthrough.* London: Colin Smythe, 1971.

Rauschning, Hermann. *Hitler Speaks: A Series of Political Conversations with Adolf Hitler on His Real Aims.* Whitefish, MT: Kessinger, 2006.

Ravenscroft, Trevor. *The Spear of Destiny.* New York: Weiser, 1982.

Regardie, Israel. *The Golden Dawn.* St. Paul, MN: Llewellyn, 1993.

Rosen-Bizberg, Fran. *Orion Transmissions Prophecy: Ancient Wisdom for a New World.* Vol 1. Jordanów, Poland: Fundacja Terapia Homa, 2003.

Runyon, Carroll "Poke." *The Book of Solomon's Magick.* Silverado, CA: Church of the Hermetic Sciences, 2004.

Ryback, Timothy W. *Hitler's Private Library: The Books That Shaped His Life.* New York: Alfred A. Knopf, 2008; Kindle edition.

Saggs, H. W. F. *The Greatness That Was Babylon.* New York: Mentor Books, 1962.

Schertel, Ernst. *Magic: History/Theory/Practice.* Boise, ID: Cotum, 2009.

Seabrook, William. *Witchcraft: Its Power in the World Today.* London: White Lion, 1972.

Seligmann, Kurt. *Magic, Supernaturalism and Religion.* St. Albans, UK: Paladin, 1975.

Shah, Idries. *The Secret Lore of Magic.* London: Muller, 1963.

Shirer, William L. *The Rise and Fall of the Third Reich: A History of Nazi Germany.* New York: Simon and Schuster, 2011.

Simpson, W. K., ed. *Religion and Philosophy in Ancient Egypt.* New Haven, CT: Yale University Press, 1989.

Skinner, Stephen, and David Rankine. *The Goetia of Dr. Rudd: The Angels and Demons of Liber Malorum Spirituum Seu Goetia Lemegeton Clavicula Salomonis.* London: Golden Hoard Press, 2007.

———. *The Keys to the Gateway of Magic.* London: Golden Hoard, 2005.

Solomon, Grant, and June Solomon. *The Scole Experiment.* London: Piatkus, 1999.

Spence, Lewis. *The Occult Causes of the Present War.* London: Rider & Co., n.d.

Steinmeyer, Jim. *Hiding the Elephant: How Magicians Invented the Impossible.* London: William Heinemann, 2003.

Swedenborg, Emanuel. *Heaven and Its Wonders and Hell. From Things Heard and Seen.* Philadelphia: J. B. Lippincott & Co., 1867.

Thomas, Keith. *Religion and the Decline of Magic.* London: Weidenfeld and Nicolson, 1997.

Toland, John. *Adolf Hitler.* New York: Ballantine Books, 1976.

Turner Jr., Henry Ashby, ed. *Hitler: Memoirs of a Confidant.* New Haven, CT: Yale University Press, 1985.

Veith, Ilza, trans. *The Yellow Emperor's Classic of Internal Medicine.* Los Angeles: Unversity of California Press, 1972.

Von Franz, Marie-Louise. *C. G. Jung: His Myth in Our Time.* Toronto: Inner City Books, 1998.

Waite, Arthur Edward. *The Book of Ceremonial Magic.* New York: University Books, 1961.

Webb, James. *The Flight from Reason.* London: Macdonald, 1971.

Wilder, Alexander, trans. *Theurgia or The Egyptian Mysteries by Iamblichus.* London: Rider, 1911.

Wilhelm, Richard. *The I Ching or Book of Changes.* London: Routledge and Kegan Paul, 1969.

Willoughby, Harold Rideout. *Pagan Regeneration: A Study of Mystery Initiations in the Graeco-Roman World.* Charleston, SC: Forgotten Books, 2007.

Wilson, Colin. *Beyond the Occult.* London: Bantam Press, 1988.

———. *Rasputin and the Fall of the Romanovs.* London: Panther Books, 1978.

Winter, Alison. *Mesmerized: Powers of Mind in Victorian Britain.* Chicago: The University of Chicago Press, 1998.

Woolley, Benjamin. *The Queen's Conjurer: The Science and Magic of Dr. Dee.* London: HarperCollins, 2001.

ARTICLES & PERIODICALS

Batcheldor, K. J. "Report on a Case of Table Levitation and Associated Phenomena," *Journal of the Society for Psychical Research* 43, no. 729 (September 1966).

Charman, Robert A. "Conjuring Up Philip," *Paranormal Review: The Magazine of the Society for Psychical Research,* no. 48 (October 2008).

Crookes, William. "Notes of an Enquiry into the Phenomena Called Spiritual During the Years 1870–1873," *Quarterly Journal of Science* (January 1874).

Horrigan, Bonnie. "Shamanic Healing: We Are Not Alone—An Interview of Michael Harner," *Shamanism* Vol.10, issue no. 1 (1997).

Keen, Montague, Arthur Ellison, and David Fontana. "The Scole Report," *Proceedings of the Society for Psychical Research* 58, pt. 220 (November 1999).

Menzel, Birgit. "The Occult Revival in Russia Today and Its Impact on Literature," *The Harriman Review,* published online at http://www.fb06.uni-mainz.de/inst/is/russisch/menzel/forschung/00786.pdf.

Popham, Peter. "Politics in Italy: The Séance That Came Back to Haunt Romano Prodi," *The Independent* (London), December 2, 2005.

ONLINE SOURCES

Alec Harris article http://website.lineone.net/~enlightenment/alec_harris.htm

Budge, Sir E. A. Wallis. *Egyptian Magic.* Online edition at http://www.sacred-texts.com/egy/ema/index.htm.

Crowley, Aleister. *The Book of the Law: Liber AL vel Legis*. Online edition at http://www.sacred-texts.com/oto/engccxx.htm.

Bhagavata <http://bhagavata.org/downloads/bhagavata-compl.html>

Bibliomania <http://www.bibliomania.com>

Bradshaw Foundation <http://www.bradshawfoundation.com>

Cagliostro's Letter <http://www.faust.com/index.php/legend/cagliostro/letter-to-the-french-people/>

Cambridge Encyclopedia <http://encyclopedia.stateuniversity.com>

Egyptian Magic <http://www.sacred-texts.com/egy/ema/index.htm>

Expectations Full <http://publicintelligence.net/expectations-full-jihadi-manual/>

Ghost Dance <http://en.wikipedia.org/wiki/Ghost_Dance>

Ghost Science >http://www.ghost-science.co.uk/2010/08/spiritualism-the-birth-of-a-lie>

Ginzberg, Louis. *The Legends of the Jews*. Online edition at http://www.sacred-texts.com/jud/loj/index.htm.

Goddess Light <http://www.goddesslight.net>

Golden Bough (James Frazer) <http://www.gutenberg.org/etext/3623>

Haunted Places <http://theshadowlands.net/places/uk.htm>

Himmler <http://www.historynet.com/heinrich-himmler-the-nazi-leaders-master-plan.htm>

Home, Daniel Dunglas <http://en.wikipedia.org/wiki/Daniel_Dunglas_Home>

Horowitz, Norman H., "Roger Wolcott Sperry," Nobel Prize Org <http://nobelprize.org/nobel_prizes/medicine/articles/sperry/index.html>

Innocence Project <http://www.innocenceproject.org/Content/Facts_on_PostConviction_DNA_Exonerations.php>

Internet Sacred Text Archive <http://www.sacred-texts.com>

Joan of Arc <http://joan-of-arc.org/joanofarc_biography.html>

Legends of the Jews <http://www.sacred-texts.com/jud/loj/index.htm>

Liber Legis <http://www.sacred-texts.com/oto/engccxx.htm>

Mead G. R. S. trans., "The Corpus Hermeticum" <http://www.sacred-texts.com/chr/herm/hermes1.htm>

Mostly Haunted <http://www.mostlyhaunted.co.uk>

Nobel Prize <http://nobelprize.org>

Paleolithic Art <http://www.bradshawfoundation.com/clottes>

Poltergeist <http://en.wikipedia.org/wiki/Poltergeist>

Poltergeist survey <http://www.themystica.com/mystica/articles/p/poltergeist.html>

Project Gutenberg <http://www.gutenberg.org>

Pyramid Texts <http://www.pyramidtextsonline.com/translation.html>

Randi Educational Foundation <http://www.randi.org>

Randi Educational Foundation Encyclopedia <http://www.randi.org/encyclopedia>

Séance Kit <http://unleashyourdreams.co.uk/Unleash_Your_Dreams/___Box_Of_Delights_Seance_Kit____.html>

Seeress of Prevorst <http://www.spiritwritings.com/SeeressOfPrevorst.pdf>

Servants of the Light <http://www.servantsofthelight.org>

Shamanism <http://www.shamanism.org/>

Society for Psychical Research <http://www.spr.ac.uk>

Society of the Inner Light <http://www.innerlight.org.uk>

Spirit Writings <http://www.spiritwritings.com>

Stanford Encyclopedia of Philosophy <http://plato.stanford.edu>

StateUniversity.com <http://encyclopedia.stateuniversity.com/pages/17660/poltergeist.html

Stein, Walter Johannes <http://en.wikipedia.org/wiki/Walter_Johannes_Stein>

Way of Laughing <http://www.fortunecity.com/roswell/barneyhill/184/ >

NOTES

INTRODUCTION

1. *Rede des Reichsführer-SS im Dom zu Quedlinburg*, no credited author (Berlin: Nordland Verlag, 1936).

2. See, for example, Heather Pringle's interesting article, "Heinrich Himmler: The Nazi Leader's Master Plan" at http://www.historynet.com/heinrich-himmler-the-nazi-leaders-master-plan.htm (accessed August 9, 2011).

3. Lynn H. Nicholas, *Treasure Hunt*, http://www.museum-security.org/quedlinburg-hoard.htm (accessed August 9, 2011).

4. J. H. Brennan, *Occult Reich* (London: Futura, 1974).

5. Heinz Höhne, *The Order of the Death's Head: The Story of Hitler's SS*, trans. Richard Barry (London: Classic Penguin, 2000).

6. Ibid.

7. Ibid.

8. Louis Pauwels and Jacques Bergier, *The Morning of the Magicians*, trans. Rollo Myers (London: Souvenir Press, 2007).

9. Ibid.

10. Psalm 96:5, Septuagint (LXX).

11. Exodus 12:23, KJV.

12. 1 Chronicles 21:1, KJV.

13. Numbers 22:22–35, KJV.

14. Job 1, KJV.

15. Luke 4:1–2, KJV.

16. Matthew 8:32, KJV.

1: FIRST CONTACT

1. Quoted from Everard F. Im Thurn's 1883 account in Jeremy Narby and Francis Huxley (eds.), *Shamans Through Time* (London: Thames and Hudson, 2001).

2. Ibid.

3. From Thévet's book, *The Singularities of Antarctic France*, as quoted in Narby and Huxley.

4. Ibid.

5. Quoted from de Oviedo's 1535 account in Narby and Huxley.

6. From Gmelin's four-volume account quoted in Narby and Huxley.

7. From Lafitau's 1724 account quoted in Narby and Huxley.

8. See http://www.shamanism.org/ (accessed September 10, 2011).

9. Michael Harner, *The Way of the Shaman* (New York: HarperOne, 1990).

10. Ibid.

11. Mircea Eliade, "Shaman," in Richard Cavendish, ed., *Man, Myth & Magic* (London: Purnell, 1970).

12. Ibid.

13. Bonnie Horrigan, "Shamanic Healing: We Are Not Alone—An Interview of Michael Harner," *Shamanism* 10, no. 1 (1997).

14. James George Frazer, *The Golden Bough: A Study of Magic and Religion* <http://www.gutenberg.org/etext/3623.> (accessed November 28, 2008).

15. S. G. F. Brandon, "Animism," in Richard Cavendish, ed., *Man, Myth & Magic* (London: Purnell, 1970).

16. As quoted in Henri F. Ellenberger, *The Discovery of the Unconscious: The History and Evolution of Dynamic Psychiatry* (New York: Basic Books, 1970).

17. David Leeming and Jake Page, *God: Myths of the Male Divine* (New York: Oxford University Press, 1997).

18. Jean Clottes, "Paleolithic Art in France," the Bradshaw Foundation <http://www.bradshawfoundation.com/clottes > (accessed November 26, 2008).

2: COMMUNION WITH THE GODS

1. Named for the village of Al-Ubaid, where their remains were first discovered.

2. See "Sumer," *Encyclopædia Britannica: Encyclopædia Britannica Ultimate Reference Suite* (Chicago: Encyclopædia Britannica, 2011).

3. Rudolf Steiner had a similar theory, postulating a time when the spirit world was more visible than it is today, but dated the beginning and end of this development quite differently from Jaynes.

4. Richard Dawkins, *The God Delusion* (London: Black Swan, 2007).

5. Julian Jaynes, *The Origin of Consciousness in the Breakdown of the Bicameral Mind* (Boston: Houghton Mifflin Company, 1976).

6. Ibid.

7. Ibid.

8. Ibid.

9. Ibid.

10. Father Joseph de Acosta, *The Natural and Moral History of the Indies* (London: Hakluyt Society, 1880).

11. Quoted in Jaynes, op. cit.

12. Ibid.

13. See http://www.blacksacademy.net/content/4791.html (accessed January 15, 2013).

14. Jaynes, op. cit.

15. H. W. F. Saggs, *The Greatness That Was Babylon* (New York: Mentor Books, 1962).

16. Quoted in Jaynes, op. cit.

17. Matthew 27:46, KJV.

18. "Heaven," *Encyclopædia Britannica: Encyclopædia Britannica Ultimate Reference Suite* (Chicago: Encyclopædia Britannica, 2011).

3: THE EGYPTIAN EXPERIENCE

1. "Egypt, ancient," *Encyclopædia Britannica: Encyclopædia Britannica Ultimate Reference Suite* (Chicago: Encyclopædia Britannica, 2011).

2. Jeremy Naydler, *Shamanic Wisdom in the Pyramid Texts* (Rochester, VT: Inner Traditions, 2005).

3. An aquatic flowering plant (family Araceae) native to central and western Africa.

4. For most people, their reflection undergoes profound changes when they gaze intently at it by the light of a single candle. For some, the changes are believed to show how they appeared in previous incarnations.

5. Sir E. A. Wallis Budge, *Egyptian Magic*, online edition at http://www.sacred-texts.com/egy/ema/index.htm (accessed September 15, 2011).

6. As a divinity himself, Pharaoh was believed to have the ear of his fellow gods.

7. Budge, *Egyptian Magic*.

8. The text on the stele relates it was the god himself who carried out the rite, but it seems more likely it was the priest Khonsu who did so, probably using the god's statue.

9. "Middle Eastern religion," *Encyclopædia Britannica: Encyclopædia Britannica Ultimate Reference Suite* (Chicago: Encyclopædia Britannica, 2011).

10. Budge, *Egyptian Magic*.

11. Ibid.

12. Bob Brier, *Ancient Egyptian Magic* (New York: Perennial, 2001).

13. http://www.pyramidtextsonline.com/translation.html (accessed September 20, 2011).

14. Naydler, op. cit.

15. Harner, op. cit.

16. http://www.pyramidtextsonline.com/translation.html (accessed September 20, 2011).

17. Harner, op. cit.

18. J. Assmann, "Death and Initiation," in W. K. Simpson, ed., *Religion and Philosophy in Ancient Egypt* (New Haven, CT: Yale University Press, 1989).

19. Pyramid texts online, op. cit.

20. "Moses," *Encyclopædia Britannica: Encyclopædia Britannica Ultimate Reference Suite* (Chicago: Encyclopædia Britannica, 2011).

21. Rabbinical tradition places the total at around six hundred thousand.

22. Louis Ginzberg, *The Legends of the Jews*, available at http://www.sacred-texts.com/jud/loj/index.htm (accessed January 1, 2012).

23. Or possibly two. A Jewish tradition holds that Aaron, Moses's brother, was abandoned with him in the ark.

24. The Egyptian *Mose* means "is born" and is the root of the Hebrew name *Moshe* anglicized to *Moses*. The form *Tutmose*, a popular name in ancient Egypt, translates as "[The god] Thoth is born."

25. Ginzberg, op. cit.

26. Ibid.

27. Ibid.

28. Exodus 3:6, KJV.

29. Ginzberg, op. cit.

30. See page 108 of the present work.

31. Exodus 24:1–18, KJV.

32. "Moses," *Encyclopædia Britannica: Encyclopædia Britannica Ultimate Reference Suite* (Chicago: Encyclopædia Britannica, 2011).

4: MYSTERIES OF ANCIENT GREECE AND ROME

1. Pliny the Younger, "The Haunted House" <http://www.bibliomania.com/0/5/159 /534/17353/1/frameset.html> (accessed November 26, 2008).

2. Average air temperatures at Eleusis during September–October, when initiations were held, range from 24.2°C to 19.5°C (75.6°F to 67.1°F). In the later period when preliminaries took place in Athens during February–March, conditions were a little easier: candidates would only have had to endure temperatures in the range 10.6°C to 12.3°C (51.1°F to 54.1°F).

3. N. J. Richardson, "Eleusis," in Richard Cavendish, ed., *Man, Myth & Magic* (London: Purnell, 1970).

4. One gift of the goddess was that air currents became visible to the recipient. I came across a remnant of this ancient belief in rural Ireland only a few years ago while chatting with a master thatcher. During a wide-ranging conversation, he remarked that "they say pigs can see the wind."

5. See Richardson, op. cit.

6. Harold Rideout Willoughby, *Pagan Regeneration: A Study of Mystery Initiations in the Graeco-Roman World* (Charleston, SC: Forgotten Books, 2007).

7. Matthew Dillon, *Pilgrims and Pilgrimage in Ancient Greece* (London: Routledge, 1997).

8. E. D. Phillips, "Healing Gods," in Richard Cavendish, ed., *Man, Myth & Magic* (London: Purnell, 1970).

9. Or, in some sources, the fumes of barley, hemp, and bay leaves burned over an oil flame.

10. The picturesque description is from the Homeric *Hymn to Apollo*.

11. Livy, *The Early History of Rome*, trans. Aubrey De Sélincourt (London: Penguin Classics, 2002).

12. Robert Hughes, *Rome* (London: Weidenfeld and Nicolson, 2011).

13. A meteoric stone discovered in the Roman citadel is believed to have been used to cast the auspices for Numa's succession to the throne following the death of Romulus.

14. Despite extensive investigation, I have been unable to determine what differ-

entiates a sacred from a profane chicken. Multiple accounts of the practice suggest that to the Romans, chickens were chickens but became sacred automatically if used for divination.

15. "Augury," *Encyclopædia Britannica: Encyclopædia Britannica Ultimate Reference Suite* (Chicago: Encyclopædia Britannica, 2011).

16. Ezekiel 1:1–28, KJV.

17. Today, by contrast, it denotes one of the most popular tanks in the Israeli army.

5: SPIRITS OF THE ORIENT

1. George Buhler, *The Laws of Manu* (Charleston, SC: BiblioLife, 2009).

2. Those listed in the ancient *Bhagavata* include *bhutas* (spirits of the dead), *pramathas* (mystic spirits), *dakinis* (female imps), *pretas* (ghosts), and *kushmandas* (demons), among many, many others. See http://bhagavata.org/downloads/bhagavata-compl.html (accessed January 9, 2012).

3. Louis Jacolliot, *Occult Science in India*, trans. William L. Felt (London: William Rider & Son, 1919).

4. Ibid.

5. "Fu Xi," *Encyclopædia Britannica: Encyclopædia Britannica Ultimate Reference Suite* (Chicago: Encyclopædia Britannica, 2011).

6. See http://www.sciencedaily.com/releases/2007/04/070402214930.htm (accessed October 19, 2011).

7. Quoted in Richard Wilhelm, *The I Ching or Book of Changes* (London: Routledge and Kegan Paul, 1969).

8. The mythologies of many other countries show variations of this theme, while the past fifty years have seen maverick scientists present evidence for the existence of an advanced prehistoric civilization with global cultural spread. For a fuller discussion, see my *Atlantis Enigma* (London: Piatkus Books, 1999).

9. Jou Tsung Hwa, *The Tao of I Ching* (Taiwan: Tai Chi Foundation, 1984).

10. C. G. Jung in his Foreword to the Wilhelm translation of the *I Ching*, op. cit.

11. William Seabrook, *Witchcraft: Its Power in the World Today* (London: White Lion, 1972).

12. Gary Lachman, *Jung the Mystic: The Esoteric Dimensions of Carl Jung's Life and Teachings* (New York: Jeremy P. Tarcher/Penguin, 2010).

13. Ibid.

14. For details of color and other associations with the five elements of Chinese occultism, see Ilza Veith, trans., *The Yellow Emperor's Classic of Internal Medicine* (Los Angeles: University of California Press, 1972).

15. J. H. Brennan, *The Magical I Ching* (St. Paul, MN: Llewellyn Publications, 2000).

16. Dalai Lama XIV Bstan-'dzin-rgya-mtsho, *Freedom in Exile: Autobiography of His Holiness the Dalai Lama of Tibet* (London: Abacus, 1998).

17. Ibid.

18. Ibid.

6: DARK AGE CONJURATIONS

1. William Eamon, *Science and the Secrets of Nature* (Princeton, NJ: Princeton University Press, 1996).

2. Ibid.

3. Ian Moyer, "Thessalos of Tralles and Cultural Exchange," in Scott Noegel et al., eds., *Prayer, Magic and the Stars in the Ancient and Late Antique World* (University Park: Pennsylvania State University Press, 2003).

4. 1 John 4:1, KJV.

5. Leviticus 19:31, KJV.

6. Leviticus 20:6, KJV.

7. 2 Kings 21:6, KJV.

8. 2 Kings 23:24, KJV.

9. Exodus 22:18, KJV.

10. 1 Samuel 28, KJV.

11. Luke 10:20, KJV.

12. *Datura Stramonium*, or "thorn apple," is a highly toxic plant that, if it does not kill, can produce intoxication in which it is impossible to differentiate reality from fantasy. Historically, it has been used as a mystic sacrament in North America and Southern Asia, while in Europe its use is believed by some to explain the prevalence of stories about flying on broomsticks to Sabbat meetings.

13. Keith Thomas, *Religion and the Decline of Magic* (London: Weidenfeld and Nicolson, 1997).

14. S. L. MacGregor Mathers, *The Key of Solomon the King* (London: George Redway, 1889) revised by Joseph H. Peterson, 2005, and available at http://www.esotericarchives.com/solomon/ksol.htm#chap7 (accessed November 29, 2001).

15. Thomas, op. cit.

7: ROOTS OF ISLAM

1. Kurt Seligmann, *Magic, Supernaturalism and Religion* (St. Albans, UK: Paladin, 1975).

2. Martin Lings, *Muhammad: His Life Based on the Earliest Sources* (Santa Fe, NM: Inner Traditions, 1987).

3. Tosun Bayrak al-Jerrahi al-Halveti, *The Name & the Named: The Divine Attributes of God* (Louisville, KY: Fons Vitae, 2000).

4. "Muhammad," *Encyclopædia Britannica: Encyclopædia Britannica Ultimate Reference Suite* (Chicago: Encyclopædia Britannica, 2011).

5. Now the site of Islam's greatest mosque, the Dome of the Rock.

8: THE VOICES AND THE MAID

1. http://joan-of-arc.org/joanofarc_biography.html (accessed December 13, 2011).

2. Ibid.

3. http://www.joan-of-arc.org/joanofarc_life_summary_visions.html (accessed December 14, 2011).

4. M. Lassois was named by Joan as an honorary uncle: he was in fact a more distant relative by marriage.

5. It was not unusual for women to travel in male garb at the time as a precaution against assault or rape. Transvestism was held to be a sin, but the Church routinely issued special dispensations in cases of necessity.

6. http://www.joan-of-arc.org/joanofarc_life_summary_chinon.html (accessed December 16, 2011).

7. http://www.joan-of-arc.org/joanofarc_poitiers_conclusion.html (accessed December 16, 2011).

8. "Joan of Arc, Saint," *Encyclopædia Britannica: Encyclopædia Britannica Ultimate Reference Suite* (Chicago: Encyclopædia Britannica, 2011).

9. The demand was refused.

10. Charles VII proved less loyal to Joan. He made no attempt to save her at any point, probably because he was trying to reach an accommodation with the Duke of Burgundy.

9: THE EVOCATIONS OF NOSTRADAMUS

1. J. H. Brennan, *Nostradamus: Visions of the Future* (London: Thorsons, 1992).

2. See http://en.wikipedia.org/wiki/Nostradamus (accessed December 2, 2011).

3. Quoted in James Laver, *Nostradamus; or The Future Foretold* (Maidstone, UK: George Mann, 1973).

4. Edgar Leoni, *Nostradamus and His Prophecies* (New York: Wing Books, n.d.; retitled reprint of *Nostradamus, Life and Literature*, 1961).

5. Ibid.

6. Laver, op. cit.

7. Alexander Wilder, trans., *Theurgia or The Egyptian Mysteries by Iamblichus* (London: Rider, 1911). Online edition edited by Joseph H. Peterson, 2000, available at http://www.esotericarchives.com/oracle/iambl_th.htm#chap4 (accessed December 2, 2011).

8. Quoted in Laver, op. cit. See also Joseph H. Peterson's 2007 corrected transcription of *De Daemonibus* at http://www.esotericarchives.com/psellos/daemonibus.pdf (accessed December 2, 2011).

9. John Hogue, *Nostradamus and the Millennium* (London: Bloomsbury, 1987).

10: THE QUEEN'S CONJURER

1. Meric Casaubon, ed., *A True and Faithful Relation of What Passed for many Yeers Between Dr John Dee and Some Spirits* (London: T. Garthwait, 1659).

2. Benjamin Woolley, *The Queen's Conjurer: The Science and Magic of Dr. Dee* (London: HarperCollins, 2001).

3. Peter French, *John Dee: The World of an Elizabethan Magus* (London: Routledge, 2002).

4. Ibid.

5. Woolley, op. cit.

6. Ibid.

7. French, op. cit.

8. See Henry Cornelius Agrippa, *Three Books of Occult Philosophy* (St. Paul, MN: Llewellyn, 2000).

9. Robert Mathiesen, "A Thirteenth Century Ritual to Attain the Beatific Vision from the Sworn Book of Honorius of Thebes," in Claire Fanger, *Conjuring Spirits: Texts and Traditions of Medieval Ritual Magic* (Stroud, UK: Sutton Publishing, 1998).

10. Dee, op. cit.

11. Israel Regardie, *The Golden Dawn* (St. Paul, MN: Llewellyn, 1993).

12. French, op. cit.

13. Ibid.

14. Woolley, op. cit.

15. Quoted in Woolley.

16. Ibid.

17. Quoted in French.

18. Ibid.

19. Woolley, op. cit.

20. Thomas, op. cit.

11: ENLIGHTENMENT SPIRITS

1. Joseph H. Peterson, ed., *The Lesser Key of Solomon* (York Beach, ME: Weiser Books, 2001).

2. Stephen Skinner and David Rankine, *The Goetia of Dr. Rudd: The Angels and Demons of Liber Malorum Spirituum Seu Goetia Lemegeton Clavicula Salomonis* (London: Golden Hoard Press, 2007).

3. See Lon Milo DuQuette, *My Life with the Spirits* (York Beach, ME: Weiser, 1999); Joseph C. Lisiewski, *Ceremonial Magic and the Power of Evocation* (Tempe, AZ: New Falcon Publications, 2006); Carroll "Poke" Runyon, *The Book of Solomon's Magick* (Silverado, CA: Church of the Hermetic Sciences, 2004).

4. J. Kent Clark, *Goodwin Wharton* (Oxford, UK: Oxford University Press, 1984).

5. Thomas, op. cit.

6. Jane Williams-Hogan, "Swedenborg," in Wouter J. Hanegraaff et al., eds., *Dictionary of Gnosis and Western Esotericism* (Leiden: Brill, 2006).

7. Emanuel Swedenborg, *Heaven and Its Wonders and Hell. From Things Heard and Seen* (Philadelphia: J. B. Lippincott & Co., 1867).

8. Quoted by John Selwyn Gummer, "Swedenborg," in Richard Cavendish, ed., *Man, Myth & Magic* (London: Purnell, 1970).

9. Robert Darnton, *Mesmerism and the End of the Enlightenment in France* (Cambridge, MA: Harvard University Press, 1968).

10. Henri F. Ellenberger, *The Discovery of the Unconscious: The History and Evolution of Dynamic Psychiatry* (New York: Basic Books, 1970).

11. Ibid.

12. Ibid.

13. Ibid.

14. At this point, it may be as well to note that from the days of Gassner onward, spirit

contact became progressively less concerned with angels and devils (although some such contacts did persist) and more involved with the souls of the dead.

15. Ibid.

16. Ibid.

17. Ibid.

18. Alan Gauld, *A History of Hypnotism* (Cambridge: Cambridge University Press, 1995).

19. Ibid.

20. Ibid.

21. Ibid.

22. Justinus Kerner, *The Seeress of Prevorst: Being Revelations Concerning the Inner-Life of Man, and the Inter-Diffusion of a World of Spirits in the One We Inhabit* (London: Patridge & Brittan, 1845) <http://www.spiritwritings.com/SeeressOfPrevorst.pdf> (accessed December 18, 2008).

23. Ibid.

24. Gauld, *A History of Hypnotism.*

25. Ibid.

26. Alison Winter, *Mesmerized: Powers of Mind in Victorian Britain* (Chicago: The University of Chicago Press, 1998).

27. Ibid.

12: REVOLUTIONARY SORCERER

1. As a novice in the Benfratelli of Cartegirone, Cagliostro substituted the names of notorious prostitutes for the names of the saints while giving a Scripture reading at supper.

2. The ability to gather information about someone by means of subtle clues in their reactions.

3. http://www.faust.com/index.php/legend/cagliostro/letter-to-the-french-people/ (accessed December 3, 2011).

4. Eliphas Lévi, *The History of Magic*, trans. Arthur Edward Waite (London: Rider & Son, 1922).

13: HISTORY REPEATS

1. E. M. Almedingen, *The Romanovs* (London: The Bodley Head, 1966).

2. Colin Wilson, *Rasputin and the Fall of the Romanovs* (London: Panther Books, 1978).

3. Aldous Huxley, *The Doors of Perception and Heaven and Hell* (London: Vintage Classics, 2008).

4. Quoted in Colin Wilson, *Rasputin and the Fall of the Romanovs.*

14: DIRECT GUIDANCE

1. http://www.controverscial.com/Paddy%20Slade.htm (accessed December 4, 2011).

2. Sheila Ostrander and Lynn Schroeder, *Psychic Discoveries Behind the Iron Curtain*, (Upper Saddle River, NJ: Prentice Hall, 1984).

3. A. H. Z. Carr, *Napoleon Speaks* (New York: Viking Press, 1941).

4. Judy Hall, *Napoleon's Oracle* (London: Cico Books, 2003).

5. Paul Brunton, *A Search in Secret Egypt* (New York: Weiser, 1992).]

15: AN AMERICAN EXPERIENCE

1. James 1:5, KJV.

2. The phrase is Smith's own, although copies of the plates show a script that appears to bear little resemblance to Egyptian hieroglyphic or demotic.

3. See http://en.wikipedia.org/wiki/Joseph_Smith (accessed January 17, 2012).

4. See http://lds.about.com/od/mormons/a/church_membership.htm (accessed January 19, 2012).

5. Richard N. and Joan K. Ostling, *Mormon America: The Power and the Promise* (New York: HarperOne 2007).

16: IS *EVERYBODY* THERE?

1. Ruth Brandon, *The Spiritualists: The Passion for the Occult in the Nineteenth and Twentieth Centuries* (London: Weidenfeld and Nicolson, 1983).

2. "Spiritualism," *Encyclopædia Britannica: Encyclopædia Britannica 2009 Ultimate Reference Suite* (Chicago: Encyclopædia Britannica, 2009).

3. Quoted in Brandon.

4. Brandon, op. cit.

5. Ibid.

6. Ronald Pearsall, *The Table-Rappers* (London: Michael Joseph, 1972).

7. Montague Keen, Arthur Ellison, and David Fontana, "The Scole Report," *Proceedings of the Society for Psychical Research* 58, pt. 220 (November 1999).

8. Rosemary Ellen Guiley, "Cooke, Grace," in *Harper's Encyclopedia of Mystical and Paranormal Experience* (San Francisco: HarperSanFrancisco, 1991).

9. Fran Rosen-Bizberg, *Orion Transmissions Prophecy: Ancient Wisdom for a New World*, vol. 1 (Jordanów, Poland: Fundacja Terapia Homa, 2003).

10. The most sympathetic of the white community were Utah's Mormons, who were familiar with the concept of visionary revelation.

11. The idea has much in common with the Mormon belief in "endowment garments," which protect pious wearers from evil. Some scholars have even argued that the Mormon doctrine was the inspiration of the Native American belief. See http://en.wikipedia.org/wiki/Ghost_Dance (accessed January 21, 2012).

17: THE SPIRITS GO TO WAR

1. A similar phenomenon occurred a century later with the publication of Stephen Hawking's *Brief History of Time*.

2. Eliphas Lévi, *The History of Magic*, trans. Arthur Edward Waite (London: Rider & Son, 1922).

3. Lewis Spence, *The Occult Causes of the Present War* (London: Rider & Co., n.d.).

4. I was to hear the same argument, half a century later, from a member of Oswald

Mosley's Union Movement.

5. William L. Shirer, *The Rise and Fall of the Third Reich: A History of Nazi Germany* (New York: Simon and Schuster, 2011).

6. Once again we have an echo of Jaynes's theories, but again dated differently.

18: THE SPIRITS AND THE FÜHRER

1. Arthur J. Magida, *The Nazi Séance* (New York: Palgrave Macmillan, 2011).

2. By, for example, the Society for Psychical Research.

3. Magida, op. cit.

4. http://en.wikipedia.org/wiki/Erik_Jan_Hanussen (accessed December 11, 2011).

5. http://www.steinschneider.com/biography/hanussen/page18.htm (accessed December 11, 2011).

6. Hermann Rauschning, *Hitler Speaks: A Series of Political Conversations with Adolf Hitler on His Real Aims* (Whitefish, MT: Kessinger, 2006).

7. John Toland, *Adolf Hitler* (New York: Ballantine Books, 1976).

8. Henry Ashby Turner Jr., ed., *Hitler: Memoirs of a Confidant* (New Haven, CT: Yale University Press, 1985).

9. Trevor Ravenscroft, *The Spear of Destiny* (New York: Weiser, 1982).

10. http://en.wikipedia.org/wiki/Walter_Johannes_Stein (accessed December 12, 2011).

11. See, for example, the training program offered by the Jersey-based Servants of the Light (http://www.servantsofthelight.org) or the writings of Dion Fortune, who founded the Society of the Inner Light (http://www.innerlight.org.uk) based in London.

12. Timothy W. Ryback, *Hitler's Private Library: The Books That Shaped His Life* (New York: Alfred A. Knopf, 2008; Kindle edition).

13. Ernst Schertel, *Magic: History/Theory/Practice* (Boise, ID: Cotum, 2009).

19: A MUSEUM OF SPIRIT CONTACT

1. Birgit Menzel, "The Occult Revival in Russia Today and Its Impact on Literature," *The Harriman Review*, published online at http://www.fb06.uni-mainz.de/inst/is/russisch /menzel/forschung/00786.pdf (accessed November 22, 2012).

2. Peter Popham, "Politics in Italy: The Séance That Came Back to Haunt Romano Prodi," *The Independent* (London), December 2, 2005.

3. See, among other works, my own *Astral Doorways* (London: Aquarian Press, 1972).

4. Samir Khan, "Expectations Full," http://publicintelligence.net/expectations-full-jihadi-manual/ (accessed November 22, 2012).

5. Ibid.

20: CLOSE ENCOUNTERS OF THE SPIRIT KIND

1. The term derives from Spiritualism where it describes the appearance of small objects in the séance room out of thin air.

2. In Ivan Cooke, *The Return of Arthur Conan Doyle* (Hampshire, UK: White Eagle Publishing Trust, 1975).

3. Ibid.

4. Jean Overton Fuller, *The Magical Dilemma of Victor Neuburg: Aleister Crowley's Magical Brother and Lover* (Oxford, UK: Mandrake of Oxford, 2005).

5. Aleister Crowley, *777 and Other Qabalistic Writings of Aleister Crowley* (New York: Red Wheel/Weiser, 1987).

6. Fuller, op. cit.

7. Israel Regardie *The Golden Dawn* (Chicago: Aries Press, 1940). Quoted in translation.

8. Tobias Churton, *Aleister Crowley: The Biography* (London: Watkins Publishing, 2011).

9. Ibid. Other sources suggest her message was that "they" were waiting for Crowley.

10. Ibid.

11. Quoted in Richard Kaczynski, *Perdurabo: The Life of Aleister Crowley* (Berkeley, CA: North Atlantic Books, 2010).

12 In reality a simple room in their apartment designated for magical purposes.

13. Quoted in Kaczynski, op. cit.

14. Aleister Crowley, *The Book of the Law: Liber AL vel Legis*, available at http://www.sacred-texts.com/oto/engccxx.htm (accessed January 28, 2012).

15. Ibid.

21: THREE CONJURATIONS

1. The account that follows draws on Elizabeth M. Butler, *Ritual Magic* (Stroud, UK: Sutton Publishing, 1998).

2. H. P. Blavatsky, *Isis Unveiled*, vol. 2 (Pasadena, CA: Theosophical University Press, 1972).

3. My version of the Inquiry's findings also draws on Butler, op. cit.

4. Edward Bulwer-Lytton, 1st Baron Lytton, a well-known English playwright, poet, and novelist with a considerable interest in the occult.

5. Eliphas Lévi, *Transcendental Magic: Its Doctrine and Ritual*, trans. Arthur Edward Waite (London: Rider & Co., 1896).

6. Elizabeth M. Butler, op. cit.

7. Gerald Brittle, *The Demonologist: The Extraordinary Career of Ed and Lorraine Warren* (Bloomington, IN: iUniverse, 2002).

22: SPIRIT TRANSFERS, SPIRIT POWERS

1. As W. E. Butler.

2. He later lost his second leg to the same condition.

3. Dolores has also claimed health benefits, notably a strengthened immune system.

4. She died on November 26, 2010.

5. 1 Kings 10, KJV.

6. Song of Solomon 1:1, KJV.

7. Ibid.

8. Emma Hardinge Britten, *Nineteenth Century Miracles: Or Spirits and Their Work in Every Country of the Earth* (New York: Lovell & Co., 1884).

9. Ruth Brandon, *The Spiritualists: The Passion for the Occult in the Nineteenth and Twentieth Centuries* (London: Weidenfeld and Nicolson, 1983).

10. http://en.wikipedia.org/wiki/Daniel_Dunglas_Home (accessed, January 31, 2012).

11. Britten, op. cit.

12. See http://www.victorzammit.com/book/chapter12.html (accessed January 17, 2013).

13. Britten, op. cit.

14. Revelation 12:7–9, KJV.

15. From Canon H. R. Charles, *The Apocrypha and Pseudepigrapha of the Old Testament* (Oxford, UK: The Clarendon Press, 1913).

16. Ibid.

17. Although it is probably true to suggest the New Age movement has carried these beliefs to a wider Western audience than at any other time in history.

18. G. R. S. Mead, trans., "The Corpus Hermeticum," *Internet Sacred Text Archive* <http://www.sacred-texts.com/chr/herm/hermes1.htm > (accessed January 19, 2009).

19. Ibid.

20. Ibid.

23: A Skeptical Inquiry

1. James Randi, *The Supernatural A-Z: The Truth and the Lies* (London: Headline, 1995).

2. http://www.randi.org/encyclopedia (accessed February 2, 2012).

3. Randi, *The Supernatural A-Z*, op. cit.

4. Jasper Maskelyne, *White Magic* (London: Stanley Paul & Co, n.d.; probably late 1930s).

5. Ibid.

6. Jim Steinmeyer, *Hiding the Elephant: How Magicians Invented the Impossible* (London: William Heinemann, 2003).

7. John Gordon Melton, "Spiritualism," in *Encyclopædia Britannica: Encyclopædia Britannica 2009 Ultimate Reference Suite* (Chicago: Encyclopædia Britannica, 2009).

8. http://unleashyourdreams.co.uk/Unleash_Your_Dreams/___Box_Of_Delights_Seance _Kit____.html (accessed February 3, 2012).

9. http://www.spr.ac.uk/main/ (accessed February 3, 2012).

10. January 2012.

11. James Randi, *An Encyclopedia of Claims, Frauds, and Hoaxes of the Occult and Supernatural*, op. cit.

12. http://www.innocenceproject.org/Content/Facts_on_PostConviction_DNA_Exonerations .php (accessed February 5, 2012).

13. http://www.ghost-science.co.uk/2010/08/spiritualism-the-birth-of-a-lie (accessed February 5, 2012).

14. William Crookes, "Notes of an Enquiry into the Phenomena Called Spiritual During the Years 1870–1873," *Quarterly Journal of Science* (January 1874).

15. Robert McLuhan, *Randi's Prize* (Kibworth Beauchamp, UK: Troubador, 2010).

16. McLuhan, op. cit.

17. Ibid.

18. Ibid.

24: THE BICAMERAL THEORY

1. Jaynes, op. cit.

2. Quoted by Jaynes.

3. Eugen Herrigal, *Zen in the Art of Archery* (London: Routledge & Kegan Paul, 1953).

4. Jaynes, op. cit.

5. *Martian Genesis* (London: Piatkus Books, 1998) and *The Atlantis Enigma* (London: Piatkus Books, 1999).

25: SPIRITS OF THE DEEP MIND

1. Ellenberger describes it as "vaguely resembling a mixture of Italian and French."

2. Back on Earth, the first sustained powered flight in a heavier-than-air machine was not made by the Wright brothers until the end of 1903.

3. Jung's family history claimed illegitimate descent from Goethe.

4. Ellenberger, op. cit.

5. Then generally believed to be caused by physical lesions of the nervous system resulting from the original trauma.

6. Theodore Flournoy, *From India to the Planet Mars*, trans. Daniel B. Vermilye (New York: Harper & Brothers, 1900).

7. Ibid.

8. Ibid.

9. Ellenberger, op. cit.

10. C. G. Jung, *Psychology and the Occult* (London: Ark, 1987).

11. Ibid.

12. Butler, op. cit.

13. Ibid.

14. Paschal Beverly Randolph, *Seership: Guide to Soul Sight* (Quakertown, PA: Confederation of Initiates, 1930).

15. Butler, op. cit.

16. Ibid.

26: PERSONAL ENCOUNTERS

1. http://theshadowlands.net/places/uk.htm (accessed February 7, 2012).

2. In a private conversation with the present author.

3. Some sources put the figure as high as twenty-seven thousand.

4. Accounts vary. In some, the armies appeared in the sky overhead; in others, the ap-

paritions fought across the fields and hills of the original battle.

5. Eric Maple and Lynn Myring, *Haunted Houses, Ghosts and Spectres* (London: Usborne, 1979).

6. J. H. Brennan, *Time Travel: A New Perspective* (St. Paul, MN: Llewellyn Publications, 1997).

7. Colin Wilson, *Beyond the Occult* (London: Bantam Press, 1988).

8. Brennan, *Time Travel*, op. cit.

27: THE GEIST THAT POLTERS

1. An East Frankish historical text composed by monks in the tenth century CE and covering a period between the reigns of Louis the Pious (died 640 CE) and the accession of Louis III in 900 CE.

2. Survey quoted in http://www.themystica.com/mystica/articles/p/poltergeist.html (accessed February 9, 2012).

3. Which stood on the site of the present Zouch Manor.

4. Richard Cavendish, ed., *Encyclopedia of the Unexplained: Magic, Occultism, and Parapsychology* (London: Penguin, 1995).

5. http://en.wikipedia.org/wiki/Poltergeist (accessed July 16, 2012).

28: THE BOGGLE THRESHOLD

1. Joseph H. Peterson, ed., *The Lesser Key of Solomon* (York Beach, ME: Weiser Books, 2001).

2. Ibid.

3. Ibid.

4. Ibid.

5. Ibid.

6. Ibid.

7. Ibid.

8. Ibid.

9. Ibid.

10. Ibid.

11. Joseph H. Peterson, ed. and trans., *Grimorium Verum* (Scott's Valley, CA: CreativeSpace Publishing, 2007).

12. Ibid.

13. Ibid.

14. S. L. MacGregor Mathers, *The Key of Solomon the King* (York Beach, ME: Weiser, 2001).

15. Arthur Edward Waite, *The Book of Ceremonial Magic* (New York: University Books, 1961).

16. S. L. MacGregor Mathers, trans., *The Book of the Sacred Magic of Abra-Melin the Mage* (Chicago: de Laurence, 1948).

17. Frank Klaassen, "English Manuscripts of Magic, 1300–1500: A Preliminary Sur-

vey," in Claire Fanger, *Conjuring Spirits: Texts and Traditions of Medieval Ritual Magic* (Stroud, UK: Sutton Publishing, 1998).

18. Flournoy, op. cit.

19. Blake W. Burleson, *Jung in Africa* (London: Continuum, 2005).

20. Ibid.

21. Ibid.

22. Ibid.

23. Ibid.

24. C. G. Jung, *Memories, Dreams, Reflections* (London: Fontana, 1971).

25. Ibid.

26. Ibid.

27. Ibid.

28. Richard Noll, *The Jung Cult: Origins of a Charismatic Movement* (London: Fontana, 1995).

29. Richard Noll, *The Aryan Christ: The Secret Life of Carl Gustav Jung* (London: Macmillan, 1997).

30. Ibid.

31. Ibid.

32. Ibid.

33. C. G. Jung, *The Archetypes and the Collective Unconscious* (London: Routledge, 2008).

34. Ibid.

35. Ibid.

36. Ibid.

37. Eliphas Lévi, *Transcendental Magic: Its Doctrine and Ritual* (Twickenham, UK: Senate, 1995).

38. Ibid.

39. Israel Regardie, *The Golden Dawn* (St. Paul, MN: Llewellyn, 1993).

40. J. H. Brennan, *Astral Doorways* (London: Aquarian Press, 1972).

41. Eliphas Lévi, *The History of Magic*, trans. Arthur Edward Waite (London: Rider & Son, 1922).

42. C. J. Jung, *The Archetypes and the Collective Unconscious* (London: Routledge, 2008).

43. Dolores Ashcroft-Nowicki, *Highways of the Mind: The Art and History of Pathworking* (Wellingborough, UK: Aquarian Press, 1987).

44. Jung, *Memories, Dreams, Reflections*.

45. Ibid.

46. Robert A. Charman, "Conjuring Up Philip," *Paranormal Review: The Magazine of the Society for Psychical Research*, no. 48 (October 2008).

47. Ibid.

48. Ibid.

49. Ibid.

50. Sourced from conversations with participants.

29: A SCIENTIFIC FOUNDATION

1. Stanislav Grof, *The Cosmic Game* (Dublin: Newleaf, 1988).

2. Quoted from a speech delivered by Leary in 1967.

3. Aldous Huxley, *The Doors of Perception and Heaven and Hell* (New York: Harper & Row, 1954).

4. Grof, op. cit.

5. Ibid.

6. Jung was self-contradictory on this area and much of his work points directly toward the idea of the Collective Unconscious as a single entity. It seems likely that with an academic reputation to protect, he took care to hedge his bets rather than present ideas so outlandish that they were unlikely to gain acceptance.

7. A principle of logic that states, in effect, that the simplest explanation of any phenomenon must always take precedence.

8. Grof, op. cit.

9. As do several recent cosmological theories.

10. "Mark," channeled through Jacquie Burgess, 1997, *The Way of Laughing,* http://www.fortunecity.com/roswell/barneyhill/184/ (accessed March 5, 2012).

11. Source: a private letter to the present author.

CONCLUSION

1. Fred Gettings, *Ghosts in Photographs: The Extraordinary Story of Spirit Photography* (New York: Harmony Books, 1978).

2. See, for example, Lon Milo DuQuette, *My Life with the Spirits* (York Beach, ME: Weiser, 1999) and Joseph C. Lisiewski, *Ceremonial Magic and the Power of Evocation* (Tempe, AZ: New Falcon Publications, 2006).

3. Carroll "Poke" Runyon, *The Book of Solomon's Magic: How to Invoke Angels into the Crystal and Evoke Spirits to Visible Appearance in the Dark Mirror* (Silverado, CA: C.H.S. Inc, 2004).

4. Barbara W. Lex, "Neurobiology of Ritual Trance," in Eugene G. d'Aquili, Charles D. Laughlin Jr., and John McManus, *The Spectrum of Ritual: A Biogenic Structural Analysis* (New York: Columbia University Press, 1979).

5. Ibid.

6. Ibid.

7. Ibid.

8. Jung, *Memories, Dreams, Reflections.*

9. "Poltergiest—Research, Major Hypotheses, Examples, Famous Alleged Poltergeist Infestations, Poltergeists in Fiction," *Cambridge Encyclopedia*, vol. 59 <http://encyclopedia.stateuniversity.com/pages/17660/poltergeist.html> (accessed February 21, 2009).

10. Norman H. Horowitz, "Roger Wolcott Sperry," Nobel Prize Org <http://nobelprize.org/nobel_prizes/medicine/articles/sperry/index.html> [accessed February 26, 2009.]

11. Ibid.

12. Anthony Peake, *The Daemon* (London: Arcturus, 2008).

13. Ibid.

INDEX